"If I could have ONLY ONE BOOK, I WOULD WANT THIS ONE! Written in rich and beautiful language, it takes us on a journey visiting a dazzling variety of places, people, and cultures, often not easy to get to or be with. It also takes us through an internal journey from trauma to letting go. There are many stories in this wonderful book. There is the story about the body being a messenger of the unconscious, a source of challenge and triumph. There is the story about connection and solitude, about dependency and independence, about competence and resourcefulness. There is a story about personal relationships told with courage and generous openness. There is a story about being a psychoanalyst and becoming a Buddhist. There is a story about animals—love, loss, and sadness. There are many stories about mountains and oceans and dangers and triumph. There is a story about illness and overcoming the fear of death. There is the story about the end of the journey and stepping into freedom. THIS IS TRULY A CAN'T-PUT-IT-DOWN BOOK, LEAVING YOU AWED, INSPIRED, AND GRATEFUL!"

**HEDDA BOLGAR**, Ph.D., ABPP, FIPA, training and supervising psychoanalyst at LAISPS, founder of Wright Institute Los Angeles, and still actively teaching, analyzing and travelling at 102!

"*Pulling Up Stakes* explores the outer terrain of Wrye's travels with her husband in Africa, West Papua, South America, the Sierra High Country, and delves into the inner terrain of her psyche, their marriage, and her spiritual yearnings. Any reader who has a long-held dream to become a citizen of the world will be inspired by Wrye's determination and courage to make her own dreams come true. A fascinating read."

**MAUREEN MURDOCK**, author of *The Heroine's Journey*

"This is an authentic and deep journey that links external adventure with inner awakening, written by one of the foremost psychoanalysts of her time. Harriet Kimble Wrye moves from the consulting room to living with primitive tribes, from healing others to being a cancer patient who needs healing, and from chafing at constraints to letting go into freedom."

**SARA DAVIDSON**, author of *Loose Change, Real Properties, Cowboy*, and *Joan*

"Grab a cup of tea and prepare to be pulled into a journey that combines cliffhanging excitement as well as the experience of calm water. Our dear friend and dharma sister, Harriet, is a kind, generous, and wise woman with an unfailing characteristic of being a risk-taker and adventurer. What makes Harriet unique is that she is both an explorer of the deserts, mountains, and rivers, as well as the inner terrain of intimate relationships, the psyche, and soul. She is equally comfortable in a hut in the Sahara, an international Jungian panel at a psychological conference, or seated serenely in a Buddhist zendo.

Harriet Kimble Wrye is a soul sister of amazement. She invites us into her explorations, into all of these worlds, even into her own marriage and family, sharing struggles, triumphs, vivid detail, and wise teachings. She invites us to inhabit each day as the miracle that it is. Her ability to be curious, amazed, alive, and compassionate is an inspiration. She doesn't hold herself back. Her trust in a friendly universe and her vow to live each moment whole-heartedly reminds us to treasure our every breath and footstep on this marvel that we call earth."

**PEGGY ROWE AND LARRY WARD**, authors of *Love's Garden: A Guide to Mindful Relationships*

"Headhunters, near-death by scuba, bicycle, llama-induced plunges toward cliff edges, long-dark falls into Bhutanese toilets—from Los Angeles to Jerusalem, Patagonia to Bali, Borneo to Kilimanjaro—and all of it psychoanalyzed as she goes, a thrilling story of adventure, tenacity, and spirit. Woven through this great read are the relational challenges, feisty and healing dialogues, and the loving support of her husband and travel buddy, Jim Wheeler."

**SAM SHEM**, M.D., author of *The House of God* and *The Spirit of the Place*; co-author of *We Have To Talk: Healing Dialogues Between Men and Women*

"Harriet Wrye's psychoanalytic writings have addressed the terrors and pleasures of the body, the long-range impact of the earliest maternal surround on fantasy, fears, desires, and basic questions of psychic aliveness and deadness. She has noticed the risks and challenges of living a full life—of, as she once put it, 'composing a life with ambition and desire.' In this personal narrative, ambition, desire, self-knowledge, and the vulnerabilities of mortality meet, as Wrye describes adventures and experiences throughout the world from quiet meditation to daring mountain ascents, along with the legacies of family traumas and repeated, life-threatening challenges to her health. Here, the psychoanalyst meets the autobiographer, as life, death, and primary relations are at stake."

> **NANCY J. CHODOROW**, Ph.D., psychoanalyst and author of *The Reproduction of Mothering* and
> *Individualizing Gender and Sexuality: Theory and Practice*

"Harriet Wrye offers the story of her pilgrimage, her inner/outer journey in an authentic and fluid style that will speak to so many who are concerned with the transformation of their lives and relationships. As a trained psychotherapist, she has been keenly able to turn the lamp upon herself to help her own healing, even when reflecting on and easing the suffering of others."

> **SHANTUM SETH**, Dharmacharya and Guide: In the Footsteps of the Buddha, buddhapath.com

# PULLING UP STAKES
## Stepping Into Freedom

**Harriet Kimble Wrye**

For Georgann,
Enjoy Stepping Into
Freedom! ~ Harriet Wrye
December, 2019

This is A Chanslor Book, an imprint of Rare Bird Books

Distributed in the U.S. by Cameron + Company, Inc.

Published in the United States of America

For information and inquiries, address Rare Bird Books, 453 South Spring Street, Suite 531, Los Angeles, CA 90013.

Cover design by Lou Beach
Set in Minion Pro

Cataloging-in-Publication Data for this book is available from the Library of Congress.

ISBN-13: 9780983925521
ISBN-13: 9780983925552 (ebook)

Rare Bird Books are available at special discounts for bulk purchases in the U.S. by corporations, institutions, and other organizations. For more information, please contact Cameron + Company, 6 Petaluma Blvd. North, Suite B6, Petaluma, CA 94952 or email info@cameronbooks.com.

Printed on recycled paper.

10  9  8  7  6  5  4  3  2  1

To the memories of my grandparents, Fred and Jessie Kennedy Prescott, who bequeathed their pioneer spirit, love of mountains and oceans, far flung travel and "Twin Brooks," our now fifth-generation homestead in the Sierras; to my mother, Martha Prescott Kimble, who encouraged me to dream; to my father, James Clinton Kimble, who always said, *Write a book!*, to my dearly beloved children Gabriel, Ariel, and Brooke; and with incredible gratitude to my husband, James Wheeler, who has gamely accompanied me, every step of the way.

# CONTENTS

# Acknowledgements

THE INSPIRATION for this book has been nourished by so many people along the way, I can hardly begin to express my gratitude: To my patients for the privilege of knowing them, their tolerance for my long sabbatical absence and for their generous willingness to let some of their stories (disguised) be shared; to my wonderful teachers, mentors and colleagues in the psychoanalytic community, especially at LAISPS (The Los Angeles Institute and Society for Psychoanalytic Studies); to my inspirations in the Buddhist community, Zen Master Thich Nhat Hanh, the monks and nuns of Deer Park and Plum Village Monasteries, my Sangha, and the community of the Order of Interbeing.

There are so many amazing people we encountered along our journeys, from our trekmates climbing Kilimanjaro, to the Stone Age tribesmen of the Baliem Valley in Irian Jaya, the park rangers in Borneo, our many wonderful guides into "the back of beyond" in Indonesia, Asia, South America and Africa, to the friends and family at home who cheered us on and supported us every step of the way and kept us grounded as we disappeared into the distance.

Finally, thank you to all of you who have directly worked on this book— my three Santa Cruz wordsmith angels, Carolyn Brigit Flynn, Natascha Bruckner and Melody Culver for extraordinary editorial guidance, my Los Angeles team, marketing guru Tyson Cornell of Rare Bird Lit, and Lou Beach for the most wonderfully apt cover design. Earlier support came from Steve Scholl of White Cloud Press, the Meredith Bernstein Agency, and Elizabeth Lyon, editor.

And did I save the least/most for last? My wordless animal support group—our llamas Machu, Hopi, Mica, Jambo, Llao Llao, Miwok, Zuni, and Sequoia, who carried our stuff and gamely went along everywhere we literally pulled up stakes—my horses Spirit, Cheyenne, Shambhala Sunrise, and little Running Bear—and our loyal canine friends, the regal Jullay, my giggle therapist Tashi Delek, and his newly minted nephew, the effervescent Bon Bon de Beau Beaune.

For so many privileged encounters with those who appear in these pages, thank you all! May you and all my future readers Step Into Freedom.

Harriet Kimble Wrye
Santa Cruz, California
April 2012

# PART I
# KILIMANJARO

# Chapter 1
## The Launch

Our jostling, dirt-encrusted jeep bounces and squeaks for four unremitting hours across a narrow desert track through the open country of Tanzania. We arrive in the middle of the night, finally stopping in pitch blackness at base camp. As I climb out of the jeep, stiff and bone-weary from the long flight and journey from the Arusha airport, I trip headlong instead into the talons of a thorn bush. Sprawled in the dark, hot sand, impaled by stinging thorns, I'm brought up short and bloody. Edgy laughter competes with fatigued tears, and I settle on giving free range to both.

My mind quickly trips to the familiar. *Whoa, now my new microfiber khaki safari shorts and Coolmax shirt are dirty. Laundry is more than a week away.* Then, as I pluck thorns from my palms, I let myself ask the critical questions. *What am I doing here? Why am I about to try to climb this 19,349' peak? Is this an omen?*

I grimace with the prick of thorny little jabs of pain. *Why am I here, sprawled in the African desert, far from home?* I enter a timeless zone of introversion, my frequent home as a psychoanalyst, beginning a familiar thread of tracking my own inner workings. My thoughts race with practiced ease. I recognize a dynamic tension between seeking freedom and the biggest challenges, traveling to the farthest outbacks, testing my mettle, stoking the fires of omnipotence and pleasure in taking control, versus my greatest trial of all: accepting limits, learning to let go, releasing the need for control. Another thorn pique bolts me back to my body. Life is short, and we're here by a slender thread. *I want to sort out the balance between living each*

*day to the fullest as if there were no tomorrow and facing the fact that*
*before I know it, I will be turning sixty.* My beloved husband Jim,
three years ahead of me and a far more reckless adventurer than I,
has already lived out a lion's share of his nine lives.

Pulling out the last of the thorns, I enumerate the list of reasons
I am here as naturally as a homemaker makes out her shopping list.
*I long to tolerate my limits, accept my mortality, and cultivate a deeper*
*understanding of impermanence.* Finally relieved of thorns, I breathe
in the sweet-scented African night air and rest a moment on the
warm desert sand.

I am suddenly surrounded by my trek mates, relative strangers
until we met a few hours ago in the airport. Their flashlights shine on
me while Jim, my tall, lean, handsome, gray-haired husband, grins
down with his sky blue eyes, saying, "So, Doctor, that's a splashy
start!" Anton, our expedition guide, trots smartly out from Jones
Camp base tent with a first aid kit, a bucket of warm soapy water and
his own impish, slightly unshaven grin, punctuated by sparkling blue
eyes. He quips in a Cockney voice, "Kind of a pointed greeting we
gave you here in the bush, eh?"

Next morning, after a stuporous sleep, our newly assembled trekking
group trudges from individual sleeping tents across a barren, dry
expanse to the cook tent for a breakfast of fresh fruit, grits, eggs, and
homemade rolls. Anton clinks his spoon on a Toucan-emblazoned
coffee mug to get our attention, his sandy hair still sleep-tousled.
"Listen up, guys!" We pull our canvas camp chairs into position.
We're going to have our first daily "chalk talk" about what to expect
in the coming days.

Outside the tent I hear the awakening chorus of the African
bush—whirring insects, birds with unfamiliar feathers and songs
chirping and singing. Anton gathers our two handsome, very black
African assistant trek leaders, well-muscled Joseph and lithe August.
We soon delight in hearing these Bantu Chagga tribesmen speak
in clipped British voices, an ironic contrast to their boss's brawly
Cockney style. Eight American climbers lean forward in our camp

chairs. We are singles and couples from all over the United States, and our trip doctor, Nihal, is East Indian. We range in age from twenty-something to sixty-three, and costumes vary from newly purchased REI and Campmore clothing to well-faded, far-traveled gear.

With a portable blackboard, pull-down maps and charts, Anton formally welcomes us: "We're about to trek through six distinct eco-zones over the next eight days of the climb and descent." He indicates with his pointer on the trail map. "We'll be leaving this high desert plain, crossing a montagne forest of dense jungle canopy, running streams, and plenty of orchids and monkeys, then we'll move into the clearing that gives the first dramatic vistas of Kili herself. We'll trek across the Shira Plateau at 11,000 to 13,000 feet with its gigantic specimens of myriad native plants, then up thousands of feet through sparse, arid volcanic scree before we reach Arrow Glacier, opening onto the glaciers at the Kili summit at 19,349 feet."

This sounds like the brochure, fascinating and challenging, but with an unexpected spin. I respond with more than simple anticipation as he outlines the daily routine on the trek, telling us how to arrange our gear and what weather to expect. It's not just that spine-tingling screech of chalk on a blackboard. In spite of Anton's enticing introduction to the geological and botanical wonders we will traverse, as an attuned psychoanalyst I'm picking up a kind of eerie energy between Anton and our assistant guides, Joseph and August. I note a few disquieted pauses, and know that something powerful is preoccupying them. Even though we are still a group of relative strangers, it is my training as an analyst to ferret out unconscious communication and my basic nature to speak up. Not willing to accept unspoken barriers to communication with leaders on whom our lives will soon depend, I ask at first gently, but then persistently: "I sense something bothering you." No answer. Then, "What is it?" Still no answer.

My query brings on a chilling silence. I swivel around in my camp chair to see what I can read in the others' faces. Seeing their attentive expressions, I'm guessing I've nailed a feeling some of them may have felt unconsciously. Nihal, the trek doctor and a Chicago radiologist by trade, trains his sharp, black, well-schooled Indian eyes first on Anton, then me. Susan, the youngest and bubbliest of the group, leans forward, the effervescence evaporating from her wide Texas smile.

Anton begins formally speaking of the dangers of Kili and high altitude. It sounds like a canned safety speech. He says the company has an almost 95% success record on reaching the summit, almost twice the average. I'm being stonewalled. Anton turns apprehensively to look at Joseph and August, who are staring down at their sandaled feet. I continue gazing at him pointedly across the breakfast table. It takes Medusa's stare to dissolve his defense.

Finally, returning my gaze, Anton drops his pointer and his teacherly mien and blurts out, "Just over a week ago, a woman on our last trek died on the mountain. We're all pretty stirred up about it. It's never happened to me in all the years I've guided this mountain. It was the second to the last trip before I retire into married life and a desk job. I'm not ready to say more."

Whoa. In spite of the rising African heat, a chill raises the hairs on the back of my neck and on my arms. I've always welcomed "goose pimples" as clinically informative; they signal anxiety and say *bulls-eye*. I rub them. At this moment, we all barely know each other and we're each cocooned in our own pre-trip anxieties. Anton's confession rips silently through the group. The meeting breaks up awkwardly, half-finished tea and coffee mugs are hastily abandoned and we scatter, shuffling in nervous silence through the hot sand to our tents to spend the day readying for tomorrow's departure. Nothing like a "to-do list" to pull you back from the brink of panic.

After dinner our group settles around a blazing campfire that lights up the starry African night. This time it is Susan who breaks the ice for us, pressing Anton for more details. She is recently divorced, a thirty-something, curly blonde and blue-eyed Texas lawyer who has revealed her spunk and courtroom savvy by effortlessly gleaning information from each of the climbers. She's a little Texas pistol who applies her vivacious good offices and impressive cross-examining skills, confronting Anton across the campfire: "You've got to tell us more."

Anton leans back in his camp chair and his Cockney accent rivets us. "A 53-year-old woman, her name was Zoe, was on our last trek with her new husband. It turns out her doctor had warned her not to exceed 12,000 to 13,000 feet due to some heart stress. But she and her husband Bart never said anything about it to me. They described their health as excellent." Anton pauses to throw a log on the fire, sending crackling sparks skyward. "But by the third day she was really struggling."

Jim, ever the mountaineer, interrupts to ask, "What signs was she showing?" Anton says, "Unsteady on her feet, breathing hard, her color was pale and she felt clammy. At 16,000 feet I told her she had no choice. She *had* to turn back. It was bizarre. She didn't want to, but I told her again she had no choice. Reluctantly, she set out with two porters to help carry her gear and a radiophone to keep in contact with me. Unbelievably, Bart wanted to continue to summit with the rest of the group and let her go down on her own." Our anxious murmurs turn to gasps and exclamations of "Oh, my god!" Susan blurts out, "You mean her husband *didn't* go with her! I would've decked the guy!" Anton, August and Joseph are all breathing hard and shifting uncomfortably on their chairs. Anton takes a deep breath and continues, "On the second day's descent, the porters radioed me. They told me Zoe had gone into cardiac arrest."

"Oh my god!" I bleat.

"'What's her condition?' There was static silence on the radio, and then I heard, 'She's dead.' Joseph and I were in total shock. There was nothing we could do."

Anton clears his throat, and in a voice husky with emotion, continues. "I told the porters to carry her body down. Joseph and I decided not to tell the rest of the group until after their ascent on the summit next morning. We waited until they had all summited. Stoked about reaching the top, none of them, most especially her husband, were focused on Zoe. It was awful. After we came off the top and were starting down, then I had to tell them of the call and about her death."

A log suddenly collapses into the fire and we all jump as coals fly dangerously close to our feet. In spite of dancing flames and crackling fire, a grim pall settles over all of us. Nihal, Susan, Jim, Janet, Ruth, the others and I all groan in horror, sympathy and disbelief. Anton pauses while Joseph pushes one of the logs back into the center of the fire. "When I told him, I found out her husband had actually known all along that she was at serious risk." We all lean forward, waiting for details. "The guy actually tells me then and there that she'd told him she wanted to be cremated if she didn't make it!"

As a group we emit a chorus of incredulous groans. "No shit!" "What a shit!"

"Yep," Anton continues, "He let her go alone. Bart and Zoe had both put the whole group at risk. They knew about her condition. Zoe'd been to see her cardiologist and he'd warned her unequivocally and outright, 'You shouldn't go above 14,000 feet!' They'd suppressed his report, never alerted the agency on the medical forms."

Flabbergasted, I repeated, "And she wanted to be *cremated* on the mountain? This is appalling—shades of *Into Thin Air* and Krakauer's description of some of those dangerously self-oriented climbers on Everest!" Anton and Joseph mutely nod.

I find myself trying to imagine their motivations. Anton says the husband was strikingly handsome but seemed like a very self-centered jock, always driven to find some new challenge. Zoe the bride sounded mousier, and was probably pushing herself to impress and meet the athletic standards of her new macho husband. I know something about this dynamic. Though mousy I am certainly not, before I met Jim—an avid skier, hiker, competitive cyclist, and macho man himself—I was pretty content with a comparative walk in the park. Here I am, about to do something I would never have dreamed of. And now it's sounding way scarier. My friends and family still can't believe what I've gotten into since I met Jim fifteen years ago. I am excited by most of the sporty challenges and adventures he's spurred me on to. We've done a lot of downhill and cross-country skiing, many miles backpacking in the backcountry, and treks up to 21,000 feet into the Land of the Snow Leopard in the Himalayas. But I certainly don't have a known heart problem.

Not only do I comprehend why Anton, Joseph, August, and the porters seemed so squirrelly and weird, but I also realize that our group has the raw death of this woman to carry with us. We each might have to contemplate our motivations. I'm ready to look into my own grandiosity and the truly unsettling implications of this story of people who could afford to travel halfway around the globe to prove something. The questions I asked myself during the thorn bush episode ratchet up.

Anton the Brit seems like a highly competent leader, a jokester, good at making light and putting people at ease. August and Joseph are young, maybe in their mid-twenties, both friendly but shy. They all seem deeply relieved to unburden themselves of this horrible experience as the rest of the story tumbles forth from Anton.

"By the time we got down to the bottom of the mountain it was clear the evacuation of a body is very difficult at best, since there are only two helicopters in all of Tanzania. They're reserved for the president and the military. In spite of how we felt about the guy, because of what her husband said were her wishes and the logistics of how difficult it was going to be to get the body back to Arusha, we decided we had no choice but to build her a funeral pyre."

This information about the helicopters, I later discover, derails us all momentarily from the unfolding drama, stirring mini panics and resentment among those of us who paid a lot extra for emergency evacuation insurance. The only way to be evacuated off Kilimanjaro, it turns out, is to be physically carried down the mountain on the back of a porter and driven for two days over bumpy roads to Arusha, the capital. We're going to have to make this climb on our own two feet and not expect to be rescued. Serious gravitas settles in the air around our snapping campfire. But for a minute, it takes our minds away from the horrible image of the funereal fire that is about to unfold.

Anton continues, "I don't think any of us are really ready yet to go back to that scene, even in our minds. You'll soon discover that there's very little available wood around on the mountain. It took the porters all day to scavenge enough to build a funeral pyre. I can't really talk about what came next. Just imagine—it was pretty damn traumatic for the survivors to see, hear and smell her body burning."

The image is excruciatingly graphic. How can you not be overcome by an image of a funeral pyre, with unimaginable smells and the sounds of flesh sizzling? Our warm, crackling campfire takes on a creepy symbolism. But for Anton, Joseph, August, and our porters, the memory of that other conflagration must still be raw and unmetabolized.

I feel that as a group we have no choice but to help them contain and defuse the intensity of this awful experience. But what will it leave us with on the eve of our climb? As I ask this question, I find myself ready to metaphorically leave the campfire. I want to move away from the intensity of the present moment, to escape the heat by going inward and taking refuge in my own free associations.

From my clinical experience with patients, and from my own life, I know that raw trauma is sometimes simply too much to contain. I have learned that we can never be inoculated against trauma. Once we absorb the energy, we may have to tolerate being haunted by it for a time. But for the moment, it's clearly a relief for these witnesses to share their grisly nightmare at last.

Though I can feel a clutch in my belly and the cold tension of hair rising on the back of my neck as I sit with Anton's story, I'm aware that I struggle with other tensions and anxieties of my own. I pray that one day I will be emotionally free enough to release them. I am concerned about my need for control and security. For example, I am such a neat freak that my son Gabriel once jokingly gave me a label maker so I could list the contents of all the drawers in the kitchen to be sure nobody, god forbid, would dream of putting the pizza cutter where the pastry brushes belonged. In terms of emotional security, I want Jim to reassure me too much about his love for me, and to tell me that he'll watch out for his physical safety when he goes on long bike rides. I also feel I have too many attachments both in the material world—to my home and its contents (that goes way beyond the pizza cutter and the pastry brushes), and to particular aspects of my identity—my professional role and my role as a mother. I fear I hold too tightly to these.

I'm brought back to the dying campfire, aware of dead silence all around. Stirred and hushed, one by one we pull back our camp chairs and head somberly to our tents for the night. Jim and I try wordlessly to expunge these distressing ruminations and morbid images with tented love. It helps, but it has an edgy aura—like the gravity of knowing a lion is crouched outside the tent.

*Monkey Business*

We depart camp next morning via Land Cruiser, driving an hour through surrounding farmlands, up into the montagne forest to the end of the road. On the way we watch frolicking Colubus monkeys, fabulous arboreal creatures with long black fur punctuated by white "lion's mane" shawls and fluffy tails. We discover them only through the rustling of leaves and flashes of movement in the forest canopy. We also see elephant dung and learn from the porters that what we smell is leopard piss on the trail. Along the first day's eight-hour hike, we find the forest a riot of new and unfamiliar wild flowers and foliage, lavishly scattered amongst familiar plants such as huge Schefflera, twining lianas, Ficus, wild impatiens, and colorful birds such as sunbirds and Turacos.

Our porters seem to practically jog past us on the trail with their heavy cargo. We were all floored yesterday to learn that the trek gear, tents, and food for our group of eight trekkers would be borne by thirty-three African porters. It seemed obscene until we realized that the gear was extensive—tents, sleeping bags, cooking and privy tents, food, radio, etc.—and that there is great competition for the high-status, well-paid portering jobs. It is awesome to see our porters, most from the nearby Chagga tribe, a Swahili-speaking subgroup of the Bantu, struggling up the mountain with sixty to eighty pounds on their backs or balanced on their heads. On their feet are the remnants of cast-off old boots, tennis shoes, and duct-taped flip-flops.

Juxtapositions of life and death, haves and have-nots, challenges and foolhardiness are so rife, my mind swims. Where *am* I headed? What unfamiliar states of body and mind lie ahead of me? Can it really be that in five days we will summit Mt. Kilimanjaro? We have been training for months, running on the beach, scaling the StairMaster, climbing Mt. Baldy and Mt. San Jacinto near our home in California, and finally donning crampons and ice axes, summiting 14,000-foot Mt. Shasta with our adult daughters Brooke and Ariel supporting us and cheering us on.

For my part, although I've accomplished a lot in this life, I've never felt particularly physically competitive. But now I want to prove to myself that I am strong and can prevail over the hardest challenge, especially as I see my sixtieth birthday and the millennium on the near horizon. I want to rise above my fears and transcent burdensome aspects of my personality. I have an inkling that the sheer grit, guts and stick-to-itiveness that I will need to rise to the summit in a few days also contain the stubbornness, willfulness and inflexibility that are the base of that burden. It's the challenge of my life: to let go of the dross and keep what is truly good.

A trek is like this: moments of deep personal reflection relieved by stimulating connections with new acquaintances. The group is definitely loosening up. Adding a story of love to death on Kilimanjaro, Anton tells us of his heated love affair with "Gretz," a trekker who climbed Kili two years ago. They fell passionately in love and braved all kinds of impediments, including, predictably, a drumming down by the head office of the adventure company, which has a strict policy against hanky-panky between guides and clients, followed by a frozen reception from her New England family at home. He tells us ours will be his last climb up Kilimanjaro. When we finish he'll marry Gretz and settle in behind a desk at the adventure travel agency's home office in the U.S.

By the end of our third day together, it's clear we've got a congenial group—no crazies like the ill-fated honeymooning couple Zoe and Bart on the last climb, Sensing a good group dynamic, cemented by the knowledge that Kili can and does kill, the eight of us establish three ground rules for the climb: absolute honesty in communications; supporting each other at whatever our pace and struggles on the climb; and unmitigated humor.

Our spark plug and most vibrant trekker, Susan, regales us with stories of her recent 30th birthday party in New Orleans, just after she left her husband and embarked on an "exorcism of bad love in Sin City" with a few of her kick-ass Texas girlfriends. Though monkeyshines and laughter abound in camp, with husbands being "offed" and figurative lions and literal leopards circling, our group seems palpably infused with the strong scent of mortality thrust into us by Zoe's death and cremation.

On our last night with firewood available, we circle around our last campfire. Jim is inspired to tell sagas of his own near-death experiences. There are three too many. His are all pushing-the-limits sports related. While I can introspectively reflect on my own grandiosity, Jim is pure action-oriented and not in the least introspective.

Jim enjoys telling his horror stories to our hardy fellow trekkers. His first near-death bike accident happened about ten years ago at sundown on a lonely strip of Pacific Coast Highway north of our home in Pacific Palisades. An unlicensed driver, headed northwest and blinded by the setting sun, turned left in front of him, cutting him off. Jim crashed—hands and head first—into the oncoming car. I scan the stricken faces around the campfire and hear our group exclaim, "Oh my god!" and "Oh, no!" and "Jeez, then what happened?"

Jim's hands took the brunt of the impact and were almost pulverized. The crash also cut an artery in his arm. Jim explains, "As my body and bike were thrown into the air, a paramedic jogging along the shoulder of the highway saved my life." This guardian angel bound the artery in Jim's slashed arm. "They rushed me to the hospital, where I ultimately had to undergo over twenty-seven hours of successive reconstructive hand surgeries and repair of the artery. Both hands were skewered by metal rods and trussed up in bandages and casts as big as boxing gloves for six weeks."

I chime in, "Naturally this made all normal bodily activity an enforced family affair. Picture this: How are you going to eat? Get dressed? Answer Nature's call? You're helpless as a baby! This was probably the most troubling aspect of the accident for him. He tried to deny how dependent he was on his dad and me, his primary caretakers for all his basic bodily functions." Nevertheless, once his hands finally healed and the bandages removed, he became the hand-surgeon's star patient; his machismo ratcheted up with even more scary gusto and the life-threatening accident became fodder for party conversation.

In the firelight, I see pregnant looks ripple across the faces of the group, especially between the coupled group members, Ruth and John, Janet and Mike. Jim and I are teetering publicly on the edge of one of our marital "issues." But then, too, Susan has just told us of the issues that uncoupled her in Sin City, and Nihal will soon lament why his wife refuses to come on adventure trips with him.

Brought together and ultimately into silent reflection by Jim's near-death story, as the second night's campfire dies down, we begin stirring from our silence and say our goodnights. I realize that climbing Kilimanjaro is densely packed with a panoply of feelings and motivations for each of us.

## CHAPTER 2
## HOW I GOT HERE FROM THERE

EVER SINCE my mother's fatal car crash over thirty years ago, when I was a young mother with two small children, I've experienced conscious, marginally disabling anxieties about losing loved ones in traumatic ways. My anxieties came from a palpable trauma: my mother, or "Ma," as we called her—the centerpiece and hearthstone of our family—had died a sudden and violent death in a side-on hit by a Mack truck. The finality of the crash totally pierced any last remnants of adolescent omnipotence I'd carried into adulthood, having never suffered a broken bone in my whole life.

My mother's accident alerted me to appropriate vigilance about the myriad safety issues children face in daily living; I had child-proof security latches on cabinets and drawers, no household poisons, and caps on electric sockets long before it was fashionable to hire an agency to "child safe" your home with Martha Stewart glam. We had very few trips to the ER and we kept the literal and metaphoric training wheels in place for suitably safe terms.

### *"Lacunae" in my Psyche*

However, mother's accident also catapulted me into a low level of lightly concealed, chronic anxiety that could escalate into near panic when anyone I loved was unaccounted for. My husband's infidelity within that first year of mourning turned the screws, piercing my psyche with fears like the holes in Swiss cheese. In psychoanalytic parlance, these "holes" in the ego are known as "lacunae," little vestiges of craziness. It was only two years after the accident that my husband finally came clean about the truth of the affair he had been having since before Mother's death. That marital deception and abandonment left me feeling deeply unsafe, and destroyed our marriage. The trauma of divorce continued to play diabolically in my mind with the loss of my mother. The truth set me free, but years of deceit on top of grief scarred me for a very long time.

Even before our divorce, my husband was traveling and filming on location for extended periods of time. The demands on a high-budget Hollywood film director are intense, and his work left him emotionally unavailable, so I was often effectively a single parent to our children, Gabriel and Ariel. Prior to their birth I had taught for eight years as a high school English teacher at Beverly Hills High School. I love literature, loved high school teaching, and thoroughly enjoyed my many wonderful students. Looking back, I realize that I was struggling with masked depression and a subliminal awareness of living on shaky marital ground, sometimes overwhelmed by a maelstrom of confusion, grief, and rage, juxtaposed against parental and professional responsibility. Eventually recognizing my frustration and the lid on what I could do as an employee within the swinging politics of state and district directives. I took a leave from teaching to pursue the exploration of unconscious processes, Plus, even Hamlet can get tiring after eight years running.

So, when Gabriel and Ariel were small, I went back to graduate school and earned my Ph.D. in social-clinical psychology. On a positive note, having completed my doctorate, seeing patients and undergoing my own analysis. I was finally beginning to make sense of my life and take control in positive ways. Internally, I was changing as dramatically as my external world was changing, and of course, I wasn't very settled in either realm. Looking back on those most difficult years of my life, I can see that while I was genuinely becoming more self-aware, less depressed and healthier through my analysis, I often felt alone and inundated by the demands of daily life.

Enamored of my two treasured children, I probably became a hypervigilant mom, and in the long run accomplished just the opposite of the security I'd set out for. I inadvertently fostered children who, by their adolescence, would periodically sneak out on me, lying about their plans and whereabouts to get me off their backs. I also created undue tension; sometimes they felt roped in more than loved. Our relationships carried scars long after I loosened my anxious grip.

As the children were growing, I continued my studies and completed psychoanalytic training. That career has kept me challenged, stimulated, and deeply satisfied for three decades now. It awarded me the great privilege of entering into psychoanalysis myself, where I discovered much of what I described about myself above including the "lacunae" in my psyche, my depressive recesses, Calvinist-induced hang-ups, a need for control, my imagination, empathy and creativity, and my arrogance. My analysis prepared me to work with very challenging and fascinating patients, moving with them through their own deep scars, metabolizing old traumas and re-sculpting ingrained character styles and defenses. My psychology practice allowed me to continue teaching, writing, and publishing, and the latter led to a widening circle of travel, consultation, and presentations around the country and the world. Psychoanalysis got me through my divorce, helped me immeasureably as a parent and continues to stimulate me to think about my own scars, neurotic knots, gifts and capacities, and to apply the tools of clinical experience to myself and within my relationships.

### The Marital Crucible

My romance with Jim, which began after Mother's death and my divorce, was forged in that psychodynamic crucible. His sister and I were high school friends and our parents had also become friends. I was drawn to Jim not only due to our common history and interests, his handsome good looks, playfulness and romantic nature, but because he was trustworthy, reliable and honest. I gratefully had no qualms about his whereabouts and always felt very safe with him. During his tenure as a banker, I could count on him to be home for dinner at a reasonable hour, and never needed to worry about who was carrying his cookies on the film set or who was warming his hotel bed at night. His steadiness and vitality, as well as the clarity of his sky blue eyes and the twinkle therein, were like a breath of pure, clear air. We were both so starved for a good relationship and good loving that we fell quite madly in love, though not without the anxieties and ambivalences that beset most recently divorced adults who have just taken a deep look at their complicity in failed relationships.

It was quite a while before residues of my silent anxiety insinuated itself into the tranquility between Jim and me. It came up big time, not surprisingly, when he had his first near-fatal bicycling accident. In 1987, seven years into our relationship and four years into our marriage, Jim was hit by an oncoming car as he cycled up Pacific Coast Highway at sunset. His accident rekindled the trauma of my mother's death; and this time, the shock was complicated by the fact that Jim had promised to clean the garage that day, but instead, without telling me, took off on his bike while I was at work. When I got the phone call from the emergency room that he had been brought in seriously hurt, I imploded with anxiety, derailing my newfound sense of safety, and stirred up a stomach-turning sour milk cocktail of resentment that was served up to me several more times during our years together.

Despite the bike accident, Jim and I shared mostly loving, sweet times, navigating the terrain of child and step child raising, work, and play as life moved us forward. Still, at the same time, quietly in my heart I craved some kind of "walkabout" in my life: an opportunity, without time constraints, to explore the recesses of my soul and to seek a greater measure of freedom from the inner demons of anxiety and abandonment fears than even my own analysis had accorded. I also passionately longed for challenge, adventure and untethered freedom. Jim always was, and still is, up for the latter.

This dream began taking shape when I was invited to give a psychoanalytic paper in Barcelona and Jim suggested we "pop over" to Tanzania afterward to climb Mt. Kilimanjaro. My plan was hatched during that climb. By then, Gabriel, Ariel, and Jim's daughter Brooke had all graduated from college and were living as independent adults and Jim was retired from banking. Not ready to retire yet from this profession I so loved, my secret dream, with careful advance planning, was to somehow take a "sabbatical" from my practice, to venture into the back of beyond.

# Chapter 3

## Kilimanjaro: The Dawning of a Dream

"Wakie wakie!" Anton calls outside our tent at 6:30 a.m. We roll out to a breakfast of ngali (cornmeal porridge) and papayas, treat our drinking water with iodine tablets, and start down the trail by 8:00 a.m. Before crossing the Shira Plateau, we begin in a forest that's rich with forget-me-nots, impatiens, small red gladiolas, and protea kilimanjaro.

Poor Jim has fallen prey to a private exorcism. With thorn bush abrasions and deep scratches on his ankle, still picking off ticks from base camp, he woke in the night with nausea and diarrhea and couldn't keep breakfast down. It isn't clear if this is early altitude sickness or a bug. As we climb the steep trail up through the heath and cross a bog, jumping from one tundra hillock to the next, Jim skids and falls into the mud, dousing his arms, belly and legs with sloppy brown ooze. Normally coordinated, he's now the portrait of an unhappy camper. I shout brightly, "Hey, you deserve the Brown Badge of Courage!" A man of few words, he groans, "I've had better days." At a time like this, a day back at work as Wells Fargo Vice President, in his hated pinstripe suit, would be preferable to the adventuring life. Anton prescribes Cipro for the diarrhea and Diamox for altitude (and attitude). Jim soldiers forward.

Mid-morning, we emerge from soupy clouds and see mighty Kili for the first time. Glaciers sparkling, she is staggeringly majestic. Like many other dormant volcanic cones, she's often sheathed in cloud, but today she rises solitary and dramatic from miles and miles of cloud. It's easy to see why Kilimanjaro is revered as a sacred summit.

We scramble up a steep, rolling scree track, gaining twelve

hundred feet in altitude, and are rewarded with breathtaking vistas overlooking the summit of neighboring Mt. Mehru (14,985') and Lava Tower, where we camped. The valley below is filled with cumulus clouds, which occasionally break to reveal glimpses of the plains beneath.

Susan also has our best interests at heart. She serves as the trek cheerleader and model of generosity. She insisted on giving her heavy-duty hiking boots to August, who's worn nothing on his feet but tattered tennis shoes, soles flopping loudly with each step. Susan also has an endless store of icebreaker questions at lunch and after dinner.

One night, Susan's question spawns a killer idea in me. She asks the group, "If you could live anywhere in the world, where would you live?" Everybody else has a dream of some faraway place, but Jim and I agree: We're already blessed. We live in a beautiful home by the ocean in Pacific Palisades, California. A family timber ranch, Twin Brooks, is our hideaway in the Sierra Nevada mountains. Our good health and creature comforts are unfathomable for some, such as the hardworking porters on this trek. I love my work; we have good friends and a very good life.

But Susan's question has stirred me. "As good as our life is," I blurt out, "I want to be free. I would love to explore the diverse cultures and geographies of the Third World. I'd love to reflect deeply inward without following a timetable." I breathe out a deep sigh of release and gratitude to Susan for offering this stirring question and inviting me to plant this seed of an idea. I look across the table at Jim's face to check his reaction. He looks a bit dumbfounded and delighted. It's out there in the universe now.

I lean in toward the Coleman lanterns on the camp table. Mesmerized by the glow on my trek mates' faces, I slide into a reverie. As a psychoanalyst in private practice, I am utterly tied down, committed to being available to my patients for as many years as they need me. I can't do anything spontaneously; I must be in my office at eight o'clock every Monday morning. Jim and I have managed to fit some amazing adventures into weekends or annual vacations. But I never traveled during my youth or first marriage. My thirst for travel has hardly been quenched.

*What if I take a two-year sabbatical from private practice?* I'm surprised to find myself thinking outside the box. We could lease our house at the beach to cover expenses. Twin Brooks could be our base, and we could take off—go where the spirit moves us! Jim's retired; he'll *love* this idea. I just have to figure out how long it would take to wind down my practice before we get too old to climb mountains! I love my work, and can't afford to retire yet, but I crave a wide bay window of unstructured time to explore the world while Jim and I are still physically fit.

"Slowly, slowly!" Anton's rejoinder echoes in my mind. I trudge up the trail, one foot at a time, my breath coming in chest-cinching gulps. But my mind is racing onward, sculpting my dream. I hardly notice the effort required for every step as I mentally review the progress of my patients in treatment. If I take only referrals for short-term couple therapy and supervision, my current patients' analyses could be finished in four years! A sabbatical could become a reality!

Awakening from my reverie, I stop, leaning exhausted and breathless on my hiking poles to look down the mountain. Realizing how far I've come, I suddenly feel my knees trembling, feet quivering, and lungs constricting. I shade my eyes to look at the summit and gasp in awe at the magnitude of its glacial face. I smile at the thought that I've hatched a killer idea while climbing Kilimanjaro.

As I resume my dogged trudge up the steep trail, my thoughts are interrupted by a blast of cold down my backside. My drinking water, carried in a bicyclist's water bladder inside my jacket, is leaking out of the valve, which I apparently failed to tighten at lunchtime. High in the thin, cold air, my hiking trousers are suddenly turning to ice. My inner Puritan mocks me with a familiar refrain: "The best laid plans of mice and men are aftly gang awry, and pride goeth before a fall." Will I be allowed to sculpt my life with freedom and possibility? Is this just too much good stuff to have in one life?

At 16,000 feet above sea level, in the dark of night, I plummet further from sublime exhilaration. I'm the last in camp to succumb to altitude symptoms we call "the timpani of farts" and "the zipper symphony." I wasn't expecting to be brought low by altitude, having managed a 20,000-foot climb in the Himalayas a few years ago. At first I think it's just a bit of altitude gas. But soon an internal volcano demands my attention. I have to get out of the tent, fast. Rushing, muttering at stuck zippers, I put on my parka, mittens, wind pants, and boots, and barely make it outside before exploding three feet from the tent.

Surrendering to the cold and absurdity, I remember how my son Gabriel at age four loved hearing me read his storybook *Drummerhof*. He would squeal in wicked boyish delight at the repetitive refrain: "And Drummerhof fired it off!" Fortunately, our guides have provided each of us with a bag containing a trowel, lighter, and toilet paper, so I clean up and return to my bag by 12:30 a.m. At 3:30 a.m. I get the call again, making it to the loo in brilliant moonlight for Drummerhof's repeat performance. The loo is a two-foot hole in the ground, with an ersatz stool and toilet seat perched over it, surrounded by a canvas tent. Shivering in the cold, I am inspired to be eco-conscientious and burn the used toilet paper. As I strike the match, my only flashlight flips lightly out of my hand and spirals into the loo hole. You know exactly what I said, of course.

We face a 7:00 a.m. departure for the strenuous climb from 16,000 feet to our highest campsite at 18,500 feet. In the wakeful pre-dawn hours, Jim and I cuddle gratefully in our zipped-together bags and talk. Jim has an overzealous laugh about my flashlight. We decide we're quite proud of each other. "This was such a good idea of yours, love," I acknowledge. "Giving my paper in Barcelona first, then coming to Africa to climb Kilimanjaro."

"Hmm. Thanks."

I think I hear a purr that could become a snore, but really want to talk. "How do you feel about it at this point, Jim?"

"Sure glad I'm feeling better. That intestinal stuff was a bummer." I feel his hand wander to my tummy, making warm comforting circles. "Hope your belly'll be okay now, and that gut rumbling is the only trouble we have. Hey, those porters are pretty incredible, don't you think?"

"Amazing spirits. They've got nothing in the material world, but they have so much fun together. Always joking," I smile.

"Yep. Singing, fussing around. I like walking with Joseph, hearing about his tribe, his family, growing up on the foot of this mountain and how much he wanted to learn to guide. He wants to learn all about the flowers." Jim and I intertwine our legs into our own familiar pretzel.

"I've been thinking of giving Joseph our copy of *Wildflowers of Tanzania* as a gift after we summit. What do you think?"

I tell him that would be a wonderful idea, knowing how much Jim loves botanizing and how eager Joseph is to learn. It reminds me of Susan giving her boots to August. All of us feel grateful to our porters, aware of how few resources they have.

"And what do you think of my sabbatical idea? I couldn't believe it just popped out of my mouth when Susan asked."

"Well, it's a *lot* to think about—"

"Mmmm. It is." I listen.

"But I know I'd *love* to be able to just take off and wander like that."

My heart gives a little skip.

"Ever since Sally and I spent that year driving all over Europe in our VW bus—"

"Yeah, but I'm not thinking Europe. We can do that in wheelchairs, Luv. How about more stuff like this?"

"What do you mean?"

"I'm dying to visit other undeveloped countries, get deep into the outback. Stuff we never have time to do on a two- or three-week summer vacation. In the spirit of a sabbatical, it'd have to be a significant personal growth experience. I'd want to be challenged physically and stretched psychologically and even more so, spiritually." I take a deep breath and sigh as we disentangle. "You know, Jim, believe it or not, it sometimes feels I've been too boxed in."

"Like this?" He pulls me into his chest. Loving it, I squeal and push against him. "Not bad! You know I've got my own laundry list of things I've always wanted to do, too—like cycle across the U.S. What about that?"

"Oops," I cringe. "That's a hard one for me after your bike accidents. When I said this was a 'killer' idea, I didn't just mean really cool. Part of me is way too aware of your mortality—you scare me because you seem totally unafraid of danger."

I feel him pulling away from me. We're approaching an edge. Not always smart, I press on. "I feel crazy when I'm the only one who voices these fears of vulnerability. I know it touches *my* worst nightmares and traumas, but I wish I knew you were aware of danger too."

I sense Jim withdrawing. Why can't I leave it alone? "That second bike accident, when you were racing in the senior Olympics and crashed headlong into the mountain wall and had to be airlifted to the trauma center? Brooke and I had to wait for two days for all the MRIs and CAT scan results and the neurologist's determination of whether you would be a quadriplegic. You act like it was no big deal."

This kind of frontal attack would usually be a cue for him to roll over and start snoring. I can't tell if he's listening. "Remember? I took that photo of you on that gurney, your eye sockets, cheekbones and jaw smashed, your neck in that immobilizing brace, your face green, blue, swollen, misshapen like some kind of aberrant squash, so later you couldn't deny how bad it was."

In a slow swivet I remember churning between gratitude he'd been spared and, it turned out, wasn't a quadriplegic, and a slow boil that he was still thick-headed enough to keep doing such things, denying their impact on our relationship. How I wished I could control him! I did extract a promise through his wired-shut jaw that if he wanted to keep this marriage alive, he would look at some of these issues in therapy. Although Jim can be incredibly stubborn, he can also use his head as something other than a battering ram. He agreed to therapy.

I snap back into the present moment. He's not snoring, but his body language tells me I'm on thin ice. "I'm sorry, Sweetie, I guess talking about your bicycling all the way across the United States gets me a bit worked up. Maybe we can figure out things we want to do together. Then maybe it'd be good for us to do some things alone. Traveling alone would surely be a huge growth step for me. Navigating in foreign languages, finding roads, trains and all that—it would be amazing if I could handle that." I can feel Jim relax back into me as we retreat from the edge. Cuddling in the pre-dawn hours, we move into our own fantasies about extended adventures.

I feel my anxiety about Jim's desire to cycle across the country. Even while I'm trying to stay soft, I sense my chest tighten slightly, my jaw compress and a hint of that odd clamminess of fear. I'm still freaked out about his cycling after two near-death accidents. Here on the "dark continent," I'm touching on some primal fears in myself. Yet I have further work to do, to plumb my own depths. I want to seek out primitive places and people off the beaten path, and explore even more of the primitive aspects of my own psyche. Plus, I spent many years raising kids, working hard, writing, teaching, and being president of a psychoanalytic institute, that I never made time to develop my spiritual side.

I also feel challenged to move our relationship to a different level, to release both of our fears of not being in control. Jim and I are very compatible and we've learned from couples therapy, but I'm too dependent and Jim can have a granite obstinacy to feelings. Can we move our stone walls? Are we both too bullheaded? Do I want too much?

### Up the Western Breach

"Wakie, wakie" again interrupts us at 5:15. Jim and I give each other one more delicious hug before we start our day of hard climbing.

"The greatest danger today," Anton tells us, "besides altitude, is that you could be hit on the head by falling rocks dislodged by the climber above. You will have to be very careful. And you'll be climbing step by step at a snail's pace because of the lack of oxygen in your blood."

As we head straight up the Western Breach from Arrow Glacier Camp, the trail suddenly becomes very steep; we're climbing hand over hand on rocks and loose scree. I've given up my hiking poles like security blankets, instead clutching the rocks above me, searching behind and beneath for a safe place to plant each boot. Rolling volcanic rocks explode from underfoot and I catch myself, forgetting to breathe. The climb becomes especially challenging as we scramble on loose rocks covered with thin ice. We reach Summit Plateau at 18,500 feet, exhilarated but bushed, and go straight to our campsite beside magnificent walls of ice up to 200 feet high. It is a spectacular, crystal clear day, and below us the crags of Kilimanjaro are covered with snow and ice.

Anton, Mike, and Jim take off to explore the eastern ice field and the volcano's inner crater. I, on the other hand, barely make it into the tent, and crash without unrolling our sleeping bags. Although Diamox has made me more tolerant of the thin air, I have a wracking, repetitive cough that yields serious phlegm. Waking up to the deep cough, I have a disquieting thought: Is this the laryngitis I contracted in Barcelona, returning with a vengeance? My trek mates are no better off. Ruth's face looks grey and wan; she's been sick with vomiting and diarrhea. Susan has the same symptoms plus a deep cough, and looks ashen and ill. Our trip doctor, Nihal, is coughing and doesn't look good either. Many of the porters look drawn; they've stopped singing as altitude stress compounds the effects of their heavy smoking.

Lacking our one fail-safe of trip evacuation insurance, we know the only way out of danger is under our own steam. We have no choice but to soldier forward. As the descent is down the other side of the peak, the only option is for us all to summit tomorrow morning.

### Kilimanjaro: Summit and Descent

It's a gloriously sunny, blustery morning. Today will be awesome and then hellacious: we'll summit the peak, then descend 9,000 feet! I'm up extra early to tape my ankle, put on *both* knee braces, and extend both Leki hiking poles. We manage to get on the trail by 7:00 a.m. and we attain the summit by 8:30.

It is spectacular. All of Africa stretches out around us in a fantastic 360-degree circularama. Uhuru Peak looks down onto the crater that Jim climbed yesterday as well as the three breathtaking

200-foot-high glaciers of Kilimanjaro. Far below us, Mt. Mehru peeks through the clouds at 14,985'. It is a fulfillment of our dream, and an awesome privilege, to stand on the roof of this vast continent. Less than 1% of Africans will ever have this experience. I am inspired and sobered by that awareness. I vow to do something meaningful with it. I realize that with such great privilege comes deep responsibility. If I am able, on this journey, to attain new points of view and embrace perspectives that lead to wisdom, I want to share that with others.

For the first time since crossing the Machame trail, we encounter other climbers who have ascended faster routes—primarily the Marangu or "Coca Cola" route, which is reportedly littered with trash. The Machame, our route, is less traveled, faster than the northern route from Kenya (Loit Okitole), and barren until it links up with Marangu Route. We meet a dozen climbers from all over the world.

After half an hour on top of the world, we begin the 9,000 foot Descent from Hell. I'm worried about my knees, ankle, and recently re-torn shoulder rotator cuff. The trail is mostly scree with rocky, steep drops—good for rocking and rolling, slipping and sliding. I've had surgery on one knee to repair a torn medial collateral ligament, and recently learned that my anterior cruciate ligament is torn as well—the price of taking up with my push-the-limit-adventurer husband. Thus far, though swollen at night, the knees have done me proud, but a steep descent is more stressful than a climb.

After three hours of descent, we reach Barafu Hut (better named "Barfo" Hut), a filthy, overcrowded mountaineering ghetto with tents and trash everywhere. Ruth is extremely weak and Susan is green at the gills, with a grave cough. Anton gives her another "Silver Bullet," an anal suppository of Compazine. We continue our descent with Joseph carrying her pack, and she manages to stumble down the trail.

Mike and Janet cruise ahead of us all toward camp. Jim, who could easily have kept up with them, kindly stays with me and guide Vincent, watching out for my knees. Two thirds of the way down, August insists on carrying my load, and I am amazed what a relief it is not to carry even a small twenty-pound pack down 9,000 feet. How do our porters carry eighty pounds? We make it to Mweka

Campsite about 5:00 p.m. and discover that Susan is in considerably worse shape and must be evacuated immediately. August and two porters carry her in the dark, 3,500 feet further down to Mweka Gate, hoping that the dramatic loss of elevation will resolve the crisis. I give her the Ceclor I'd brought for my respiratory infection, in case she has pneumonia, and off they go—another marathon at the end of an incredibly difficult day. By eight o'clock, with sentries posted on guard all night to watch our gear, Jim and I are zonked.

Joseph arranges to have hot chai brought to each tent for wake-up. We're up and moving at 6:30 a.m., assuming this will be a straightforward half-day descent of the last 3,500 feet. I note nervously that while everyone else's is improving, my cough is getting worse instead of better, and I've given away my antibiotics out of concern for Susan.

Our hike starts out lovely and gradual, prompting Janet to say, "I could handle this all day!" We soon reach the forest zone and hike among ferns, lobelia, and impatiens kilimanjari. The forest is festooned with moss called "Old Man's Beard" and long, strong vines known as liana. The montagne forest here is more lush and beautiful than on the other side of the mountain. Now we can relax and enjoy it more with the summit behind us. I still have to pinch myself. *I really have done it!*

But I should know the dangers of hubris by now. Suddenly, the trail gets wetter, steeper, and muddier. Janet and Mike effortlessly lope ahead. Slipping down a rocky chute of boulders, vines, roots, and greasy mud, I thank God for poles and knee braces. Jim tries his mountain goat two-step descent, which usually leaves me behind. But this time, it leaves him in the mud, covering his boots, pants, and part of his pack. I jest, "More stripes for your Brown Badge of Humiliation." Further down the tedious descent, he slips and falls again, soaking his shirt as well. We take pictures of each other looking like pigs in a wallow. Slimy with mud, we reach Mweka Gate shortly after noon, to whoops and cheers from a much-revived Susan, Anton, August, and others. A lovely lunch picnic table is set up. The Kili Climb is over!

Already nostalgic, I ask our porters to sing their "Kilimanjaro Song" in Swahili so I can record it. At this moment, in this setting, though we have heard its lovely strains several times before, the song is poignantly moving. But in my excitement I fail to push the record button, so their lovely song remains only a memory—a metaphor for letting go.

Listening to the porters sing the Kili Song, feeling gratitude and awe at the yeoman's work they have done for us, I decide to find a porter with small feet and pass my boots on to him. These beloved Asolo Italian leather boots have trekked the Inca trail in Peru, the Torres del Paine Circuit in Patagonia, Mt Ranier, Mt. Baldy, San Jacinto, and many high Sierra miles, but they still have a lot of good wear left. Watching the porters climb in tennis shoes, flip-flops, and worn-out sandals has been a sobering reminder of the material poverty here, although there is no poverty of spirit. After a short Cinderella-like quest with a muddy hiking boot in place of a silver slipper, I discover just the right fit on an appreciative young man. We have a little boot ceremony, and I go happily off in my socks and he in my Asolos.

My persistent cough is not relieved by the descent, and I discover I've been climbing Kilimanjaro with bronchial pneumonia. Susan, on the other hand, is much recovered from the effects of altitude sickness. She tells me an amazing story. Having given her size ten leather hiking boots to the only Chagga tribesman they fit, she wore lighter-weight boots throughout the trek. As she bumped along the muddy descent carried piggyback by a porter, weak and nearly unconscious, she blearily looked down and saw her leather boots on his feet. August was carrying her. She gave him a hug of gratitude and thought, "Truly, what goes around comes around." August squeezed her back and carried her on down the mountain. "*Asante Sana*," they murmured—Swahili for *thank you.*

*Asante Sana* to my fellow trekker, Susan, for providing the impetus to help me formulate a millennial life dream, to let go of all that's familiar, to pull up stakes and reach for the stars.

# PART II
# BENCH VALLEY:
# LOOKING INWARD

# CHAPTER 4
## FINDING A MUSE IN A MEADOW

AT CRABTREE LAKE, 10,400 feet above sea level in the Sierra Nevada Mountains, an August day is dawning. I'm savoring Jim's deliciously warm body sleeping close to mine, waiting for sunrise to warm our tent and signal it's time to get up, move the llamas across the verdant meadow, straighten up camp and fix breakfast. We are five days into an eleven-day, seventy-mile summer pack trip with our poodle and five llamas. After a long, challenging day of hiking and a sound night's sleep, I'm indulging in my morning reverie, reflecting on how much has changed in the four years that have elapsed since we summited Kilimanjaro.

I've been sculpting my sabbatical plan and we're preparing to make it reality. Three years ago I stopped taking new patients, except for short-term work and consultations. Each of my current patients is finishing analysis, a bittersweet process that brings freedom, completion, and relinquishing our deep relationship that has, in many cases, extended for years. We're preparing to lease the Pacific Palisades house I've lived in for three decades. We've built a storage barn at our Twin Brooks ranch, my great grandfather's homestead, midway between Sequoia and Yosemite. It's daunting but exhilarating to imagine shifting our base from an overcrowded city to a remote outpost, so far back in the mountains that the only way out during winter's harshest snowstorms may be several miles on snowshoes.

It feels like the right time to loosen our ties and set out for new adventures. The sense of time passing, of attachment to the familiar over the risky, and the sense of holding on too tightly have been bubbling up in my psyche and fueling this dream. Letting go is a sad, scary proposition, but learning to let go may be the crux of this wisdom journey.

Yesterday I experienced lesson number one in letting go. We left our camp on Fall Creek expecting a relatively easy climb, but things "aftly gang awry." As we covered miles of rugged territory, scrambling cross-country the last 1,500 feet above the trail along the North Fork of the Kings River, Jim and I launched into several of our typical "discussions" as to who could read a topo map better. Jim, a no-nonsense former Marine and former bank officer, likes to solve problems in a very direct (and directive) way, by himself. I prefer to work things through in a sensitive way that yields mutual decision-making. But that involves a lot of talk. My "Can we talk?" signals him to run for cover—like when you lift a log and sowbugs, centipedes and newts scatter to find dark hiding places.

As we went toe-to-toe over the topo map, a belly-flipping feeling came over me. I felt a chill of anxiety and a clammy sensation through my body. *I'm about to cut loose from all of my familiar support systems: my closest friends, our children and family, the home I've lived in for thirty years, my colleagues and patients, a secure professional identity, my favorite yoga teacher and my beloved animals—to set out alone with this ex-Marine as my sole companion?*

I crave close interaction and intimacy while Jim fancies himself the stalwart sort with little use for dependency. Even though the outside world may see me as a competent "can do" person, inside, I can be afraid of abandonment and failure. As we stood at an impasse in our argument on the trail, I thought: *Maybe he's right: I'm a high-maintenance woman. Oh, God. Will I drive him nuts? Will he want to leave me? Can I ever just be quiet and let him be who he is?* I realized I'd best let go of proving him wrong and address my own compulsion to prove I was right. Suddenly I was in touch with how steep the mountain really was. My knees and hips felt torqued from climbing, my thighs were quivering, my feet ached, and I was irritable and famished. The llamas restlessly shifted this way and that.

Jim prevailed, as he usually did in this sort of argument, and the llamas gamely followed us across logs and streams, through thickets and deadfall, up against barrier rocks and back again, oblivious as to whether their route was determined mutually, to the satisfaction of the smaller, more agitated human, or by executive fiat by the larger, more secure of their two trail bosses. We searched the terrain for signs to match contours on the map that would guide us to Crabtree Lake, which we'd heard was one of the most beautiful and rarely visited lakes in the High Sierras.

Hours on, I pleaded, "Let's look for a picnic spot as soon as we reconnect with the stream."

Jim growled, "No, we've got too much ground left to cover. Better push on."

We pushed and pushed, realizing there was still more pushing to do. Zuni, the youngest llama, finally kushed. (As camelids, llamas have inherited Moroccan camel driver vocabulary, which includes "kush" from the French "couchoir," to lie down). I felt like kushing myself, so we stopped in the middle of nowhere.

Wearily we ate lunch in stony silence, not in the bonny spot beside the stream I'd fantasized but on a dirt heap, not quite here and not quite there. I felt like the proverbial unhappy camper waiting for a care package full of goodies that clearly wasn't coming. As I packed up lunch, Jim decreed, "I'm going ahead" and took off with three llamas in tow, either assuming I'd follow close behind, or worse, wanting to put some distance between us.

Spent from the morning's rough climb and stiffened by the lunch stop, which fed my disgruntlement as much as my belly, I got up from the dirt pile picnic, slowly leading Miwok and Jambo up the trail. Jim, out of sight, had declined to indulge me by keeping in touch with walkie-talkies through the cross-country terrain. He reluctantly carries the walkie-talkie I bought him, but keeps it turned off in the bottom of his fanny pack. He's the minimalist, seeds-and-nuts type, while I relish words, psychological innuendoes, and labyrinthine complexity, and prefer cuisine over power bars.

My thoughts ran their contrary course. *What are we doing? We've backpacked together in the Sierras, the Wind Rivers, the Uintahs, the Rockies, and the Hilgards. We're doing what we both most love to do, the same thing we were doing when we met at East Lake in the Sierras twenty years ago. But sometimes in the midst of doing what I think I want to do, I have to stop and wonder, what are we doing?*

Suddenly, I was jarred out of my pity-fest by a weird sound, like a strangled alarm or a woman's cry. Spinning around, I saw Miwok with two heads and six legs. The weird sound was a noise llamas make when under distress or very excited, onomatopoetically called "orgelling." Jambo and Miwok stretched their entwined necks skyward together, orgelling a sound track for the llama version of "Love in the Afternoon." At the moment I was most worried about my own romance, young Jambo had come into his manhood and mounted Miwok. Toggling along on his back legs with front legs on top of her pack, he appeared to be trying to create a new llama for our pack string.

Looking at Miwok, I wondered: *Are you enjoying this, girl? Where's Jim? Damn! He's got the walkie-talkie turned off!* Torn between savoring my bad temper and amazement at this demonstration of llama love on the trail, I sounded off my loudest two-fingered New York taxi whistle, hoping to alert Jim's attention. Jambo's ardor was increasing and in his literally mounting excitement, he managed to wriggle out of his training pack and set himself up for arduous work ... or play. He appeared to be experiencing incredible pleasure, which Miwok seemed to share—she obligingly bedded down in the middle of the trail, accepting his advances and turning her head to playfully nuzzle his neck.

My whistle roused Jim. Before long, he turned the corner with three llamas in tow to find me, breaking up with laughter, my wearying snit forgotten. My mood had rocketed from crotchety angst to hilarity. We became spectators (awash in waves of consternation and mirth), awed by the ubiquitous power of sexual attraction; there was nothing to do until they finished except enjoy the show. Chuckling, together again, we reloaded Jambo's pack and set to retracing the contours up Fall Creek, looking for Crabtree Lake. We decided Jambo had earned his name  Inspired by our Kilimanjaro trek, we had named him "Hello!" in Swahili. We'd just witnessed his inimitable version of the Tanzanian two-step. Humor and flying pheromones had brought us happily back into sync.

Dusty, sweating and tired, we climbed higher and higher, rising above the forest into god's own high country. Every now and again, one of us chortled out loud, recalling Jambo's afternoon delight.

Finally we surmounted a high granite knoll that led us around the nose of a rocky butte and into the Bench Valley drainage. Without a soul in sight, and practically no evidence of a trail or old campsite, we found heaven on earth—the way we often do together. Here was the most verdant meadow overlooking a pristine High Sierra lake with a beckoning island in its center, set against the cathedral-like backdrop of a jagged granite face, and not another soul in sight.

We stopped in the meadow to stake out the llamas. But before we could tie the animals out on the stake line, we had to scour the meadow for potential danger. Just as Kilimanjaro's staggering majesty was intensified when we imagined the acrid smell of a funeral pyre, so the grandeur of this High Sierra backcountry was made poignant as we remembered the horrifying recent death of one of our llamas by plant poisoning.

A month before, during a brief warm-up pack trip, Jambo's mama llama, Hopi, had browsed on a toxic plant. We watched helplessly as agonizing death throes overtook our beautiful chocolate brown llama. She was far too sick to move and we were too far from the trailhead to get help. As poison coursed through her veins for hours, she kept trying to throw herself into the campfire, and we worked ourselves to exhaustion, trying to control her and force her to drink water to dilute the poison—in vain. Our memories of the sheer terror in Hopi's brown eyes, the foul smell of her singing soft brown fur, the paroxysms of her death throes, and our utter impotence to save her, are still raw.

Jim has studied toxic plants to try to avert such a tragedy with our animals. After that fateful trip, with the help of a U.C. Davis lab, he identified a plant sample as kalmia polyfolia or bog laurel, a member of the heather family like rhododendrons and azalea, sharing the same chemical toxicity that lethally attacks the nervous system. He encouraged me to write an article to warn llama packers of this heretofore-unidentified danger in high meadows. He taught me that nature's most poisonous plants are among the most beautiful wildflowers, including shooting stars, lupine, labrador tea, mountain heather, elephant heads, swamp whiteheads, larkspur, water hemlock, and monkshood. In this practical way, he shows support for me and care for the animals he loves to berate at cocktail parties. Note to self:

when on the verge of a self-indulgent snit, please remember Jim's quiet devotion and caretaking.

Dusty and bone tired from the long hike, in a meadow bathed in alpenglow and singing with grasshoppers and birds, we undertook a task nobody wants to do on vacation: an hour of weeding. As we worked, I wondered: *how often are any of us drawn into fateful danger by the allure of something unknown and fascinating?* For urban folk, increasingly exposed to human destructiveness such as gang wars, drive-by shootings, and acts of terrorism, it's easy to forget how stealthily Nature herself can unleash destruction. As a recently traumatized, helpless observer watching nature wreak havoc on our innocent Hopi, I can testify to the cruelt of her death.


Yet Nature is magnificent. In our gorgeous campsite, the tent's back window opened onto the reason this hard-to-reach place is called Bench Valley: a sheer insurmountable rock wall rose in a semicircle around Crabtree Lake and the top of the drainage basin at over 12,000 feet. Our poodle Jullay, whose name in Ladakhi also means "Hello," celebrated her freedom from her own backpack by wriggling and rolling gratefully in the dirt, turning her curly black poodle fur dusty brown as we pitched our tent overlooking the lake.

When I turned fifty and decided I'd had enough of lugging a weighty backpack, llamas seemed a great alternative to giving up the backcountry. Gratis the llamas, back-country dining merits four stars. I unpacked my two baking ovens and reviewed our cold boxes full of fresh nectarines and blueberries, sugar snap peas, jicama, red and yellow peppers, fresh tomatoes, and even fresh basil and tarragon, Belgian endive, avocado, and cabbage. I had makings for quiche, homemade pizza, polenta, gorgonzola pasta, and other cuisine that tastes especially tasty in the backcountry, for giant appetites make a cook's best sauce. While we've eschewed four-star Parisian hotels, saving them as dessert for later life, we've shared sublime moments at the end of difficult trails, finding unparalleled ambiance and lighting, and for music, the melody of lake water lapping quietly at the shore. This night, I whip out my backpacker's oven, make a quiche, and serve it with fresh salad greens, avocado and wild onions.

Boots off aching feet, bellies full, relaxing in low chairs in front of a campfire crackling with resinous pine cones, we relished our arrival in the heavenly high alpine valley. We let the fire burn down and watched myriad stars come out, no city lights dimming their stellar splendor. A starry firmament is one reward for the toil and hassles of backcountry packing. I felt comforted by the Milky Way and innumerable constellations, evoking other stargazing nights—in Patagonia, hiking the Torres Del Paine Circuit at the southernmost tip of Chile; along the Inca trail in Peru; surmounting Mt. Kilimanjaro in Tanzania; trekking in the Himalayas in Kashmir and Ladakh. What new stars in which hemispheres await us on our sabbatical nights?

I felt deep satisfaction: exercised, well fed, surrounded by natural beauty and cozy with Jim among the stars, with Jullay curled up in the warmth of the campfire and the llamas safe and sound. Didn't my western settling forbears savor such moments at the end of blistering days on the trail, and didn't they look up after a good meal and see the same stars and enjoy the same satisfaction?

After the fire burned out and we had our fill of starlight, we tucked Jullay into her bed in our tent portico and retired to our own zipped-together sleeping bags to enter the dense sleep that befalls the body after a day of hard physical activity.

As first light splashes the peaks in rose and gold, a spark of an idea ignites in me. *What if I write a book about all this?* Excitedly, I slip out of our cozy sleeping bag and look for something to take notes on. As I root around for paper, shivering in the alpine chill, the phrase "pulling up stakes" pops into my mind. It marks the way of the Old West—pulling up tent stakes and moving from familiar safety into new territory. The thrill makes my head spin. Is this how my great-great grandparents felt as pioneers, crossing the continent for California? Scouring eagerly but unsuccessfully for paper, I sigh. Never mind. I'll just scour up used cooking packets, book jackets, and paper scraps to write on. That's the pioneer spirit!

I repeat my vow: *I'm really going to pull up stakes in my life.* When I feel hungry to process new experiences, I won't have to rely solely on

Jim for release. Writing will be my way to foster continuity between the life I'm leaving and the unknown journeys, internal and external, lying in wait. Writing will be my companion, my therapy, and a wonderful way to relish every moment and remember my journey. As I relinquish my psychoanalyst role for now, I can take on the role of author. It will be a bright, smart step toward letting go, giving Jim the breathing room he loves, and opening the same for me.

# CHAPTER 5

## CHICKEN JIM AND THE EXPULSION
## FROM EDEN

AFTER EIGHT LANGUOROUS days in our own alpine lakeside garden, I understand how Adam and Eve might have felt cast out of Eden. We've spent our days hiking, rock climbing, fishing, exploring with Jullay, reading and writing by the lake, tending the llamas, swimming or paddling in my child-sized inflatable boat, relishing the alpenglow, and savoring our delicious meals.

We've resumed our favorite campfire ritual, reading aloud to each other. This trip's treat has been Bill Bryson's *A Walk in the Woods*, describing the author's adventures along the Appalachian Trail with geographically compromised "Chicken John," who regularly managed to get himself lost. Bryson figured Chicken John, a solo through-hiker (one who hikes the entire two-thousand-mile Appalachian Trail in one year), probably traveled an extra thousand miles because he kept wandering off the trail, ridiculously far off course. Last night, as the campfire crackled and shooting stars blazed above, Jim read to me Bryson's description of this hapless soul:

"He had been walking for the better part of half a year, and he was still only three-quarters of the way to Katahdin.

'What kind of'—I didn't know quite how to put this—'what kind of miles are you doing, John?'

'Oh, 'bout fourteen or fifteen if all goes well. Trouble is'—he slid me a sheepish look—'I get lost a lot.'"

That was it. Chicken John was forever losing the trail and ending up in the most improbable places. Goodness knows how anyone could manage to lose the Appalachian Trail. It is the most clearly defined, well-blazed footpath imaginable. Usually it is the only thing in the woods that isn't woods. If you can distinguish between trees and a long open corridor through the trees you will have no trouble finding your way along the AT.

I asked him the most lost he had ever been.

'Thirty-seven miles," he said almost proudly. "I got off the trail on Blood Mountain in Georgia—still don't know how exactly—and spent three days in the woods before I found a highway. Thought I was a goner that time. I ended up in Tallulah Falls—even got my picture in the paper. The police gave me a ride back to the trail the next day, and pointed me the right way. They were real nice."[1]

Unfortunately, the selection was to prove apocryphal. Yesterday, we left paradise early to begin our journey homeward. It was a doleful day, saying goodbye to Crabtree Lake after a glorious eight days without seeing another soul. We'd planned a circular route along Bench Valley lakes we had not yet visited. According to the topo, the route would include a steep downhill traverse billed "not acceptable for stock." We were undaunted. Our llamas are more like members of the family than common "stock." After their first successful pack trip several summers back, I hosted a celebration in our Twin Brooks kitchen with oatcakes for Jambo and Miwok, who came to the party dressed in gold paper crowns. Like mountain goats, these animals can navigate terrain that horses and mules cannot. So, ignoring the warning, we set off, planning to hike to Maguire or Guest Lake, camp for the night, then proceed to Long Meadow and the trailhead.

By 9:30 a.m. we'd climbed the steep granite escarpment from Crabtree Lake to gaze at a vista of magnificent lakes awaiting us on the other side. In a few precipitous places we threaded between boulders and scrambled over downed trees, descending into the other side of Bench Valley drainage toward Colt Lake and Filly Lake. So far, the five llamas, Jim and I had made it without incident.

1 Bryson, Bill. *A Walk in the Woods: Rediscovering America on the Appalachian Trail.* New York: Broadway Books, 1999, 206-207.

But Jim's pre-GPS navigational system—his decades of Sierra backpacking experience, honed by altimeters and topo maps—utterly failed us. He misidentified Horsehead Lake as Maguire Lake. I disagreed, but he insisted and prevailed. The error, discovered after four hours of hiking, landed us in serious trouble. (The topo showed a steep cross-country trail following the drainage of Maguire Lake, leading to the Fall Creek drainage and back to the main trail.) Cairns (stone markers) led us to believe we were on the right track, so we proceeded down a rugged, steep embankment that led to a sheer drop.

I was in the lead with Jambo and Miwok. We edged down the vertical trail, deeper into the yawning divide, until Jambo lost his footing, fell, and rammed into me. He knocked me head-over-teakettle down the mountain and across several switchbacks, tumbling over boulders until I came to a stop, face-down on a narrow granite ledge overlooking a chasm. Terrified, with the wind knocked out of me, I lay dazed until my senses returned.

I slowly gathered myself and looked up. Jambo was prostrate on an outcrop above me. When faced with serious danger, llamas fight, flee, or faint. Jambo had fainted as we fell toward the chasm. Miwok, unhooked from Jambo, stood above us on the trail. She saw her new boyfriend collapsed on the trail and freaked out, orgelling until he recovered and scrambled to his feet. Jambo had probably saved both our lives, for if he'd panicked, he could have taken us over the cliff. I lay there on my ledge, panting in horror as I absorbed not only what had happened, but worse, what might have happened.

I wiped gravel out of my skinned arm and shin and figured I'd have a good bruise on my hip. I hadn't been able to catch my fall, as I was babying my right shoulder's torn rotator cuff and torn left anterior cruciate ligament, despite the sturdy mechanical brace protecting my knee. I'd kept my arms at my sides, so hadn't injured my shoulder again. My heavy-duty vinyl-covered custom brace was torn up, but it had saved my knee from further injury.

Slowly I pulled myself up and struggled back to Jambo, then clambered up to Miwok and our anxiously waiting compatriots. Jim, Jullay, and the other llamas all checked us out to their satisfaction. We discovered that after seventy miles of hiking, Jim's right knee had swollen to the size of a grapefruit. Sobered and acutely aware of our vulnerability in the wilderness without another sign of human life, we decided there was no choice but to return to Crabtree and start out the next day via the route we'd hiked in.

Reconnoitering over the topo map at what he'd thought was Maguire Lake, with my teeth-clenched help, Jim realized his error. Tension was thick. Realizing that I could have been killed in the fall, and that Jim could become too lame to hike out, we were scared into fight mode. Psychoanalysts call this well-worn defense "turning passive into active." We might have done well to learn the llamas' peace-preserving strategy and faint instead of fight, but we just weren't there yet. We sat down by the misapprehended lake and ate lunch in stony silence until I blasted Jim with my best and worst verbal arsenal, and he retaliated with his.

"You're so sure you know what you're doing, you don't think about how others may get hurt! Your pig-headedness nearly cost us our lives."

"Give me a break. I wouldn't be here if it weren't for you."

"I knew it! All along you've been hostile to the llamas and me. Part of you would secretly celebrate if you strategically knocked a couple of us off a cliff!"

"I am NOT hostile. Stop psychoanalyzing me. I'm a very good sport. You and your llamas would drive anyone off the edge. You're always trying to control me—just ask the kids."

"Damn you. First, you insisted on having your way interpreting the map. It's not for nothing others call you the Wander FUHRER. Second, you know better than to invoke the kids as your Greek chorus in an argument. And third, I KNEW it! You just admitted you are hostile. You've been nit-picking and negative and denying it!"

"Well, maybe I have. This is a goddamned army operation. I'm a simple man. I just want my freedom. I'd much rather be off by myself."

"You like to think you don't need anybody. Remember our couple therapy session when Larry called you Jeremiah Johnson the Mountain Man and you thought it was a compliment? That is, until he explained about Johnson's schizoid personality, his hatred of dependency and his various sadistic assaults, including scalping Indians, including women. Oh, he was onto you!"

"You really piss me off. Really."

"When you deny you're angry and do some dumb hardheaded thing, I get agitated. I feel like I can't get through to you, so I badger. I was really scared back there. Sometimes it feels like you're not thinking of me at all."

"Well," Jim said abruptly, "we've got to get going."

The Big Fight usually occurs once a year, and it constellates around our core issues. Typically, Jim's final salvo means the conversation is over. We've both gotten our rocks off; we haven't solved anything, but we'll do less permanent damage if we cool off by ourselves.

I began to think about our predicament, and realized I was really sad to be leaving our alpine Eden. I was unhappy about having to part with my furry friends, the uncomplaining llamas, leaving them at Twin Brooks for the winter, returning to the city, smog, freeways and a locked-in work schedule. Jim didn't feel the same way about the llamas, and he didn't have to go back to work. I'd felt scared and hurt on that rock ledge, dangerously close to a fatal fall. It all constellated my sour mood.

Then I realized that Labor Day would mark our twentieth year in the backcountry together. Why get into this mean-spirited fracas now, just a couple of weeks before our anniversary? *I LOVE this rugged mountain man. Beyond a shadow of a doubt, he loves me too. Maybe we have to clear the pipes of the annual undercurrent of our personalities. Jim does like things simple, while I love the complex. I am aware of my dependency on him but he completely denies his reliance on me. We're bound to tangle. I'd better just leave it alone for a while. Maybe he will have second thoughts while he's hiking. He usually does if I can just button it up.*

We looked at the map again and decided not to go all the way back, but to set out for the trail I'd seen earlier and thought was the right one. If this was indeed Horsehead Lake, we could hike another few miles to Maguire Lake and camp there. We somberly resumed our trek. A couple of miles on, Jim—bless him—turned around and cut through it all. He grinned at me and said, "I guess you might as well start calling me Chicken Jim."

Humor is the best icebreaker. Suddenly, we were back in the warmth of the campfire on Crabtree Lake, reading about "Chicken John" who was so clueless that he had no idea why he earned the epithet "chicken." Relieved we were back on track relationally and geographically, and didn't have to climb over the boulder-strewn scree into Bench Valley, we stopped and kissed passionately. After a precious moment of tenderness, we hiked down to the real Maguire Lake and found the correct cross-country trail, marked clearly by major cairns. Finally on the right track, ready to go home, we boldly decided to keep going and camp on Fall Creek.

"Cairn" is an old Celtic term used for stones that mark the way, in this case, down switchbacks, over boulders, and across streams. When you've been lost, they appear as heartwarming markers from folks gone by. Most cairns (or ducks, as some backpackers call them) consist of a single good-sized stone placed atop a boulder to mark the path. Toward the end of our day from hell, I saw one that delighted me. At the bottom was the requisite boulder, maybe three feet in diameter. On top of that lay a flat twelve-inch rock, and then on top of that was an eight-inch flat rock, making a tower. This tower ascended with six or eight rocks in descending size, each more precariously balanced, up to the topmost four-inch stone. I was sorely tempted to put a pebble on top, but on the tenth steep mile of a thirteen-mile day with many rugged switchbacks, I had to just think the thought and smile. I enjoyed fantasizing about the next hiker to travel this way, maybe this year, maybe next, adding a few grams of sand on top of my pebble.

We continued downward to aptly named Fall Creek, our final resting point on The Day We Were Expelled from Eden, falling into an exhausted, tentless, ten-hour sleep beside the stream.

As I emerge sleepy-eyed but refreshed from our sleeping bag, I can't believe my eyes. I rub them twice to make sure. There's Jim, up and dressed, chatting to the llamas, telling them they were amazing yesterday and amiably offering them their morning grain. Now that is a sight for sore eyes. Although we plan another fourteen-mile hike today, it will be at a comfortable pace on a good trail, following the picturesque North Fork of the Kings River. Today will be a piece of cake.

# CHAPTER 6

## ANIMAL SPIRITS

AFTER OUR FOURTEEN-MILE 2,000 foot descent, with a knee still the size of a grapefruit, Jim has gone to bed early. Jullay has cratered and the llamas are bedded down in one of the lushest meadows they'll ever see. Already nostalgic for the backcountry and feeling pensive, I make notes from the day on my last remaining scraps of paper. I stoke the fire and sit quietly by the dying embers, gazing out through virgin timber, watching the full moon rise over the meadow.

My mind is in a quiet reverie of tiredness, satisfaction, pleasure, and a sense of sadness as a rare and exquisite time draws to its close. At the edge of my consciousness, though, I notice a hint of wariness. For the first time in ten days, I feel apprehensive. Little bowlines in my stomach and half hitches in my neck signal something might be up. Is camp secure?

For the first time in over a week we've encountered humans, prompting a slightly edgy anti-sociability, prompting us to think, "What are these humans doing in our wilderness?" We met two young rangers with axes and handsaws heading in to clear deadfall off the trail. They warned us to expect a string of horse packers. With that postcard from the edge of civilization and the anticipated arrival of packhorses, my mind tripped into staccato interruption mode. Interruptions are typical of a weekday in the city, but here, they're Herculean intrusions into my peaceful reverie. The notion of modern consciousness occupied me for several miles past the horse packers and all the way into the final meadow, as we encountered two young men so tuckered they'd plunked down their sleeping bags in the middle of the trail. We skirted the llamas around them, and they confessed that they'd been too fatigued to go a step further the night before. They were certainly no threat, so exhausted they hadn't even lit a stove to cook.

At this hub where trails branch off to Red Mountain Basin, Big Maxon Meadow, Blackcap Basin, and Bench Valley, there are always a number of backpacker parties or an encampment of horse packers. Even as we hunkered down emotionally for re-entry, a troop of Boy Scouts was waiting for us, roaring around, dizzy and wild. Then, approaching camp in the setting sun in the middle of the meadow, we came upon an exuberant group of young female gymnasts doing back flips and cartwheels, and building towers of bodies. My anti-social negativity ebbed as I remembered with pleasure my own young days of tower building.

Someone else is camped close behind us in the woods. We heard them as we were setting up camp. Never saw them. Why is a feeling of protective wariness encircling me like an invisible radar fence? Is this anxiety brought on by today's contact with people? Suddenly I remember our first long llama trip, five years ago, on our way to Blackcap Basin. Other backpackers warned us to hang our food in trees because of bears. I remember a semi-comical night in dense woods, when we tried to toss a rock with a string tied around it over a high branch, then balance the food bags, elevating them out of bears' reach, but not so high that we couldn't retrieve them. *That's it. I'm probably worried about bears.* As I stoke the embers and toss another log on the fire, a series of bear associations tumbles into my consciousness.

Bill Bryson wrote about a terrifying night on the Appalachian Trail when a large bear with acrid breath lurked outside his tent. His buddy offered to ward it off with toenail clippers; Bryson wasn't amused. Then I remember Jim's bear story, camping with his first wife. As newlyweds they went car camping near Yosemite and a bear visited their camp in the night. Jim woke up but his wife, zipped snug into her mummy bag, didn't awaken. A macho ex-Marine with a testosterone surge, he reached out of his sleeping bag, grabbed a rock and heaved it at the bear before racing into their VW Beetle and locking the doors. That annoyed the bear and woke his wife, who roared to her feet, clutching her mummy bag around her neck, hopping like a drunk in a sack race to the other side of the Beetle, banging on the door at Jim to let her in. He obliged. I don't suppose she ever forgave him that one. I begin to feel more empathy for her, especially after yesterday's episode with Chicken Jim.

But Jim's first marriage isn't on my mind; it's bears. I search for a sign in the campfire light, but there's nothing, no sound in the dense forest. The llamas are kushed in the meadow. I faintly hear Jim's even breathing inside our yellow tent and picture Jullay, curled up in her down vest in the tent foyer near his feet, her nose twitching in dog dreams.

Stirring the fire, settling back onto my low backpacking chair, I remember the Big One: the grizzly that almost ate Uncle Ross, my Great Grandpa Kennedy's sheep ranching partner. Few letters remain in our family archives, but Uncle Henry Ross's 1874 letter to his brother and sister in the Midwest remains as a testimony to the dangers early settlers faced in the old West. His letter describes an incident close to their high Sierra sheep camp, near Kennedy Meadows in present-day Sequoia National Park:

```
Fresno City, Feb. 20th, 1874
Dear Brother & Sister,

     In answer to your last letter of December 11th
this leaves us all well hoping that it will find you
well. You wish in your letter how I came by my ac-
cident.
     The way that it happened was that I came on the
Bear by accident laying in the long grass with her
two Cubs -so she jumped on me at once and caught my
face in her mouth at the first leap. I had nothing to
fight her with at all, so I thought the only chance
was to make on that I was dead - but it was hard to
do when she was chewing me up so I had a shepherd
dog along with me, and when she thought I was dead
```

she went after him, then I sized (sic) the opportunity and tried to get a safer place so I struggle
to a small tree and got up it about five feet but - I
could not climb fast - as my left arm was broken in
two places. I had only one hand to hold on by, so
she came at me again and chewed my legs fearful and
tore off all my cloths and blooding like a oxe so I
gave up to die in earnest then. So her two cubs came
up then and they all went off together - so then I
got to my feet to get a look at myself - so I concluded that I was the most pettyable sight speechless. So I stayed then and sent for the Doctor - so
it took three days to feach the Doctor - by that
time I was pretty low but then things took a turn
and I commenced to get better.

I congratulate you on the arrival of the third
person to your family and thank you for his card.
I am so glad that you are started on your own hook
by thus time. I wish you great success. This is a
busy time with me as this is lambing time. Be sure
and write soon. Thank you for the card of Father's
and Mother's gravestone. We all unite in sending our
kind love to you.

Signed, Henry Ross

Uncle Ross survived one year after he wrote this letter before finally
succumbing to the complications of the bear attack. Recalling his
story as I sit by the dying fire in the moonlight, although I am relaxed
and pensive, I feel a disturbance. It's too late to hang the food and too
dark to do it alone. Besides, we have two bear-proof pannier boxes,
stamped and dated by the U.S. Forest Service. I get up and move
around camp, zip up a few things, make sure the grain and dog food
aren't wide open. Bushed from thirteen miles on the trail, I return to
my seat. And that's when I see them—two dark eyes shining at me
across the crackling fire. I freeze. My heartbeat races. Is it a bear? I
call out to rouse Jim in the tent.

With a quick shiver and rising hairs on the nape of my neck I
flash back to 1978, when a bear ravaged our Tiger Lily Creek cabin at
Twin Brooks. I had retreated there with five-year-old Ariel and eight-
year-old Gabriel to finish my doctoral dissertation and avoid losing

the NIMH fellowship I'd won for postdoctoral study. Three times that summer, a rogue bear found its way to our cabin. It ripped the screen door off the hinges, found storage tins of flour and sugar and ravaged them, and then, in a coup de grace, pulled the refrigerator door off its hinges and bent it in half before pulling its contents out with a swipe of its mighty paw. We learned that the bear, which had three tags in its ear, had marauded campsites in a nearby national park and was relocated to "the wilderness"—our land. I feared for our safety, and especially for the children.

I am not a huntress. My father took me on a dove hunt when I was twelve, and when he shot the first dove, I ran to where it had fallen, sobbed, cradled it in my arms, and made a grave for it. My father was duly unimpressed. I was never invited on another hunt. However, when that bear threatened my children's safety, we made a distress call to the National Forest Service to report the marauder, and the rangers requested that we keep the animal around "until Thursday when we can get out there." Right. *Here bear, just sit in that rocking chair until the rangers come.*

A primal force coursed through my veins and a mighty huntress was born. With ferocious resolve, I marched to the ranch caretaker's cabin and asked to borrow his hunting rifle. Reluctantly, sizing me up as a "girl" but recognizing a fierce mother with her jaw set like Annie Oakley's, he handed me the heavy gun.

When I returned to Tiger Lily cabin, I lifted the rifle to my shoulder. I teetered under the weight of it, but when I sighted through the telescope I was amazed at the power of the scope and the exactitude of the cross hairs. I put it and the shells under my bed, where they remained until an afternoon ten days later, when the children and I were decorating t-shirts with sun dye. The children had been unable to talk about anything but the bear all summer, so they were painting a teddy bear's picnic on their shirts.

With cups of dye and brushes, we sat at the screen porch table as the afternoon sun slanted warmly through the screen. We were singing, "If you go down to the woods today, be sure you don't go alone ... Today's the day the teddy bears have their picnic!" All of a sudden, from below the table, our Rottweiler Aaballou began a deep, sonorously chilling growl. The hair rose on the nape of his neck. He lunged from under the table, nearly upsetting our cups, and bolted out the door to give chase. As Aaballou barked and branches broke outside, the young househelper from my parents' home came running down our drive, waving his arms wildly, yelling, "The bear has come into our yard. He's climbed a tree in front of the house. You have to come now!"

He took the children by their hands. I went to my bedroom for the rifle and shells. Shaking, I loaded the rifle as we walked to the main house. My parents and their guests stood on the front porch, lined up as if for a Wild West show. My mother motioned for Gabriel and Ariel and gave me a look that only prairie women in danger would recognize. I saw the bear, 20 feet up an alder tree in the front yard, his arms around the tree, his back to me. I dropped one knee to the ground. With my elbow steady on the other knee, I raised the heavy rifle to my shoulder and took aim. I got his left side in the cross hairs and slowly squeezed the trigger. *BOOM!* The kickback threw me nearly onto my back as the bear fell stone dead out of the tree, landing with a thud in the garden. My heart was racing, I was hyperventilating, but I was exultant. I shot the bear! I felt as if I had climbed Everest. That primal force and dead-eye accuracy must have come from deep in my ancestral past.

He was a medium-sized brown bear, probably 250 pounds. He had loomed over us and terrorized us all summer, but now his lifeless form seemed shrunken. My Dad announced that we must all be sworn to secrecy. "This didn't happen. Even though the Forest Service inflicted danger on us, and refused to help when the bear threatened us, they can arrest Harriet for this. So it didn't happen." He instructed the caretaker to collect his rifle and to bury the carcass far from the houses. "No one is to speak of this again."

At the apex of my courage and bravery, my father's anxiety trumped his pride in my marksmanship and gagged me into silence. Amazingly, fearing arrest for illegal hunting, Dad seemed more worried about taking matters into our own hands than concerned about the safety of his daugher or grandchildren. It wasn't his cabin the bear kept breaking into, and he didn't have little children any more. I hadn't yet fully understood the extent of his emotional insensitivity and narcissism.

The children's excitement and pride, however, couldn't be silenced. When their father called from his film shoot location, they blurted out, "Mommy shot the bear!" Donald damnably replied, "You mean Mommy shot Winnie the Pooh?" That retort was one key nail in the coffin of our marriage.

Because the two most important men in my life responded in the way they did, I began to feel guilty and ashamed, as if I had done something reprehensible, not brave and protective. Although I was not yet so conscious of this pattern of behavior or its implications, I know I felt deeply hurt and humiliated. Thus, without reflecting on the complexity and perversion of guilt and recriminations, I began my atonement to "the Great Bear" that lasted for many years.

Is this night in the forest yet another haunting of my guilt-ridden soul? Are those a bear's eyes I see in the firelight?

No, the eyes belong to a deer. It looks like a big buck with impressive antlers, but then I realize those antlers are branches silhouetted behind a doe, luminescent and white in the moonlight. It's too late to take back my reflexive, adrenaline-driven outcry. Still, she gazes calmly at me with her large brown eyes, her healthy, lithe body literally glowing. She daintily lifts her left hind leg up to scratch her chin, turns to look at the llamas in the meadow, looks back at me, then vanishes.

Awe and reverence settle over me like a soft blanket. At the threshold between wilderness and a return to daily life, an incandescently moonlit doe with huge soft eyes just approached me in a peaceful, trusting state, dissolving my suspicion and paranoia. *That was Zuni!*

I'll explain about Zuni. When Jim and I hiked the Himalayas in the early 1980s, we had an extraordinary experience that inspired our passion for many subsequent adventures. The native Kashmiri mountain boys who guided us, cooked for us, and tended to ponies that carried our gear, could not wrap their tongues around "Harriet." It came out in many different funny ways. I finally laughed and said,

"What would you like to call me?" Two young brothers looked at each other and simultaneously said, "Zuni." I was Zuni for the whole trek.

My associations were to Native American Zuni Indians, but when I asked the Kashmiri boys what Zuni meant, they said, "It means Goddess of the Silver Moon. We like you. You have a special spirit, Zuni." Needless to say, I felt blessed. I love the name, and have decided that the next llama born at Twin Brooks will be named Zuni.

The doe, shining silver in the moonlight, looked like a moon goddess. I sense a kinship between us, and also between her and the llamas. Their tracks are very similar—while the deer print is made by a cloven hoof, the llama walks on a cleft pad, soft like a dog's paw, covered by a sturdy toenail. Their scat is almost indistinguishable; llama beans look like the tiny oval balls left by deer. They both have large, expressive eyes and beautifully alert ears. Is the doe's visit a sign that Miwok is pregnant with Zuni? Is this a lunar blessing? A chill runs down my spine and I feel awe and gratitude for this gentle farewell encounter in the Sierra.

This is an auspicious portent, like the emerald hummingbird that alighted on my hammock at Crabtree Lake. If we are open, such moments are there for us, but how often do our internal barriers—anxiety, fear, negativity, and the preoccupations and interruptions of daily life—block our capacity to truly receive? One of my clear intents, as I envision taking a sabbatical from conventional work, is to explore my capacity to truly receive.

Feeling deeply connected to all the vibrant natural presences around me, I feel a philosophical affinity to the great Sierraphile, Scottish kinsman John Muir, who believed in a spiritual force present in all matter—including the inanimate world of stones and trees. John Muir thought it was presumptive to imagine a universe in which humans have souls and everything else is "dumb." Muir believed in a spiritual force present in all matter—including the inanimate world of stones and trees. This is certainly not the Judeo-Christian Scotch Presbyterian theology I was raised on, where "man shall have dominion." In spite of my upbringing, I feel a kinship with Muir's philosophy, and to the Eastern or Buddhist understanding of the oneness of all sentient beings.

At U. C. Berkeley in the early 1960s, I took a physics course taught by Edward Teller, the "Father of the Bomb," who invited Aldus Huxley into our class as a guest lecturer. Like subsequent physicists who have come forth in favor of the ultimate mystery of things, Huxley offered us his view of matters of the spirit. I've never forgotten that class. He believed there was a spiritual energy present in all beings and likened this energy to water molecules, which, when frozen, form into solid matter. For Huxley, each person's spirit forms like a distinct piece of ice. When we are born, he posited, our own unique portion of spirit shapes itself from the infinite body of spiritual energy, like ice crystals form within water. At death, like the molecules of our physical body returning to earth, the ice melts back into the pool. It doesn't end; individual forms simply cease to exist as they gradually melt back into something larger. No ego or personality remains over time; we evolve into disparate forms in an ongoing process of evolving spiritual energy.

By the last glow of firelight, I am left in a state of wonder. I believe I have met and been touched by Zuni herself. I crawl into our sleeping bag beside Jim. His lean, warm, muscular body beckons me into a dreamful sleep, only awakened in the morning when he arrives at the tent portal with a smile and a cup of steaming cowboy coffee.

When I emerge from the tent in the sunlight, I see that our camp is surrounded by gooseberry bushes laden with ripe berries. If there had been any bears within miles, they'd have come to feast on those gooseberries. Those berries had been dripping red yesterday but escaped my notice, so my nighttime fears, though valid, were all internally driven. Another life lesson. How often do we ignore the signs that would allay our anxieties, preferring instead to plunge into melodramas of fear? How often do we hook ourselves to neurotic engines that carry the freight of our earliest traumas, reliving juiced-up drama from the past, which we could instead recognize as past, release, and let fizzle out like the death of the wicked witch in the *Wizard of Oz*?

# Chapter 7

## Outward Bound

Back in sync with Jim and my world, quietly hiking the last dozen miles out of the wilderness, I find ample opportunity to meditate on Aldous Huxley's spiritual metaphor of water and ice as the birth and transformation of a soul. The morning's sunny skies over the meadow have given way to darkening clouds, followed by thunder and lightning, then hail, then ice crystals frosting and dripping from the leaves. As we descend in altitude, the torrents of cold rain become warm, composing a rather dramatic finale to our trip.

We all have good rain gear; the llamas each wear a rain fly to cover their packs. Over the years, we have scoured many outdoor adventure gear sales, particularly at the venerable mountaineering outfitter known as Patagonia. Jim evaluates foul weather gear by taking it home, putting it on and testing it in our shower. Our rain gear was chosen for our wickedly wet trek around Torres del Paine in the original Patagonia, the stormiest Eden we've ever traversed. So today, we're ready for the downpour. Suiting up as the thunder claps is like retreating inside a snug house, lighting a fire, turning on music, pulling out a good book and settling in for the storm. In this case, roof, walls and floor are a gortex hood, jacket and rain pants; the door is a zipper; cozy warmth is generated by hiking; the music comes from a mini cassette player with earphones, and the good book is found as I turn the pages of my own mind.

My mind is a mesmerizing travel companion. During this un-interrupted walk in the silent woods, I'm free to drift along the stream of my own consciousness for hours. It's a rare luxury, since my modern brain is constantly jangled by interruptions: deadlines, emails, faxes, phones, stop signs, news flashes and tax time. Except for precious moments lying sleepless in the night or on awakening, my mind rarely has the unfettered ease to flow wherever it may.

The rhythmicity of simply walking and breathing provides a free-form "walking meditation," a Buddhist mindfulness practice I recently read about in a compelling book by Vietnamese Zen monk Thich Nhat Hanh. It's a fitting end to our eight days in wilderness without human contact or interruptions—a rare, languorous voyage along the river of my consciousness. In *Remembrance of Things Past*, Proust gave us the modern stream of consciousness style of writing, similar to Freud's invitation to his patients to recline on the analytic couch, imagine they were on a train ride through their minds, and narrate all the ideas and feelings they passed along the way. It's like following a river down its tributaries and side streams, one to the next, meandering wherever the river flows.

Listening to intermittent rain splashes and the staccato pulse of small hailstones on my "roof," I muse about my patients back home, wondering how they have fared over our three-week break. As we approach my sabbatical and the conclusion of their therapies, I consider each patient's psychological signature around endings. I trust that any feelings of rage, abandonment, panic and withdrawal— representing infantile protests against the powerlessness of being left behind—have been worked through in therapy, and are evolving into more gentle feelings of sadness, coping, and appreciation. I wonder whether my patients have any idea how often I think of them when I am away. This is often the nub of therapy; we tend to be pulled toward the darker vortex of partings, imagining that we're helpless, out of control, forgotten, or even worse, abandoned because we're unwanted and bad.

Savoring the pungent humus smell of summer earth greeting the first heavy rain of fall, I think about one patient, "Gareth," a powerful entrepreneur. His childhood attachment to his parents was so tenuous that he adopted an arch veneer of imperviousness, while underneath he starved for affirmation and support. Gareth came into therapy at his wife's behest, acting as if it were a tedious obligation that drained him of time, money and energy, keeping him from his important real work. Early on, Gareth welcomed my vacations as a relief from the meaningless bore of our meetings. Over time we've mined feelings deep beneath the veneer, and recently shared poignant sorrow over our parting. I genuinely hope Gareth has been able to take pleasure in a family vacation that coincided with mine, and that he's relinquished his need to work like a drone.

I think of "Jeb," the young professional with core feelings of being a terrible burden on a mother who, herself an orphan, was literally abandoned as a toddler. In their household, both parents and children competed as if they were all needy orphans. Jeb became an "Infantus Tyrannous," and as an adult, he alienated family, co-workers, and strangers with bullying obstinacy. This ingrained pattern has taken years of our combined effort to shift, sometimes moving at the glacial speed of grinding rock into sand, sometimes changing with lightning fury. Initially, when I went on vacation, Jeb would cavalierly cruise public bathrooms, risking his reputation, his health and the health of his fiancée by looking for homosexual liaisons. He acted out his core conviction that he was a tiring, demeaned piece of shit I couldn't wait to get rid of. He has stopped that behavior now, and we've moved into a humorous and rewarding therapeutic alliance; I believe he holds a sense of my devotion to helping him grow into a fuller, more connected person. I miss him and look forward to hearing about his recent honeymoon.

"Eva" is a young woman who just made a huge breakthrough in analysis. As a little girl she was traumatized by an abusive, volatile mother and overstimulated by her father. We uncovered one apocryphal trauma: when Eva was five, her mother, in a fit of rage, tried to drown her in the bathtub. She repressed the memory, but remained terrified of bathing and swimming. Her mother told her she would absolutely drown her if Eva ever told a soul.

Eva's sexual and emotional guardedness has played out in our relationship. Initially she "forgot" to come to her sessions, finding herself "zoned out, on another planet," approaching analysis with dread. I often felt emotionally flat with her, as if she were dead. I felt incompetent and guilty for accepting fees, especially for missed sessions, because I wasn't sure how I could help her. But we both persisted and the deadness has vanished: she never misses her sessions now, and I've discovered in Eva a bright, creative, engaging person, whom I look forward to seeing.

I daydream about every other patient I will return to next week, as well as former patients from as far back as twenty-five years ago. Where are they? How are they doing? By the time I return my focus to the muddy trail, several miles have gone by, the rain and occasional hail have stopped and started a few times, the trail is wider, and we are clearly at lower elevation.

To banish my sorrow about leaving these extraordinary mountains, I put on a tape of Telemann's Concerto in D Major for Three Trumpets. As the trumpeters play their antique, valveless trumpets and earnestly reach for the high notes, the sound soars in breathy effort, speaking poignantly of human aspiration—a fitting celebration of a successful trip once perilously close to the edge.

We have another hour's hiking left, and the rain is coming down in sheets. Still snug in our rain gear, we realize we haven't seen another soul today. Then we spot them: two guys hunkered forward under soaking backpacks, almost running down the trail. I cheerily call out, "Nice day, eh?" Jullay wags her tail and barks in greeting, but one man raises his fist at her as they pass, and the other one snarls. Stunned by their hostile behavior, I notice they have a dog traveling with them. One of them growls, "You better look out for him. He's a pit bull in a real bad mood." "Good god," I think, as Jullay's weight is a snack-sized 35 pounds. Fortunately, the pit bull responds to Jullay's slender poodle tush in a more romantic than nasty vein. Shortly after these sour apples and their pit bull are out of sight, I reflect, "Many are the ways to travel the same path."

Soon after, we pass another pair of folks who are plum perfect fodder for a William Steig New Yorker cover. Out for a picnic lunch a mile from the trailhead, they are hovering in the unanticipated rain. He is shivering in pink plaid Bermuda shorts, wetly plastered to his skinny thighs, with water soaking into his socks. She looks miserable in a large, formerly chic straw hat now flopping around her brow and dispensing rivulets into her picnic basket. They are huddled together under a tree and don't look up, and I don't have the heart to emit a greeting, as we are so enviably rain-clad.

We begin to see the glint of chrome bumpers, and soon rest assured that we have survived every backpacker's fear—yes, our truck and trailer are still parked at the trailhead, and yes, the windshield is still intact. I turn off my tape as Teleman's gorgeous trumpets fade, and we arrive back where we started, but deeply nourished, refreshed, newly focused. We unload, give the llamas their last feed of grain and watch them hop eagerly into the trailer for the ride home.

# PART III
# THE LAUNCH

# CHAPTER 8

## LUMINESCENCE, IRIDESCENCE,

### AND TRANSCRUDESCENCE

SINCE OUR SIERRA backcountry trip nine months ago, each therapy session with patients has been intensely poignant, as we complete analytic relationships ranging from two to sixteen years. I'm truly hearing each doorbell ring, noting each person's entry into my small consulting room, savoring each splash of jeweled light through the stained glass entry door from my grandmother Sassie's long-gone Victorian house, smelling and feeling the gentle rocking of my well-worn Eames style brown leather consulting chair, watching patients' hands run along the familiar sage green velvet cushions on the couch.

It's an extraordinary event—my whole practice, and all my patients, are engaged in what psychoanalysis unfortunately labels "termination." I hate the word; it evokes the Terminator or a terminal illness, when in fact this is the beginning of "real life" after analysis, better described by words like threshold, transition, embarkation, launching, imparting, or birth. Whatever we name it, my patients and I are all riding the wild emotional roller coaster of parting and imparting.

Our sessions have been inscribed with tenderness, anger, resentment, tears, gratitude, bittersweet sadness, nostalgic reminiscing, attempted shanghais, brave and fearful anticipation, and occasional bursts of exhilaration. More than once I have quoted "I Never Promised You a Rose Garden," as we've ruefully acknowledged our own limits and the restrictions of analysis. We are working to weave this ending chapter into a positive goodbye, in contrast to many patients' earlier partings that left deep scars and feelings of rejection or abandonment. As I partner with patients in this concluding dance, I sense them absorbing my voice and my bodily presence as well as details of the consulting room, or "womb." While they are drinking me in, I am doing the same with them, savoring the uniqueness of each one, knowing I will miss them terribly.

I am reminded of the children's story *Frederick*, which I read to Gabriel and Ariel when they were little. Frederick was a mouse poet who lived in his own ethereal world. While the practical mice busily gathered bits of wool and feathers to make nests in the stone wall for winter, and collected nuts and seeds to eat during the snowy season, Frederick was gathering sense impressions. He gathered memories of flowers, birds, rainbows, colors, images of light and dark, and textures. The other mice chided him mercilessly for his foolishness, but neither man nor mouse can live by bread alone. During the dreary siege of winter, Frederick's poetry brought vitality and warmth to the little colony in the wall. I identify with the little mouse poet as I prepare to enter a figurative winter in the woods and on the road, and nourish my spirit with writing and memories.

Thinking of Frederick, the mouse poet preparing for his winter not so much by the conventional way of gathering nuts but by drawing on his internal world, I realize that during the impending "winter" of this sabbatical, after having been intimately engaged with many people every day, I'll be relying primarily on my own inner world and the company of one person, my taciturn husband. And we are so different. Jim is like the more practical mice in Frederick's colony; he's been loading the trailer, securing a post office box, arranging mail forwarding, paying taxes. I've been sitting in my office on the verge of weeping with the poignancy of it all. I comfort myself with a reminder that the mouse poet and his action-oriented brethren needed each other, and each provided vital sustenance for the other.

This morning I gathered poetry from several sessions. One patient, who has long struggled with distrustful cynicism and sarcasm, is now deeply aware of his vulnerability and dependency. He has been letting me in on this well-guarded secret as well as the shame of never feeling lovable. Today he cried openly in a good way, something he was never able to do before. Instead of a hard-edged

"I can do it by myself, thank you very much," he can now value and appreciate others in a way that is more likely to make him accessible to intimacy and romance.

Another patient, "Adele," finished writing a book, finally finding her own strong voice after many years of forfeiting her prodigious talent and turning unsuccessfully to men for affirmation. She just returned home from a highly prestigious national book tour, which concluded at her birthplace. Her last stop was at the rest home where her once-mighty father resides in frailty, and she read aloud from her book, surrounded by invalids who marveled at her gumption. Adele inspires me. She has struggled against addictions and fearful distrust of intimacy to become much calmer and more present. She has embraced the authenticity of her own story and the authority of her voice, while her aged father, her childhood idol, wanes dramatically but gracefully. Knowing his death will come soon, and our ending sooner, I quietly relive the dying of my own powerful father who was both my hero and my consternation. Pulling up stakes is iridescent, luminous with shared meaning.

Another woman spent her session lying down on the couch for the first time. It was a breakthrough for her, here "on the clubhouse turn," to relinquish control and outward focus and to enter into meaningful discourse with her inner life. "Mimi" has long been trapped in tortured performance anxieties and the pressures of her demanding profession. It was difficult to invite her to move past the dailies of her life into awareness of her inner world. Today she shared two richly evocative dreams and played comfortably in the land of metaphor and illusion that is dream work.

Gareth has overcome crusty layers of cynicism and resistance to his wife's insistence that he "see a shrink." To his own amazement, he has found our sessions valuable to him in his family life as well as professionally. After a weekend ski trip, possibly the first pleasure-seeking outing he has ever taken with his family, he told me with newfound delight of teaching his small son the rudiments of skiing. Gareth described how frustrating it was for both of them the first day; there were many tumbles and tears and not a little rage. But he had an idea. He went into the ski shop, purchased an "Edgy Wedgie," and attached it to his son's ski tips. This little gizmo held his son's skis so that he began to turn successfully, then gleefully, until he begged to ski again as soon as possible. Seizing the obvious metaphor, I suggested that our therapeutic relationship was Gareth's new Edgie Wedgie gizmo, to help him approach the turns of his life in a new way. He liked the metaphor and agreed that he would be flowing more smoothly with his life rather than becoming enraged at every turn.

Among many moving exchanges in these closing hours, I received a letter from a patient whose struggles have been huge, and who has been an enormous challenge to me:

> When I came into analysis with you, I was a broken person, or so it seemed then. Confused, unaware, feeling abandoned. Somehow, through the long and short years together, I managed to feel a sense of connectedness to you. Of course, we know I had to get past that cynical, disbelieving nature first.

> Although I still stumble, don't always know how to deal with situations, I feel more able to see the other's point of view, look at my part in the situation, attempt in a more knowledgeable way to ameliorate misunderstandings.

> Have I found love??? Love of self is still a hard one for me, but I do have more confidence in my ability to be kinder to others and myself. Love of others, I'm a work in progress although I feel like I've made great strides. Your love for our work together, your loyalty to this effort makes me feel love is present between us. I know I'll be sad to end this "affair" that became such a comforting place in my universe. When life dealt me a blow, I felt I could run under your protective wings.

> Now those wings will fly away, as I have so often done. Gee, I don't like you being the flyee. On to new challenges, destinations, experiences for us both! You, on the wings of airplanes and the safety of your faith in the universe. Me, to those challenges of doing this life on my own wings, with my own God and with you ever present in my core.

> Thanks for putting up with my abuse and rage, for the laughter we shared, the love we felt and the hope of a future when we might even see each other on the terms of friendship. I would like that very much.

Biggest hugs, much love, have fun, be safe, feel peace and come back to the Palisades.

It's going to be hard to leave my swiveling leather chair and this little monastic cell of a consulting room. Every bit as much as my patients are going through the throes of the long goodbye, I am doing the same. With many of them, I've enjoyed juicy and potent therapeutic relationships, and felt I should not accept fees for the privilege of being invited into their rich inner worlds. I feel deeply grateful to them for the honor of participating in their psychological growth, and fortunate to be leaving one extraordinary experience to begin another. I'm hoping that they, too, can adopt the notion of "westering" when it is time to pull up stakes, take the leap and follow a dream.

### Order into Chaos into Order

Jim and I are hitting the road—Highway 5, that is, heading north out of L.A. toward the San Joaquin Valley and the Sierras, and, unfortunately, the other side of iridescence. I think I'll call it transcrudescence. I think you'll know what I mean.

It's the weekend before my last two weeks as a psychoanalyst, and we are moving our household gear from L.A. to the Sierras, readying to lease the home I've lived in for three decades. The green Ford Explorer is loaded to the gunwales, listing slightly, sea kayak lashed on top, and towing our llama-trailer-turned-moving-van. Inside the trailer are Jim's recumbent bike, my mountain bike, backpacks, kayak paddles, snowshoes, skis, boxes of books and CDs, plus a few arcane items such as the scarecrow from our vegetable garden, wearing cast-off bits of favorite clothing from everybody in the family, too familiar and comical to leave with a tenant.

As we climb the Grapevine, a truck driver passing our overladen vehicle motions vigorously to Jim, indicating that we've got trouble. When a professional road warrior signals trouble, you listen. We pull onto the shoulder, somewhere near the summit of the ridge between the Los Angeles Basin and the San Joaquin Valley. Jim gets out and sees it. The trailer has a very flat tire. Our jack is in the back of the Explorer, which is crammed to the gills.

We start unloading stuff onto the shoulder of the highway. A lot of stuff. Then some more stuff. I take a moment to appreciate my husband's practical side. He has packed both the car and trailer with soldierly precision, maximizing our carrying capacity. Finally unearthing the jack from a side panel, he approaches the flat tire, only to discover more bad news. The lug nuts on the trailer are too big for the car's lug wrench, and his other wrenches are still back in L.A. Moreover, he remembers that he moved the trailer's spare tire up to the front of the trailer. The spare is inaccessible unless we unpack the entire trailer as well. The first and only four-letter word uttered that day is hissingly exhaled, sotto voce.

I take this as a cue to open my cell phone and call AAA for roadside assistance. The next challenge is to communicate our location to a dispatch operator, a next-to-impossible task for me because I have been waxing poetic on my laptop about poignant therapy sessions, paying little attention to landmarks on the road. Jim has been in his own reverie, listening to *Mars and Venus in the Bedroom* on tape, harvesting and storing sexual secrets for a sybaritic sabbatical. But with the help of our map and any visual remnants we can muster, we learn from the AAA operator that we may be at the Vista Del Lago overlook by Pyramid Lake. And then I mention that the flat tire is on our trailer. "Oh. Sorry," the operator says. "Emergency Roadside Service anywhere and anytime applies only to your vehicle, not your trailer. You'll have to call a private tow truck."

We make the call to Joe's Towing, then begin unpacking the trailer with an urgent but markedly silent edge. Soon the highway shoulder looks like a yard sale. Out come Jim's recumbent bike, my mountain bike, backpacks, kayak paddles, snowshoes, skis, boxes of books, CDs, wine, and the fully outfitted scarecrow from our vegetable garden.

As we unload, I find myself singing a childhood ditty to the tune of "Mary Had A Little Lamb." "Mary ate some Johnny cake. Mary ate some jam. Mary ate some bread and cheese. Mary ate some ham. Up came the Johnny cake. Up came the ham. Up came the bread and cheese. Up came the jam." Jim is not singing. Like Mary, he seems to be upset.

Later, he divulges that while unloading the trailer, he too was singing to himself a childhood ditty: "Nobody likes me. Everybody hates me. So I'll eat some worms. Long, thin slimy ones. Short fat juicy ones. Fuzzy wuzzy, itty-bitty worms. Down goes the first worm. Down goes the second worm. Down goes the third worm! Long, thin slimy ones. Short fat juicy ones. Fuzzy wuzzy, itty-bitty worms. Up comes the first worm! Up comes the second worm. Up comes the thirrrd woorrrm. Long thin slimy ones. Short fat juicy ones. Fuzzy wuzzy, itty bitty worms." Reverting to childhood vomit songs in the face of overwhelming circuit overload, by the way, is technically called "regression in the service of the ego."

Joe's Towing finds us when the driver recognizes our gypsy wagon-style trailer, on whose tailgate I painted one of our llamas, Machu, standing on a mountainside under a sunny sky, belly deep in a meadow full of wildflowers. (I once had aspirations to become an artist, but realized I couldn't make my living that way, so now find outlets in projects like this mural.) Joe's in a better mood than we are, and with the help of his lug wrench, the flat is soon off and the spare is in its place. Giving us directions, Joe takes the flat to his garage for repair and departs, looking rather bemused at us and our attempt to reload the chaos into order.

Methodically, tacitly agreeing not to talk while engaged in serious mental and physical work, we slowly refit the jigsaw puzzle. On the road to Joe's, I feel impelled to tell Jim that I think we've handled this set-to with good grace and well-oiled precision. I can imagine another husband of mine reacting with physical and verbal bluster. And I can certainly picture my own pre-analyzed self, becoming accusative, martyred and depressed. Jim says, "Yeah, and you sure got a bit for the book!"

As we motor into Joe's Towing to reclaim the tire, I think it's time for a celebratory glass of wine. "Where's that wine, Sweetheart?"

"No problem. You'll find it under my recumbent bike, your mountain bike, the backpacks, kayak paddles, snowshoes, skis, scarecrow, boxes of books, and CDs...right there in that cardboard box."

# Chapter 9
## How the Elephant Got His Trunk:
### Adjusting to a Lifestyle Change

She is not only a haven but a grand Mediterranean beauty, nestled on a hillside overlooking the Pacific Ocean. We call her "Villa Porto Marina"—the house where I raised my son Gabriel and daughter Ariel, endured a divorce, launched my career as a psychoanalyst, opened my home office, lived with Jim for nearly twenty years, wove his daughters Brooke and Erin into our recombinant family, then weathered the deaths of both our parents. Over the years we've strolled many moonlit nights on "Sunset Beach" in front of her, the children learned to surf and ridden innumerable waves on their boogie boards here, and we've jogged on her beach with our llamas. She's hosted many parties, psychoanalytic convocations and a friend's wedding. We've aged together and provided for and protected each other well. She's been remodeled several times, survived two major earthquakes, mudslides, and encroaching Santa Monica mountain forest fires. For nearly three decades, she has been my safety net, my hearth and home, and our family home together.

Now, uncomfortably close to the eleventh hour, we've finally found a tenant to lease our dearly loved home. A hotshot New York filmmaker coming to L.A. to write and direct a movie, "Jake" is going through a divorce. His young kids live with their mother back east, but his real estate agent has assured ours that the children will rarely visit. She says he will be working long hours under contract, can pay a lot of money, and is looking for a tranquil, furnished place. Our house is perfect. Remembering how hard my ex-husband worked when he was on location, I know the tenant's story is plausible. This will be our first experience with passive income; we'll be free to travel while the rent checks roll in. Our tenant is a creative guy who will hardly spend time in the house. What can go wrong?

But when Jake drives up in a huge black Hummer, blocking the driveway, I get a slimy taste in my mouth. I remind myself that people don't ordinarily rent furnished houses long term, and we were lucky to find a tenant just before our launch. We already have the first leg of our travels planned: we'll journey to the Middle East, building the trip around an invitation for me to lecture in Jerusalem and Haifa. After a respite at the ranch, we'll then embark on the next leg in the Indonesian outback. Jake pumps Jim's hand, saying he is a fellow athlete, a jujitsu expert. I can see Jim silently resisting the urge to pull back from the man's grip.

It's surreal, walking room-to-room through this place, showing it to a stranger who will soon call it home. Childhood memories of these cabinets and chairs from Sassie and Punky—my dear grandparents—and their old Victorian house in Fresno flood over me, while Jake fairly prances through the house, oohing and aahing. I float back decades with the whole family—my mother and her sister Marion and cousin Betty and their husbands, the three Kimble brothers from Hanford, all the kids sitting on these chairs at the long table dressed in bright red oil cloth for Christmas dinners in Fresno. I can practically smell the sweet potatoes bubbling in butter and brown sugar, the turkey glazed and sizzling in the oven, the biscuits rising as we chop fresh cranberries and oranges for dressing. But I'm jolted into present-day reality, recoiling from Jake's grossly sweet cologne. He's like an alien in our house, sitting with slick black designer jeans on my family treasures!

Our broker and his, anxiously seeking reassurance that this sweet deal will go through, chatter with small talk. Jake says he'd be delighted to hire Miriam, our loyal Salvadoran housekeeper, to continue caring for the house she has lovingly tended for over fifteen years, so she won't have to look for another job. He doesn't object to our request to keep the downstairs office by the garage operational, so our assistant Martha can pay our bills and maintain her routine, as long as he can share our fax machine and copier. My consulting room with its gated entrance, adjacent to Martha's office, will remain locked, off limits, and outside the lease, and I will retain the right to use it when I return to Los Angeles and may need to see one of my former patients.

In spite of Jake's perfume and big black car, we are relieved to close the deal, find someone who we hope appreciates the beauty and tranquility of our home, and is so flexible. We sign a two-year lease.

Working feverishly, we take three final round-trip trailer loads from L.A. to Twin Brooks Ranch. Stressed from the pressure of a huge move, both of us bolt awake every night between 3:00 and 5:00 a.m., each haunted by to-do lists of tasks remaining before our final departure.

Driving into the mountains with our last load after working like dogs for weeks, we decide to stop for a treat in the little town of Auberry, an hour from the ranch. It's our closest town and the home of our post office box. We figure we'll check out the neighborhood pub for the Friday night country music scene we've heard about.

As working weekend road warriors over the years, we've always wanted to get as far away from people as quickly as possible, and have never stopped on the way in. But now we'll have all the isolation one could wish for, especially as our road isn't plowed in winter. We're curious about the local cultural scene and might even find a good band to hire for my upcoming 60th birthday Twin Brooks retreat.

I make it up the canyon well ahead of Jim and the trailer, to find Auberry's Friday night scene well under way. As soon as I pull my Mercedes into the S & J Social Club parking lot full of old trucks and vans, a small crowd of well-oiled locals and their kids gathers around my car. I am definitely driving the wrong car for my new neighborhood, and tasting the downside of my own prejudice about Jake's Hummer. Letting our poodle Jullay out, I think, "Oops, wrong dog!"

Kids swarm her, saying, "What is it? It's got funny curly hair!"

"She's a poodle," I respond. "Her name's Jullay."

"Oh, yeah. I heard of 'em. That's a funny name, but she's kinda cute. It's all right for you to take her inside. We like dogs around these parts."

Jullay and I stroll into the bar together. Heads turn on every barstool. The bartender greets me, jovially introducing himself and his wife as the proprietors. Feeling smartened up and not wanting to stick out, I alter my drink of choice from wine to beer. Unfortunately, however, I order a Heineken. Wrong car, wrong dog, and wrong beer. I've probably just been sized up by the entire neighborhood as an effete auslander, which—even though my great-grandfather settled his lumber mill here, and I've spent summers in these mountains since I was three weeks old—I guess I am.

"Where are you from?" the bartender asks.

"We're moving from L.A. to our ranch at the old Peterson Mill," I explain.

From the barstool next to mine, my somewhat juiced and toothless neighbor offers: "I can come any time of the day or night to fix anything that needs fixing, pretty lady."

A couple of others make similarly generous offers while I pray for Jim to drive up soon. Am I being picked up? Is unemployment at an all-time high in this particular county, even though it is at record lows everywhere else? I notice remarkable lack of dentition on some of my older compatriots. I've been looking for new cultures and change, and it's right here!

Then the music starts, and all the cultural, educational, aesthetic and economic gaps instantly seal over. The spirited female singer knows all the Patsy Cline, Merle Haggard, Judds, bluegrass, blues and pop you could ask for, so on a break I ask if they'd like to play a birthday gig in July. We make a date on the spot. Jim walks in and we enjoy the next set before hitting the long winding road to our new home.

True to our new early-rising ritual, Jim and I wake at 4:00 a.m. Last night's scene is replaying across my brain when Jim plaintively asks, "What am I going to do? No Starbucks!" In the Palisades, Jim had come to savor his early morning coffee launch, thanks to his daughter Brooke's campaign to convert us to the joys of Seattle life by plying her dad with Starbucks gift cards. He hadn't considered missing his coffee ritual until now.

His innocuous question sets me to recognizing the magnitude of the changes in our daily lives. On our infamous flat tire trailer run, I'd brought my laptop to the mountains to check out Internet access. Unsuccessful in getting connected, I'd searched the ¼" rural Ponderosa Telephone Company yellow pages for a local computer techie. I only found two listings that mentioned computers; I called them both and heard pleasant messages, such as: "I'm probably outside for a bit, please leave your name and number. If it's anyone calling for Carrie, she's sleeping over at Mary Sue's and said to call her there." I left messages, and the return calls yielded no luck. One man was an outpost worker for a national software designer, and the other said he had no Macintosh experience, and that no one on the whole mountain sold or serviced Macs. No coffee, no computer, no Internet? And Jim is not Peter Mayle, nor is this going to be *A Year in Provence*. And I'm not Frances Mayles living *Under the Tuscan Sun*, either!

"Well," I muse in response to Jim's plaintive question. "Whatever is there to do? I can't think of a single other thing to do here in Oz but initiate a new sabbatical morning launch. Are you thinking what I'm thinking?"

"Yeah." Getting right down into the country, Jim says, "How about we make our own morning kick and call it 'Starfucks'?"

"Great idea! We've been so preoccupied with moving, we've forgotten the real joys of early morning awakening." Cheering to the prospect of awaking to love, I ask, "So, what is it you usually get at Starbucks?" There is a pause. Then, rather sheepishly but with a degree of glee, Jim says, "A Grande Drip!" We collapse into rolling waves of laughter.

And that is how the new sabbatical morning ritual is born, and how we come to try the Grande Drip, and the Double Vente, and the frothy Cappuccino. And if my maiden name were Kipling instead of Kimble, I would say it's how the elephant got his trunk.

# PART IV
# OH, JERUSALEM!

# CHAPTER 10

## INTO THE ANCIENT DEEP:
## CONFESSIONS OF A NEWBORN DIVER

### *Scubaphobia*

OUR RATTLETRAP plane lands in the middle of a midnight sandstorm that is pummeling Hurgada, a dive resort on the Egyptian banks of the Red Sea. I stare through my cracked, duct-taped window at the opaque sky, its eddying sand mirroring the anxiety churning in my gut. I am frazzled from Los Angeles departure mania, lost luggage, and transfers from jumbo jet to prop to this tiny plane, whose threadbare carpet reveals missing bolts and screws. Smelling of dried vomit unsuccessfully covered by ammonia, this little aircraft reminds me that it's been exactly two weeks since Egypt Air's Los Angeles/Cairo flight inexplicably crashed off Nantucket Sound, killing hundreds.

Before leaving the states, we read a *Los Angeles Times* piece on the crash investigation, highlighting complex cultural differences. U.S. journalists reported that the little black box showed no mechanical failures, but the flight recorder captured the co-pilot repeatedly praying to Allah. As he was found to be in financial distress, Americans called it a suicide/homicide. The article argued that Muslim culture virtually denies mental illness, protects families from public scrutiny, and views newspaper speculation about a man's finances as utterly inappropriate. Egyptians, distrusting American technology, reportedly believe there really was a mechanical failure and that Americans have been too quick to show their anti-Arab sentiment by blaming a praying man as if he were taking his own and all the passengers' lives to avoid debt.

Opening a rumpled copy of *The Egyptian Gazette* on the plane, Jim reads the headline aloud: "'The U.S. Is Wrong' to steer the crash probe in one direction, brushing aside any accusation against Boeing. An internal or external explosion could have occurred in the rear of the plane and damaged the cockpit voice recorder." He then reads from another article entitled "The Snake in the Grass," which offers: "Religion has never been a barrier to Israel's perpetuation of the most vicious crimes of mass killing, torture, detention without trial and bashing the bones of Palestinian children." Even during this rare period of peace between Egypt and Israel, and renewed peace talks between Israel and Syria, we are rudely awakened by this taste of intense xenophobic tension between the principal parties comprising the Middle East. These political concerns compound my burgeoning anxiety about our trip.

Egypt Air lost my dive bag and all my gear in Cairo, and my apprehension is at a peak, fueled by fear of the unknown and "stranger anxiety." This is the feeling that sets in with babies around eight months old, when they deeply sense an attachment to their mother. Stranger anxiety is one of the root causes of xenophobia, our fear of foreigners. Another cause of stranger anxiety is projection of our own unacceptable flaws onto others. In this sense, xenophobia is a first cousin to paranoia. Add to that the fear of losing control and the security of one's attachments—in this case, my dive gear—and it's all swirling around in my gut like the sandstorm in which we have landed.

I am particularly anxious about this Middle East trip because it signals a huge life change. My preparatory obsessive list making, trip planning, luggage packing, and ticket buying are simply focal points for a freewheeling apprehension about leaving the security of my known world. I am forced to acknowledge that pulling up stakes is not just a physical act of moving a tent, so to speak. This journey might—hopefully, *will*—lead me toward letting go, not only of my attachment to our home, my career, our familiar life with friends and family in Los Angeles, but also this remarkable level of anxiety that I hadn't known I carried, until now.

Our dive master welcomes us by reporting that our boat's course has been altered due to adverse weather conditions. My reflections give way to escalating concerns about deep sea diving. Our first serious scuba trip won't be safe in a Malibu swimming pool or the familiar pacific waters off Catalina Island where we got certified, but deep in the Third World. The good news: after a sleuth circus in Cairo to find the London-bound passenger who retrieved my look-alike bag in customs, my dive gear has been found and is being unloaded off the plane. With no time to celebrate, we stuff ourselves into a transport van to motor south through the sandstorm. Crammed like ducks in a box, we ride with four French-speaking passengers, presumably divers, and an Arab driver and navigator, both swathed in traditional cattans and keffiyehs. We will drive two hours south to a sheltered mooring.

Wind and sand buffeting the van, I scrunch into a corner with my pen and travel journal, recounting the sleepless flight from California to Cairo, my lost dive bag and frustrating encounters with airport security. We cross several checkpoints where armed, turbaned solders menacingly lean into the vehicle, gesturing at our documents with glinting rifles, to verify that we look like the photos on our passports. At 3:00 a.m., jet lagged and unsettled, Jim and I and the other dive passengers lurch unsteadily down a swaying gangplank to board Miss Nouran, who strains at her mooring in rocky seas. We find our cabin and collapse into bunks, briefly chuckling at the sheets inscribed with red and purple puckering lips and the word *Love*.

In the morning, we arise as Miss Nouran travels southward, still pitching against the swells. We gather in the boat's lounge, our dining room, kitchen, card room, rec room and meeting center for the week. Miss Nouran appears shipshape; the lounge's mahogany paneling smells of fresh varnish mixed with sea air and naugahyde upholstery. In clipped British tones, dive master Mark announces: "Hey, mates, listen up. Our first dives will be checkout dives. I need to see everyone's PADI or NAWI dive certification cards and dive logs to verify that you're all qualified."

Reassured that this will be a professional operation, I head to our bunkroom to retrieve my travel notebook with my dive log and certification. The bunkroom is tiny, with no place to unpack, so I have only to look in my carry-on shoulder bag. My journal can't be missing! I was writing in it last night. Jim has his papers and our passports and tickets in the fanny pack. All I have to keep track of is my journal and purse. In the sleepy mayhem of crawling out of the cramped van and boarding the boat, could I have dropped my notebook? Distraught, I tear into my duffel and dive bag, but find nothing. My notebook contains my travel journal, scuba certification papers, dive log, and other travel documents to boot.

Back in the lounge, Mark, the snowy blond dive master who looks younger than our kids, stares at me with light blue eyes and sunbleached eyelashes and confidently assures me that I will never see my journal again. "If you dropped it for a minute, it was probably swept into the van driver's caftan, and no doubt it's already the prized possession of his nomad family." Mark allows time for me to emit a pained, barely audible gulp. After examining Jim's valid PADI certification card, Mark says to me, "I'm willing to give you a go on a test dive without your papers. I'm a dive master. I'll know soon enough if you know what you're doing."

It's clear we are about to be more than literally in over our heads. We're the least experienced of fourteen divers. And I can't even keep track of my dive log and notes, journal and PADI papers, let alone my mind. When we emailed the British dive company, querying whether this voyage was appropriate for us novice divers, they responded: "Don't worry, you'll be in good hands. Mark's a pro and by the end of the week you'll be much more competent." But as we meet the other divers and note their sun-bleached dive suits, well-worn boots and casual demeanor, we become fully intimidated—not to mention insecure about the company's assurances. The Egyptian economy is in rather desperate straits. Is a credit card more important than a PADI card here?

Five male divers and one female diver are from the U.K. The woman is a Navy frogwoman. Two of the men are diving instructors, including Mark; the other Brits are certified masters who dive in the frigid North Sea just for fun. The four Frenchmen are highly experienced divers, including one pro underwater photographer. In winter, they saw holes in the ice of alpine lakes to dive. There is one other woman, a Dutch-American diver from Amsterdam, who seems to be on this journey more to recover from heartbreak than to dive. But her presence is not reassuring and I'm really not up for healing broken hearts at sea.

My mind swims. *Why don't we ever do things like most people? Why did I let my cousin talk us into starting scuba diving at sixty, and why didn't we go to a nice warm tropical dive resort? What are we doing here in high winds, choppy seas, strong currents, and most dangerous of all, this mounting anxiety in my gut? Mark is talking in centigrade and metrics; what if I can't convert critical information to Fahrenheit and inches?*

Pummeled by fear, I manage to talk myself down. My options are limited. We're in the middle of the Red Sea with no plans to touch land for a week. I can either go for it or spend the week fetally curled on love lips in my cramped bunk. I might as well go for it. I pull on my obviously new Titanium wetsuit, custom-made to accommodate my torn shoulder rotator cuff. Dreading I've forgotten all instruction, shivering before I even get in the water, I check my tank, my weights, my computer pressure gauge. Snapping into my inflatable vest or BCD, I check that my hoses are in place. I descend the dive ladder, pull on my dive mask and take a huge breath. Holding my nose and goggles, fighting my impulse to hold tight to the ladder, I remind myself that the deeper agenda of this sabbatical is letting go. I let go, release the ladder and plunge into the dark choppy water.

Only my cheeks and neck feel the cold. My suit feels familiar and good. Yet as I descend, I quickly discover my mask is leaking, my goggles are fogging, and my new reading lens inserts don't work. I can't read the strategic numbers on my dive computer, and even if I could, I seem to have forgotten how to interpret them. Startled by a warning beep, I squint at my dive computer and make out a flashing pair of lungs. I am pretty sure this is a bad sign.

Neutral buoyancy is an art form I have not yet mastered; neither has Jim. It is the art of smoothly maintaining oneself at one depth without bobbing up and sinking down. Our test dive turns out to be a humiliating no-no called a "yo-yo dive." Mark calmly reminds us to "buddy up," stay close together and remain relaxed, but we don't do very well. Jim has a characterological habit of taking off by himself, so I've brought a boogie board leash to attach to his ankle in case he forgets about me. It's a perfect metaphor for his denial of dependency and my desperate need to hold on. Am I too embarrassed to bring the leash on the next dive?

In spite of everything, Mark accepts me to dive and brightly insists we'll improve. I'm sure it's about the credit card.


After dinner, totally exhausted from two more deep dives, we fall into our bunks and sink into the nitrox induced stupor of jet-lagged scuba divers. Every few hours I awaken, pitching from port to starboard, seized by a new wave of survival anxiety. Restless dreams of death by suffocation and drowning crystallize into a fear of strangulation by the "octopus" of my buoyancy control device hoses.

The night seems endless as I oscillate between recuperative rocking and primitive dread. What washes over me is another form of anxiety: compression anxiety. The bodily experience of being encompassed in a tight scuba suit, constricted by the pressure of much deeper dives than we've ever done (or are certified to do), has rekindled a submerged birth memory.

It is as if the scary diving experiences I had today, under such intense pressure at the ocean floor, liberated a deeply repressed memory of being stuck, backwards and upside down, in my mother's birth canal. Five years of psychoanalysis never triggered this palpable, kinesthetic terror of my own birth trauma, a prolonged breech birth I heard about but never recalled. I feel pressure on every surface of my body, along with a primal fear of asphyxiation, being stuck with no way of getting out to safety. I know I am close to my beloved (mother/husband) but I'm utterly unable to be saved. Rocking and pitching in the ancient waters of the Fertile Crescent, I am reliving—in vivid bodily detail—that traumatic passage of sixty years ago.

We sleep for more than fourteen hours, "gassing off" dive-accumulated nitrogen like we're on drugs. I awaken sweat-drenched from intense dreams. What is curious and amazing is that I feel I have passed to another side. After spending a night in terror of suffocation and drowning, then lying in my bunk in the early morning processing the myriad anxieties that have fed my "scubaphobia," I arise with the new day, strangely peaceful. Simply being able to recognize the primitive roots of my anxiety in a long-forgotten birth trauma brings incredible relief. I've been miraculously released.

I feel grateful for my experience with psychoanalysis, as both patient and practitioner. Like Eva, my analytic patient who carried a mysterious terror of bathing and swimming until we uncovered the repressed trauma of a near drowning by her mother, I have never understood my lifelong fear of dark water and suffocatingly tight places. I rock rhythmically on the bunk, greatly calmed by my new understanding. I reach my foot up to jostle Jim in his upper bunk and he sleepily drops his arm over the side to tousle my hair. Slowly, he slips his body over the edge of his bunk and down into mine, and we tumble deliciously in the red-lipped sheets.

It's time to get up. I feel ready to read and retain the complex functions and tables of my dive computer. I am ready to find and maintain the deep relaxing Ujjayi Pranayama breathing that is an integral part of my yoga practice, and to bid adieu, for now, to the dozen variegated forms of traveler's anxiety. I am ready to become a competent deep-sea diver.

### A Psychedelic Undersea Garden

OVER THE NEXT SIX DAYS, we make more than a dozen descents into the Red Sea. Some are shallow at forty feet; most are between sixty and eighty feet, in a rich coral reef zone of plenteous and varied marine life. I see all kinds of fish—moray eels guarding their lairs like dark swaying sentinels, white-tipped reef sharks resting like Navy submarines along the bottom, shoals of glinting silver barracuda, brightly striped yellow and blue snapper—all swimming among hard and soft corals in resplendent white, pink, blue, red and gold, evoking the psychedelic undersea gardens of the Beatles' Yellow Submarine.

We encounter bright coral Serranidae or groupers, and Labridae or wrasses, remarkable not only for their beauty but for their ability to change sex. I think Freud was all mixed up about penis envy. I have discovered wrasse envy. Freud's sample was restricted to repressed Victorian women; he never analyzed a female wrasse. Why settle for one sex? A female wrasse can change into a male at will, and back again. On the other hand, don't ask to become a cleaner wrasse; your lifetime job will be to clean other fish of parasites, dead scales and pieces of skin. Though fish willingly submit to this service, and even line up to wait their turn like cars at a car wash, this job doesn't ring my bell.

We marvel at the spectacular colors of different Angelfish, including striped Emperors, Royals, Arabians and Zebras. Little butterfly fish are funny-looking fellows with long narrow faces and tiny lips more puckered than Goldie Hawn's after collagen injections. The seemingly limitless species include aptly named clownfish, parrotfish, puffer fish and porcupine fish. We see gobies who share their ocean floor domiciles with crustaceans. Around them swim dozens of the iridescent, blue-spotted, bottom-dwelling stingrays ubiquitous in the Red Sea. Camouflaged triggerfish and stonefish are immobile as rocks, waiting for prey to come within striking range. And for the first time in his native habitat, we meet the familiar face of the lionfish we called Leon in our saltwater aquarium at home. Before long we see Leon's relatives, stunning brown, orange and white striped fish sporting huge "manes" and fins of poisonous floating tendrils.

My absolute favorite reveals herself during one of our night dives on the reefs of Nabba Abu Dabbab. A floridly scarlet nudibranch—actually, a mother/daughter pair—is out for the evening, taking a leisurely dinner on the reef. Mother is about eighteen inches long, five inches across, and daughter measures eight inches. Mother propels herself with fluffy, psychedelic red mantles that run her length on each side, as her white-tipped red skirt wafts in the current. On her back is a reproductive center fringed with ruffles. Crimson nudibranchs are the most beautiful sea creatures I've ever seen. Their common name, "sea slugs," is an affront; they are more aptly called "Spanish dancers" for their brilliant, gyrating ruffles that swirl like the seductive skirts of gypsy flamenco performers.

The next night, sixty kilometers away, I discover their luminous phosphorescent velvet lace fans. Iridescent black fan worms, these "Spanish fans" open and close as my halogen light shines upon them. An old prejudice has washed away: slugs and worms can be extraordinarily beautiful! And as I observe my own deeply hushed rhythmic breathing, I realize with joy that my scubaphobia has been replaced by calm and awe. It's astonishing how quickly and profoundly I am letting go of old anxieties and preconceptions, rewarded for "coloring outside the lines" of conventional travel.

### Call to Courage in A Rough Sea

That is, until next morning's dive. I shade my eyes and search the horizon for the northern end of Elfin Stone, a famous unspoiled reef in the South Red Sea. Well rested and confident, facing a sunny morning, I feel ready for this premier dive. Jim cocks his head and gives me a thumbs up, reflecting my high spirits. We kiss, lips soft and warmly reassuring. Within forty-five minutes, Miss Nouran has set anchor, we're suited up, and I jump into the blue-green sea with a satisfying splash. Jim follows. I signal my readiness and Mark leads us down. Jim and I are grateful we've had him as our private dive master this week, as the others are so accomplished they prefer to go off on their own.

We dive deeper and deeper and the surrounding waters turn darker and darker. *At least,* I think, *it's calm.* I glance at the dive computer on my wrist. One hundred and thirty-two feet. My heart thuds against my breastbone. I suck in a breath and kick hard to propel myself three yards to Jim's side. He points to a small hole in a coral outcropping, but I stare at him. He's gulping oxygen from his tank. He's asthmatic and at this depth we must make several seven-minute decompression stops before we can safely surface. Otherwise we'll get the bends.

I draw close to check Jim's dive computer. The flashing lungs sign is bad enough, but then I read that his tank is getting low. My heart pounds. My love for him and the joy of our life together flash before me. I curse myself for allowing us to be led so deep by our juvenile dive master. *I've been letting go of control, and look what's happened.* I see Mark observing an undulating octopus in a rock wall. I make a quick decision: Jim first, then Mark.

I grab Jim's arm, then send divers' signals with nervous hands that don't want to cooperate. Jim's computer beeps, warning of low air and continuing excessive air use. I stare through his black-rimmed goggles at his eyes. He looks scared. I know our safety depends on staying calm and I signal that. I wonder if he's thinking, like I am, of the two Brit dive masters yesterday who surfaced too fast due to leg cramps. Their computers have "locked them out," forbidding further diving for forty-eight hours. Suddenly I realize how much worse things could get. At more than a hundred and thirty feet, we're well below twice the depth we were certified to dive. Jim signals his worry, and we catch Mark's attention to indicate we're heading up.

At our first decompression stop, around eighty-five feet, we have to wait eight minutes to allow respiration to clear nitrogen out of our bloodstreams. Blood absorbs nitrogen as you descend, and without the decompression stop, the ascent can boil your blood, leading to "getting bent" and possibly to death. Jim's computer indicates he's out of bottom time and has only 300 psi of pressure left (we started with close to 3,000). We have no choice but to wait, trying to maintain slow and measured breathing. I check my own gauge and extra hose, mentally reviewing the buddy breathing technique we learned in case he needs to breathe off my tank.

Slowly, the minutes tick by. We gradually ascend to our next decompression stop at thirty feet. Jim's computer continues beeping, warning he's still gulping air too fast. I signal my concern to our dive master, who simply indicates the need for calm. When the decompression stop is over, we continue a slow ascent to fifteen feet, where we must wait for seven minutes. Jim's tank is nearly empty. Barely enough oxygen remains to inflate his BCD, turning it into a life jacket, which is critical because we know the surface will be extremely choppy. We resort to buddy breathing whereby I share the oxygen in my tank with Jim, offering him my auxillary breathing hose to reach the surface. Thank god he's finally breathing fresh air through his snorkel. Miss Nouran has disappeared in the waves; Mark inflates a neon safety signal buoy so the captain can spot us and dispatch a Zodiac to pick us up.

The sea is too rough for me to breathe through my snorkel. Besides, unconsciously clenching my mouthpiece, I have bitten it in half. Since plenty of air (1300 psi) remains in my tank, I signal to Jim that I am going to descend below the choppy surface to wait. I follow

Jim and Mark's fins underwater until a dark shadow comes over me. The Zodiac has finally come. It is too rough to climb into the craft, so we hang on to a towline and return to the boat.

By the time we reach Miss Nouran, the dive ladders are flying crazily in the air and slamming into the boat's transom. Jim and Mark manage to climb back on the boat. I struggle to remove my fins. Each time I grab the ladder it slams me down. I am afraid that with almost 100 pounds of gear on my back, my shoulder will be yanked and my torn right rotator cuff will tear again. I've spent the last twelve months babying it back to health. *God*, I ask, having forgotten the beautiful Spanish dancers, *why are we doing this?*

Finally, on a down swell, the crew hauls me aboard from where I've been thrashing, trying to get my fins off. Jim, Mark and the other divers are clustered near the transom, watching. As I reach the deck, they excitedly yell, "Sharks!" Drawn by my thrashing, sharks have come to circle the boat. Never mind my safety—the Frenchmen are thrilled that I've brought a great show right to their feet.

Shivering, I climb out of my BCD, peel off my wetsuit, sort out my gear and trade cold salt water for a hot shower. My soft, warm sweat suit feels comforting to my skin. Back from the deep! At lunch, the pro divers crack open Egyptian beers and drink a toast to our guts, telling us they have each a minimum of two thousand dives all over the world, and that we have been diving in seriously rough seas. They call it courage. We look at each other, wondering if it wouldn't better be called foolhardiness. Warm from the shower, spaced out from relief, nitrogen and the midday beer, I lean back to muse on the question I'd asked myself at one hundred thirty-two feet. *What are we doing?*

Before meeting Jim, I never did anything this bold or risky. But no international crew of frogmen ever toasted my courage, either. I have ridden horses my whole life, starting as a newborn when my mother cradled me in her arms and rode around Twin Brooks, and I've skied since I was nine. But I have always felt safe and relatively in control. Summiting Kilimanjaro, I was unaware of how sick and vulnerable I was. This dive trip felt dangerous—it resurrected my fear of losing Jim, the possibility of getting bent, the small matter of an agitated school of sharks, and myriad issues of trust in strangers. Still, we are safe, we've had a thrilling and beautiful adventure deep under the ancient Red Sea, and I feel pleasantly relieved by my own cool under pressure. I maintained my composure and safely shepherded Jim a hundred and thirty feet to the surface.

Every day is a new day. The sun rises warm and bright, and the seas are calmer. Jim, ironically rereading Ann Tyler's *Breathing Lessons*, is breathing much better. We decide we've got to get back in the proverbial saddle or never ride again. We agree on a nice shallow dive at Il Kaessara before our return to Hurghada. We make our intentions clear to Mark. This morning's dive is "only" eighty-six feet—a piece of cake! Il Kaessara is a relaxed, enjoyable dive, and we gaze at beautiful corals and sea urchins—especially the long black spiny Diadema urchins. Jim calmly has three white-tipped sharks practically sitting in his lap. Another lesson: when we remain calm, the sharks are quite tranquil and attractive. As a further reward for earning our scuba stripes, a giant sea turtle swims right over our heads.

After our last night dive, we gather in Miss Nouran's lounge with our new buddies, the Frenchmen, the Brit South Enders and the Dutch woman, who is feeling more whole after a week of sleeping, writing poetry, diving, and talking for hours to a psychoanalyst who happens to be aboard. She leads us all in dancing and celebrating the international friendships that have flowered in this extraordinary place. The others exchange tales of diving the Maldives, the Caymans, the North Sea, the Hebrides, Madagascar and the Seychelles— favorite dive sites for Europeans. We've been so preoccupied with not drowning, we hadn't noticed that all but two of the divers are young enough to be our kids. Heavily ensconced in building their careers, they drool as we talk of our plans for next spring, diving off the coast of North Suluwesi in Indonesia, and next winter, among curtains of hammerhead sharks and whale sharks migrating north through the Galapagos.

The Brits toast us: "Really sporty. Brilliant, actually!" We have officially earned our stripes. Even if I no longer have my PADI diving certification card, there are twelve souls somewhere out there in the world, several of whom are dive masters and instructors, who will swear to my competence.

# CHAPTER 11
## FREUD IN THE TWENTY-FIRST CENTURY

LAST YEAR I received an email from my Israeli colleague, Emanuel. "We're organizing an international millennial conference on Freud in the twenty-first century in Jerusalem next December. Would you give a paper on film from a psychoanalytic perspective?" Since neither Jim nor I had ever visited the Middle East, such an invitation was a juicy way to initiate an adventure. It was easy to send back an enthusiastic "Yes!"

My dear friend and colleague, Diana, was also invited, so the three of us planned the adventure together. Diana had spent her first five years living on an Israeli kibbutz with her since-deceased archeologist father and photographer mother, and was eager to search out her roots. In addition to taking part in the Freud conference, we wanted to visit the West Bank and Gaza, the Dead Sea and Masada in Israel, Diana's kibbutz and surrounding lands, as well as the Sinai, the Pyramids of the Lower Nile valley, Petra in Jordan, and Bethlehem.

Baptized by our adventure in the Red Sea, I've nearly repressed memories of all the obsessive wardrobe-related phone calls with Diana in the weeks before we left. We'd both been awash in nitpicky little details about what to bring, how to pack, and what we desperately needed to order from the online travel store at the last minute. I've forgotten all that until we meet Diana at the Jerusalem airport. I love seeing her as she comes through customs, her blonde hair, finely chiseled features and warm smile fresh from New York. As we greet each other, it becomes clear that while we've been undersea for the last week, Diana has been stewing in her own obsessional pre-trip details. She spent all night packing and repacking before the flight. Diana is brilliant as a psychologist, clinician and researcher on attachment theory, but she trumps me with her mind-spinning travel anxieties.

Settled into our Jerusalem hotel, Diana and I share stories about our pre-trip preparations. I read aloud from my travel journal, recounting my own gerbil-on-a-habitrail activities. Many authors have written eloquently, humorously, even mystically of travel in the Middle East: the Valley of the Kings, the Nile, Jerusalem, the Holy Land and its unholy terrors, the gut-wrenching pain caused by violence, and the depths of the Red Sea. But, this being Freud in the twenty-first century, before I embark upon our travels and written explorations of Egypt, Jordan, Israel and Palestine, I need to process the psychic knots that manifested planning for our trip. Writing helps me explore the myriad kinds of anxiety, ranging from insignificantly personal to universal, which came to a head in frightening moments at one hundred and thirty-two feet under the Red Sea. As I read my journal aloud, Diana bursts into gales of appreciative laughter. "Just about every female I know goes through this!"

Most of the time, the anxiety isn't even conscious. It's a subdued underground background noise that I don't even notice. Sometimes it surfaces, just catching my attention like a fly inside the house; I'll notice it, then go back to whatever I'm doing. But when it marches on the scene like a brass band, it can knock me off my pins, and then I have to stop, focus, and process it, giving it its due.

That near-death scuba diving experience so knocked me off my pins that I have had to breathe very deeply, regroup, and retrace my steps. Like Ariadne in Crete, following the threads leading out of the Minotaur's labyrinth, I have to travel backwards in search of the earliest signs of signal anxiety that, like a slow-burning fuse, ultimately reached my powder keg of panic and ignited. Many a traveler has stepped on this initially small fuse of signal anxiety while heading into the unknown.

Anxiety isn't a bad thing. In its most common form, we psychologists call it "signal anxiety;" it works like a yellow light at a traffic intersection: *Proceed with caution!* It helps the deer notice a light whiff that possibly signals a mountain lion's scent. Separation anxiety in infants is designed to assure that mothers and babies don't lose each other. A toddler plays raptly in the park, his mother engrossed in the daily news with her neighbor, until one or the other stops and looks up anxiously to check out the other's whereabouts. It's a good thing.

Stranger anxiety, which precedes separation anxiety, is a necessary part of attachment behavior, though tribal and group attachments can lead to cultural and racial xenophobia and the political paranoia that has caused so many wars. When you give in to paranoid and persecutory anxiety, you escalate your fear as I did on the Bench Valley pack trip, ignoring that the ripe gooseberries pendulant from the bushes remained untouched, clear evidence that hungry bears were not haunting the area.

Like a candle, anxiety can light a darkened room, but if the flame leaps out of control, it can consume all in its path, burning the house to the ground. Panic is contagious and  spreads. The source of the blaze needs to be discovered, contained and processed. Since awakening on Miss Nouran, beset with panic about death by suffocation, I have slowly retraced my steps back through the maze to its innocent inception: an ordinary little bit of pre-trip anxiety that circled around like a cat and held me prey to inchoate memories of my own breech birth.

Pre-departure anxiety has familiar a ring; most travelers recognize it. While it is usually logistical, it's also spiced with excitement and mediated by lists. List making is a time-honored defense against the fear of loss of control. I should know, as I am the "llamandant" of llama packing, which means lists of lists, labels, measures, and signs.

Prior to coming to the Middle East, I spent two weeks mildly to momentarily lost in my most inane form: wardrobe anxiety. Jim, who always packs the same minimalist bag, sees my anxiety as absurd and refuses to be hooked into discussion of my elaborate lists: "Get over it. Just pack." But admittedly, analyzed or not, I find myself lying awake mornings, mentally packing my bags, like a nine-year-old filling a trunk for Barbie's honeymoon.

I sent a slightly veiled email to my Israeli colleague. "Emanuel, what's the garb for Jim for the Jerusalem conference?" Humorously, but indicating an end to the conversation, Emanuel responded, "I'm not the one to ask. I've spent my lifetime in trouble all over the world refusing to wear (or own) a tie." Sight unseen, Jim immediately bonded with Emanuel and looked forward to meeting him in Jerusalem. Left to my own devices, I emailed Diana, the perfect wardrobe play partner. She was up in the same tree, so together we narrowed our packing choices and even introduced the sisterly notion of sharing clothes. "I'm bringing this and you can borrow it. Do you have anything extra for the hike up Mt. Sinai?"

The conversation boils down to a variation on a theme: What do we need for mountain climbing? Camel riding? Scuba diving? Desert travel with scorching days, freezing nights, no layovers for laundry? Professional meetings? Dinner dancing? What matches what? What wrinkles? What doesn't? I worried: what luggage will each airline allow? How can I possibly schlep all this? Will I re-tear my rotator cuff hauling the bags? Where can we store scuba gear? Should I get new bags with wheels? Such questions can unleash a shopper's feeding frenzy: midnight internet orders, extra charges for overnight delivery, anxious waiting for the FedEx truck.

Enough! Clearly, beneath all my obsessional pre-trip nonsense lie deeper fears of separation, loss, disorientation, and health and safety dangers, nicely masked by worry about something I can control.

Sometimes I pray for the simple intelligence to practice what one travel writer described as a family ritual. After everything is packed, they gather to sit on their luggage for half an hour. He says if you've forgotten anything, as you sit there (and before it's too late) it comes back to you; if you've actually packed everything, the extra time allows you to relax and quiet yourself before setting off. It's a surefire way to leave with peace of mind. Will I, over the course of this odyssey, become that wise? Will I be able to let go of my hamster-on-a-habitrail worry about wrinkles and what could go wrong, and instead really breathe into the present moment?"

Having shared my journal with Diana, we do begin to settle into the present moment: our happy reunion, the launching of our time together on these Middle Eastern adventures and the richly provocative Freud conference in Jerusalem.

# CHAPTER 12
## BORDERS, BOUNDARIES, AND THRESHOLDS

AT THE LAST CHECKPOINT as we cross the Israeli border, the underbelly of our car is thoroughly scanned by mirrors and magnets, and we nervously leave it and our Israeli guide at the border to walk across the barren, dusty no man's land separating Israel and Jordan. Although we cross an armed border, the same hot desert air flows freely and follows us across the line. Baka, a Bedouin Muslim, greets us in Jordan, announcing himself as our new guide. The transition into Jordan immediately stirs new feelings in me, and I recall the words of Arab poet Mahmoud Darwish:

> I am an Arab
> & colour of hair: jet black
> & colour of eyes: brown
> distinguishing features
> on my head a camel-hair headband
> over a Keffiyeh
> & my palm is solid as rock
> scratching whoever touches it
> & to me the most delicious food
>     is olive oil & thyme . . .
> However
> If I am hungry
> I will eat the flesh of my usurper
> Beware beware of my hunger
> And of my anger.[2]

---

2  Darwish, Mahmoud. *From Leaves of the Olive Tree*. Trans. I. Wedde & F. Tiroan. Manchester: Carcanet Press, 1973.

As this border crossing becomes more threshold than boundary, I am intrigued by how fickle my identifications turn out to be. Until today, we have been eating, talking, driving, laughing and thinking Israeli with Johanan Moses, from whom we parted company at the final border checkpoint. Israel felt familiar. The average secular Israeli dresses casually, similar to Californians. Yet after a few hours in Jordan, I find myself moving from stranger anxiety to chameleon-like identification with my new hosts.

The clothing is very different here, and the change is far more substantive than a wardrobe adjustment. I soon discover the ample soft cotton headscarf, also called a shel or keffiyeh, embroidered in the black of the Gebaliye or mountain Bedouin, or the red of the desert Bedouin; it can be a practical protection against the wind and sun of the desert, left loose or swaddled about the head, depending upon weather. When I don one, I notice any potential antipathy toward foreigners melting a little. Some of the men wearing the shel nod appreciatively as they walk past. As the barrier of my stranger anxiety dissolves, I feel the poetic in-your-face poignancy of Mahmoud Darwish's lines: "I am an Arab. You usurped my grandfather's vineyards & the plot of land I used to plough…and left us & all my grandchildren nothing but these rocks."

With American passports, Jim, Diana and I are able to move back and forth between cultures far more freely than most of the local people. We are finding ourselves opening up and becoming more tolerant of complexity. Since our bodies and minds were purged of toxins with a wonderful wallow in Dead Sea muds, our pores have been open. Here, in a roadside coffee house over cups of sweet, inky black Arabic-style coffee, we feel like blotters soaking up learning as much as we can, porous to the smells of aromatic spices, animals, dust and sweat, and sounds of myriad voices speaking Arabic amidst the hustle bustle of daily life in a new culture. The sensory experience is exhilarating, and it's one of the main reasons we're on this journey.

Preoccupied with borders, boundaries and thresholds, I remember my favorite John Sayles film, the classic 1995 *Lone Star*.[3] Sayles is interested in the lines of sex, class, race, and age we draw between

3 Wrye, H., Lone Star: Signs, Borders and Thresholds. *International Journal of Psychoanalysis*, 1998, 790:2.395-398.

ourselves and others, and he describes his film as a "story about borders," both geographically—set in the mythical border town of Frontera, Texas—and psychologically. He explains that "a border is where you draw a line and say, 'This is where I end and somebody else begins.'" Recovering from our own border-crossing tensions, Diana and I lose Jim to a copy of the *International Herald Tribune* as we sip our coffee and settle into conversation about *Lone Star*.

Diana is not only my psychoanalytic colleague, travel wardrobe maven, but a fellow film junkie; we've each written several articles and co-edited a journal about psychoanalytic film interpretation. Warming up to the topic, a propos our morning, and since we are both *Lone Star* fans, I say, "I love it that Sayles was so interested in thresholds, border crossings, epiphanies.

Diana replies, "Right! In contrast to boundaries which are meant not to be crossed, he shows that borders can be consciously crossed, and invite transformation!"

"Yes, I love it because I feel we are living it here and now with these border crossings and major cultural forays. Sayles is a cinema master . . . he creates a dialectic in the film showing where rigid points of demarcation can be softened and transformed. In numerous dramatic scenes in *Lone Star*, both within the film and between the screen and the audience, these 'thresholds' occur."

Diana sighed, "It's so cool to be feeling that transformative energy here."

"Yes, you've got it," I nod. I lean back in my chair, savoring conversation with my wonderful friend. I've missed this kind of dialogue since closing my practice, moving away from the urban scene in L.A. Jim is just not up for this kind of talk. "But, you know, there is this third area, the notion of a threshold, a particular kind of space.[4] Crossing a threshold, we can extend and enrich ourselves. At one moment we're holding simultaneously a glimpse of the familiar and the new. Threshold experiences are transitional. They're potentially transformative in the sense of promoting change. Something that's never quite existed before in either opposing culture or within a

---

4 More in Welles, J. *Rituals: Cinematic and Analytic. Psychoanalytic Inquiry,* 1998. 18:2. 207-221 & Wrye, H. & Welles, J. *The Narration of Desire.* Hillsdale, N. J.: The Analytic Press, 1994.

person. Threshold experiences may prove momentary or lasting, depending on the course of events."

Diana nods reflectively. "Yes! And while we're here together, let's make sure the softening changes we are seeking are not fleeting, but really do transform us!"

Jim looks up from his paper with an "Aren't you done yet?" look. Diana and I give each other that sisterly nod that women share when an alien intrudes, finish our coffee, and pack up to resume our travels. Little do we dream what is in store. Before midnight on this day abroad, a bold threshold experience will present itself to our open pores.

But first, Baka takes us to the fabulous Greco-Roman ruins of Jerash, the most stunning ruins of a Hellenic and Roman city any of us have seen outside Rome or Athens. As we cross the huge, circular, colonnaded reception court and make our way to the amphitheater, I think I hear...could it be? Bagpipes? This is tribal music for Jim and me, and we hardly expect it here! As we enter the ancient amphitheater of Jerash, there he is, a Jordanian soldier wearing a kilt and playing the bagpipes!

Baka reminds us that Jordan was formerly a British protectorate, and Jordanian society is permeated by such anomalies. The piper plays beautifully in this ancient, acoustically superior amphitheater, an imposing temple to Artemis on the hill above the ruins—awesome in scale, engineering, and aesthetics. Since Greek Artemis is Roman Diana, we photograph our Diana here in front of her temple. Baka shows us how the huge columns were designed to slightly rock on their foundations, withstanding high winds and earthquakes.

We wend across the desert for five conversation-filled hours, arriving after sunset and a hard day's travel to check into our hotel in Petra. We'll arise before dawn to explore the city's miraculous ruins as the sun rises. But first, Baka offers to initiate us into an experience of crossing borders, boundaries, and thresholds: "Have you ever had a real Turkish bath?"

After dinner, we set out in the dark for the village of Wadi Mousa (or more prosaically, "Moses Wash"). Wadis are dry riverbeds carved in the desert by flash floods, and this one was where Moses (Mousa) reportedly stopped as he crossed from Canaan to Egypt. Wadi Mousa is home to an old Turkish bath. As we tread tentatively into the dimly lit, incense-permeated reception room, a caftan-swathed young man greets us with a tray of tea. Baka translates, "It's a sweet herb-laced mint tea. Relax on these wide velvet cushions while they heat the baths for us."

Mid-December is not high bath season, so the marbled rooms need time to be steam-heated. After we sip our calming tea, one man escorts Jim to the men's baths, and another guides Diana and me to separate dressing areas, indicating by hand gestures that we are to completely disrobe and then wrap ourselves in long cotton sheets, like sarongs. A guide then leads us all into the baths, from a steamy room into a steamier room, until there is zero visibility. I arrive in the innermost sanctum completely disoriented.

Where are we? Have I been time warped back to the Roman Baths of Beit She'an, or of Aquae Sulis in Bath, England? Reclining on marble slabs in a room so densely, sweetly steamy, I relax, conscious that decorum won't be an issue. It is impossible to see other bodies at all, and I think the only people here are Jim, Diana, Baka and me, as the "guides" have mysteriously evaporated. It is a strain to converse over the hissing steam. In contrast to the morning's border crossings and accompanying traveler's anxiety, we are suddenly swaddled into a passively regressed state of pleasure.

We loll in the marble steam room for about an hour. Time becomes elusive until a new guide takes my hand and leads me into a different steam chamber, where I embark on the most unusual and intense massage experience I've had—among many I've sampled around the globe. Like me, my young Turk is wrapped in a wet sarong, shrouded in a gauzy mist. Oh, my god. Shades of Omar Sharif! He unpeels my sarong and places me on a hot, wet, marble table. With a stiff brush and a bowl of soapy water, he scrubs my limbs vigorously. All residue of desert grime, mud and sand from Beit She'an, Masada, Ein Gedi, the Dead Sea and Jerash are sloughed away.

My astonishment gives way to separation anxiety. *Where's Jim? Where's Diana? What's this young Turk going to do next? Can I, like Ariadne escaping the Minotaur, wind my way out of this maze? Why am I so trusting and open? Why do I say yes to every new caper? If she were still alive, what would my mother, the only other person to have bathed me so freely, say to this? What would my conservative sister from Pasadena do? She would be giggling.* Imagining my sister's nervous laughter offers me some levity and relief.

The Turk flips me onto my belly with a splat on the marble slab, like a fat flounder being tossed on a wet deck. Any fantasies about a steamy seduction scene are brought to an abrupt stop. Omar vigorously scrubs my backside, pours buckets of warm soapy water over me, and begins a wet massage. He combines acupressure and reflexology on my feet, hands and temples, then strenuously rubs my limbs, then decisively pummels my back. Next, he turns me over and, keeping my breasts and pubic area covered by a towel, begins an abdominal organ massage that is both pleasant and unnerving. Not knowing whether to sigh, laugh nervously, or cry, I settle for Lamaze breathing, but it's too steamy to focus on a relaxation point. That fact is mildly reassuring. Giving myself over to the bathing experience, I begin moving into an altered state. I realize that his movements are carefully orchestrated and that this must be a Turkish ritual developed over centuries.

But the gender boundaries are confusing. *How have I crossed these borders to give this stranger, in his foreign and authoritative way, access to my body? Do local Muslim women, assiduously covered in public, participate in this?* My Turk and I have no common language except the language of the body. He continues to rub, scrub, and massage me until I've lost track of time. He douses me with buckets of hot, then cold, then hot water, again and again, before signaling me to sit up. Before I know it, he has cracked my neck and back in a move I would only allow my chiropractor daughter to do. But I had no vote. I wasn't even offered a ballot. *Is he licensed? Knowledgeable? Careful?* Then he crosses my arms across my chest, firmly and quickly encircles them from behind, and *crack!* Another adjustment.

*Insha'Allah—god willing—I won't be injured. I would never submit to this at home.*

But I feel much better. I am reeling, released, purged, cleansed, more than after immersion in the Dead Sea, more thoroughly than I can remember. My young Turk stands me up, wraps my sarong around me, and slides my water sandals onto my feet. He leads me down one steamy corridor after another until I am in a shower room. A man awaits with thick white towels to dry me off after a shower, then leads me through the maze, back to the original dressing room where Diana is waiting, as wide-eyed as I am. We locate Jim, all three agape with disbelief. Traveler's anxiety has met its match and been expunged. We compare notes, reassured that the massages were discreet and professional. We feel fantastic, as if we have crossed a new bodily threshold.

### Haunting Maze to Hidden Treasure

"Match me such a marvel save in Eastern clime
A rose-red city half as old as Time."
                                        —John Burgon


Purified by our deep cleansing and even deeper slumber, we arise before dawn to become time travelers in the Nabatean tomb city of Petra. With Baka, the three of us walk in open-mouthed awe as the first light of rosy-fingered dawn marks the coming of day. We are silent, entering this wonder of wonders of the ancient world. I feel a chill up and down my spine, not only from the pre-dawn cold, but because I feel like Alice falling into the rabbit hole—spell-bound and disoriented by a sense of mystery.


Known only to a small Bedouin tribe who guarded its secret mouth fiercely for over seven hundred years, Petra was discovered by the outside world in 1812. Johann Ludwig Burckhardt, a Swiss disguised as a wandering Arab, was determined to find this marvel referred to in ancient texts. Petra, meaning "stone" in ancient Greek, remained shrouded in relative mystery to many westerners until three years ago, when King Hussein opened Jordan's borders to Israel and the outside world.

The Nabateans, who originated in Southern Arabia, settled here to reign from about the fourth century BCE until cataclysmic earthquakes in 363 CE and 747 CE destroyed their life. The ancient nomadic Nabateans partook of many surrounding cultures with which they traded goods and spiritual ideas. They osmosed elements of ancient Arabic, Hellenic, Pharaonic and fertility cults. As a polyglot Californian with newly adopted Arabic, Egyptian and Semitic identities, I feel quite at home. They carved their City of the Dead, magically weaving elements of Greek temples and Egyptian tombs with figures of Baal and Astarte out of Nubian sandstone. For centuries, Petra remained completely hidden down a long, narrow, winding sandstone gorge deep within the mountains.

Hushed, shuddering in the morning chill, we wander through the ten-foot-wide, pink and beige sandstone gorge or Siq, towering over two hundred feet above us. We wind almost a mile as dawn brings flecks of sunlight to the top of the Siq walls. Along the way, we see enclaves of tombs and figures of elephants and temple goddesses carved into the walls. Surely I am Alice and this is yet another dreamlike excursion down a rabbit hole. Suddenly, we come to the end of the narrow Siq and to a dramatic opening where we face the huge columned temple of Al Khazneh, known as the Treasury. We half expect to discover Abe Lincoln gazing down at us from his colossal chair. We're not surprised to learn that the director of *Indiana Jones and the Last Crusade* scouted and chose this location as the final resting place of the Holy Grail.

At just the right moment, sunrise is complete and the Treasury and surrounding courtyard are bathed in rose-hued light. A lone shepherd sits on a large stone far across the yard from us, playing a haunting ancient melody on his flute. After an awe-filled pause and further explorations deeper into the canyon, we hear the flutist finish and watch him disappear with his few sheep down a mysterious path. We retrace our steps back out, hearing first a few, then more and more voices, as the morning's first covey of tourists arrives, dispelling the magic.

Later, at the Freud Conference in Jerusalem, colleagues recount stories of candlelight visits to Petra. On a special occasion, they were given lighted tapers and escorted along the Siq in candlelit silence. After nearly an hour of quiet marvel, winding through the cut in the rock, they came to the open court of the Treasury, where a trio of Bedouin musicians serenaded them with a flute concert as the moon slowly rose. That compellingly visual and acoustic fantasy of envelopment by candlelight and music beckons us to return to Petra and the Siq, years hence. But that will be another journey. Nothing can compare to a traveler's discovery of the unadvertised and unexpected, the opportunity to transform borders into thresholds and celebrate a voyager's greatest accompaniment: basic trust.[5]

---

5 Months later, on a small plane in Venezuela, Jim turned to me, his face ashen, as he held up an old Spanish language *Newsweek*. The article reports that Jordanian and US State Departments have revealed their blocking of a plot by Osama Bin Laden to capture and kidnap American tourists in Petra, the exact dates we were there. Hmmm. Whew. Basic trust.

# CHAPTER 13

## FLIGHT INTO EGYPT

BECAUSE IT IS A FRIDAY during Ramadan, the Muslim Sabbath in the holiest of holy months, the only safe ferry across the Red Sea to Egypt will depart an hour and a half early. That leaves Mohamed, our driver, only three hours to complete a five-hour drive through Wadi Ram to the Gulf of Aqaba. Wadi Ram is known as the gorgeous Painted Desert, but Diana and I keep our eyes shut tightly as we hear Baka crying, "Look out!" Each high-tension utterance is followed by the whoosh of a huge cargo truck that roars past us, inches away from our crazily rocking van.

My optical escape is suddenly disrupted by Baka's piercing scream: "Look out, Mohamed!" I open my eyes to see two lorries, neck and neck, heading for us—one trying to pass the other, neither giving way on the two-lane desert road. Diana screams, "Oh, my god!" Mohamed slams on the brakes and we fishtail. At the last nanosecond, the driver barreling down our lane backs off and slides behind the second lorry. With no time to spare, they swoosh by, honking, grinning devilishly at our pallid faces.

Miraculously, Mohamed and Baka get us to the dock in one piece, just in time for the ferry crossing from Aqaba to Nuweiba on the Sinai Peninsula. In a blink, we've traversed a landscape that, in biblical times, encompassed Canaan, Gilead, Ammon, Moab, and Edom. Baka explains coolly, "The later ferry takes four times as long, and is dangerously overcrowded. This morning's news described a ferry sinking only yesterday in the Indian Ocean, drowning a hundred and fifty passengers." Though torqued, I feel unequivocally grateful to have survived a ride from hell in order to take the safe ferry, a brand new, ultra high-speed hydrofoil. Baka and Mohamed wave us off and we bid farewell to Jordan. We're zipped across the Gulf of Aqaba, the hydrofoil creating salty plumes of wake.

Ashore in Nuweiba, where Moses and his people wandered homeless for forty years, passing immigration guards, once again we cross a no man's land as our identification shifts this time from Jordanian to Egyptian. Our new guide, Ramy Riszk, is waiting to help us reach our goal, sunrise on top of Mt. Sinai. Ramy is a well-informed, handsome young Bedouin, a devout Coptic Christian and a New Testament scholar. We will behave.

We are soon taken by Ramy's engaging manner. His young wife is expecting their first child any moment now, he tells us. Diana and I maternally share his nervous expectancy every time his cell phone rings. Will he get home in time for the birth? Will the baby be healthy? Will it be the girl he hopes for? But why is Ramy here with us instead of at home with his wife?

"I must work hard whenever work is available so I can support my wife and new baby," he explains. "Though we are Bedouin, we have given up the nomadic way to live in traditional Egyptian family style in a stacked house. On the ground floor we have our kitchen, living room and my parents' bedroom. On the next floor up, my pregnant sister and her husband have set up housekeeping. Above that, my wife and I are adding another floor for our own housekeeping."

This explains why the rooflines of Egyptian towns and cities along the Red Sea look like works in progress. Rebar talons extend upward, waiting to be built into brick or stone walls for the next floor. People here do not take out mortgages; they build floor by floor, as they can and when they must. The typical multigenerational family lives in a single brick domicile crowned expectantly in rebar. Most of the houses and commercial buildings along our route in Jordan, Egypt and Palestine share this unfinished look. According to Muslim mythology, the purpose of needlepoint minaret towers, such as those of the Blue Mosque in Istanbul, is to pierce the sky so the prayers of the faithful can readily make their way to heaven. Do these mundane rebar spires help carry entreaties heavenward from domestic quarrels in the houses below?

As we drive across the desert, Diana, Jim and I pepper Ramy with questions about Egyptian family life. How does he live as an adult in such close proximity to his parents? He explains matter-of-factly that throughout Egypt, boundary squabbles, financial and family issues are commonly settled by the father, who remains the true patriarch, the gatekeeper at the point of ingress and egress of the home. If the issue is an emotional or domestic one, it is directed to the mother or mother-in-law for resolution. What the elder says goes. Ramy asks us, "I don't know, I can't imagine it another way, can you?" It seems prudent to nod quietly.

From Ramy, we learn about the deeply etched genealogical and cultural identities of the peoples here. He proudly states, "I can recite by heart the names of my grandfathers eight generations back and I will teach this to my sons." Am I surprised no grandmothers or daughters are mentioned? No, but I'm confused; Ramy told us he longs for a daughter, yet his genealogical legacy is reserved for sons. Rarely one to hold back my questions related to gender and culture, I ask. Ramy explains, "A son must know the generations by heart so that he can intermarry within the family line to keep it strong, but not more than every third generation to avoid the diseases of some Bedouin tribes. Close genetic inbreeding results in children who cannot speak or see." We soon witness some of these genetic anomalies wandering along the roadside: Bedouin families with club-footed children, and others with eyes clouded by blindness. Here, entrenched tribalism leads to somatic degradation.

As we near Nuweiba, Ramy asks the driver to stop. "Wake up, everybody. Let's get out and walk a bit. I want to show you an oasis." It feels good to stretch and breathe in the Sinai desert air. We round a bend in a path to the oasis and a huge sandstone wall, where a seven-branched menorah was carved by wandering Jews several millennia before Christ. I am awed. I've never been in the presence of such ancient evidence of human habitation. In this desert of shifting sands, many tribes—Semitic and Arab and Coptic—have deeply engraved their identities on mute stones, testaments of their passage eons ago.

### Rebirth in Sinai's Colored Canyons

After a deeply restful Nuweibian night, Ramy takes us hiking in the Sinai's Colored Canyons. The brilliantly painted gorges remind Jim of the Slot Canyons of southern Utah and northern Arizona, cut by flash floods and grinding sand out of red, purple, beige, golden and white sandstone and limestone. For me, the canyons recall the narrow Siq of Petra. We walk in pensive silence, moved by nature's majesty and history's magnitude here in the cradle of civilization. At one point we slither our way down a long, twisted, narrow sandstone tube into a slender canyon below. For a moment it is not clear whether I will make it. Stuck in mid-passage, I am suddenly plunged back into the rocking nightmare in the Red Sea, wrestling with my own primal breech birth memories. My hips are too wide. I can't go back up, and for a silent agony of moments, it seems I cannot go down. Then, as suddenly as the space between peril and freedom that opened on the highway, I slide free, reborn. Released from the narrow passage, I feel free to swell from pinched infant back into my adult hips, fill my lungs with air and let out a long gutteral sign of relief, grateful for another threshold crossing, a symbolic birth on my way toward stepping into freedom.

Shaken from the impact of my latest re-birthing, I dissolve in Diana's arms. The unspoken shared experience is so intense that Diana, unbeknownst to me, is moved to write an extraordinary poem, which she dedicates to me. She saved it until the following year to give to me during another shared rite of passage, my sixtieth birthday retreat.

*On Mastering Birth Anxiety in the Colored Canyon:*
*For Harriet on her Sixtieth Birthday*

We hiked through the colored canyon
Wound ourselves through its torqued walls
Of purple, rose, lavender and gold
A cathedral made of sand
Spires, whorls, cut into rock
By ancient waters that left their mark.

Multicolored layers in the sand
Made shapes of animals, faces, human hands
That we imagined as we walked and talked
Learning the striations of each other's lives and thoughts.
The sedimentation of old acts, wishes, loves, regrets
Assumed new configurations in our friendship

So that when we came upon a tunnel
The end of which was barely visible
It was your hand that guided me into an ecstatic slide
And my eye that caught the grace and beauty of your ride
As you freed yourself forever from an atavistic tie
And slide towards 60, heart open and soul wide.

# CHAPTER 14

## CLIMBING JEBEL MUSA
## IN THE FOOTSTEPS OF MOSES

THE HOSTEL at the base of Mt. Sinai is close to Saint Catherine's Monastery, one of Coptic Christianity's oldest standing churches, built by a decree of Emperor Justinian between 527 and 565 CE; it is named after the Alexandrian martyr Catherine, who died in 395. Her body, Ramy tells us, was said to have been carried away by angels, and found centuries later at the top of the mountain bearing her name. The monastery is a treasure house of ancient manuscripts in Greek, Arabic, Syriac and Egyptian, as well as a breathtaking collection of Byzantine icons. In the monastery courtyard grows a huge bush; the monks say its rootstock survived from the burning bush revealed to Moses by Yahweh to signal the covenant between God and the Jews. A room off the courtyard holds an eerie treasure collected by ascetic Catherine monks over centuries. The skulls and bones of their deceased brethren are stacked in piles in the dimly lit room. We peer in and gasp at the skulls, which are stacked ghoulishly, their empty eye sockets confronting us, reminding us of our own mortality. Although it is hot and dry, I shiver, feeling the hairs on my arms rise.

*Pilgrimage on Moses' Mountain*

Like countless other pilgrims over the millennia, we are drawn to the sacred rocky mountain Moses climbed to talk to his god and receive the Ten Commandments. Ramy describes two main routes up the mountain. The most direct is called the Steps of Repentance, a nearly vertical climb of 3,750 steep steps hewn out of the rock by a penitent monk. The other route is a serpentine camel path that ascends the eastern slope and joins the penitent's stairs two-thirds of the way up the mountain. Where the two paths converge, camels cannot proceed; the last 750 steps to the summit must be ascended on foot. The latter route, which we choose, should take four or five hours. We must depart soon after midnight to arrive for sunrise on the peak. Stirred by visions of wise men bearing gifts, swaying majestically on their hairy ships of the desert, I relish the prospect of climbing Jebel Mousa on a camel.

Like Kilimanjaro, Fujiyama, Machu Pichu, Denali, Shasta and Anapurna, Mt. Sinai is famed as one of the greatest spiritual mountains of the world. People living near these mountains regard their mountain reverently as a vortex for psychic and spiritual energy. Such energy is palpable when one's pores are open; I have sensed it powerfully while climbing Shasta, Kilimanjaro, Machu Pichu and sacred peaks in the Himalayas, so I am prepared to approach Moses' 7,500-foot mountain as a pilgrim.

Phil Cousineau writes that "pilgrimage" derives from the Latin "pelegrinus," foreigner or wayfarer, and refers to the journey of one who travels to a shrine or holy place. An older, more poetic derivation reveals that "pilgrim" has its roots in the Latin "per agrum," meaning "through the field." "This ancient image suggests a curious soul who crosses fields, walking beyond known boundaries and touching the earth with a destination in mind and a purpose in heart. This pilgrim is a wayfarer who longs to endure a difficult journey to reach the sacred center of his or her world, a place made holy by a saint, hero or god." [6]

Jim, Diana and I are escorted to an austere, triple-cot room at the hostel near St. Catherine's, where we gratefully settle in for a few hours of sleep before our pre-dawn 3,500-foot climb. Before bedding down, practical Jim admonishes: "You know we'll be climbing a mountain in winter in the dead of night. This means...really cold, you guys." Wardrobe anxiety resurfaces. Jim and I left our scuba gear in Tel Aviv, and we all left our city clothes in Jerusalem. Rather than

6 Cosineau, Phil. *The Art of the Pilgrimage: The Seeker's Guide to Making Travel Sacred.* Berkeley: Conari Press, 1998, 13-14.

turning in, Diana and I launch into Barbie's trunk ritual, pooling our warm garments in a pile on the hostel floor and bargaining in Middle Eastern bazaar fashion. Jim snores on his cot, having won the prize for preparedness and parsimony, while Diana and I settle on a distribution plan for our motley assortment of gear. On impulse, I add the keffiyeh, the black and white cotton headscarf of the Gebaliye mountain Bedouins, which I purchased as a souvenir in Jordan; it turns out to be a godsend.

Exhausted, we flop onto our hard, narrow cots for a few hours of sleep. But Diana begins ruminating on a new incarnation of traveler's anxiety. "What do you think, Harriet? Should I or shouldn't I ride a camel? You know I've had surgery on both knees. I had a lot of meniscus damage and a torn ACL. Which would be worse, climbing or riding? I really don't want to ride. I don't even know how to ride a horse. Those beasts are huge. They have nasty reputations! But I'm worried about my knees. What should I do?"

Her anxiety is contagious. I am supposed to wear my mechanical ACL knee brace on any unstable terrain, and 3,500 feet up a rocky path in pure darkness surely qualifies. But my knee brace is bulky. Hiking poles wouldn't fit into my bag, and it wasn't worth the security hassle to carry two sharp-ended, telescoping poles over seven Middle Eastern border crossings. I had resolved to leave all prosthetic devices at home. But Diana gets me stirred up. I waver until we fall asleep.

A few hours later, shivering in freezing darkness, I swath my head and shoulders with the keffiyah, wrapping my face so only my eyes are uncovered. Ramy hints that Moses climbed this mountain on foot and that riding a camel might not please God. Diana wrestles with her decision from an orthopedic, rather than spiritual, perspective, until we reach the camel drivers bedded down with their camels, hoping for business. Unlike Diana, I awakened resolved to ride a camel.

Hearing our voices, the sleeping camel drivers arise and surround us insistently. like a flock of flapping geese. In pitch darkness, the band of Bedouins elbowing and yelling insults at each other in Arabic, pawing our arms and squeezing us into their midst, threaten a panic of body boundary violation. Ramy parts them like the Red Sea and selects two camels he knows well.

Realizing that Diana has no experience with rugged adventure travel, let alone camel riding, and clearly needs help, I take matters into my own hands. As I have done with novice cohorts on trailheads around the world, I become my friend's adventure psychologist, mother, hypnotherapist and Zen breathing specialist. "Calm, calm, Diana. Let's breathe together. Feel the aura of this place. We are about to fulfill one of our dreams this amazing night. Breathe..." We breathe deeply as I talk her onto the back of Abdul, the kneeling camel, who wins her heart after ten uncertain moments. Like Abdul, my camel Navam kneels down, I mount, and we begin our trek in utter darkness.

Jim, who wants nothing to do with camels, is not happy; the camel driver accompanying us has instructed him to walk right behind the behind of a camel. When Jim tries to move to the front, the driver, who carries a stick, threatens him. Ramy explains firmly that passing the camels makes them uncontrollably competitive. Jim, chastised like an unruly boy, is banished to walking below us, stuck behind the huge swaying beasts. For our benefit, he narrates the plethora of perfumes that emanate from a hardworking camel's ass. Knowing Jim's need for control of his physical situation and macho "I *will* do it myself" attitude, I am torn between empathy and perverse amusement at his plight. I'm also concerned about the delight he will take in translating this malodorous experience into cocktail party chatter, to the detriment of my PR efforts for these camelids' cousins, my llamas.

I, on the other hand, am swaying rhythmically aboard my mighty ship of the desert, Navam. As my eyes accustom to the darkness, I see an extraordinary starry night, the kind we are blessed to witness only far from city lights on crystal clear moonless nights. Orion's Belt is comfortingly familiar, as are the Big Dipper and North Star. This is the same starry sky that Moses saw when he crossed the Sinai Peninsula from the land of the Pharaohs back to Canaan, as did all the Jews of the exodus, including Joseph, Mary and Jesus. A moving sense of timelessness washes over me.

Diana sighs, almost passionately. "I'm bonding with Abdul. I'm blissed out! This giant beast knows every step of the trail by heart! My knees are being spared!" Meanwhile, my hips testify that Navam's saddle is narrow and cramped as if made for a child. Unlike a horse's saddle, a camel's has a wooden frame with tall cylindrical horns in front and back, covered by an odd assortment of padding and tasseled blankets.

Navam hits his stride, passing Diana and navigating a zigzag course in front of Abdul. I think he is trying to add switchbacks to the steep trail, but I learn from Ramy, who has learned it from the driver, that Navam is a young stud competing with Abdul for leadership. Visions of Jambo, our youngest llama, and his macho adolescent tricks come to mind; but I am captive on this camelid's back, six feet off the ground, towering over the others. *Breathe,* I think, *this isn't a camel race. It's a pilgrimage.*

I ask Ramy, who guides visitors up this mountain for a living, if he ever rides a camel. He seems reluctant to discuss the matter but says something to Jim, sotto voce. Chuckling, Jim explains, "Ramy is young. He wants to have more children." I'm slow on the uptake, whereupon Jim says simply, "Prostate." Of course! I'd wondered why these nomads, who spend long, cold nights in darkened tents, don't have huge families. Camel riding must be Bedouin birth control. *Insha'Allah.* It is Allah's will.

We approach a dim light: a rock hut lit by a lantern, with a Bedouin proprietor offering hot tea, chocolates, and drinking water. I've never climbed a serious mountain with a teashop, though I've wished for it many times! Climbing higher in the wintry night, we pass more tiny lantern-lit caves along the way. Soon Diana's and my camels and their driver Ideh have outdistanced Jim and Ramy, surely freshening up their air.

By 3:30 a.m., our caravan arrives at the end of the camel trail. Navam kushes, followed by Abdul. While "to kush" comes from the French "couchoir," to lie down, it is not the seductive verb that adolescent Americans delight in learning: "Voulez vous couchez avec moi?" A camel's kush feels like a perilous lurch that might jettison you over the animal's loopy neck. But Navam's too-tall legs and bony knees gracefully fold up, and we are safely on the ground. In fledgling Arabic, Diana and I offer praises to our beasts for carrying us steadfastly to this point, where only 1,000 feet remain to be climbed. Diana praises Abdul's eyes, long eyelashes, woofily nose, and character.

Standing at a Bedouin tea shop near the top of Moses' Mountain with our camels and their driver, Diana and I are now quite in the dark, so to speak, about another traveler's concern: gratuities. Since negotiations were conducted in Arabic between Ramy and the camel driver, we don't know whether "service is included." Moreover, our Egyptian pounds and piasters have been changed from Jordanian dinares, which were exchanged the day before from Israeli shekels, which once were our dollars. The rapidity of these conversions adds to our calculation difficulties. Then there is the gender issue. Diana and I are independent professional women who earn our own keep, but we are appreciative of our husbands' acumen in the area of tipping. Finally, we give the camel drivers a generous tip, and they are deeply grateful; other travelers are not so kind. Ramy later tells us we will not be forgotten, not only for our tip, but also for the obvious pleasure we are having. And that is not so bad, since I remember feeling like a grain of sand in the millennia of time only yesterday.

Ramy suggests we wait out of the wind in the nearby Bedouin hut for an hour. The top of the mountain will be blustery and dawn will not come until after 5:30 a.m. After a lovely cup of steaming tea and a little sign language with our host, I curl up in the back room on the Bedouin's very own bed, a rock bench carved into the wall of his mountain cave. Warm under his heavy woolen blankets, I fall fast asleep.

Ramy shakes my shoulder at 4:30 a.m. "It's time to climb the last, most rugged part of the trail, that series of tight switchbacks up to the summit." I crawl out from under the Bedouin's blankets and rejoin Jim and Diana for more tea while Ramy explains: "Egyptian King Farouk, during his reign, gave the money to carve these switchbacks. He offered it as a gift to visiting pilgrims and the people of Egypt." Recalling the siren song of Rita Hayworth's affair with the Egyptian king, we perk up at this tidbit of 1950s news. The steep trail, like the penitent monk's steps before, is difficult in darkness and hard on our knees. Descending later by light of day, we are impressed by this well-engineered stairway, but each narrow step is nearly twice the rise allowed for human ergonomics and safety by American building codes. The trail is too narrow to climb side by side, so Ramy and Jim lend Diana and me their hands for support. We stop again for hot tea. Bundled Bedouin-style, grateful for my Arabic keffiyeh headdress, I feel quite cozy from exertion and the tea.

Climbing Gabal Mousa is a pilgrimage. Still in darkness, we reach the peak, where the monks of St. Catherine's have built a tiny private cell for solitary retreat. We are joined by a slowly growing group of pilgrims from all over the world, huddling together and softly conversing, awaiting the dawn on Moses' Mountain. It is here that "the glory of the Lord abode upon mount Sinai, and the cloud covered it six days and the seventh day he called unto Moses…and Moses was in the mount forty days and forty nights…and the Lord gave unto Moses…two tablets of testimony, tables of stone written with the finger of God." [7]

Mountaineers nearly all report awe at first light in the high country. At dawn on Mt. Sinai, an awed hush comes over the group. We're greeted by a stunningly clear and beautiful sunrise, and the surrounding craggy peaks are bathed in a golden and pink glow. Dawn slowly extends her rosy fingers across several mountain ranges to the east as twenty-five climbers stand in reverent silence. From Europe, the Middle East, America, and Japan, some of us are secular pilgrims, but others may represent the three religions—Judaism, Christianity and Islam—that honor Moses as one of god's greatest prophets.

Little is spoken. There is a palpable communal wonder at the sheer beauty of the sunrise. I deeply feel the impact of this place on the course of history. The international group seems to grasp the effect on human consciousness of what happened on this mountain. The Ten Commandments formed the backbone of an ethical code that still abides many centuries later.

In the silence I reflect on my sabbatical experience. *What was the point of all that anxiety? When I leap with faith, I am rewarded.*

---

7 Exodus 24:16.

*If we hadn't had warm gear, it wouldn't have mattered. We were more than warmed by the hospitality of a stranger we couldn't even talk to—and I was offered his very bed for rest. St. Catherine's hollow skulls speak in eloquent silence: carpe diem! Seize the day and live fully in the moment. Breathe deeply and show up for the adventure! I will dedicate myself to lightening up on anxiety and embracing the power of life itself as a pilgrimage. Letting go will be my mantra.* Jim, Diana and I nod, smiling, our faces bathed in morning sunlight, each in our reverie on Moses' Mountain.

On our descent, we encounter the ascending climbers who either prefer climbing a mountain by daylight, or who curse themselves for having indulged in an extra hour of sleep. Further down, we pass Abdul and Navam, engaged by a Bedouin guide who wants to save his knees and is apparently content with the size of his family. Diana enjoys one last murmuring swoon over Abdul while I wish Navam a hearty Swahili greeting: "Jambo!" Ideh smiles and thanks us warmly one last time before he and his camels sway down Moses' Mountain ahead of us, out of sight.

## CHAPTER 15
## TUTANKHAMEN'S UNCOMMONLY COMMON
## LITTLE TREASURE

In Egypt, I loved the perfume of the lotus. A flower would bloom in the pool at dawn, filling the entire garden with a blue musk so powerful it seemed that even the fish and ducks would swoon. By night, the flower might wither but the perfume lasted. Fainter and fainter, but never quite gone. Even many days later, the lotus remained in the garden. Months would pass and a bee would alight near the spot where the lotus had blossomed, and its essence was released again, momentary but undeniable.

—Anita Diamant, *The Red Tent*[8]

IN HONOR of Navam, and missing our llamas, I decide to try camel riding again in Cairo. Diana, my camelid-loving companion, has returned to Israel to revisit her childhood kibbutz before we rejoin her for the Freud Conference. Jim gamely agrees to leap out of character and join me on the camel's back. We engage a camel auspiciously called "Super Fly" for a get-acquainted folie à deux around the Pyramids.

One-humped dromedaries are truly among nature's most unlikely constructions. They remind one writer, Bruce Feiler, of clowns, "with everything misproportioned, the too-tall legs, the bony knees, the molded jowls…(and) hooked nose that looks like a bunch of bananas…Clowns design their costumes to accentuate their oddities; camels seem to come that way naturally."[9]

8  Diamant, Anita. *The Red Tent*. New York: Picador, 1997, 321.
9  Feiler, Bruce, *Walking the Bible*. New York: William Morrow, 2005, 252.

We climb aboard Super Fly, who groans, snorts, and lurches—back legs up, then front—from his kushed position to a towering height. We lumber around the desert, swaying and gaping at the Pyramids, basking in the absurd juxtaposition of Super Fly with one of the seven wonders of the ancient world, a sharp contrast with the quiet awe we experienced atop Mt. Sinai.

One of my favorite record albums is Paul Horn's mystical 1960s trumpet solo, Inside the Great Pyramid. Dismounting from the comedic in search of the sublime, I must venture inside the great pyramid, dragging Jim into the tomb with me. Recalling the uncommon marine beauty, peace, and soul nourishment of the Red Sea's depths, I wonder what age-old knowledge may be gleaned inside this ancient edifice.

However, crawling into the pyramid's belly with a crushing crowd of tourists in suffocating heat is a decidedly nonspiritual experience. My descent into the Great Pyramid shares only one element with Paul Horn's mystical composition: hope. Unlike my passage through the sandstone birth canal spiral in the Painted Canyon, this feels like a descent into an incubator containing a potpourri of microbes. I briefly consider holding my breath for the duration, but opt for germs over suffocation.

Gratefully returning to daylight, I discover Super Fly's proprietor waiting to relieve me of more Egyptian piasters. After creeping through the belly of the necropolis, my ship of the desert's contemplative mastication of viscous green camel spit comes as a welcome relief. Appreciatively stretching my limbs, I realize that our tortured underground moment is nothing compared with the lives of slaves who labored in the Pharaoh's pyramids during their construction.

The next morning, Jim and I welcome a change of pace. Hannah, a gorgeous Egyptologist with almond-shaped amber eyes outlined in black kohl, jet-black hair, and haunting lotus-scented perfume, shows us the unforgettable Egyptian Museum. I hope that a full day in the museum with a graduate Egyptologist will allow us to explore its byways extensively, but Hannah reassures me that we cannot. She says, "In my five years of university studies in Egyptology, I actually spent five days a week, for four solid years, cataloging and studying this museum's vast treasure. We will only be able to see a fraction of its wealth."

Hannah leads us to the treasure all visitors want to see: the fabled fortune of King Tutankhamen's tomb, amassed to protect and guide him into eternal life following his brief eighteen years on earth. I recently savored the New York Metropolitan Museum's exhibition of the early Pharaonic period, including some of Tutankhamen's dazzling treasures, and was awed again by the familiar articles, many of which had electrified me at the Los Angeles County Art Museum in the 1970s.

The Egyptian Museum contains rooms and rooms of King Tut's chariots, royal beds, jewelry, funerary icons, statuary, and giant sarcophagi—golden mummy cases inside of mummy cases, nesting like Russian dolls. Justly famous the world over, the iconic, fifty-four pound, solid gold death mask is emblematic of both Tut's and Egypt's importance and power in the ancient world.

But it is in a dark, out-of-the-way room, where Hannah leads us to a dusty glass display case, that I have quite a touching experience. The case holds an unexpected marvel—an uncommonly common remnant of Tut's treasure. In this rarely visited room rests a tiny, finely woven envelope of ancient white linen with two linen straps sewn to the top. It is the boy king's first condom, a linen sheath sized for a juvenile penis.

Apparently, after Tut's regal wedding to Queen Nefertiti, the thirteen-year-old Pharaoh's younger bride suffered two royal miscarriages before she turned thirteen. The Pharaoh's court physicians judiciously recommended that the young queen needed time to physically mature before bearing children and before her own capacity to bear an heir would be permanently compromised. Seven centuries ago, Tut's doctors prescribed birth control—the delicate item we behold. To give the royal queen's body time to mature, the cloth was soaked in lemon juice as a spermicide. "Once in place," Hannah explains, "this little linen sheath was secured with a narrow sash around the young boy's waist, tied in a bow behind his back to keep it securely in place."

It looks so small and delicate. Hannah's story of these two children, thrust by birth into a wealth and power beyond the world's wildest imagination, is poignant and touching. In this homely little piece of 5,000-year-old linen, there is something strangely, timelessly vulnerable.

After days deep under her seas, inside her tombs, and atop her great desert caravans, saying goodbye to Egypt is sad, but I am expected in Israel to deliver lectures at the University of Haifa and in Jerusalem. We again cross borders guarded by well-armed soldiers, reminded of a peace process as vulnerable as any in history. The durability and fragility of King Tut's common piece of cloth, the ordinariness of its purpose juxtaposed with the power of its owner, representing the fleeting transit of glory, is the metaphor that accompanies me.

# CHAPTER 16

## OH, JERUSALEM!

JIM AND I SPEND a few days visiting Israeli war zones, Roman and Crusader fortifications, and ruins of Caesarea on the Mediterranean. We traverse the Golan Heights, stay in a kibbutz and then tour the West Bank. Everywhere we look, we see visual proof of a small country under siege from neighbors who contest their right to an ancestral homeland. Our Israeli guide, Johanan Moses, proudly talks of his Lithuanian family's history in the settlement and defense of Israel, of his father's heroic role in the 1948 war for the survival of the Jewish state, and of his own work as a tank commander in the 1967 war.

Johanan explains that the Golan is the only historically fertile valley in this tiny land. The mountains on either side, which belong to the Syrians and Palestinians, are perfectly stationed to allow inhabitants to peer enviously down from their dry, desert hills onto this "land of milk and honey." Such is the food of envy; it seeks to despoil the prosperity of the other. I think of Melanie Klein, a British child analyst who added much to psychologists' understanding of envy. She pioneered the powerful concept of the infant's envy of the mother's breast and womb for their capacity to generate babies and milk, and to this she added the concept of the envious impulse to spoil that which the other has. We covet, she said, not only actual wealth but also the creative capability to imagine and generate it.

From where we sit, in the car of an Israeli whose family—men and women, side by side—farmed, fought and died for this land, it is easy to think about the geography of envy. You can practically smell it in the defensive bunkers and battlements along our route. The Golan Heights are a critical strip of high ground that protects this fertile valley and its inhabitants from living like sitting ducks in an entrapped pond. Driving along exposed roads lined with barbed wire and warnings of mine fields, I give considerable thought to the attacks that have been launched the world over out of projected rage, envy, paranoia or greed.

Passing the signs of civilization and peoples who have inhabited this Holy or Unholy Land since the beginning of recorded time, we are taken aback by the rapidity of historic and geologic time—the Canaanites, the Hittites, the Phoenicians, the Pharaonic people, the Babylonians, the Hellenes, the Romans, the Jews, the early Christians, the Byzantines, the Ottomans, the Muslims, the Crusaders, and so on, into the present day. Like the brief blink of time King Tut enjoyed with his child bride, we are like grains of desert sand, so small in the scheme of things.

Our journey once again bears a resemblance to Alice's Adventures in Wonderland. For one warped moment, I imagine myself so big the entire country seems consumed by the anxieties I've felt during our travels—these battlements and soldiers are here to either fire on me or protect me from lurking dangers. The next moment, truth prevails and I know I am tiny. My life has little significance in the scheme of things. I am strangely calmed by this knowledge, and by the realization that any relevant dangers only threaten my peace of mind, not my homeland and my life.

### Culture Shock at the Intersection of Tribes

I greeted dawn as a pilgrim in dusty hiking boots, head wrapped in a Bedouin keffiyeh, and at the end of the same day, I walk into the psychoanalyst-packed Jerusalem Hotel, where an opening reception for "Freud at the Threshold of the 21st Century" is underway. We've crossed yet another border, this time into the enclave of my own tribe of Freudians.

Just as I underwent culture shock upon entering an Arab culture, I feel it again in this Israeli hotel, a popular gathering place for another tribe: orthodox Hassidic men. Striking in long-jacketed black suits, formal crowned beaver hats, white prayer tassels, and long side curls, they stride into elevators and restaurants with an air of entitled superiority. Hassidic boys are similarly attired, although they wear yarmulkes on their close-cropped hair, just revealing their curled side locks. In contrast to the men, Hassidic women stand out as startlingly frumpy in long-sleeved, long-skirted print dresses and bowler-like, flattish hats with rolled brims pulled low over their foreheads. Some decorate the brims with artificial flowers. The women look so resolutely and intentionally anti-erotic that one wonders how the swarms of children encircling them are begotten, if not by duty.

Overhearing conversations, we realize the extreme tension between the secular and orthodox Hassidic Jews. The latter males study the Talmud and are exempt from the army or work, providing an economic drain on the country's highly taxed secular Jews, many of whom deeply resent the scholars. They also reproduce at a disproportionately higher rate, which adds to the resentment their non-religious fellows feel. But all in all, they are somewhat familiar to us as there was a large Hassidic community where I worked in the Fairfax district of L.A. In Israel, I move from stranger anxiety to identification with the secular majority.

We retrieve our "city" baggage from the checkroom and shower quickly. Rejoining my own psychoanalytic tribe, I don the appropriate attire: stockings, pumps, jewelry and the basic black dress that is a trademark of the professional American woman's travel wardrobe. Within twenty minutes after checking into the hotel, I've shed one persona for another, pinning on the name badge that identifies me as a psychoanalyst visiting from the U.S. I am transported to Freud's Vienna via the strains of a chamber ensemble playing Mozart's "Eine Kleine Nachtmusik."

For the next four days I am plunged into the intellectual maelstrom of a conference that convenes distinguished scholars and clinicians from all over the world. We examine Freud's impact on 20th-century culture, and anticipate how contemporary psychoanalytic thought may be translated in the 21st century. We discuss the myriad ways Freud's discoveries of unconscious process have influenced the study of art, music, literature, film and history. An unexpected highlight occurs one day, on my way outside for a breath of fresh air, when I stop in the hotel lobby near the psychoanalytic bookstalls. A bookseller recognizes me from a book jacket photo and goes out of her way to apologize that there are no more copies of my *Narration of Desire* on display because it sold out on the first day. It may not be a galloping palomino, but I do float out on a cloud.

### A Dazzling Stone City

The beautiful old city is breathtaking at night. It is situated upon a hilltop, surrounded by a huge stone wall built by Herod. Every building and fortification in the city is white. The only building material available is white limestone, so Jerusalem is ancient but pristine, a dazzlingly bright stone city. Lit by floodlights at night, it is an exquisite historic jewel. One night, we crawl through recently excavated tunnels under the old city, along the original walls and through literal layers of history. It is quite a moving experience, evocative of a psychoanalytic metaphor of trying to get to the bottom of things to understand the roots. It is a great privilege to be here. I decide that this is the moment to place a note that one of my patients has entrusted to me into a chink of the Wailing Wall. Since the tunnels follow the original foundations and underpinnings of the Wailing Wall we visited in the daytime, I hope my patient's prayers will be answered.

The following morning, we take time off to explore the old city's four quarters: Moslem, Jewish, Armenian and Christian. We're deeply moved by the palpable density and layering of history here. It is formidable walking along the Via Dolorosa, replete with spice shops, to view the Stations of the Cross, climb the battlements of David's fort, and witness the intense muddle of overlapping life. Despite the potential enmity among various ethnic groups, they share the same city and the same contiguous walls. We see boys wearing yarmulkes playing ball with Arab boys, and we are awed. God willing, they should never be at war.

The Chihuly millennial glass installation in open courtyard gardens at the Tower of David is our last visual treat, a fitting finale.

We arrive late in the day, just as the midwinter sun is at its most glorious, spectacularly backlighting these monumental pieces of glass. Created in honor of the millennium, this exhibition is the largest showing Seattle glassblower Dale Chihuly has ever mounted. It has been mounted in Jerusalem because the Phoenicians developed the art of glassblowing here in the Eastern Mediterranean some 2,000 years ago. The exhibit is built from over 10,000 pieces and 42 tons of glass that were shipped to Israel.

In the sunlit courtyard are spectacular "trees" of glass fourteen meters high, a huge "Crystal Mountain" of rose quartz glass on an iron armature, a tower of blue glass, and a star-like silver chandelier mounted on fortress battlements. We are impressed by the power of art to transgress time and culture, and by the exquisite metaphor of this fragile medium, so potent in this politically precarious part of the world, appreciating that diving deep in the Red Sea, we were privileged to see how nature herself could put on an exhibition that was just as colorful and spectacular, and much older.

# PART V
# INDONESIA LOG—
# BALI to BORNEO

# CHAPTER 17

## MEETING THE RANGDA IN BALI

A FEW MONTHS LATER, another departure day barrels down on us. On May 18 at 1:15 a.m., on Singapore Airlines, I am buckled for the first time in my life into business class. Jim, because he's parsimonious about spending his frequent flyer miles, is buckled into coach. Twenty-five hours later—and with infinite gratitude that I spent every single one of my frequent flyer miles on the upgrade—we climb off the plane, into the blanket of damp, warm air that is Indonesia.

After another incredible crunch of folding up our lives, seeing to wills, taxes, post office boxes, clinical coverage, and car storage, and tearfully leaving Jullay with the caretakers, five llamas, and five ranch dogs at Twin Brooks, we decided to start easy. Before embarking on offbeat tracks into the jungles of Kalimantan (Borneo), Suluwesi, and Irian Jaya, we will spend the first week at our ease in sybaritic and artistic Bali, at a time in history when it still seems the most peaceful place on Earth.

Bali is a beautiful blur of beaches, mountains, frogs, rain, damp clothes, sweet breezes and kites. We encounter exquisite fresh fruit and fragrant floral offerings, sweet smiling people, sarongs, fruit drinks, amazing dancers, textiles, carvings, paintings, and hypnotic gamelan music. And little temples everywhere! Amidst gorgeous psychedelic green tiers of rice paddies, what blows my mind are the fence posts. I've never seen fence posts *growing*! Chop down a tree, peel the logs, split them into fence posts, put them into rich volcanic soil, keep them liberally moist, and before you know it, they're growing again. All the fences have sprouted leaves! That's about as astute an observation as this jet-lagged correspondent is up for, her brain having apparently decomposed into verdant vegetable matter. Hopefully, that will be a temporary state; in Bali, all kinds of creatures are constantly, mythologically morphing into new forms.

We delight in performances of Legong, Kecak and Barong dances. The Barong is a highly stylized ritual dance depicting the transmogrification of a Balinese version of the Hindu pantheon. A mythological animal called a Barong represents the spirit of goodness in perpetual struggle against the spirit of evil, the mythical monster Rangda. Both creatures are fantastical. The Barong is portrayed by two men occupying a fabulous costume with flowing mane and hair (somewhat like a huge Pekinese) and a wooden mask with gnashing teeth that clatter as the hinged jaw snaps shut. The Rangda is a grotesque beast with red and black snakes issuing from its bizarre, obese body. When things go badly for the Rangda, it changes itself into another form: a *garuda* (eagle-like bird), a witch, or a wild boar. Legions of loyal followers line up in both camps to participate in the perpetual struggle between good and evil.

While this portrayal of Balinese Hinduism is primitively animistic and magical, it reveals timeless wisdom. The struggle between the Rangda and the Barong recognizes the universal forces of dark and light, and parallels the struggle between the life force or libido and the death instinct or aggression; hence, the dance is not far from Freud, Jung, and my own philosophic backyard.

### *The Birth of the Bali Llama*

In addition to its extraordinary dance, Bali's arts and crafts are world-renowned. We visit the homes and workshops of master weavers and carvers who work exquisite magic in bone, ivory, stone, and myriad woods, including mahogany, teak, ebony and sandalwood. It occurs to me to inquire of a wood carver about a sign to hang over the gate to Twin Brooks. Finding such a mission more interesting than shopping, we set out to locate a master carver and meet Dewi, a lean and beautiful young Balinese whose work we immediately admire. "Yes. Is possible," he says. "What you want on sign?"

The floral, animal and bird motifs in Dewi's studio inspire me to conjure up a sign decorated with the flora and fauna of Twin Brooks: pine, cedar and fir trees, wild columbine and tiger lilies—and, of course, a llama. This seems like a capital idea until we realize that we have our feet planted firmly in the middle of a very comical caper. How to describe a pine tree to a tropical islander who has never seen one, and whose languages are Balinese and Indonesian with just a smattering of English?

I start drawing pine trees, pinecones, and lilies, to gales of laughter from Jim and the Balinese who gather around us. Although I was a studio art minor at UC Berkeley, it was in the era of pure abstract expressionism, so my translates into an exuberant russet splotch. Somehow, combining my stylized Christmas trees and Dewi's expertise with bamboo, we come up with a rather credible pine tree. Lilies are easy; all we have to do is add dots on the petals to make the Balinese lily into a Sierra tiger lily.

But Dewi has never even heard of a llama! I try gesturing a deer with ears like a rabbit, and he and Jim both snigger. Then I try drawing again. After all, I painted a mural on the Twin Brooks Timber Llamas trailer. But Dewi can't accept that a beast with banana shaped ears really exists, and he insists on giving the ears points like the winged caps of Balinese Legong dancers. Now he has Jim and me collapsed. It's a Bali Llama!

Finally, Jim asks Dewi for a computer and tries www.llamas.com. Bingo! A rather bizarre web page shows a cartoon llama driving a motorcycle, and it is all Dewi needs to get the ears just right. We shall see what we shall see when the Bali Llama arrives in a container crate at the dock in Los Angeles.

## A Balinese Dream

Today we follow a procession of devoted villagers in the lengthy observations of a death and cremation ceremony. Rather than the somber tone of Western funeral processions, this one has an air of celebration. Led by musicians playing a gamelan, surviving generations of the family of the deceased, as well as neighbors and friends, walk slowly through the winding streets, accompanying the body to the cremation site. Men and women, dressed in traditional sarong skirts and many wearing white overshirts, carry beautifully arranged plates of exotic fruits, tropical flowers and baskets of food. For the Hindu Balinese, burning the body is a sacred ritual that returns the form to its five elements, earth, air, water, fire and space, liberating the soul to join the ancestors who watch over the living, and freeing it to return in the body of a soon-to-be-born child. Squeamish with the memory of the Kilimanjaro cremation story still too fresh, we do not stay with the procession to see the log pyre lit and smell the burning flesh.

Clearly we are back amongst a culture absorbed with death and the afterlife. But unlike Egyptians, who perceive death as the aim and purpose of life on Earth, the Balinese simply believe that the afterlife is more paradise, like Bali! Impressions from the ceremony and reflections on life and death filter into my unconscious mind. This night, fast asleep in our carved Indonesian bedstead elevated on a dias and made into a sleeping palace, I dream a Balinese dream about my own dead parents. In the dream:

*My mother is ill and suffering from dementia when I visit her in her hut. She beckons me inside and greets me. I know she recognizes me, but she can't retrieve my name. It is exquisitely painful to be close to her again, yet to know that our very close mother-daughter connection has broken or is at least seriously compromised because of her dementia.*

*I turn to my father, who is close by. I tell him that it is hard to see her this way because as a staff psychologist on the oncology ward, I have seen so many young men demented and dying from Kaposi's sarcoma. He seems quite calmly aware of Mother's decline and approaching death. He says he knows that I am sad about Mother but that he is very proud of me for taking myself into difficult and painful places to help people in need. He says developing that capacity is part of the meaning of life. His words move me deeply for I have never seen such sensitivity in him before, and I realize that in my dream, he has empathy of which I had never thought him capable.*

I awaken feeling calm and moved, as if a lifelong wish for a different sort of father has been fulfilled. I recognize the reversal.

Once, after my father got a pacemaker, when I visited him in the hospital, he didn't recognize me. He said, "Hello. I'd like to introduce you to my wife, Mrs. Kimble," and indicated his third wife sitting at the bedside. It was very painful for me; he didn't know me, and my mother, who I felt to be the real Mrs. Kimble, had died in the accident years before. It was Jim's mother who died of Alzheimer's. It was my Ma, not Dad, who deeply appreciated my work with the terminally ill in the oncology unit at Cedars-Sinai, as she always had deep empathy and social responsibility. My brusque father, on the other hand, could be brutally hard-nosed. He often reduced my sister or me to tears with his blunt pronouncements and his demeaning tendency to grade people as either "winners" or "losers." He'd crush us with statements like, "Looking from a snake's eye view on Mars, that boyfriend of yours couldn't box his way out of a paper bag."

But my Bali dream suggests hope for an evolution of spirit. The spirits of deceased loved ones are carried in the living; what if, wherever it goes, our spiritual energy keeps developing beyond the capacities we revealed in life? I smile to the spirit of my dead father, remembering that in life he was a devoted and generous provider, and had a great sense of humor as well as a capacity to see well beyond the details. Without his encouragement, my own capacities might have remained stunted, as so many women of my generation were. I know he would have celebrated my spirit of adventure on this journey and would have insisted I write about it. "Be a winner!" His voice rings in my ear, propelling me up mountaintops and to professional heights. But I love the newly dreamed softness in his voice.

I emerge from the dream and these reflections with a sense of peace, which I attribute to the palpable spiritual grace of Bali. On this day we make a fitting pilgrimage to Pura Besakih, known as the "Mother Temple" north of Ubud in the foothills of Mount Agung. It is a steep climb, and to honor our ancestors, all pilgrims are required to wear sarongs. The climb is worth the challenge; with my dream still so fresh, I feel the energy of deep connection with my own mother. Plus, for comic relief, I love watching Jim's antics as he wrestles both mentally and physically with his sarong. By the end of the day, though the temple visit on top of the mountain is wonderful, we've had enough of Balinese traffic, motor bikes, vans, oxen, men pulling carts, and women carrying huge loads or floral offerings on their heads. We want to get out of the car and be physical, so we arrange a white water rafting trip down the Ayung River on the following day. The Ayung flows through the culturally rich area of Ubud in central eastern Bali, right past our balcony in the interior tropical rainforest.

The rafting course follows a 300-meter deep winding gorge lined with massive fig trees, ancient fern trees, giant philodendrons, and tangles of liana vines filled with birds. As the monsoon has only recently (and not definitively) ended, the river is up and the rapids thrill us and our fellow paddlers, a truly international conglomerate of Japanese, Hawaiians, Germans, French and Balinese, and a curious old pair from Auberry who gain friends and enemies by dousing everyone with water. The ride is physically and visually exhilarating. We are back in our element and ready to embark on a real adventure away from the tourist track. But first, I have to link up with my email and news from the home front. After a seafood feast on the beach in Sanur, I find an Internet cafe.

### Rangda Attack on a Cyber Isle

I am excited at the prospect of being able to pull up stakes and still have an internationally accessible mailbox. We have certainly gone to enough trouble, especially since computer/internet trouble became my middle name in the year before our departure. In addition to phone line problems and no possibility of satellite or DSL at Twin Brooks, our Los Angeles server seemed bollixed with overloads and disconnects. My Mac frequently succumbed to the hegemony of our neighbor to the north in Seattle, Mr. Bill Gates, who seemed bent on quietly squeezing Macs off the net. Finally, I reconfigured my modem, changed servers, and cleared the phone lines. Tonight on this honeymoon isle, I look forward to cyber union. I hope it will be the first of many connections with the kids, our friends, my patients and Martha, who is our lifeline, handling all of our daily financial and business affairs at home.

Practically salivating, I get online. Up comes "Harriet's Page," right here on a beach sidewalk cafe in Sanur! "You've got mail!"

Since I don't have time to correspond much, I only read the news from Martha. Wrong choice. Her email is titled "Slam Bam." With a pounding heart and a deep sigh, I open it. It is what I feared.

Our new tenant's flexibility and generosity lasted only as long as it took us to get to LAX and board a plane. He's told Martha that he would never have signed a lease for a house like ours unless he could raise his six children (count 'em, six!) in it. He would like her to close the downstairs office and decamp promptly so he can turn it into a bedroom. He doesn't intend to have her "policing" the place. The Rangda has crossed the Pacific, morphed yet again, and taken on the form of a Tenantus Tyrannosaurus!

Martha and our beloved housekeeper Miriam, in a frazzle, are frantically moving our filing cabinets, computers, etc., into the closet we had agreed by lease to keep locked. Martha's email sounds totally distraught and I know that my attempt to send a reassuring reply about alternative office space won't assuage the problem. So much for our island paradise. I leave my first Internet cafe with a major bellyache. It's time to unplug and head into the jungle.

# CHAPTER 18
## WAYFARING AT BOROBUDUR

WE'RE EXCITED. Our plane from Bali touches down on the north coast of Java in Semarang, where we are to meet Leksmono, the Javanese ethnographer we've heard so much about. Jim's Stanford classmate Dick Mobilio arranged this meeting. Mobilio has been following his passion for exotic adventure, scuba diving and ethnography since the tech boom days, when he mined the fertile soil of Silicon Valley and retired early to pursue travel as a sojourner and leader of like-minded adventurers. For years, we've salivated over his exotic destinations and ethnographic explorations. But we could never go; the constraints of our family and careers always precluded such peregrinations. We've been educating kids and saving spare change, enviously wondering if we would ever make such adventurous travel happen for ourselves.

But today it's actually happening. Here we are in Kalimantan, Borneo! If this isn't the beginning of a trip into the "back of beyond" I'm not sure what would be. The group trip Mobilio originally organized was cancelled, but better yet, he's arranged an expedition just for Jim and me. We disembark yet again into the warm moist air that is Indonesia, heavily perfumed here with the smell of sea salt and cut timber. In moments, my blouse is already clammily stuck to my back. At the same time, coming off the small plane onto the tarmac, I feel almost breathless with excitement to finally meet Mobilio's contact in person, the ethnographer who is responsible for the extraordinary journeys on which we are about to embark. Leksmono steps forward to greet us, a sturdy, muscular man with bandy legs and a mane of curly black hair. He looks stockier and more Tonganese than the Balinese, who are remarkably slight and delicately boned. Since he is the first Javanese I've met, I wonder if his build is characteristic of this island's people. He wears a dozen silver and brass bracelets collected during years of exploring many of the 666 inhabited and 17,000 total islands of Indonesia. He looks every bit the part of an ethnographer famous for his research into the cultures of Irian Jaya, Sumba, Suva and Kalimantan. As we perambulate through the street markets of Semarang and feast on a dinner of Javanese seafood, we learn more about Leksmono's interests.

As an adolescent, he began voyaging to the remote islands of his country. He brought back extraordinary primitive sculptures, bark shields, spears, headdresses, and textiles. He decorated his own room at home, then adorned his parents' small house with these treasures. His mother regarded this as the eccentric rambling of a teenaged son who was wasting his time on old junk. While he was away on a trip, she gathered it all up, threw it away, and proudly painted the house a bright new color. He came home to the devastating loss of what he, rare among his countrymen, valued so highly. He still winces, recalling the irretrievable waste of those national treasures. His interest in Indonesian ethnography was way ahead of its time; unfortunately, his mother's values prevail today, as many Indonesians are enamored of first world materialism.

Until age forty, he lived "free like a bird," following his interests from island to island, studying the tribal cultures, beliefs, and art that were inaccessible to outsiders. He used Bali as a base for ten years, guiding visitors to some of the exotic peoples and places of his deepening knowledge. But like a woman's bio-clock sounding at age thirty, his approach to forty sounded a nesting alarm; he was ready to wed. Try though he might to find a suitable bride among his own people, as his parents insisted a traditional Javanese should, none of the Muslim women shared his wanderlust. Three years ago, he met a passionate world traveler, an American professor destined to become his wife. He promises to introduce us to Linda after we come out of the jungles of Kalimantan and fly to Jakarta, their new home.

*Merpati Gone Flatty*

But now we are on a mission. We'll fly across the Java Sea to meet Wan Tu, our assistant guide. We will journey upriver on a live-aboard riverboat called a *klotok*, chugging up various waterways into the world's greatest orangutan reserve, the Tanjung Puting Harapan Ranger Station. This is what we have been told. However, as I am destined to learn yet again, "the best laid plans of mice and men are aftly gang awry." After waiting in the Semarang airport for two hours, we are notified that our Merpati Airlines plane has engine trouble and today's flight is cancelled. Deplaned passengers clump morosely around the airport.

We make the acquaintance of two ladies: Roni, an American here to visit the factory of furniture she imports, and Simone, a young French veterinarian carrying a huge duffel bag full of medications for the orangutan hospital where she serves as a volunteer vet. Carpe Diem! Within moments, we devise a plan to return our luggage to the hotel for another night and embark on a daylong adventure. Roni will visit her associates in Solo, while Simone will join Leks, Jim and me for an unexpected bonus, a trip to the ruins of Borobudur, the world's largest Buddhist temple, built in the early 9th Century AD., Isaac, a fellow psychoanalyist and wander buddy, raved about the beauty of Borobudur before we began this leg of our adventures, but we didn't expect to have time to visit it—until "Merpati went flatty" (Jim's phrase) and bestowed this chance on us.

For three hours, we thread through carbon-fumed traffic, jockeying for position with trucks, buses, bicycles, pedicabs and foot traffic that make the Balinese byways look like a quaint tea party. At last, we reach the interior of central Java. It is well worth the journey to this high plateau surrounded by volcanoes, rolling hills and beautiful landscaping.

Borobudur, the most fantastic of all Buddhist stupas in the world, was buried under a thousand years of volcanic eruptions and jungle encroachment until 1814, when it was miraculously discovered by Colonel Raffles, an Englishman. For the next century, excavations unearthed and preserved this extraordinary world treasure. In the

1980s the United Nations spent almost twenty million dollars cleaning and copying all the carvings and friezes, and shoring up Borobudur's foundations for posterity. What has emerged is an extraordinary monument to the Bodhisattva, modern by pyramid standards but predating Angor Wat in Cambodia by three centuries, and Notre Dame and Chartres cathedrals by 200 years.

No written records have been discovered, but archeologists speculate that thousands of laborers, slaves, engineers and carvers used only hammers, mallets and human effort to construct this temple out of two million cubic feet of volcanic stone over several generations. It was consecrated 1100 years ago and abandoned soon thereafter, when Hindus overruled the Sailendric sect of Tantric Buddhism, which designed, built and sanctified it. Muslims, who dominate Java and most of Indonesia today, subsequently confiscated the temple.

Borobudur looks like an enormous, splendid wedding cake, with ten terraced layers ascending in elevation while descending in size. The layers represent greed, desire, lust and death, in progressive steps up from the basest level of earth. With each stage of ascent, a pilgrim aspires closer and closer toward the loftiest height of spiritual enlightenment, unattainable by any but the Buddha himself. On every level, carved friezes depict scenes from the life of the Buddha, set off by more than seventy-two stone stupas shaped like inverted openwork baskets atop lotus flowers. Within each stupa, a statue of Buddha sits in meditation. This colossal temple's name probably derives from Sanskrit "bhumian bhara hudara," roughly meaning "the mountain of the accumulation of the merits of the ten states of the Bodhisattva."

While the temple is visited by pilgrims and a few awed travelers like ourselves, it has only one religious ceremony each year, which, we learn, took place just last week. Called Waicak Day, it falls during the full moon on the most auspicious day in May. Thousands of Buddhist monks in saffron robes advance solemnly, chanting and praying, processing in circular ascent clockwise toward the main stupa at the top. At that holy place, they await the rising of the moon on the horizon, symbolizing the birth of the Buddha.

Well worth the frustrations of a delayed flight and Javanese traffic, Borobudur will long remain in my mind as a profoundly holy place, like Mt. Sinai and the Old City of Jerusalem. We are also rewarded by the opportunity to get acquainted with Dr. Simone, with whom I converse all the way back from Borobudur. Jim calls such discussions my "wayfaring sessions," as they seem to pop up unexpectedly along the road. They provide me with an interesting and privileged window on the soul of a fellow wayfarer, who may be at a point of struggle. Catnip as they may be to me, these sessions are not Jim's cup of tea; he soon nods off, leaving Dr. Simone to talk in privacy.

I immediately liked Dr. Simone. She appeared somewhat shy and isolated, partly by nature and probably due to being the only French-speaking person in this part of the Indonesian jungle. She has been living and volunteering on the orangutan preserve for five or six months and is still getting her bearings. My romantic notion is that I am meeting a young Jane Goodall. Already she's succumbed to a 105-degree malarial fever and a major bout of depression. She is the first of several Western women I will soon hear of who were drawn to the intrigue and romance of the jungle, yet subsequently experience depression and psychic introversion characterizing a kind of psychological jungle fever.

Though Dr. Simone is of a much younger generation, it occurs to me that her upbringing in a French Catholic family might share some commonality with mine in 1950s conservative Pasadena. I see parts of myself in her; we were both raised traditionally but with a passion to undertake a nontraditional career and to move "outside the box," as well as a vulnerability to depression and insecurity. But while Simone is alone in the jungle with her internal demons, I had the soul-saving rescue of a wonderful psychoanalyst. My own analysis revealed to me how constrained I was by "proper" values that included sexual repression, suppression of aggression and patriarchy. Under my compassionate psychoanalyst-father's guidance, I became able to express myself boldly, embrace my sexuality and follow my star by leaving an unsatisfying marriage and pursuing a fulfilling career as a psychoanalyst. All incomparable antidepressants!

Later, our new friend Roni tells me stories of several American women in Guam who married Filipino men then found the adjustment impossible. Among them, too, bouts of depression are common. They had babies with their husbands before encountering their true isolation and status as outsider women. Deciding to leave the islands, they discovered they cannot take their babies with them.

Dr. Simone remembers her adolescent self, champing at the bit in a very traditional and conservative Provençal family. It was expected that she, like her sisters, would marry, settle into a well-paying profession and have babies. But this was not for her. She always had dreams of "a life of meaning," and rebelled. After she completed university studies and received her degree in veterinary medicine, she studied for a time at the London Zoo. But she soon realized that she still felt as caged as her caged patients.

She withdrew into a depressive psychic cocoon. Her depression was so debilitating that she sought out a psychoanalyst in France. She discovered that she had always been unconsciously striving to make her kind but undemonstrative parents tell her they were proud of her accomplishments. Although she's sure that they are pleased with her, they never proclaimed their pride. She found the psychoanalyst's initial observations useful, but quit after only one session to contemplate her frustrated efforts to gain her parents' approbation. She managed to crawl through the depression on her own, and a pathway was revealed to her. She would make her way as a wild animal veterinarian. She was offered a two-year position as resident veterinarian at the orangutan clinic in Pasir Panjang, founded by world-famous Canadian primatologist Birute Galdikas. She now feels exhilarated at the prospect of life among the wild apes of Borneo.

I am impressed by Dr. Simone's spunk and independence, though I detect something that is beginning to worry her. What is the psychological cost to other areas of her life of this resolution/escape? She has relinquished the impossible dream of winning her parents' praise, and set out on a healthy path to satisfy her own dreams. But in the bargain, I offer, perhaps she has also forfeited her faith in the capacity of another person to meet her deepest needs. She nods sadly. I say that while she benefited from her session with the French psychoanalyst, her "flight" after just one session probably presages her anxiety about intimacy and dependency.

Dr. Simone looks away and lowers her voice. It's true, she says. She has never been able to maintain a successful relationship with a man. She always tends to bolt. Winding along on the road from Borobudur, we talk of the importance of cementing her dream among the wild apes. Facing extinction without the intervention of rescue efforts, perhaps their plight parallels her struggles between freedom and dependency. At some point, when she has worked out the pursuit of her dream of freedom as far away from the constraints of home as she can get, it might be time to return to the good doctor to seek an experience of satisfying dependency. Her willingness to face the music may enable her to find and maintain intimacy. Completing our on-the-road session from Borobudur to Semarang, we hug, express our hopes to visit her at the orangutan clinic, exchange email addresses, and agree to keep in touch, wherever our paths might take us.

I sigh with gratitude for the richness and fulfillment my own analysis provided. It allowed me to be present here, not running away from an unresolved past, but—as the Bali dream revealed—freed from residual conflicts with my parents, and able to pursue my own dream. I have come a long way in letting go of the sorts of struggles Simone is enmeshed with; I have pulled up stakes and embarked on this adventure with less baggage. But I still carry the baggage of anxieties and fears, and I look forward to softening them through this pilgrimage.

I realize that while I have essentially closed down my practice, I'm still a psychoanalyst. This serendipitous encounter on the back roads of Java has enabled me to practice my art. While I may have let go of the trappings of my tribe, thousands of miles from my office, I am still that person in my heart. That feels good. I want to practice letting go, but not of everything.

# CHAPTER 19
## KALIMANTAN: HAIRY LOVE IN A BUCKET

WE'RE FINALLY AIRBORNE the next day from Semarang, Java, in one of Merpati Air's "best." The window next to Jim's seat is taped in with packing tape, which makes the missing screws on Egypt Air's "best" look pretty good. Despite the plane's imperfections, an hour and a half after departure, we touch down safely on the airstrip of tiny Pangkala Bun, Kalimantan. Inside the tiny airport, a small polisi (policeman) rushes up to greet Jim and vigorously shakes his hand. He looks Jim up and down admiringly, pausing with particular awe to gaze at Jim's very large feet, and says, "You army?" He means that Jim and his feet are so big he must be in the army—or maybe he IS an army!

In 1997, our new ethnographer friend, Leksmono Leks, as we call him—helped establish FNPF (The Friends of the National Parks Foundation) to aid in saving threatened orangutans and their habitats in the interior of Borneo. Orangutans are dwindling at an alarming rate, prey to poaching, the massive deforestation of Indonesian rainforests, and the tribal upheavals that have ensued on the ravaged lands. FNPF supports park rangers who rescue and rehabilitate orphaned orangs. Leksmono will guide us upriver to visit three ranger stations. The first station is a full veterinary care infirmary for newly rescued apes, and the others—each one farther upriver—are designed to foster greater and greater independence for the animals. At the furthest outpost, established by primatologist Dr. Birute Galdikas, orangs rarely come in, as they are able to maintain themselves in the wild.

Leks recently became aware of the financial hardships of local national park rangers, whose pay is miniscule. He realized that while he has been raising money to rescue orangutans, their human volunteer helpers have no money even to buy shoes! Our project in Semarang is to round up a dozen pairs of shoes to take to the rangers. While we join Leks to gather his "shoe booty" in the public market, one saleswoman wants to sell us shoes, until she glances down at Jim's size 13 EEEE feet and nearly faints. After a flurry of giggles, she summons a crowd of compatriot shoe salespersons to marvel at the platters this foreigner has for feet! Some years back on a trip to Patagonia, we learned that when Sir Francis Drake's expedition rounded Cape Horn and encountered the Mapuche Indians, the travelers were so impressed by the size of the Indians' feet that they named the territory Patagonia, "land of big feet." Hearing that, we immediately christened Jim's impressive feet "the Patagons."

After Jim and his patagons are given an awed once-over, we meet our local guide, Wan Tu ("one two"), who lives at the first orangutan rescue station. Charmingly engaging, he greets us with a beaming, white-toothed smile and the traditional bow of respect, palms together in a gesture of reverence. Wan Tu escorts us to a taxi that transports us and our gear to the Kumai Harbor, where we find our klotok, home for the next three or four days, waiting to take us up the Kumai River.

Chugging upriver in the "African Queen," we cannot miss the heartbreaking evidence of deforestation, with mahogany, ironwood and teak logs stacked high on the docks. Yet, in spite of our pain and horror as we bear witness to the deforestation, the journey is serene and lovely. The klotok's motor kloks and tocks us through jungles of mangrove and palm. Jim and I look at each other, and he reaches out to squeeze my hand. A cool breeze wafts over us as we recline on soft cushions under the boat's canopy. He asks, "Are you feeling what I'm feeling?"

"Absolutely," I say. "Very, very content."

Wan Tu says, "You like the African Queen?" I nod happily. I feel like Katharine Hepburn going upriver with her Bogart, the cares of the world receding.

Jim asks Wan Tu how he came to this beautiful place. He delights us by telling us that as a boy, he saw a film of Johnny Weissmuller as Tarzan, and decided when he grew up, he would leave his native Java for a life in a wild jungle with apes.

I ask, "And what about Jane?"

Wan Tu looks wistful. "I'm looking for her... now she's only in my dreams." Looking for a suitable Jane for Wan Tu becomes our play project over the next few days as we study the habitat and ways of the true Tarzans and Janes, the extraordinary orangutans of Kalimantan. We are up against highly unfavorable odds, though, as we discover almost all the rangers and caretakers in these outposts are young men.

After several hours chugging upriver among the mangroves, we arrive at the ranger station where Wan Tu lives. The park rangers and resident vet joyfully greet Leks. They're beyond grateful for the new shoes. One young ranger shows us his hut, which he has decorated with considerable artistic talent. To while away the lonely evenings in this distant outpost, he reads a lot and shows off a large, hand-hewn bookcase full of books. Twining around the walls and windows he has painted a mural of a long, elegantly colored serpent. He proudly displays the chair he just built; on its back he lovingly painted a portrait of his guitar—looking very feminine—to keep him company in his solitary retreat.

Near this Tanjung Puting Harapan #1 Feeding Station, Leks, Wan Tu and the crew sleep on the klotok, but they have arranged for us "guests" to sleep up the Sekonyer River at Rimba Lodge. With a down-at-the-heels jungle lodge look, Rimba reminds me of the rustically charming Tambupati Lodge in the heart of the Amazon Basin, fortuitously upriver and upwind from the armpit of Amazonian Peru, Porto Maldonado. Rimba Lodge is a series of teak and bamboo huts built on stilts above the tidal current wetlands. Each tin roof house is surrounded by ironwood walkways connecting the main lodge and restaurant with the cottages.

Before retiring to our cottage, we are served a huge, tourist-oriented, "western" repast in the restaurant. We try reading in the large mosquito-netted bed, but it is so humidly close that we decide to slather on more mosquito dope, don our backpacking headlamps and take our books onto deck chairs in front of our room. No sooner have we settled in to read than we hear an enormous crash, then a squeal and splash. It seems this is macaque monkey central, and our room is right next to their favorite playground.

Although Jared Diamond's Pulitzer prize-winning *Guns, Germs and Steel* is fascinating, it can't compete with the monkeyshines that keep us in rapt amusement for a couple of hours. The initial *kersplash* is just the first of several, brought on by monkey miscalculations as they roar along the branches, get them swaying like rocket launchers, and jettison hopefully over the water to the next tree. Their engineering acumen is sometimes a little off, and they crash into the water, squealing wildly.

We finally tear ourselves away to sleep. I enjoy a stuporous jungle slumber until our macaque gymnastics troop starts another round of play at 3:30 a.m. Jim and I sit bolt upright in the dark, looking at each other and mouthing, "Oh, shit." It sounds like they're throwing coconuts at our tin roof from the tallest palms. Monkeyshines continue unabated until dawn, when our alarm sounds. But awakening around 3:30 a.m. has its advantages for a writer. I relish my predawn jungle writing during the coolest part of the day.

The next day, we beg to sleep with the native crew, Leks, and Wan Tu aboard the klotok. Their food is fabulous, unlike the attempt at western cooking on shore. The only hitch, other than sleeping on the open-air deck with its nightly midnight rain scramble, is the klotok's bathroom, which Wan Tu describes as a "semi-wild jungle toilet." In the night we have to navigate across a deck of sleeping bodies to the stern, where the jungle toilet is located—an enclosure hanging over the back of the boat, with a floor slatted close enough to stand on, but wide enough for relevant matter to fall into the river. There is also a bucket full of water with a dipper to wash off the slats.

While we're concerned about the long-term ecological impacts on the river, from a personal standpoint it beats a lot of Asian toilets. It definitely outclasses the wickedly smelly airport latrines of Porto Maldonado, and it wins hands-down over the vile-smelling squat toilets of the islands off Hong Kong. The latter elicited a core conflict between incipient diarrhea and the wish to never defecate again. Well, enough scatological diatribes. The unfortunately un-ecological "semi-wild jungle toilet" has other advantages; it's moored at the end of the dock mid-river, ergo, no midnight monkey forays.

In the morning, Wan Tu and Leks shepherd us along a board pathway to the infirmary to visit recently rescued orangs. In no time at all, I am dangerously close to succumbing to the call of the wild that lured Dr. Simone, Wan Tu and Leksmono. It calls to me from a black rubber bucket at the Tanjung Puting Harapan Ranger Station. There, on May 27, 2000, I meet Adung, an orphaned eight-month-old baby orang. He was abandoned to certain death in the forest, when illegal loggers probably killed his mother. Baby Adung was rescued just one month ago. Whenever he is here at the station, Wan Tu sleeps with him and feeds him his bottle faithfully, even at midnight, 3:00 a.m. and 5:00 a.m. I approach the bucket where Adung is curled up on a cloth that serves as his diaper, looking warily at me, the approaching stranger. As Wan Tu gently tends to him, I try photographing him on the dark porch of the jungle house where he, Wan Tu, the vet, and another ranger have their bunks.

But as the photographer, "taking" memories, I feel separated. My heart dearly wants more. Something about this little redheaded orphan tugs deeply at me. Do I see in him an image of my own dreaded abandonment fears? Though I was almost forty and twice a mother myself when my own mother was killed, that gut-wrenching loss cut through my adult defenses and found its mark in the heart of my inner "orphan" girl. I'm identifying with little Adung.

We spend an hour talking about the plight of the apes and the terrifyingly rapid deforestation occurring throughout Kalimantan. Most of the Western world is aware of the deforestation of the Amazon, but few know what's going on in Indonesia. 60% of the logging is illegal and occurs *within* the national parks. The Indonesian government is too preoccupied with cleaning up corruption left by Sukarno and then Suharto, and perpetrating more of its own. The national parks are not staffed, and the only support for rangers is through private efforts such as the FNPF trust.

Indonesians unwittingly perpetuate the tragic destruction of their own nest. The poor Dyak tribal people, displaced from the isolation and integrity of their ancient hunter-gatherer ways in the jungle, seek modern goods and the money to buy them by hiring on with logging operations and cutting down the very forest that has sustained them for millennia. Great teaks, mahoganies, and ironwoods are being ransacked and shipped to foreign ports. The horror is that the vast majority of this rare wood does not even become valued handcrafted furniture or exquisite carvings, but is shipped to Japan to make plywood for concrete construction forms. Once used, it is thrown away.

As the sun slowly sets behind the trees, we listen in dismay to the story of the careless decimation of a precious resource and the last remaining habitat of the great apes. I feel so sad. Our conversation about the destruction of our planet's forests is not an intellectual report we might hear on NPR or public television. It is right here and now. This little orphan ape's beseeching brown eyes make the tragedy achingly real. My whole journey, pulling up stakes, is intentionally about letting go. I'm releasing attachments to my house, professional identity, secure situations, and everything that can become antithetical to psychological freedom. Yet I am now teetering on the precipice of a powerful new attachment.

Little Adung, who cannot possibly understand this conversation or what has happened to his mother and his home, gazes up at me with huge coffee-brown eyes and hooks my heart. During our hours-long conversation, sitting next to his bucket, I sense his longing for a maternal presence. He seems aware that I'm a woman and decides I'm okay. He tentatively starts fingering—with hands and prehensile long toes—my hair, my face, and me. Next, he cautiously ventures one foot out of his bucket, then the other, and soon he is in my lap. I am transfixed. He settles in to suck on the coin of Alexander the Great that I have been wearing as a necklace talisman from the Old City of Jerusalem. As he leans back, he extends his amazing toe into the porches of my ear. Jim takes several photographs of us, Adung's great brown eyes gazing into my face out of his halo of red hair, and me in a state of maternal bliss. I can practically feel the let-down reflex awakened in my breasts. This furry, redhaired, big-eyed baby has touched the mother and the bereft little girl within me, and I feel we are destined to be bosom buddies. No letting go here.

Jim and I take turns giving Adung his late afternoon bottle. We return to visit him again at night, when he's sleeping in his bucket, before we take a walk through the jungle with Leks and Wan Tu. We find ourselves fascinated by a chorus of myriad singing insects, our way lit by phosphors on the forest leaves.

I ask how much it costs to take care of an orphan like Adung until he develops enough to be repatriated into the jungle as an adult male.

Jim immediately recognizes the signs. He says, "You're thinking of adopting Adung, aren't you?"

"Yep."


After the jungle walk, I dream of little Adung in his bucket, and make the decision that I want to adopt him. Jim agrees; he too has bottle-fed the little guy and discovered quite a bit of melted butter in his usually stoic heart. We are truly impressed by the quality of care the orangs receive from the FNPF camp vet and rangers, and equally impressed by the magnitude of the danger to this endangered species. Adung and his ilk desperately need help. It's so much more gratifying to support a creature you know firsthand, who's insinuated his toe into your ear and sucked on your coin necklace, than to write a check to a distant charity from a desk at home.

This decision allows for a new and nourishing attachment quite free of self-interest. I have all the heart-expanding benefits of falling in love, but at the same time I relinquish control and embark on another heart-expanding journey—trust and the practice of generosity. My "baby" will be entrusted to the care of others, and we will both be the beneficiaries. I feel smitten, elated and light-hearted. New synapses are firing in my brain. Am I learning that letting go of conventional attachments can provide spaciousness and a less self-interested generosity? A seed is planted. I vow to explore this question further on another sabbatical pilgrimage: a retreat with those who are truly practicing this path in a monastery.

But now it is time to tear myself away from my new baby and continue upriver to visit the other rescue stations. For the next three days, during our foray deep into the Bornean jungle and primatology's heart of darkness, I am besotted, thinking of little Adung and his toe in my ear.

# CHAPTER 20

## JUNGLE FEVER:
### PARANOIA, PRIMATOLOGY, AND BAPTISM

JUNGLE HUMIDITY doesn't agree with my electronic Palm operating system. A green bubble, accompanied by the words "fatal error," slowly spreads across the screen of my Handspring, signaling the crash of my writing tool. Losing my electronic journal is clearly an opportunity to practice letting go, and it grates on me. So far, pulling up stakes has mostly felt liberating. Leasing the house, closing my practice, saying goodbye to friends and family, and dramatically paring down our possessions have all felt light and exhilarating. But losing my written journal feels like a stab. Nonetheless, it's one I will have to accept.

I consider reverting to pen and ink to reconstruct our expedition into the deeper jungle. But after writing on paper in the Middle East last year, I returned home and tried to decipher and transcribe my hieroglyphics for months. It was such a frustrating exercise that I now decide to hope for an electronic miracle rather than take up a pen. In this land of death and ritual rebirth, who knows?

As we travel upriver, we are lucky on several counts. First, the monsoon is over. The weather, though punctuated by periodic showers, occasional brief downpours and omnipresent humidity, is pleasantly clear. Second, because of the current political instability of Indonesia and the Philippines, hardly any tourists have had the temerity to venture forth. Said instability includes the recent capture of an international group of scuba divers in the Philippines, the ongoing internecine strife in East Timor, and a major currency crisis, which has had a tremendously deleterious effect on those who can bear it least—the peasant majority.

We reconnoiter at Pondok Tangui Camp to observe the outpost feeding of rescued orangutans. As we make our way to the feeding station, the rangers hoot and roar, simulating orangutan language, to alert the jungle orangs that fresh grub is on the way. We hear crashes and watch high branches wave wildly in the trees above us. Before long, we spot the source of the racket: a mother orang with one baby aboard and another following close by. Swinging their enormous arms, hand over prehensile foot, they hoot back and travel over our heads in raucous celebration of our gifts of fresh buckets of milk and huge bunches of bananas. The station consists of a feeding platform where the rangers place the milk and bananas, as well as logs lashed together to form makeshift benches for observers.

The first trio to arrive is the repatriated orangutan, Rosemary, and her two children. She lost a baby shortly after its birth, but with the help of other rescued orangs, managed to break into the cage of an orphaned baby at the first camp. She stole the baby and adopted it as her own, which worked out beautifully for everyone. Shortly thereafter, Rosemary conceived again and successfully bore a second offspring. Now adopted baby Damino and biological baby Rika travel with her wherever she goes.

In addition to Kopral, Ramono, Oscar and Linda, we also have the good fortune to encounter Ludo, a wild orang who has befriended the repatriated apes at this station. Of the estimated seventy orangs who periodically appear for feeding here, eight answer the call today. Mothers and babies, juvenile males and females show up and provide us with an incredible show. Some are bold and swing exhuberantly hand over hand from the trees to the feeding platform, practically grinning at us. Others, younger and shyer, catch a free ride by clinging to their mothers. Still others seem to enjoy clowning around, swinging first hand to hand, then flipping to travel upside down from their prehensile toes. When the sun catches their red hair from behind, they appear to be wearing psychedelic red haloes. Between our two cameras—one with a 300mm telephoto zoom lens shooting slide stock, the other with a 38-105 mm lens shooting print stock (Recall, this is before the digital revolution,)—Jim and I, intrigued with their antics, fire off three rolls of film. These primates seem the picture of health, relishing their own habitat and receiving occasional feeds and veterinary care as needed.

We've excitedly anticipated our next stop upriver; it's on a par with visiting Jane Goodall and her chimps or Dian Fossey with her gorillas. But in a disturbing disappointment of our expectations, we witness the apparent dissolution of an internationally based effort. The Orangutan Fund International's efforts to protect the apes, spearheaded by Canadian primatologist Birute Galdikas, seem to be unraveling before us. In the early 1970s, Dr. Louis Leakey trained Galdikas in the study of orangutans, as he trained Jane Goodall with chimps and Dian Fossey with gorillas. These three gifted female primatologists became world-renowned as "Leakey's Angels."

Galdikas came to Kalimantan to collect data on orangutans for her doctoral dissertation. She and her husband established an outpost observation station and named it Camp Leakey after her African mentor. For several years, like Fossey and Goodall, she embarked on what she called her "follows" into the jungle, tracking primates and gathering the first comprehensive data on orangutan feeding, breeding, and social patterns. The *National Geographic* publication of her research findings, plus a number of scientific journal publications, put Galdikas on the international map. She enjoyed growing fame and received a permit from the Indonesian government for ongoing research in the Tanjung Puting National Park out of Camp Leakey.

But something seems odd as we head upriver for Camp Leakey. Evidence of logging, which has been ubiquitous along the river, mysteriously slows to a trickle. One or two tugboats pull strands of over one hundred logs downriver, but this is well below the six to eight log-laden tugs of a typical day. Why, after years of ineffectual lobbying against the logging, is there such a dramatic curtailment now?

Watching him pace nervously on the crowded deck of the African Queen, we can tell that Leks is increasingly concerned. His recent efforts to visit Galdikas' new orang clinic in Pasir Panjang, where Dr. Simone is working, have been stymied. Though it is an internationally funded orangutan urgent care center, it's been kept as closely guarded as a cruise missile installation. In spite of the Friends of the National Parks Foundation's efforts to share data with Galdikas group, the latter has been shunning them. Leks is clearly worried about the group's stewardship of the orangs.

Before parting from Dr. Simone, our French friend in Semarang, we said we wanted to visit her at Galdikas' new clinic. She was nervous about the idea, not sure if that would be possible, and reluctant to explain why. She said she was still getting settled there, trying to figure out her role. She revealed that in the past, her rebellious nature has gotten her into trouble, and she'd vowed to move slowly this time. What was up?

Our curiosity roused by the veil of intrigue over Galdikas' projects, we continue upriver. Mystery gives way to the enticing promise of water clean enough for swimming, and we stop for a dip. We also encounter the few intrepid (or crazy) souls who are on the "orangutan circuit" with us. Roni, our plane mate from Guam, has showed up here, as well as a refined young Englishwoman, Leonora, who has been volunteering at Camp Harapan for a month. All of us dive off the klotok and the dock like the kerplonk launch of a bunch of monkeys, swim hard across the swift current, and head for the poles driven into the river bottom for mooring boats. We enjoy a refreshing international confab—an Italian and a Spaniard midway through a one-year Asian odyssey, two Irish boys and a girl who met in India, two Dutch primatologists here from Sumatra to study orangs, local klotok crews, and us, all clinging to poles in the river and shouting merrily about where we've been and where we're going and where the best deals are. We garner some good tips for our upcoming travels. The river water, darkened with tannin, stains us all a deep, tan color, giving new meaning to the phrase "going native."

Refreshed, we all trek up the trail toward Camp Leakey for the afternoon feed of Dr. Galdikas' research animals. Our jovial mood darkens upon finding the camp messy and disorganized. We are shocked to find the animals raiding the pantry and making off with buckets of food. One ape breaks into the kitchen and runs out the door with a plate of prepared rice and vegetables, while the cook ineffectually yells at him. We witness the local native "researchers" teasing the animals. What kind of research project is this?

Leks and Wan Tu lead Jim and me deeper into the forest, to the feeding station. I am flummoxed when an orangutan comes flying out of a tree onto my shoulders. Before I can do more than let out a whoop of surprise, she climbs down onto my chest and settles in, arms around my neck. I'm informed that this is Purawasih, a six- or eight-year-old female weighing 22 kilos, or 50 pounds. Apparently she prefers a ride to the feeding station, and she's used to being accommodated. Her weight adds up in the tropical heat as we walk a couple of kilometers. But Purawasih will not release me, so I carry her all the way to the feed. She's a fickle lassie; the minute bananas and milk appear, she springs off my shoulders and onto the feeding platform.

We forget our queasy incredulity about the operation at Camp Leakey, because in no time, we've drawn not just the mothers, babies, and juveniles to feed, but also Kosasia, a 250-pound male, who has earned the title "The King." With his intimidating demeanor, accented by the signature cheek pads and chin pouch that develop in these huge, dominant males, he is staggering to behold. When he arrives, humans and orangs cut him a wide swath.

### Another Pretty Woman and a Great Ape

The King's legendary status was exponentially enhanced a few years ago when, during the shooting of a documentary film called "Julia Roberts and the Orangutans," he pulled a real King Kong or "Me Tarzan, you Jane." He loped into the midst of the astonished group and dragged Julia Roberts into the forest, to the utter horror of the director and film crew. The assembled rangers had to hurriedly find a strategy to chase him and avoid injuring her. The King knew a pretty woman when he saw one!

Sobered by his appearance and this cautionary tale, we keep to a tight huddle ten feet away from the giant primate, even though the most delicious photo ops beckon me to creep away from the group and catch his inscrutable face. Unlike the other apes, The King is not airborne; he's too big for the trees to bear his weight. Instead, he lumbers along the ground, his huge hands dragging on the forest floor.

After recovering from the adrenaline rush of encountering this truly great ape, we return to Camp Leakey. We are stirred again to wonder what Birute Galdikas was doing. Wan Tu tells me, "Doctor, we need you to figure it out!" Taking the bait, piecing the story together, I discover that the Indonesian government has recently rescinded Galdikas' permit to do research at Camp Leakey because she stopped producing and reporting on scientific data. She has left her Indonesian 'research assistants' in charge of the apes there. But the apes are being kept in what sounds like a kind of demeaned and demented dependency, apparently more for the juvenile staff's amusement than for their own independence in the forest. Dr. Galdikas left Indonesia to raise funds for her urgent care compound downriver, where Dr. Simone is trying to get her bearings.

I tell Wan Tu that it sounds clinical: brilliant primatologist Birute Galdikas, like Dian Fossey after too long in the bush with her chimps, may have gone round the bend, and emerged from the forest as a classic paranoid personality—charismatic, omnipotent, controlling and smart, but loopy. Leks offers a sinister sequellae of my paranoia hypothesis. He posits that Dr. Galdikas, though demoted by the government, still exerts considerable power because the government is very corrupt. He thinks the cessation of logging coincides with a prestigious primatology conference she is planning. She wouldn't want things to look bad for her guests, and she's convinced the Indonesian government that the conference attendees are good for Indonesia. The bad news about her psychotic behavior has not reached major donors in Europe and the U.S., so the Indonesian government continues to reap the benefits of her former reputation.

She can still raise charitable donations abroad, and the funds will be spent in Indonesia. It won't benefit the orangutans, but the government doesn't care. Galdikas appears to be building herself a walled paranoid palace at her tropical urgent care clinic.

In spite of these unsettling discoveries, like well-fed Miss Marples pursuing a case, we enjoy another fabulous meal on the klotok. Our sleeping stations are spread out again for our last night on the Kumai River. Rocked gently by the boat, lulled by the sing-song of the tropical forest, we sleep like babies. At dawn, it's time to head back to Pangkalaban, but with an important stop at the Tanjung Puting Harapan #1 Feeding Station. We'll drop off Wan Tu and partake in a commitment ceremony and ritual baptism for my adoption of little Adung.


Back aboard the klotok, I lounge on a pillow while Wan Tu sits on the African Queen's deck, weaving a celebratory Dyak palm fiber anklet onto my ankle. The anklet symbolizes the ceremony to be performed this morning for my formal adoption of Adung, the baby orang who—in the tradition of rescued orphans—carries the name of his rescuers. A Dyak tribesman named Adung found him last month, abandoned in the forest near a logging operation. His mother was probably shot for sport or meat. Having been carried into the care center, the orphan will henceforth be known as "Dr. Adung" to honor both of us, his benefactors—a rescuer and an adopted human mama!

Wan Tu is always smiling and gracious, asking "Mr. Jim" and "Doctor Harriet" if we would like water or snacks, or if we've seen the proboscis monkeys clamoring in the trees along the riverbank, or if there's *any*thing he can do for us. Now he's smilingly holding, in his teeth, a large porcupine quill he uses like a needle for weaving palm fibers into intricate bracelets, necklaces and anklets. He works intently, his quill moving swiftly, while I work with my own tool, a PalmPilot stylus.

Just when I readied myself to "let go" of my attachment to my Handspring, my patience was rewarded with a resurrection. After three days, my operating system dried out and reconstituted, and now I resume tapping with my stylus and typing on my small portable keyboard as Wan Tu taps with his quill. There is something remarkable about sitting together thus, each embedded in our own culture, each fascinated by the other's, he with his porcupine quill, me with my mini computer stylus.

The day dawns sparkling clear after midnight rains. After a breakfast of hearty, dark-roasted Indonesian coffee, succulent mango fruit, and creamy rice porridge, we set off downriver to the Tanjung Puting Harapan Ranger Station for the adoption ceremony. I put on a clean shirt and shorts, Jim loads the cameras with film, and we bask in morning sunshine as the Kalimantan jungle speeds by. We are met at Harapan Station by the rangers, the veterinarian, and Leonora, the British volunteer we met upriver, who is waiting to give Adung his final bath before she returns to London. It will be her farewell ceremony to the little ape, and it will also be a baptismal bath as I adopt him and bestow his new full name, Dr. Adung.

Wan Tu picks flowers for my hair, and we gather Adung and his bucket to go down to the river dock for the ceremony. This time, Adung is not hesitant with me. He climbs right into my arms, grasps my shiny coin necklace, and begins sucking on the familiar Alexander coin with delight. Leonora and I take turns holding and bathing him. His bath is exactly like the baths I used to give my own babies, years ago! We use Johnson's baby shampoo, a soft washcloth, and a cup to rinse the baby.

Adung usually cries during his bath, which is part of a routine to keep his skin free of parasites, but today there's not a whimper. He cuddles in for the warm suds, looking up at us with extraordinarily engaging brown eyes. It is incredible to wash his little neck, his fuzzy head, his small back, exquisite long-fingered hands, and even more astonishing feet. The skin on the bottom of his baby-sized feet is so smooth. His toes are as long as a baby's fingers, and he loves to grasp with them! Jim snaps pictures while Leks pronounces us mother and baby, and Wan Tu beams paternally.

Michael, the resident monkey, cannot restrain his jealousy. He flies out of a teak tree and lands on top of my head, attempting to pull on my hair and avert my gaze from Adung. Jim snaps a picture of this perfect simian expression of sibling rivalry while I, with little Dr. Adung's help, try to extricate Michael from my hair.

When the bath is over, we rinse Adung and dry him with a baby towel. Leonora gives me a baby t-shirt to put on him, and he reaches his little hands through the armholes. I am completely smitten. I look at Jim, who is grinning broadly too. "Poor Brooke and Philip!" I say. "Here they are getting married in October, and how in the world can they ever compete with our first grandchild? Our little redhaired, brown-eyed, sweet-smelling Dr. Adung!" Just then, my new little one baptizes me, squirting my chest and clean clothes with warm baby orangutan pee!

On this journey of letting go, each attachment leads to a new farewell. Leonora and I burst into tears as we say goodbye to our baby, who looks as if he fully understands that he's about to lose a mother, yet again. Wan Tu will stay with him, and tells us that he knows Dr. Adung will be very sad for several days, as he is very sensitive. Leonora and I cry even more and pray for his well being. We feel grateful that he is in the very good hands of FNPF staff, who seem genuinely devoted not to self-aggrandizement, but to responsibly repatriating orphaned orangs into a healthy natural habitat in the national park.

Further downriver in Pasir Panjang, we disembark and drive up a long, imposing driveway to the new, white-walled Galdikas Urgent Care Compound. Inside, workers are constructing another new building. Whatever is going on here, it's clearly well funded. A European woman in Indonesian dress sees us coming, turns on her heel and disappears. Leksmono tells the construction workers who he is and reminds them that this is Monday, visiting day. He explains that we're here to visit the facility and Dr. Simone, the new vet. But the workers have been instructed not to allow anybody in, and a standoff ensues. Leonora enters the fray, telling them that she was a major fundraiser for this project in England, and that she personally adopted one of their babies and has a right to see him.

Eventually, we wrest permission to walk around the immediate area. We notice bales of barbed wire awaiting installation. Why would anybody who is trying to protect orangutans put up barbed wire, which could easily slash their tender skin? We removed all the barbed wire fencing around the Twin Brooks pasture so none of the llamas would get hurt. This place has the eerie aura of a Columbian drug compound. I sneak out to the back and discover a huge cage with two orangutans inside. They look to be about eight to ten years old. Their feces are smeared on the floor of the cage and they are playing with a kitten, which looks like it is getting mauled. The sight is most disconcerting. We are not allowed to speak with Dr. Simone before we have to leave.

At the airport, we run into Roni again. She has succeeded in talking to Dr. Simone, but the encounter was disquieting. The formal awkwardness of their conversation unsettled her. Roni shows us an article from an issue of *Outside* magazine, written by Linda Spalding in 1998. On the plane back to Semarang, we pore over the article with rapt attention. It is an impressive piece of investigative reporting; at the same time, the documentation is sickening.

Spalding had wanted to write a book about Galdikas and had begun researching the esteemed primatologist, for whom she had the greatest respect. Before long, Spalding encountered the same strangeness we found in Indonesia, and through interviews, she pieced together the story that, as I had surmised, Galdikas, like Dian Fossey, had indeed "gone round the bend." Rather than continuing her work as a researcher, she left behind a sham operation at Camp Leakey and began adopting orphans, but not to release to the national park. She "released" them occasionally to her own private property at the compound. Her first husband left when she began sleeping with the apes. She then married a native Dyak man several years her junior and had two children by him.

When volunteer researchers came to Camp Leakey to do field studies, she permitted it, but cavalierly left their notes to rot in the kinds of cabins we'd seen the apes rifling for food. My clinical speculation about a paranoid decompensation appears to be confirmed. Leksmono's assessment of the parasitic/symbiotic relationship between Galdikas and the government is probably on target, as well. Donors all over the world, believing in a good cause, are being taken advantage of at the expense of innocent creatures they want to support. This is the sour, sad note on which we leave parts of our hearts in Kalimantan.

But Galdikas' decompensation, like Zoe and her asinine husband Bart's on Kilimanjaro, manifests the psychotic behavior of educated people, not of primitive tribesmen. I'm compelled to revisit a question that provided my greatest impetus to journey to the "back of beyond," especially our next destination, Irian Jaya. How do the primitive mental states of my seriously disturbed patients, which I've spent my professional life trying to untangle and heal, compare with the psychology of so-called primitive peoples? We are about to embark on a trek into the Baliem Valley among Stone Age headhunters. What will their psyches reveal? Are they psychotic? Are they impelled by paranoid fantasies to behead their enemies? Or is it something else entirely?

Galdikas' story seems to give testimony to a dysfunctional spiral of corruption and political collusion we've encountered throughout Indonesia. The opportunistic government here appears only too willing to collude with the situation. It brings to mind lines from W.B. Yeats' apocalyptic vision in "The Second Coming":

> Turning and turning in the widening gyre
> The falcon cannot hear the falconer;
> Things fall apart; the centre cannot hold.
> Mere anarchy is loosed upon the world,
> The blood-dimmed tide is loosed, and everywhere
> The ceremony of innocence is drowned;
> The best lack all conviction, while the worst
> Are full of passionate intensity. [10]

---

10 Yeats, W.B. "The Second Coming" in *Michael Robartes and the Dancer*. Dublin: Irish University Press, 1970 edition.

# CHAPTER 21
## IRIAN JAYA: A DREAM DEFERRED

IN 1961, the Peabody Museum of Harvard sponsored an expedition into the highlands of a virtually unexplored wilderness, the Baliem Valley of Irian Jaya. Two of the expedition's members made that journey world-famous: Michael Rockefeller, who disappeared mysteriously during the trek, and Peter Matthiessen, well-known author of *The Tree Where Man Was Born* and *The Snow Leopard*, who later published *Under the Mountain Wall*, a fascinating account about their expedition. Rockefeller, the trip photographer and a recent Harvard grad, never returned; some say he drowned in a wild river, but many feared worse. Our guide Leksmono, who has extensively explored the Dani, Yani, Yali, and Asmat tribes of that area, has reason to believe Rockefeller was eaten by the Asmats, a headhunting cannibal tribe living in forested lowlands along the southern coast of Irian Jaya.

I have harbored a dream to visit Irian Jaya since 1963, when I was an impressionable 21-year-old graduate student at Harvard and the Peabody Museum arranged a screening of Rockefeller's footage from the New Guinea expedition. The film revealed an extraordinary encounter with Stone Age people who had probably seen only a few, if any, white men. Sitting in a comfortable theater in Cambridge, Massachusetts, I was awed by footage of the small but fierce Dani people, naked men wearing nothing but penis gourds and a few feathers, who were clearly intrigued by the outsiders.

We were barely past the parochial and patriarchal 1950s, and the expedition was all male, so my dream to see Irian Jaya seemed unfathomable. I doubt that I would have scripted a drama in which I'd celebrate my 60th birthday fulfilling that dream while taking a sabbatical from my work as a psychoanalyst. But here I am! My heart is pounding as I peer out of the plane window while we drop out of the clouds to behold the verdant northern coast of Irian Jaya. It is beautiful. It looks like a sylvan and unpopulated piece of northern California coast. What is in store for us here? What has happened to the Stone Age culture that remained undiscovered until World War II, and in little more than a half century, has been exposed to "civilization"?

We land with a jolt in New Guinea, and Jim declares it the worst landing he's ever experienced. Shaken, I realize I have been savoring a dream of forty years ago. Much has transformed here since the Peabody expedition, and much is still transforming. We are in a 737 from Makassar, touching down on a modern landing strip. Although our Garruda Airlines tickets were written from Ujang Pendang to Jayapura, Irian Jaya, we find that on the same itinerary, we've flown from newly renamed Makassar to newly renamed West Papua. And a major American tribal custom surrounds us on the plane: we are in the middle of the Jayapura football team, flying home to West Papua as heroes from their latest victory over Manado in South Suluwesi. There isn't a penis gourd in sight; they are all wearing Nike shoes, Spalding T-shirts, and American baseball caps. However, the men are noticeably black and stockier than the Indonesians among whom we have been traveling. Papuans come from indigenous Irian Negritos stock, sharing a common origin with Australian aborigines who settled this Ring of Fire 30,000 years ago.

Irian Jaya, or West Papua, New Guinea, was fought over by a succession of Spanish, British, and German colonialists. It was officially annexed by the Netherlands in 1848 and held by the Dutch until Japan drove the Allies out during World War II. Before General MacArthur stormed the beach in 1944, the Dutch reclaimed it as their last bastion in the West Indies. As the land contains the world's richest copper deposits, oil fields, and important uranium, gold, and timber resources, the Dutch fought against relinquishing it to the new, post-war Indonesian Republic. No one ever asked the Papuans what they wanted. By contrast, after the war, the larger Papuan portion of the island of New Guinea was placed in a protectorate by Australia, which developed schools, hospitals, and roads, and helped the natives develop their government before granting them autonomy.

While the developed world has greedily fought over the natural riches of West Papua (or Irian Jaya as the Dutch call it), the ancient peoples on this part of the island have benefited little, if at all, from the occupations. West Papua's resources have been, and continue to be, exploited. Indonesians with whom they share almost no genetic or cultural commonality now colonize them. For these and other reasons, the West Papuans met in Congress last week, when Jim and I were exploring the depths of the Suluwesi Sea. They want to rid themselves of all colonialists. They are taking steps to separate themselves from Indonesia, work toward autonomy, and return to their own name for themselves, West Papuans.

In Jayapura, we are the hotel's only guests except for the Indonesian flight crew. We've been out of the world news loop for some time now, but on our arrival here, we learn that there is more fighting breaking out all over Indonesia.

In Aceh, Sumatra, fighting between Christians and Fundamentalist Muslims started over essentially nothing. Apparently a Christian driver hit a Muslim's car, the two drivers got out into the street, argued about whose fault it was, and drew a crowd. The ensuing fight escalated into a war. Most fights here are based in ethnic factionalism. In Fiji, all the tradesmen are East Indian, including one who was elected president; a native Fijian, George Spate, objected to the election, gathered an army, and is now holding the president in captivity.

Conflicts have erupted in Jakarta since we arrived, because student protesters spearheaded a movement to jail former Indonesian President Sukarno rather than allow him the comfort of house arrest. Meanwhile, an investigation is being conducted into the excess of four billion dollars he is accused of siphoning out of state coffers into his large family's extensive holding companies. So, for a variety of reasons, including one of the few forms of traveler's anxiety I don't fall susceptible to, most travelers have opted to be either elsewhere or at home watching CNN. This leaves the heart of West Papua undisturbed for our personal peregrinations.

As promised, Leksmono's Irian assistant guide, Marius, meets us at the airport. He will guide us throughout our time in New Guinea, first here in the capital and then deep into the heart of the Baliem Valley, where Michael Rockefeller disappeared. We feel an immediate connection with Marius. He is Molukun, from the most famous of the Spice Islands off the north coast of Irian Jaya. He is a gorgeous human being with a broad grin, dancing eyes, dark skin, and a sturdy bandy-legged body. Marius apologizes for his English, but he is easier to communicate with than our Suluwesi guide, the more educated Nadja. Marius is fluent in four of New Guinea's more than 250 different languages. He speaks Molukuan, Dani, Yani, and Lani, as well as the Indonesian taught in schools throughout the region, and some French and English.

We must wait until tomorrow for the local flight across the mountains into Wamena, at the head of the remote Baliem Valley, to see if any remnants of my dream can be found. At our hotel, we drop off our duffel bags and heavy scuba gear from diving in Suluwesi, and set out for nearby Lake Sentani, where we take a lovely sunset boat ride to the island of Aroyo to see the island women's traditional bark paintings. It is a sweet-scented lake and island marked by a large cross on the hill above the village. Aroyo villagers live in stilt houses at water's edge and work mainly as fishermen and artists on this clean and charming island. Their bark cloth is pounded and dried, then painted with organic dyes in black, brown, red, yellow, and white designs that are both traditional and individually inspired. Their fabulous creations are a little like the Tanah Toraja geometric designs and colors of North Suluwesi, but these also have animistic creatures woven into them.

When I discover that this uniquely beautiful form of bark art is done only here on this island, that there have been virtually no tourists here for a long time, and that the betel nut-chewing women are hungry and need to sell their work, I ask the price of a bark painting. A gorgeous bark cloth wall hanging is only 20,000 rupees, less than three dollars. I select six, which can be rolled up to bring home as gifts. Marius and Jim laugh about how women are born to shop. I am completely undaunted, and the three Aroyo women are as happy as I am—now they can finally afford to go ashore and shop for flour, sugar and other essential staples!

Sunday we are up at dawn for the flight over the mountains into Wamena, at the head of the 4,000-foot-high, 40-mile-long Baliem Valley. We are the only Europeans or whites on the small plane. Ascending over Jayapura, gazing over a landscape that could be Marin County, California—undulant green hills and ridges accentuated by stands of trees—I am delighted. When we disembark, we know we have finally arrived someplace far, far away.

The people here look totally different from people anywhere else in Indonesia. They're very dark-skinned with nappy hair and short stature. Their short, broad feet are heavily calloused from years of barefoot trekking, though some men now don sandals with shorts and T-shirts, and women wear skirts and blouses. Most of the men's teeth appear deeply stained from chewing tobacco or smoking cigarettes. Irian women's teeth, lips and tongues are stained Bloody Mary red-brown from chewing betel nuts. Though shy, they offer broad, infectious, red grins when I smile at them.

In Wamena, while preparing for our trek, we'll stay at Leks and Linda's small Balinese-style Sinakma Elok bungalows. They are an enclave of thatched-roof huts around a lovely garden of bougainvillea, hibiscus, cosmos, daisies, coreopsis, and a plethora of other native plants and flowers that lend the place a riot of color. We have the cottages all to ourselves.

As soon as we enter our bungalow we spot Linda's unerring artistic touch and Leksmono's ethnographic collection of art from the islands. The mosquito canopy bed is covered with Batik and Balinese pillows. The grass mat walls are adorned with beautiful Asmat carvings and masks. Grass skirts separate the sleeping room from the modern bathroom with toilet and hot shower, and lovely handwoven ikat textiles hang on the entry wall, beside carved gates to a sleeping bower. There are vases of fresh flowers and Javanese puppets hanging in the doorways with beaded and grass skirts. But we will have to enjoy the cottage's fine décor later; now it is time to go hiking to a nearby village.

Marius introduces us to two of Leksmono's helpers here, Sudi and Eli, young boy/men who soon ingratiate themselves with us. They will be among a large number of porters for our trek. Sudi is maybe four feet, nine inches tall and wears a Levi jacket and a baseball cap, all celebrating the hopefully newly identified West Papua. Eli is heavily into cigarettes, betel nuts and joie de vivre. He has a Papuan hairstyle involving a short bowl cut with locks spun into short spiky tendrils, making a remarkable halo around his face. Eli also under five feet tall, demonstrates his impressive strength when he carries all of Jim's 180 pounds, and then me, on his back across one of the dozens of streams and irrigation ditches along our hike.

It is Sunday, time for our Lariam, and that's good, for we are in malaria central. Many travelers who take the anti-malarial drug Lariam are rewarded with nightmares, vertigo, and even depressive or psychotic episodes. Fortunately, Jim and I discovered in Africa and South America that we can tolerate Lariam easily. We're glad we can stomach the preventive medicine, because malaria—with its high fever, sweats, and nightmares—would probably induce major depression. We remember the malarial curse that infected our guide and some porters when we climbed Kilimanjaro. So we've been taking every precaution, including vitamin B1 to amplify the sweat smell that we've heard mosquitoes don't like. We've dipped our entire travel wardrobe in Permethrin, a floral extract discovered by the military to be effective in repelling mosquitoes. Finally, we use DEET and wear long pants, socks, long-sleeved shirts, and hats. If any malarial mosquito penetrates that quadruple defense, we've at least done our best.

A fifteen-kilometer drive, west into the valley, leads us past a rich tapestry of daily life. Women carry babies, coconuts, piglets, tobacco leaves, cabbages, sweet potatoes, taro root, carrots, corn, or any combination of the above, inside hand-woven net sacks called *nokias*.

These sacks are worn with the handle over the brow, the weight borne by the head, down the neck and the back. To my surprise, I learn that one's back can bear considerably more weight if it is carried not knapsack-style, on the shoulders, but Dani-style, from the forehead.

### Lia Village

Leaving the vehicle behind, we head on foot for Lia village. Though only about an hour's walk off the Wamena road, the villagers had apparently never seen an outside visitor until Leksmono found and befriended them. Two years ago, he brought his wife Linda, who became the first white woman to visit the village, and our friend Dick Mobilio, the first white man. We will be their next white visitors. Marius tells us that the chief and Lia villagers have planned to welcome us with a feast and entertain us with singing and dancing.

We approach along a wooded footpath, climb the stile over a lashed bamboo fence surrounding an enclave, and call out to the thatched roofed huts encircling a central gathering area. We are met with uncanny silence. No one is here. The silence creates an unnerving pall. I feel the hairs rise on my arms, but don't know why. We have plunged so quickly from a familiar world into the unknown; once again, it feels like Alice's wonderland descent into an altered reality. We continue toward Lia village and eventually see a number of women bowed, their faces eerily covered with skeletally white clay masks, digging sweet potatoes in the fields. It is a strange juxtaposition of the strange and the familiar. They look downcast and do not want to be photographed. Marius speaks to them, and tells us that they have covered their faces in white clay as a sign of mourning.

Eli and Sudi trot ahead to alert the Lia villagers of the arrival of visitors, setting up a traditional "Whoop, whoop, whoop." We cross high above another stream, balancing precariously on a slender log, then arrive at the fence that surrounds the village. Sudi and Eli's calls are answered with mock birdcalls and whistles, and a few villagers quietly materialize, shyly smiling at us. We tentatively climb over one of the stiles made with notched trees, constructed to keep pigs inside the village. Lia villagers beckon us into their village commons. The chief, identifiable by his crown of red feathers, apologizes profusely for his tribe's inhospitality, explaining that a young man of his village passed away last night. The people cannot make a feast for us today as they are in mourning.

Through Marius, we extend our understanding and sympathy and ask if we might know who died and how. The chief explains that a youth, about thirty years of age, died a natural death. He mimics a kind of palsy, indicating that the young man died of a neurological disease. With a stab of recognition, I think of my nephew who is suffering from advancing multiple sclerosis. We ask if the man was married, and the chief says, "No. He had not married because of his condition." His parents both survive him and will be arranging the funeral. His body is resting in the eerily quiet village next to this one, awaiting the funeral cremation ceremony to be held tomorrow.

The Lia chief invites us into his hut, which is low-roofed thatch over a dirt floor, with four neat fire rings along its thirty-foot length. The chief explains that each ring is for one of his four wives. He asks if we would like to visit the women's hut across the central courtyard, and of course I would. Whereas the king's house is long and narrow with one door midway down each end, the women's home is a round thatched hut on stilts with a wooden, grass-covered floor. In the center, a single fireplace is covered with log framing where firewood can be dried above the heat of the coals.

Custom has it that a man sleeps with his wife until she becomes pregnant. At that point, she withdraws from his house and moves into the women's hut to sleep, birth, and nurse her baby until the child is weaned, typically at age three or four. At that point, she returns to sleep with her husband in the conjugal hut. This arrangement guarantees birth control for the tribe. It also explains why the king has four wives; he is assured of sexual relations with at least one wife at any given time.

After again expressing our sympathy for their loss, we leave the Lia villagers in early afternoon and walk through fields and streams while Eli and Sudi sing and laugh and make fantastic floral and leaf adornments for our hats. Jim hikes under a luxuriously leafy crown decorated with huge golden lilies. My hat's brim is a crown of yellow lupine-like flowers woven with tall, fluffy grasses, almost like pampas grass. It's great until I start sneezing uncontrollably, to the impish merriment of Sudi, Eli and Marius. I have no choice but to remove my hyper-allergenic crown. They resume boyishly joshing each other, whooping, making birdcalls, and decorating their nappy hair with leaves, feathers, and flowers. Their hair makes a much better flower holder than my short, straight, fine hair—which they are quite fascinated to feel, and which sends them into gales of giggles.

I ask our guides about the Lia village women who raised their hands in front of their faces today, ambiguously as if they both did and did not want me to photograph them thus? With shock and horror, I noticed how many women's work-worn hands were missing two digits on several fingers. Marius explains that although the government banned headhunting thirty years ago, and more recently banned finger amputations, both traditions continue in outlying villages. A child, typically four to eight years old, no doubt under intense tribal pressure, offers her fingers to commemorate the loss of a tribesman. Marius confirms that after the untimely death of the young man in Lia village yesterday, one of the girls of the village underwent such a mutilation this very morning.

I am appalled. I remember reading about this tribal custom in Matthiessen's *Under the Mountain Wall*. The girl child's fingers are lopped off, hopefully with one blow of a stone axe, at the second knuckle. To stop the blood, the finger is bound tightly in palm or banana leaves and elevated above the heart. The bandages, changed several times during the healing process, are stuffed with chewed pabika leaves to help deflect the pain. This knowledge doesn't deflect my pain and outrage as I think about the grown women who presented their hands to me to photograph today. Their faces bore enigmatic smiles, like the Mona Lisa. Were they proud of their sacrifice? Or did they sense that I would be a witness for the outside world of the story of mutilated womanhood in their culture? We have seen many of them digging for potatoes, using maimed hands as their only tools. The image seared into my brain and carried on film is horrifying.

I wonder if their black sister in California, Alice Walker, who has exposed African "female circumcision" as female genital mutilation, knows about this "memorial rite." I reflect on the intensity of my unexpected feelings, stirred by this experience in a Stone Age culture. I will have to try to calm down with John Muir's cautionary advice about traveling in the backcountry, which he learned from the Indians: to tread lightly, not even leaving the mark of your moccasins. *Slow down. These people have an intact culture that has survived since long, long before whites even thought about colonizing the Americas, let alone overpopulating, polluting and exploiting it.*

At the same time, it is impossible for me as a psychoanalyst to miss the significance of this tribal culture's enhancement of male genitalia with elongated gourds, juxtaposed with the castration equivalent of the females' lopped-off fingers commemorating the death of a male. Here, women are utter chattel, bought and sold with pigs. It is not psychotic, but it is surely primitive.

### Wamena Village Market

We intersect with the road and find our jeep waiting to take us back to the village of Wamena. After an impromptu lunch of noodles, rice, and vegetables at a small café, we return to Sinakma Elok bungalow for a rest. But we are more curious than tired, and Eli and Sudi agree to accompany us on a walk to one of the Wamena farmer's markets, which will be quieter today, as it is a Sunday. I love community markets; they're fascinating windows into the daily life of a village, offering a glimpse of what the local people eat and grow and how they relate to one another.

This market offers further confirmation that women bear the brunt of the labor in this primarily agrarian culture. Men till the fields, but women plant, cultivate, harvest, and carry enormous loads of produce to spread out on the ground in front of them at the market. We see little evidence of tools, and their hands, with fingers missing, are hardened and calloused from digging and carrying. The men gather to talk, and a few, carrying bows and arrows, have apparently been hunting and spear fishing in the river; they are selling freshly caught birds and fish.

The marketplace is abuzz with excitement about the unanimous decision of the National Congress in Jayapura to change the country's name from Irian Jaya, which is a reminder of Dutch rule, to West Papua, the name by which the people know themselves. As the Congress closed just yesterday, we see many delegates who have returned from the capital, dressed in native finery, spreading the good news.

The people want to declare independence from Indonesia but have learned from hard-won experience that this must be done in stages. They are tired of a central government that sells their precious natural resources to the highest bidders from all over the world. With a long history of government corruption during both Sukarno's and Suharto's long regimes, the people have come to be cynical of political promises. Foreign companies have paid fees to the Indonesian government coffers and undertaken huge gold and diamond mining operations. Strip mining and exporting copper, gold and diamonds at tremendous profit, they offer no benefit, not even decent jobs, for local people.

We see incontrovertible evidence of Pacific racism at work. While the indigenous people are Negroid in features and choose to maintain their rural Stone Age culture, they are looked down upon by Asian/Polynesian Indonesians who possess most of the government jobs and all the power. Chinese Indonesians hold the financial reins in businesses throughout the region.

While perusing the market, we meet a commanding young man wearing a magnificent feather headdress he has made to celebrate the Free West Papua movement. On the front of the headdress, above his brow, is the new flag of West Papua, a red, white, and blue design with stripes and stars. The flag is framed in cowry shells, the traditional currency here, and encircled with a bark frame into which is woven an array of beautiful feathers, including the prized black feathers of the dangerous cassowary bird. Collecting those feathers is a mark of manhood, as the flightless cassowary is capable of disemboweling a man with one swift kick of its powerful feet. At the apex of his crown are gorgeous, highly prized plumes of the rare bird of paradise, native to New Guinea. This proud young man and his feathery Free Papua crown are quite wonderful. As we continue walking, he falls into step, accompanying us as we tour the town and its water and power generating plant.

Since we are the only white faces in the village, we soon notice that we have attracted an impressive Pied Piper trail of children and the curious. The Papua patriot wants to sell me his magnificent crown to show and tell Westerners about West Papua's struggle for independence. All he wants is a modest four or five dollars for his efforts making a headpiece fit for a king. I know that this extraordinary plumage could not survive several airline flights, and reluctantly decline, though I take him up on his offer to photograph him, promising to show his image and convey his message back home.

By evening, after our perambulations through town with Eli, Sudi and the plumed Papua patriot, the word is out that foreign visitors are in town. When we walk outside our bungalow to the dining hut for dinner, a crowd of men awaits us with handcrafted wares. It is, as Dick Mobilio had promised, "incredible shopping." Each man has his own offering that includes well-worn necklaces of pig's teeth, boar's tusks, cowry shells and white beads, and bracelets woven of reeds, orchid fiber, and river fossils. Jim, who rarely perks up for shopping, brightens at the prospect of hunter-gatherer penis gourds for all his male friends back home.

Penis gourds have made *National Geographic* poster boys of the Dani, Yani, and Yali tribes of the Baliem Valley. Each tribe decorates its gourds somewhat differently, just as each tribe has a distinct language, with New Guinea boasting over 250 unique languages. We have been startled to see Dani men strolling along the roadside stark naked except for their feathered crowns and the long gourds or "horim" they wear to protect and dramatize their penises.

Darius explained how a man attaches his three-foot-long, ochre-colored, straight or curlicue gourd onto his penis, which is tucked safely through a hole into the hollowed large end. The man then ties a short loop of woven orchid fiber twine around one testicle. Another long loop comes out from the tip of the gourd and ties around his waist or chest, depending on the length of the gourd, so that it points heavenward at all times. The weather here is so clement that no further covering is needed. The larger Lani style gourds, open at the top, provide a kind of purse for cigarettes and other items. Before the night's shopping is over, Jim has chosen two splendid, well-worn penis gourds from the Dani tribe, but he will only be satisfied with what he likes to call the "party style," adorned for chiefs and elders with cassowary and duck feathers.

I have an inspiration for our daughter Brooke's wedding, planned for October. I had intended to wear a hand-dyed, dark-colored silk voile sheath as my mother-of-the-bride dress. While packing up our goods at Porto Marina, I found an old hat box of my mother's, which contained a snug 1940s black velvet hat, a "cloche" with bronze feathers rakishly set on one side above the ear. I thought such a smart and sentimental little hat might be just the touch for my wedding finery, but here, surrounded by exotic feather headdresses, I wonder: *How about a small cassowary wreath?* Unable to decide between cassowary and black rooster feathers, I settle on two wreaths to take home; the girls can help me decide. Unlike the proud Papuan's stunning headdress, from which exotic feathers shoot up two feet above the head, at least these flat wreaths can be carried. On the other hand, I have to wonder if I've gone round the bend. Wearing rooster feathers as the mother of the bride would be a major faux pas, but would an exotic cassowary wreath, so beautiful here, look absurd at home? Is this what happened to Birute Galdikas? I'd better keep my mind screwed on straight as we descend deeper into the jungle among even more primitive tribes.

I then make a highly ambivalent purchase: a small stone axe of the type used for amputating the fingers of a young girl when a tribe is in mourning. I make the decision reluctantly, but resolve to bring the axe with my photographs of maimed women, to bear witness to this primitive ritual.

# CHAPTER 22

## IRIAN JAYA:
## TREKKING INTO THE BALIEM VALLEY

AFTER A BLISSFUL ten-hour sleep in the mosquito-netted Baliem bower of our Sinakma Elok bungalow, we arise to a glorious sunny day. We have apparently become famous overnight. Word has spread of our purchases of penis gourds, nokias, feather crowns, and the stone finger axe, and as we head for breakfast, we are greeted by a chorus of singing, penis-gourded men waiting to show us their treasures. But by now, unfortunately for them, we are finished shopping.

I have been recording audio tapes of our travels thus far: the gamelan music and Kecak dances of Bali, the klotok chug-chugging upriver in Kalimantan, the whoops and hollers announcing orangutan feeding time in Borneo, my adopted baby, "Dr. Adung," sucking on my microphone as if it were a nipple, the songs of North Suluwesi guests at a wedding, and the funeral wailing of Taja Torajans. Here in Papua, Eli loves to make music and sing as well as play with the tape recorder, and his Lani buddies join him. Eli, Sudi, Wagmena and others from the Sinakma Elok staff, backed by a big morning chorus of tribal vendors, run to turn on my microphone and record themselves. When they are satisfied with the song, they learn how to rewind the recorder and replay the tape, and gather around to listen, oohing, aahing and laughing with delight, hearing their own recorded voices for the first time in their lives.

This gorgeous sunlit morning, we're setting out deeper into the Baliem Valley. We'll walk about fifteen kilometers, or ten miles, past many small mountain villages on the north side of the valley, to our destination of Ibiroma village. Leksmono and Marius have arranged for porters from the valley to help carry our gear. Led by Marius, our entourage includes not only Sudi and Eli but also a host of Dani and Lani porters and cooks, most ranging from eighteen to twenty-five years of age. Wearing black and red face paint and crowns of leaves, feathers, and flowers, they are gorgeous specimens of young manhood with fabulously colorful style—the real deal, not a Las Vegas facsimile. All naked except for their impressive penis gourds, they greet us with shy, wide grins.

The Lani tribesmen's gourds are different from the Dani; very large in circumference, some are four inches across and open at the top end. Seeing them makes me think of Fellini's 1960s film *I Vitelloni*, which portrayed young studs strutting about, exuding testosterone in their small Italian town. These Lani young studs wear armbands with ferns, flowers, and feathers tucked into them, and their penis gourds are bound up around their torsos with blood-red cloth sarongs and scarves.

Marius introduces us to our twenty-three-year-old cook, Pinius, a Lani tribesman who distinguished himself by regularly carrying twenty-five kilos on his small frame and was therefore promoted to chef for this trek. In addition to the six colorful Lani porters, plus Pinius, Eli, Sudi and Marius, there are also Wagmena and Geerson, a housekeeper and houseboy from Sinakma Elok bungalow. Because no tourists have visited the bungalows for ages, these two are bored and want an outing. Counting Jim and me, we make an unlucky thirteen, but that doesn't last long; after less than an hour, south of town, we are joined by more tribal travelers heading down the valley. The pre-departure atmosphere is ripe with festive anticipation.

Jim and I have changed as many rupiahs as we can into small bills. This means a small wad of 500, 1,000, and 5,000 Rp notes for anticipated goodwill gifts to people who let me make their portraits, as well as for shopping. We are carrying not much more than sixty dollars, which will prove to be ample. We set off in high spirits, wearing shorts and hiking boots and using our Leki hiking poles for stability, while most of the porters skip along the rocky terrain in bare feet or, like Eli, in well-worn rubber sandals whose outer sole has long since separated from the inner sole. For Eli, this offers an excuse to devise a new musical instrument. Whenever we stop for a rest, Eli takes his separated sandal soles and becomes the spirited percussionist of a makeshift trailside singing band.

We climb past Courima village, heading south above the Baliem River. New flower garlands and wreaths are made for our hats, and generous assistance is offered each time we cross a stream or a fence between villages. The hike is refreshing, and the crisp mountain air is welcome after weeks at sea level in high humidity. After two or three hours we reach Polimo, a missionary outpost with a grass landing strip and a few buildings. This will be our lunch stop.

Tatami mats are unfurled under a big tree and Pinius produces fried rice, fried egg strips and onions for lunch. The porters take this occasion to strike up the band while enjoying their ubiquitous smokes (we are traveling in tobacco and coffee country where both are grown and freely used). In a moment, Jim and I realize we are the only people eating. Everyone else entertains themselves, but without food. This is disconcerting. We have plates mounded up with more fried rice than we can eat, and they have none.

Then Marius approaches us apologetically, saying that the police in Wamena have radioed the missionary outpost to tell them that he must return for further questioning. This seems outrageous. He was detained for almost five hours in Jayapura with our air tickets and passports, securing our permits to travel to the interior. He spent another hour and a half this morning in Wamena, reconfirming arrangements that had been confirmed the day before. We'd asked him earlier about the detention in Jayapura, and in his typically soft-spoken and deferential way, he had suggested that the permits are issued to protect tourists going into the interior.

We understand wilderness permits. Before backpacking in the Sierra high country, we have to secure permits from forest rangers and tell them our route plan. Issued on a first-come, first-served basis, these permits serve multiple purposes; they confirm that fishermen have fishing licenses and limit overuse of any single trail system. If backpackers end up missing, the permit gives a clue as to where they were headed in order to plan a rescue. But here, if permits are meant to protect tourists from disappearing into the backcountry and a cannibal stewpot, it doesn't make a blink of sense for the Indonesian polisi to recall the expedition's only English speaker and leave two Americans alone in the outback with a retinue of naked tribesmen, knowing only a few words in Dani. We can say "lauk" for hello, greet a woman with "nayak," and offer "wa" for thank you. We also know "wa wa" for "very good," and "wa wa wa" for "thank you so much."

Polite, soft-spoken Marius is about to be heisted from us for no good reason. We ask him who these intimidating polisi are, and he reluctantly replies that they are largely members of the Indonesian government-supported exportation of Javanese to the unpopulated islands. They are functionaries who have been "deported," a real winning combination. Whenever they see a darker-skinned person, they feel they have license to harass, like the Ku Klux Klan in Mississippi.

This permit policy has nothing to do with protecting foreign tourists and everything to do with assuaging the pique of would-be bureaucrats deported from over-populous Java. No wonder West Papuans want independence from Indonesia! Marius does not dare cross the polisi. Jim says I like to push the envelope; I ask, "What would be the consequences of ignoring them?" Marius laughs nervously and gives the universal sign for slitting one's throat. Like it or not, he has to go back to the trailhead and give the Wamena Police more time and money, while we continue trekking into one of the world's last great wilderness areas without a guide. No problem.

In my past, this would have been an occasion for traveler's anxiety. Curiously, prior to our Middle Eastern trip I seem to have spent my entire "worry wad" with pre-departure anxieties about inconsequential issues like wardrobe and luggage. Now, when one might really have heart palpitations, I feel as cool as a cucumber. We are becoming more comfortable with the unknown curves of travel off the beaten path. We insist that Marius share our rice and take my halogen flashlight in case the police detain him for a long time. He heads back toward civilization while we head further away from it.

## Alone in the Back of Beyond

At 6,000 feet of altitude, we carry on toward Ibiroma village along a narrow track reminiscent of the Himalayas of Kashmir and the Andes in Peru. In these areas, you are relatively remote from modern civilization, but never far from human habitation. There are always herders or farmers, adults and children along the way to greet you with eager but shy curiousity. We swing along, our perambulations accentuated by the singsong of Eli and the porters. We pass pigs and piglets, many turnstiles and many more stream crossings, as well as an intermittent flow of tribal people on daily errands to and from other villages.

In mid-afternoon, Pinius approaches me on the trail, smiling. I discover that he actually speaks some English. He asks, "How old are you?" Rather than blurt out the answer, I remain quiet, to let him continue. "I think forty, maybe," he speculates. Whoa! I tell him that this trip is a celebration of my sixtieth birthday, just a few weeks away, and he looks amazed. Right here and now, I decide: *Carpe diem!* This day, this hike, this place is precisely my heart's desire for my birthday. I don't need candles or cake. I've got everything I dreamed of. The countryside is dramatically gorgeous. I'm coloring outside the lines, which I love to do. As far as I know, our children are thriving. I trust that my former patients are weathering their independence well. Our dog, Jullay, is in good hands at Twin Brooks with the ranch caretakers, and my newly adopted baby, Dr. Adung, is well cared for in the jungle of Kalimantan. Jim and I are fit, and we enjoyed another gloriously loving morning in our Balinese Baliem bower. I can't want for another thing. What a perfect day to celebrate! We sally forth in fine spirits, leaf hats bobbing, past every kind of penis-gourded male you can imagine. Not bad, in lieu of birthday presents!

During the trek, my narcissism fluffed up by Pinius' two-decade underestimation of my age, I think about his perception. I am blessed by genetics and a healthy lifestyle with a youthful demeanor; my father died at eighty-seven, his hair having finally just begun turning gray. However, it occurs to me that Pinius' reference point is the women he knows. The indigenous women are overworked field hands with mutilated digits and no fancy Smith & Hawken garden tools, unceasingly cultivating sweet potatoes, carrots, cabbage and pigs with nothing but their bare hands here on the steep slopes of this valley. While they eat vitamin-rich vegetables, their diet is shy on protein. It's likely that pig grease doesn't compare favorably with Lancôme for complexion care. The many women I'm taking to be grandmothers, carrying babies in their nokias, are probably mothers aged dramatically by excessive exposure to sun and overwork. Papuan women look at least twenty years older than women I know. My reverie makes me incredibly grateful for the freedom of choice, lifestyle, health, education and travel I have been granted as a woman.

Before we reach our destination, rain droplets start. But Pinius, our ad hoc leader in Marius' absence, indicates that we've almost arrived at a village, an enclave of thatched huts and missionary houses on the mountain wall. Rain starts pelting us heavily, stinging my cheeks and arms like little porcupine quills, just as Jim motions me inside a missionary house. Before long, the rain commences in earnest, and where we had walked in sunny ease, rivulets of mud and rock start pouring off the slope. But it's no worry; we've arrived at the home of the village schoolteacher and his family, who offer us refuge for a home stay.

The teacher's house has a tin roof, and I can't imagine how it got here, except by airlift. His hut is modest, but it's all we need to get out of the storm. Since we've arrived before dusk, there is time to sort out our packs in the waning daylight. I find a good corner in the teacher's modest house and enjoy writing for an hour or so. But before long, I am visited by the sick and the lame of our group. Word has spread that I am a doctor, since Jim often casually addresses me with, "How's it going, Doctor?" I note with fascination how quickly news travels in this non-electronic world! There's no point in correcting their fantasies about what kind of doctor I am, because I'm certainly the only doctor of any kind in the region.

### My Outback Medical Practice

Eli tentatively approaches with one of our porters in tow. It looks like he has sustained a nasty second-degree burn on his calf from the cooking fire. Could the "doctor" help? Although I try explaining to Eli that I am a head doctor, the magic operant word is still "doctor," and before long, I have set up a makeshift infirmary. I sit cross-legged on the ground in the last rays of the setting sun on the birthday of my dreams, doing what I love best; trying, if I can, to offer some healing.

This young man's burn is about four centimeters by one and a half centimeters. I clean it thoroughly with sterile wipes until the nasty, raw wound is clean. I swab it with Traumeel, a homeopathic painkiller, and then with antibiotic ointment, cover it with a sterile gauze pad, and tape the leg with adhesive. As the sun sets on my infirmary, I look up at my squatting patient, who faces me toe-to-toe in the falling dusk. He is a nineteen- or twenty-year-old tribesman wearing only feathers, his penis gourd, and a large white bandage. After I finish with him, others shyly show me their wounds and I dress them until I am almost out of adhesives, gauze, swabs, and Band-Aids. I should have brought more.

Eli gestures to his back, which he says is sore—no doubt from showing off his prowess when he carried Jim across the stream yesterday! I give him two aspirin and explain that it comes from a tree that helps ease muscle pain. He accepts them gratefully, and later lets me know through sign language that he feels better.

My last patient, Nali, is another one of the porters. He has stomach cramps, nausea, and diarrhea. It is interesting that local natives can be afflicted with microbes from the water, as we learned when our Suluwesi scuba diving buddy came down with the same Manado menace that I had. To Nali I dispense some Cipro and hope that by morning he'll start to feel better. I find myself reflecting on the power of belief in healing. Though I am not a medical doctor, they believe I have magic like their shamans and witch doctors, and they will probably respond well to my "medicine." I bow to the universe for the privilege of this extraordinary sixtieth birthday gift, the opportunity to help heal the wounds of these extraordinary young men.

Pinius and his kitchen crew serve dinner, but again only to us. Marius returns from his ordeal in Wamena, arriving just in time to ward off a cultural faux pas. Jim and I are about to insist that everybody is tired and hungry and we should eat together.

But Marius says that in his country, honored guests must always be served and finish their meal before anybody else eats. We feel awkward, but realizing that this is their way, consent to eating alone. The dinner is impressive considering that they have carried all the food and cooking gear on their backs. Pinius and his assistants have produced fried rice and eggs, steamed rice, potato fritters, vegetable fritters, and a rich vegetable stew, with only a single pot over an open fire on the earthen kitchen floor.

After dinner, our schoolteacher host lights a gas lantern and everybody else eats. We begin to accept their custom. Once the dishes are cleared away, it is about half past six, and I have an opportunity to write for a few hours. When my headlamp flickers, dims and goes out, I realize I am the only one still awake in the house. Marius has gone to bed on the floor in one corner, exhausted from his ordeal. The schoolteacher and his family are asleep in another room, and Jim has retired inside our tent, which the porters have set up inside the house because of the downpour. Marius has told us that we need the tent to protect us from malarial mosquitoes, which are so thick here. So the tent is a considerate touch, if a bit comical inside the house. We feel like kids playing camping.

### A Capella Testosterone Sing Sing in a Grass Shack

It is only 9:00 p.m., and I'm still feeling high from the hike, the countryside and the people when I hear the voices of porters coming from a grass hut behind the schoolteacher's house. I decide to take my tape recorder and see if they mind a visit. I climb up the ladder into the hut, finding it much warmer and cozier than the concrete block missionary house where we are staying. The grass hut walls and roof provide insulation, as does the grass-covered floor. The fire pit in the middle is glowing with coals, and I count a dozen men reclining in the firelight. None are wearing anything but their gourds, and in some cases, feather crowns. They smile and through gestures, graciously invite me in. After my brief interruption, they resume their sing-sing. Their singing is communal, the words and counterpoint known by all. They clearly love vocalizing and harmonizing. My arrival seems to give them a second wind, and when they see I am recording, they put on quite a musicale: "A Capella Testosterone in a Grass Shack."

The only nonvocal instrument in the hut is a solid wood ukulele. Penis gourds are being tapped to keep the beat. Each song starts when someone sings a refrain, which is picked up and carried contrapuntally. Other voices enter as the bass, and in many songs, one deep voice serves as a one-note drone. The music is repetitive, hypnotic, and haunting. When a song ends, there is a loud, appreciative "wuh!" intoned in unison, and then someone starts up a new song. In some ways, especially by the drone, I am reminded of medieval plainsong. I record for almost an hour in rapt pleasure and fascination.

In the middle of the sing-sing, it occurs to me that I am alone in the company of strangers, having just had the best birthday celebration I could have ever dreamed of. It has been a fabulous day, hiking in a beautiful mountain valley among interesting people. My dream deferred forty years has come true, and I am a very happy woman in this time and place. Finally tired, we all retire to bed as the rain drums endlessly on the tin roof. It is a good thing they have their cozy grass hut on stilts and we have our indoor tent, or we would have all camped in a torrent.

### Pigs Are the Coin of the Realm

Morning brings abatement of the rain. This is to be another trekking day, so we get up and ready, noticing that word of our arrival has spread via jungle telegraph. Ibiroma villagers bring whatever they think we might want to buy. There are pig's tooth necklaces, woven bags, decorated bones, tobacco, woven orchid fiber skirts, and penis gourds. Jim eagerly enters into a selection of penis gourds for more friends at home, and winds up with six thoughtfully chosen gourds to be rigged for sartorial scrotal use. Some are huge, some are curlicued, and some are decorated with feathers. The total cost for these fantastic gifts is 15,000 Rps, or under two dollars each, plus airfare. Other items, such as a child's woven orchid fiber skirt, seem to have inflated in price since Dick Mobilio was here, so I pass.

We commence hiking as the clouds part and the sun comes out. A wiry little old woman carrying a child runs along the path to catch up with us. She wants to sell me the skirt she has woven of orchid fiber. I had passed on it in the village, and she has now cut her price in half; we settle at six dollars. She is exuberant and shakes my hand in approval. It is so painful: three of her fingers are missing from one heavily calloused hand, and one from the other hand. How in the world has this old woman intricately woven such a beautiful skirt with only one finger and thumb on one hand and three and thumb on the other? And is she as old as she looks? Or is she my age, appearing twenty or thirty years older due to the extraordinary wear of her daily life? Ten minutes down the trail, I rue that I bargained instead of paying the twelve dollars she'd asked, probably as much as she'd see in at least a year.

Today's hike is on a higher and less traveled path than yesterday's. Quite rugged and often obscure, it zigs and zags, up and down, over ridges, down into valleys, across recently slashed and burned fields and others terraced and growing taro, sweet potatoes, carrots, cauliflower, gourds, and corn. The ridges all the way up from the valley floor have been intensively farmed, generally with two crops per year, as crop rotation permits the fields to rest and regenerate. All along the trail we see the tiny worker bees of the Baliem Valley. They're women, young and old, all slight and wiry. Their feet and hands—or what's left of them—are calloused from long barefoot walks over rocky paths, and from digging in the fields. Most wear well-worn, old, tattered skirts and no tops. They each carry two or three hand-woven string nokias over their brows, hanging down their backs, either empty or full of cabbages, potatoes, produce, babies, and or piglets.

Pigs are the coin of the realm and receive grand treatment. They are carried about as piglets and even nursed by women along with their human babies if a sow dies, leaving orphans. As they grow, piglets are marked in the ear for identification and given free reign over the family's gardening plots, together with a special hut called a "wamai," or pig hut, where the animals rest in the evening. Each plot is cleared of stones and divided by stone walls or wooden fences to keep the pigs at home. In addition to looking carefully to stay on today's trail, we also have to be alert for abundant pig poop.

We hike at a vigorous pace along ridges for three or four hours, covering seven or eight miles before stopping in a village to make lunch. Pinius buys fresh carrots, green beans, potatoes and onions along the way and makes an impressive "caplay" or stir-fry of mixed vegetables, served with fried noodles and fried potatoes. He accomplishes this all in one large pan shaped like a wok, over an open fire in an outdoor enclosure that serves as our host's kitchen.

While Pinius cooks, clumps of children gather to peer curiously at us. Many of the children have naked distended bellies, indicative of malnutrition and protein deficiency, and almost all have constant streams of snot from chronic respiratory infections. But they also have large, beautiful, brown eyes full of curiosity and wonder, and though shy, they delight in peek-a-boo, making faces, Jim's hand-slapping game, and my soap bubbles.

We observe the youngest baby's nursing and watch his mother's eye contact game with him. After his feed, she hands him off with a folded cloth under his bottom to his sister, aged only seven. His sister tucks him into her head sling and walks him to sleep. Women's work begins very early and seems unceasing here. Theirs are literally "hard rows to hoe." We see firsthand how women are the beasts of burden, the stoop labor and chattel. They are bought and sold for pigs. Pinius tells me he has already paid two pigs for his bride-to-be, but since he is prospering, her parents are keeping her until he offers up two more pigs. He matter-of-factly explains that he will just have to work hard to buy these two additional pigs, as they are worth two to four million rupiahs each.

Later, Marius gives us more subtext. It seems Pinius was with his wife for two years, but she ran away to her village, and now her parents are demanding more pigs to deliver her back. Marius has told him he's crazy to comply, and that they should give him back his original pigs since she ran away from him. Eli told him the very same thing last night in the sleeping hut. We add our voices to the chorus. It isn't fair for the wife's parents to up the ante two years later when their daughter runs away.

Regardless of how Pinius resolves his marital problems, it will be very difficult for him. Even though he has deservedly been promoted to head cook on this trek, he will have to make many, many more treks to earn enough to buy one pig, which will cost the equivalent of $250 to $500! Jim and I are clearly the only game in town, and the political situation is worsening by the moment in Indonesia; it is unlikely that he will find any work as a cook and guide in the foreseeable future. This makes the small drama that unfolds before us when we resume trekking even more significant.

As we climb the turnstile over a wall into a village, a man trots down the trail with a full-grown pig, front and back feet trussed, carried upside down on his shoulders. When we ask what's happening, Marius explains that the man apparently raped a woman in this village and the villagers have decided that he must pay her family a full-grown pig or risk banishment or worse. Take note: the fine is paid to the woman's father, not to the raped woman.

We continue hiking after lunch, passing villagers going about their daily business in both directions. More than a few times, we pass through villages where Christian missionaries have endeavored to "improve the lifestyle of the people" by building wood houses with tin rooves like the schoolteacher's house in Ibiroma village. But most remain unoccupied and the villagers shun them. Marius' impish grin gives away his prejudice against the self-importance of outsider colonialists, whether they are Javanese bureaucrats looking for wealth or Christian missionaries looking to harvest souls. He invites us to peek inside one of these missionary-built houses, and we see that the "improvements" are standing empty, while people are living cozily and comfortably in their traditional grass huts. Unfortunately, the sylvan landscape is marred by tin roofs on unused houses that will take ages to rot.

Swinging along the trail, I press Marius further. He tells me that he was raised a Christian and always bows and crosses himself before partaking of a meal, but he believes the missionaries are robbing an indigenous and stable society of its traditional ways. Convincing natives to give up cannibalism and digital mutilation can be argued as a plus, not only for victims' rights, but also insofar as it has stemmed the progress of a disease like Kuru, a fatal spongiform brain disease that wiped out natives, and that is spread only by the consumption of human flesh, as cited by scientist Jared Diamond. But it doesn't make sense to change people's customs of living, dress, language, and values just because you think your religion is better than theirs.

Beware the zeal of a former zealot. I observe my own judgmental reformist's tone on this topic, having once upon a time been fired with adolescent missionary zeal of my own. As part of my local Presbyterian Church youth group choir, I rode a bus from the privileged enclave of San Marino, California with a large sack of grass lawn seed bound for Chinle, Arizona. Our mission was to devote our Easter break to planting grass at the Indian mission there. Before we were done sowing seeds, a creeping doubt about the logic and validity of our efforts began to cross over me. First, we were in the desert, where a lawn made no sense. Second, these Navajo Indians had lived in their pueblos since probably 3,500 BC without lawns, and had not put in a request for the same. After returning from that misguided 1950s missionary effort, increasingly filled with doubt, I embarked on a fateful teen prayer retreat that culminated in the terminal crisis of my religious faith.

When our Presbyterian youth minister told an assembled group of high school girls first to walk into the woods and gather a pine cone, then later to throw our pine cones, symbolizing the cravings of our adolescent flesh, into a fire, he enjoined us to rid ourselves of the "sinful temptations of the flesh, which must be purified." It was still the dark Fifties and we lived in ultra-conservative Pasadena and San Marino, but the Sixties and college life at UC Berkeley were just around the corner, and I felt an incipient revolutionary surge brewing in my tender breast. My flesh was bona fide untouched and pure at age sixteen, but a voice from the other side of my genetic makeup balked at this act of religious compliance. If Little Lord Jesus loved me, as they kept proselytizing in Sunday school, why would he give me wicked flesh?

In a crisis of faith, I shuddered and resolutely turned away from the youth minister, the campfire and my peers, and headed off into the woods, refusing to burn my pinecone. My friends pleaded with me to change my mind, but I wouldn't budge. I would not burn my pinecone. I was subsequently counseled out of the teen retreat. When I returned from the retreat and told my iconoclast father, he applauded my spunk, raising a bourbon toast to my budding capacity for questioning authority.

By the time I entered Vassar College I had drummed myself out of the church, but not spirituality. I'd shifted toward my lifetime direction of irreverence combined with sympathy for John Muir's theistic belief that God is in every living plant and animal as well as every rock and grain of sand. All things great and small deserve human respect as sacred. Without recognizing it, I had already begun leaning toward a Buddhist philosophy.

Years later, in the same Santa Cruz bookstore where my nephew had come upon William Prescott's *History of the Conquest of Peru* and *History of the Conquest of Mexico*, I found an out-of-print book, *The Prescott Chronicles*, a literary saga of our Prescott family history. Bingo! Besides describing Prescotts as the Conservative Pillars of Everything Important, these chronicles also presented some Prescott radicals. They included northerners who helped slaves escape, and gifted visionary historians like the blind William Prescott who, way ahead of his 19th century cohorts, took the side of the indigenous peoples over the Conquistadors, writing sympathetically in his famous histories of the Mayans and Aztecs in Mexico and the Incas in South America. I took considerable cheer imagining that my great-great-great-great-great-granduncle Prescott had paved the way for my own ethnographic explorations.

### A Baliem Dream Dreamed

Such are my musings as the sun sinks lower and lower toward the horizon, illuminating the Baliem Valley's hills, trails and stiles with a magical golden glow. This night, I have a dream that may be prompted in part by these musings. I dream of a woman whose professional life has threaded through mine. I met Helene at Beverly Hills High School, where I was teaching and she was a guidance counselor. Later I taught at the middle school where she had become principal. We met again when Jim was Senior Vice President of a bank in Beverly Hills and was expected to attend civic functions and black tie charity events. Helene had married a prominent surgeon and had been elected to the school board. She was on the same rubber chicken dinner circuit as we were, and we enjoyed catching up again. Finally, Helene and I met again when both of us, by then Doctors of Psychology, were in clinical practice and she had been elected President of the Los Angeles Psychological Association. I have always liked and admired her. In my Baliem dream:

*Helene appears as an official functionary of Beverly Hills, asking me to be the marshal in a civic parade. I agree, but am distressed to discover that I am airborne and viewing the parade below me. But it is floating above the city too. Floating past is a bed on which there are two young men whom I recognize as fairy tale characters, maybe Winken and Blinken of "Winken, Blinken and Nod." They are wearing nothing but stocking caps and penis gourds, and I know they are nice Beverly Hills Jewish boys who have been my students. No sooner have I recognized them than I begin to worry about what is keeping me aloft. I have a vague sense that I am in another of my flying dreams, but I soon touch down gently.*

*Next, I am swept into an underwater museum in which there is a dramatic performance by colorful underwater Balinese puppets. I swim through galleries, down a tunnel, and through a small door somewhat like Alice's door in Wonderland, and find myself emerging from the stage door of a very luxurious, plush, seated theater. The audience is waiting expectantly in their seats. Not wanting to be obtrusive, I begin creeping up the aisle toward the back where there might still be empty seats.*

*Creeping up the aisle, I am met by a fantastical creature, a perfectly wizened little man with bright eyes and tiny hands. He has sought me out and seems to be beckoning me to him, almost like a shaman. I make my way toward him as he reaches out his hand. Then, with an impish grin, he flips over, presenting his bottom, and emits a flood of pee and little rat-sized turds that soon became a river running down the aisle. He is delighted by his performance and my chagrin and humiliation.*

When I wake up and tell Jim the dream, he laughs and laughs. He may not be trained in deep psychoanalytic interpretation, but he's on target with what psychologists call "day residue"—images from the previous day that lodge in the unconscious and make their way, barely disguised, into our dreams. Right away he says, "Oh, you were thinking of the trail and the streams of pig poop." Yes, probably so.

I think the flying parade marshal echoes my anxious disquietude about being too powerful as a privileged American tourist, perhaps flying so high as to imagine that the fates have convened to provide me with a serendipitous birthday sing-song on the trek. Maybe it also reflects my anxiety about being the omnipotent observer-writer in a place and land belonging to others. My fear of a crash landing gets my attention as I reflect on the dream. But as a counterbalance, perhaps the figure of my friend Helene, who has been so successful at everything she's taken on, is a reassurance that it's okay to aim high and give expression to your dreams and ambitions. Besides, we share the same initials: H.W.

The underwater Balinese puppet show I recognize as the fabulous display we enjoyed when scuba diving in the North Suluwesi Sea. The theatrical setting may represent my experience as a wide-eyed traveler awed by the drama and construction of meaning in this very foreign culture. The debacle in the theater may be a humbling revisiting of my own arrogance in assuming that this extraordinary small creature would be a shaman offering me some kind of transcendent moment. I think about the many tiny, bright-eyed, very wrinkled people I've smiled at, shaken hands with, and exchanged "lauk" and "nayak" greetings with along the valley. What are they really thinking? How do they view me? Am I the monkey?

This association also reminds me of Eli singing a song as we walked together, counting on me to join in the repetitive chorus. When I did, however, Wagmena literally fell down laughing. She collapsed in gales in the middle of the trail and could not speak, and I knew Eli had played a major trick on me. What bad word had I been tricked into saying? When I asked Marius, he too convulsed into giggles, but said that he just couldn't speak the word.

Along similarly humbling lines, my last association is that the little dream critter is Dr. Adung with his adorable wizened face and perfect little hands and feet. He surely reached out to me, and I, carried on waves of euphoric transport, embraced and adopted him. And my little baby buddy peed on me ceremonially after his baptismal bath.

My Baliem dream reminds me of the importance of humility in traveling. Just as I once set off as a missionary with grass seed to Chinle, Arizona, what unexamined but warped assumptions might I be carrying now? Back then, we thought we had answers. Now, I come mainly with questions. My questions tend to cluster around the cultural wherefores of everyday life, government, decision-making and education, and issues relating to gender, class and culture. As I think about my dream, one question arises in particular. Clearly, the culture of psychoanalysis supports the idea that dreams are communications from the unconscious, usually relating to wishes, fears, anxieties, and conflicts. They often address aspects of the self that may be socially or personally unacceptable; for example, in my case, omnipotence. How do the Dani, Lani, and Yali people view their dreams?

On the next day's trek, I seek out Titus, who speaks a little English. He tells me that dreams are very important to his people, particularly when they trouble the dreamer. While children's dreams tend to be viewed as expressive of typical childhood fears of such dangers as cassowaries, snakes, wild boars, and the like, adult dreams are often felt to be portentous. They are enough to send the dreamer to a shaman in search of dream interpretation. The dream interpreters of the Baliem Valley are the village's healers or witch doctors. They usually receive their training when they appear promising to the old witch doctor, who looks for gifted successors to train first in his own family and village and then in the tribe at large. The witch doctor interprets the dream's portents and may administer homeopathic treatment if necessary. Both men and women avail themselves of the witch doctor's services and payment generally follows according to the usefulness of the doctor's interpretations and the efficacy of his herbs.

Titus imagines that in my culture, I am a shaman. That's food for a new omnipotent fantasy, which, in the spirit of letting go, I'd best release right away. Humility is the exquisite message of this journey. I explain to Titus that in my "village," witch doctors like me are paid for our time, regardless of the outcome. He diplomatically replies that every culture is different. I can't help but think of the pandemonium that would ensue if I came home preaching a change of fee structure among health practitioners dependant upon the success of the treatment.

# CHAPTER 23
## PAPUAN POLITICS, SALT, AND TRICKS

TODAY'S TREK is at Jim's request. His scientific curiosity is piqued. It's as if he's read my mind. I want more of this adventure. How did ancient people satisfy their need for one of most life's most essential substances, salt? In the morning, we head out in the direction of the very wall Peter Matthiessen made famous in *Under the Mountain Wall*, his account of the Peabody expedition's six months in a Dogon village. We will climb the mountain path to find the salt pool Matthiessen described and Rockefeller photographed, where women gather salt as they have for millennia.

We are told the hike will last only an hour or two, but we soon learn it is much slower, up a steep, rocky, slippery trail where frequent rains keep the muddy path slick. In addition to the support of my two Leki walking sticks, we gather a small entourage of friendly, very curious women and children who help Eli assist me at the least sign of loss of footing. I find myself so swarmed with well-wishers that it is actually more difficult to ascend the mountain. Jim and Marius, who love to get competitive, take off up the mountain like a pair of racing goats, ignoring the mud leaving me tangled in a pod of earnest women and children. Not to worry; I am in my own delicious if muddy reverie, celebrating this ongoing fulfillment of my dream.

Farther up the mountain, we come upon two old men tending a fire by a stream. What strikes me first is not their penis gourds, which my eyes would have been drawn to when I arrived in the Baliem Valley. No, I notice the remarkable evenness of their front teeth. It appears they have been filed to perfect smoothness. I realize that this is what happens to teeth that have been used for a lifetime of cutting, grinding and chewing. They have worn into a short, perfect, even cutting edge.

Eli talks to them and tells us that one of the men, Ushia, is the patriarchal custodian of the salt pool for his village. For these inland landlocked tribes, territorial domain over the region's one major salt pool is more valuable than gold, so Ushia wants to know our business. Though I don't see anything change hands, I imagine a token toll is paid and stored in the only place Ushia can deposit it, his Papuan bank account, the security of his penis gourd. With Ushia as our guide, we have a formal escort and my posse of followers drops away.

Ushia and his silent partner are eager to talk to Marius and Titus, as they have news. The Indonesian government wants to build a guardhouse at the salt pool. Ushia and his tribe are offended by the idea, as they have successfully guarded their territorial domain for centuries with daily patrols along the trail. They are deeply and rightfully suspicious of the government's motives and have called a meeting of the head chiefs of the Yalis, Danis, and Lanis, who all depend on this salt. Yesterday the chiefs met, smoked, and agreed to take a united stand against the construction of a guardhouse. Through Titus, we tell them that we think they are wise to protect their traditions from the cupidity of the corrupt Indonesian government.

## The Stone Age Customs of Salt Gatherers

Slipping and sliding up the muddy mountain path, we occasionally see women heading down the trail with banana-leaf-wrapped parcels strung on poles. We learn that the women are returning from salt gathering. Finally achieving the mountaintop, we enter a fairly large clearing in the forest, facing a pool eight to ten feet across, full of milky water. This is the heavily salinated water from the same natural spring that Matthiessen visited and described in his book forty years ago!

Two beautiful, pendulous-breasted young women arrive, wearing only beaded pelvic girdles, which indicate they are married. They are joined by a young, firm-breasted, unmarried girl, her hips wrapped in the traditional maiden's grass skirt; all three, topless, are wearing orchid fiber nokias secured to their brows and hanging down their backs. The young girl's nokia contains a sleeping piglet; she is the keeper of her family fortune.

They have climbed up from Sumpaima village to gather salt, and Ushia invites us to watch and learn their millennial salt gathering technique. From below, they have gathered and carried leaves and stalks from banana trees for the project. First, bending in consort around the edge of the milky pond, they scrape a reddish coating off the stalks with bamboo knives and then begin peeling the stalks, which come apart in cylindrical layers like hearts of palm. When they've peeled all they need, they take them into the pool and stand knee-deep in brine, crushing the fibrous layers.

At this point, fascinated but reticent, I am emboldened enough to ask in sign language if I may join them in their work. The two married women smile shyly back, indicating an affirmation that it will be okay. So the three of us bend together to the task of crushing and wringing the banana plant fiber into a pulp and dropping the pulp into the pool where it floats, absorbing the salty, briny liquid. Once all the pulp is beaten, given time to absorb the salt, then wrung out, they put a chew of the fiber in their mouths and contentedly suck the salt from it. When they offer me a chew, I find myself up in a cultural tree. These timid aboriginal sisters have been very hospitable to me, and on that count, I should clearly accept the offer. On the other hand, this pool looks like a more extreme breeding ground than the polluted Manado harbor in Suluwesi, where I recently got sick. I take the tiniest bit to taste, smiling a bit too broadly in gratitude and praying that the microbes that brought me down in Suluwesi do not like salt.

It appears I have tiptoed across the cultural bridge satisfactorily enough. Now it is time to bundle the dripping salty pulp in banana leaves to carry home. Once our parcels are assembled, wrapped, and tied to bamboo poles, and we've taken just about all the photographs we want, Marius explains that when the women return these soaking bundles to their village, they will spread the pulp out on their thatch rooftops to dry. Then they will burn the leaves and collect the salt-drenched ashes as their life-giving salt source.

The younger girl in the grass skirt, who is far shyer than the two matrons, comes forward from the bank to tentatively show me what she is carefully carrying in her nokia. Nestled among the leafy greens lining her sack is a tiny piglet. I am delighted to meet such a petite piglet, and understand why young girls enjoy carrying them around like kittens or puppies. In no time, the piglet is nestled in my lap making little grunts, while his corkscrew tail spins around like an excited whirligig.

I'm stirred to wonder: *Was my dream prescient? Was this charming piglet the little creature beckoning to me? And if so, am I about to have piglet poop or pee deposited on my hiking trousers?* I take this thought as a sign to return the little piglet to its caretaker, and the animal nestles comfortably in its nokia nest again. One of the married ladies bashfully indicates that I might like to buy one of her large net nokias. With hand signals we settle on a price of 20,000 Rps, between two and three dollars. It is hard to fathom that such handiwork goes for so little. But Marius has guided us to enter into traditional negotiations and to understand that we are among the rarest of visitors to this place and our cash is very valuable. Once a price is resolved, my new friend shakes my hands warmly, and I tell her, "Wa, wa, wa," while feeling the stubs of two of her fingers in my hand and realizing that as a young girl, she was chosen to honor a dead warrior with her fingers.

We traipse together back down the muddy trail, she to her village with brine-soaked leaves, no doubt happy with the coins she has received, and I to join Jim in our mosquito-netted Baliem bower in the Sinakma Elok bungalow in Wamena. After twenty rugged miles of walking, having made a full circle trek and feeling much more deeply linked to the peoples of the Baliem Valley, we welcome a shower and a bed for sleeping. We've had far more than just a good climb.

### Headhunting, 21st Century Style

Our last day's plan is to visit Jiwika village near the mountain wall. Leksmono has prearranged this visit with his adoptive father, the village chief, a charismatic Dani leader known as Yali. Partly accessible by jeep, Yali's village is north of Wamena and not far past Dogon village, where the Peabody expedition camped. The route to Jiwika is a stretch of the 600-kilometer dirt road now under construction between Jayapura and Wamena. The road has been under construction for eight or nine years, and probably won't be finished for another three or four years, because every monsoon season, most of the previous year's work washes out. It is hard to imagine that transit on this long bumpy road through malarial highlands would appeal to anyone. Having nearly worn the enamel off my molars bumping across the trans-Tanzanian highway, that person would not be me.

After a couple of hours, we bump to a stop at a turnoff and start trekking into the forest toward Jiwika village. A few paces into a large, open field across a stream, we hear a great "Whoop!" and look up to see a huge wooden lookout tower looming over us. A small, athletic, wiry warrior is shouting from the top landing brandishing bow and arrows; his face is covered in black paint and a long boar's tusk inserted through his septum adds to his fearsome demeanor. He appears to be calling to the village, warning of our arrival. In no time, the grassy field is swarming with painted warriors with bows, arrows and stone knives, standing off against each other in an opposing phalanx. There is a sudden war cry and they charge, hooting and feinting. My adrenaline coursing, I gaze back up to the tower and raise my camera, focusing, ready to shoot. The lookout sees me photographing him and scrambles nimbly down from his tower, running toward me while drawing his bow and aiming an arrow right at my eye. Through the viewfinder of my Nikon, I see him ever closer, menacing me.

It is utterly unnerving to be charged by a Stone Age man with boar's tusks through his nose, his face and body black with pig grease, and his impressive penis gourd tipped in feathers. The lookout looks very pissed off. I stand my ground with the improbable thought that if he does shoot, my camera will take the arrow, not my eye. If he gets me, I will go down with this one great photograph in my Nikon.

Seeing me unfazed, he turns and charges Jim. I just have time to note that Jim has not leapt in front of me to shield me from danger.

In fact, he seems to have fallen behind me. I quickly store this information for some future marital altercation, but soon realize that Jim is taken aback by the charge. For an eternal moment, we both hang there, when suddenly the warrior stops in mid-charge, his arrow poised three feet from Jim's heart. That moment is indelibly imprinted not only in my camera, but also in my own pounding heart. Then, frozen in mid-assault, the man starts to grin.

It turns out to be Chief Yali himself, Leksmono's adopted father! Like Coyote or Kokopeli, he is a major trickster. We realize that Leksmono probably pre-arranged all this with his adoptive father for us. Jim and I both draw our cameras again and now actually enjoy taking aim right back. Meanwhile, in the big open field, the battle continues with each side menacing and rushing the other amidst shouts and whoops and great posturing. The war paint is quite fantastic. Most of the men are decorated with white clay, applied with great individual style. One man's upper body is covered with white dots, his eyes ringed with white and his lower half white-striped. Another's dark naked body is covered in white clay handprints, obviously applied by one of his kinsmen. They all have great and varied feather headdresses, and we can see that our Dani guides' and Lani porters' love of crowns, decorative feathers, leaves, grasses, and flowers is shared by the Dani men of Yali's village.

While the real mortal battles that occurred until forty years ago have been banned by the Indonesian government, tribes still periodically engage in mock ritualized and choreographed battles—testing their prowess with spears and bows and arrows, solidifying tribal honor and the warrior code without killing an enemy. Although the government's ban is ostensibly humanitarian, apparently there has been misogyny and rarely reported political genocide of these tribes to keep their populations well under control so that actual war is no longer functional. A new and far more insidiously dangerous enemy, the Indonesian government, has been identified.

I see Eli gesturing and laughing. On the sidelines he gestures toward a young boy who seems to be having trouble keeping his penis gourd on straight. He looks to be about ten. He's probably only recently graduated from the simple training string that little boys wear with small half gourds until they graduate to the full-length gourd, which is long enough to be tied from its tip to the waist. This young warrior, deeply mortified, has had to retreat from the battle to fuss with his string. Finally he gets it sorted out and rejoins the fray, but not without providing us with considerable merriment as the giggles spread from Eli to Marius to Titus, Geerson, Sudi, Jim and me.

We learn that the tribesmen are just as humiliated and embarrassed about losing a penis gourd as any city dweller would be ashamed to have his or her pants fall to the ground on a busy street. This embarrassment is palpable with the young boy. We realize that in all our days trekking on the trail, though Jim and I have taken to the woods to heed nature's call on several occasions, we've never noticed our guides or porters heeding the call. They are extremely modest and private. Reflecting on the separation of husbands and wives into different huts during pregnancy, parturition and lactation, and the huge pig fine levied against the man who slept with a woman of another village, we realize that these "primitive" people are considerably more modest and sexually restrictive than people in our culture. Westerners wear more clothing and are shocked to hear of the "penis gourd" culture, but they indulge in sexual peccadilloes and pornography.

### Yali's Village

The exuberant whooping and charging subside, and Chief Yali beckons us to follow him and the sweat-drenched warriors off the field. They lead us along a jungle path into their village compound, where women and children, also decorated, have been awaiting our arrival. A group of white-painted Dani women approach me. One small woman leans down behind me, thrusts her head between my legs, and stands up, suddenly propelling me onto her shoulders. Speechless and breathless, I'm borne aloft on her shoulders into a procession of women marching around the village, chanting and singing. They seem even more delighted when I do my best to sing along; as I've become familiar with the chant and recitative reply, I can sort of keep up. After half a memorable hour borne on these small but sturdy shoulders, singing and parading, I am gently released to the ground to continue on foot, round and round the village.

I catch Jim's eye on a pass. We're both clearly transported by this show for our benefit. When we ask how long it has been since the tribe has put on such a display for guests, Yali indicates it's been several seasons. In astonishment, we calculate that the last time this tribe greeted outsiders was probably for Mobilio and company, who were here a few years ago on Leksmono's visit to his adoptive father's village. Knowing this, we feel free to cut loose and let it rip with the dancing and singing that ensues. Now that we've learned that they really are genuinely celebrating our arrival, and haven't had a pig feast like this for more than a year, "dancing with headhunters" clearly trumps dancing with stars. We totally savor it.

After the dancing and singing, the young boys chase a pig. The little porker gives them a real chase by scrambling over the turnstile and escaping outside the village. Having recently cuddled a baby pig at the salt pond, I'm silently cheering on the escapee. Finally, however, with the whole adolescent contingent of the village on his tail, the miscreant pig is captured and brought back to the encampment. One young man takes its front legs and another its wiggling hind legs, stretching it out squealing until Chief Yali takes aim and thrusts an arrow through its heart. After it falls limp, it is placed on banana leaves and prepared for butchering.

I have a hard time with the death. On the other hand, what follows is so strangely fascinating and seems so natural to the villagers that I have to suspend my inclination to look askance at the carnage. I also have to realize that one pig has been sacrificed for this feast and divided among the whole village for a rare occasion; it has been seasons since the last such feast. This is infinitely more parsimonious than our Texas-style barbecues, McDonald's gazillionth burger, or the acres of plastic-wrapped pork chops, bacon and tenderloin in most major supermarkets.

The honor of butchering the pig is ceremonially bestowed on two young men and one older man. Their only tools are a stone ax and three bamboo knives, razor sharp. First the ears and tail are excised and removed to a banana leaf pouch to be stored in the chief's hut with the village's ceremonial archives. This is the method they use to keep track of how many pigs have been ritually killed over the years. Nearby, another young man starts a huge fire in the Stone Age way, pulling a rattan cord back and forth quickly through a groove in a piece of wood, which is held over dry grass. Smoke appears from the friction for a fraction of a second, then sparks, and finally the dry grass bursts into flame.

Someone carries clumps of burning grass to the men and women's sleeping huts to rekindle the fires that will keep the people warm tonight. Others carry big clumps to another part of the common area, to the waiting huge pile of volcanic rocks, wood and grasses. Before long, a bonfire is roaring; the pig's bristles are singed and its skin is scraped clean with a bamboo knife.

Next, the three chosen males carefully butcher the pig, working over a pile of leaves to catch the blood. Though their noses are twitching with hunger and excitement, most of the village dogs have learned to keep clear of the carcass. Two young puppies that have yet to learn appropriate canine decorum stick their noses up into the leaves before earning an unceremonious removal by their ears as they yelp. After a couple of forays and removals, the puppies learn to keep clear of the butchering. After the pig has been gutted, the innards are taken to the stream to be washed. The heart and liver are wrapped in banana leaf packets and set aside.

When the mounded volcanic rocks are hot, an amazing feat of tribal cooperation unfolds. The men have already dug a pit near the fire, while the women have encircled it with bunches of leaves tied in bundles. Then the women arrive with net nokias full of freshly dug and washed sweet potatoes. They line the pit with the leaf bundles. Using long ironwood tongs, all the villagers—men, women, adolescents, and even younger children—carry hot stones from the fire to line the pit. They follow a carefully orchestrated pattern, arranging leaves, hot stones, leaves, potatoes, leaves, stones, leaves, potatoes and so on, until the pit is full and all the potatoes have been placed in the pit and covered with big leaves. Water and more wet leaves go over the whole heap.

The steaming mound is topped with the pig and the banana leaf packet containing the heart, liver and innards, then another layer of leaves and hot stones. More hot stones are carried swiftly but amazingly, without one error. Finally, the entire mound is covered in long, damp, wild grass cuttings and encircled with long coils of rattan. This archaic choreographed tribal ritual ends with a whoop of approval. "Wa! Wa!" Satisfaction seems to permeate the whole village. It has all been accomplished by barefoot adults and children in a veritable beehive of high-risk activity; miraculously, no one is burned.

Everyone relaxes as the feast cooks, and we have another opportunity to observe the warmth and gentleness of parents and siblings for younger children and babies. Chief Yali proudly introduces us to four of his six beautiful children, ranging from a two-year-old to teenagers. We also meet Maio, Yali's wizened, blind father who looks to us to be well over a hundred, but is only about seventy. Yali, who looks seventy, is probably only about forty-five, the same age as his adopted "son," Leks. No one, including Yali or his own father, knows or cares what age he is. These people are not interested in clock time at all.

They really do have the gift we westerners are striving for, the capacity to live fully in the present moment. The guessing of my age at forty begins to be contextualized. Due to the difficulty of their lives, adults here look decades older than most in our culture. For me to internalize their native gift of living fully here in the present moment, I have to consciously breathe, meditate, and focus on what I am feeling, seeing, hearing and experiencing here and now. My mind wanders to another dream, my desire to spend part of my sabbatical in a Zen Buddhist monastery with Zen master Thich Nhat Hanh. But there I go, "planning" the future rather than paying attention to this remarkable moment.

We meet Yali's four wives. Two are Dani, like him; one is Yali and wears a grass skirt in her people's tradition. The other is Lani and wears a woven orchid fiber skirt. The Dani wives wear beaded girdles like the one used by the tribe to garland Leksmono's bride, Linda, for her wedding. We also meet Natalis, a handsome young warrior in splendid war paint with a pair of impressive boars' tusks lacing through his nasal septum. He wears them turned upwards, indicating he is friendly. He knows Marius, Eli and Titus well, and has been eagerly awaiting our visit. Natalis, too, was trained as a guide by Leksmono. But because there haven't been any ethnography-seeking travelers for a long time, there has been no guide work. Natalis has doffed western t-shirt and shorts, donned bones and feathers, and returned to the traditional life he knew amongst his tribe in Jiwika village.

Natalis knows English fairly well from studying with Leks and is a welcome fount of information. He proudly tells us that he has already purchased two wives for a total of five pigs. But both his wives are preadolescent. One, he tells us, doesn't even have breast buds yet, so he is waiting for them to come into bud before they begin married life. Jim inquires of Chief Yali about this arrangement. Yali explains that more and more young women are "running away" from tribal life and heading toward Wamena to look for work. Apparently, the girls have hopes of finding jobs like the one Wagmena was lucky enough to land at the Sinakma Elok bungalows. Working at Leks and Linda's bungalows with all one's digits intact is a far easier life than the life of a traditional village wife. In an effort to keep his tribe together, Yali is arranging marriages of younger and younger girls. This seems like a thumb-in-the-dyke effort. We realize that we are witnessing the end of an era as this Stone Age culture disappears within half a century of its discovery.

Once again, I feel ambivalent. While these villagers clearly enjoy the stability of their tribal life, the fact that women are being bought and sold for pigs seems horrendous to me. Many of the women in the village shyly approach me now, grinning through missing teeth to show me over distended bellies how they hold their cigarettes between finger stumps. No wonder the younger ones run away. I feel a profound inner conflict between the values of the cultural anthropologist, whose role is to observe without judgment, and the feminist activist who sees her sisters oppressed and in pain.

We enjoy more conversation with Yali, whose hospitality is generous and whose showmanship is almost legendary with the fortunate few who have been his special guests. Yali's enterprising idea of bringing his village together as a kind of living anthropological museum is impressive. Leksmono, a world-savvy ethnologist, has arranged for his "father" to be a guest at the University of Chicago, where he will have the opportunity to explore with scientists how they might document his culture and he might save it.

We enjoy talking to Natalis and Yali, but it is getting late and the sky is threatening rain. Maio, Yali's blind father, has been shaking his fist at the clouds, telling them to go away. There is just time for the villagers to invite us to peruse their handicrafts. Whereas I've come to regard the men who cluster around our bungalow with made-for-tourist trinkets as tsetse flies, this modest capitalistic enterprise offers us an opportunity for cultural exchange. We are invited to select special objects that have been used by these people in their daily lives, and whose purchase contributes to the tribe's meager economy. I select a well-used chicken feather ruff worn by one of the young warriors as part of his battle regalia, an old stone axe, a cassowary bone knife, and a rectangular shell and bark pendant hung from another warrior's neck. Jim rounds out his selection of penis gourds and Eli buys a beaded necklace for his wife.

I am disappointed yet again to find there is no woman who speaks English to converse privately about tribal customs from a female perspective. I am left to brood over my conflicts alone. In my heart and my camera, I carry provocative images of these women's proud faces and mutilated hands as the sole language between us—plus, the extraordinary experience of being carried aloft for almost half an hour by a powerful, dancing, bare-breasted, war-painted Dani woman probably only four-and-a-half feet tall.

# Chapter 24

# A Poignant Papuan Farewell

WE RETURN from Yali's Village to our own farewell dinner celebration at Sinakma Elok bungalow. Marius has ordered a very artistic and festively presented final feast. In the center of a huge platter is an 18-inch-high, cone-like tower of saffron rice. Around the tower is an array of fresh, local river crayfish, sweet soy-sautéed peanuts, boiled water greens, green beans, and tomato, cucumber and potato fritters. One last time, Marius waits politely while we eat, a custom we feel honored by but can't really enjoy, as we still are uncomfortable not sharing the feasting together. But having learned not to swim against the river, we do feel celebrated with this sumptuous fare and know that Leksmono's eye for cultural drama has undoubtedly contributed to this fete.

I order a celebratory Bintang beer, only to discover later that it costs more than all the penis gourds Jim purchased put together. The tariff for a bottle of beer is high and there is virtually no alcohol here, as everything must be flown in on rickety cargo planes. Until now, I hadn't even noticed that the lack of imported or home-brewed alcohol anywhere, another interesting contrast to the "civilized" world.

After feasting, we are invited to join in a charming cultural tradition, a kind of mating ritual with the young men and women of the valley. We sit cross-legged in long parallel lines on mats on the floor, facing each other. Though we're all mixed up, I see that every boy sits opposite a girl. Soon the familiar sing-sing begins, led by Eli. All but one of our Lani porters is here, having waited to see us off before returning home to their villages. Now a few of them have put on Western wear, including Wagmena, the rare, independent, spirited young woman who is in t-shirt and shorts tonight. They all wear leaves and feathers in their hair, plus beads and cowrie shell collars.

In time to the singing, we learn to lean closer to the person we are facing and to do a kind of seductive hula with our hands. Just when we almost touch, we pull back into ourselves. This rhythmic sexual tease goes on until villagers begin removing their jewelry, dangling it enticingly from their hands, and finally, in a particularly close encounter, dropping beads into the other's cupped hands. When this occurs, a shy murmur of approbation oscillates through the group.

Eli, who already has two wives, isn't into enticing a third from the line of pretty young maidens playing the dancing game. As Jim and Eli struck up quite a yodeling friendship on the trail, Eli has invited Jim to face him. I'm sitting opposite the young Lani porter whose burned leg I'd bandaged. He seems to want to show his gratitude, but at the same time he is entangled in his shyness; he probably feels like I could be his grandmother, and a white witch doctor to boot— and here he is, involved in this seductive dance with me. I too feel awkward. We sing and dance with our hands, back and forth, but I don't have any beads to contribute. The only "jewelry" I am wearing is the special palm fiber anklet, armband and ring Wan Tu had woven tightly onto my ankle, arm and finger when we were in Borneo, plus my watch and wedding ring. I feel very sentimental about the palm fiber ornaments as reminders of my commitment ceremony to my baby orangutan, Dr. Adung, and about the wedding ring, as a deep symbol of my devotion to my world traveling partner, Jim. I might be ready to forfeit the watch, as I love losing my sense of clock time, but I realize our visit is coming to a close and there are planes to catch. Heartache all around.

Wagmena sees my dilemma and graciously leans over to contribute several bead strands for my hand dance. Her gesture, the rhythmic music, and the sweetness of these young peoples' faces overtake me. I feel great sadness about leaving this magical, ancient valley and her people. I'm afraid I'm going to cry and spoil the fun, so I cast my eyes down and do my very best to stem the tide of coming tears. Marius, astute and sensitive as always, gestures at me by wiping a tear from his eye. That does it. I can't keep concealing my feelings.

I lean back to explain to Marius, who is standing behind me, that I'm feeling moved by their friendship, their exquisite generosity, the fulfillment of this forty-year dream, and that I'm sad to leave. I'm also happy, I tell him, for their new, free West Papua movement, which will be marked with big festivals all over the country tomorrow, but I'm also deeply worried for them. I explain that when we left our mountaineering friends in the Kashmir Himalayas many years ago, a terrible war undertaken by Pakistan broke out. Endless bloody fighting continues to this day. We have received reports that many Kashmiri trekking guides and helpers, whom we came to cherish, were killed or injured in the ensuing melee. I want Papua to be free, I explain, but I'm afraid there will be reprisals from powerful Indonesians who don't want to let go of a mineral rich cash cow, or by the army and the government, which does not agree with President Gus Dur.

Marius leans over and takes both my hands. He translates my words to the young men and women swaying in the line. They seem moved. One of the porters gets up and comes over, removing a bracelet from his wrist, offers it to me. Marius explains to me that he wants to give it to me as his new friend. He translates that the well-worn bracelet says in Lani, "Greetings my sweet, from Wamena." What a touching gift! Somewhat embarrassed by my tears, I excuse myself, saying, "I'll be right back."

I go to our bungalow and scour through our things for any items I can give as gifts. I wasn't prepared for this, because Leks, Dick and other friends advised us to come here with the Sierra Club philosophy: "Take nothing but memories. Leave nothing but footprints." It's pretty slim pickings as I have learned since our Middle East packing frenzy to pack very light. Other than the bubbles I brought to entertain children on the trail, I find a tiny Swiss Army knife Jim can give Eli, and a pair of Masai earrings made of recycled aluminum that I bought in Africa. They will make a nice present for Wagmena, who has been especially thoughtful. I also find a little sewing kit and two sample packets of complexion cream that the porters can take to their wives and girlfriends.

With these Spartan offerings I return to the sing-sing to find that Jim has been draped in Eli's beads and the young men and women have exchanged more necklaces. One by one, and still in the style of the dance, I weave among the seated dancers, slipping little remembrances into their hands. We enjoy a tender farewell as Wagmena removes one of her orchid fiber bracelets and slips it onto my arm. Finally, emotionally wrung out and physically tired from our Baliem Valley adventuring, we retire to our bungalow.

Tomorrow we have a long travel day via Merpati Airlines to Jayapura. From thence, via Garruda and Biat Airlines, we'll travel to Makassar, Jakarta, and another night at Leks and Linda's in Jakarta before our final Indonesian stop in Sumatra. Though Leks and Linda are off sailing the waters of the island of Sumba, they have urged us to stay under the care of their houseboys, cook and driver, and Rudhy, their office manager.

In the morning, Marius discovers that once again, "Merpati has gone flatty." The flight is canceled because the plane, they tell us, is "broken." Marius arranges for us to go out on a Tringale cargo flight as extra baggage. So, on a prop plane that looks seriously compromised, in a cargo hold redolent with gasoline fumes, we join the cargo plus an Indonesian Army soldier and a couple of other hapless souls sitting on bundles and seats that are duct taped together. Jim and I hold each other's hands tightly, vowing our love for each other, while making a sign of gratitude for the good life we've shared together, just in case. We grimace as the smelly old, tired bird groans slowly off the runway and miraculously lurches up and over the mountain passes that encircle this magical, mystical island out of time, the Baliem Valley.

### Papuan Politics

Over the next few days, Jim and I hunker down with Titus, Marius, and Henki, all Papuan guides trained by Leksmono. Henki is the most political of the three. From him, we learn more about the

political history and plight of the Irian Jayans—now West Papuans—
and how they suffered terribly as a colonized people while the Dutch
East Indies Company established a strong colonial foothold here. We
also learn that they still experience considerable anxiety even talking
about the politically volatile situation in public.

Henki tells us how before World War II, as the Dutch Empire
waned, the Japanese invaded and won control of this, the third
largest island in the world. General Douglas MacArthur centered a
bloody Allied campaign here, and only gained control after bombing
Japan's military tunnels, entombing the Japanese. MacArthur then
established his successful Pacific military command from a mountain
headquarters overlooking Lake Sentani near Jayapura.

After World War II, the Allies somewhat arbitrarily drew a line
across the island on a north/south axis. Under the name of New
Guinea, they bestowed administration of the eastern portion to the
Australians, who developed infrastructure and later granted New
Guinea its independence. The western part of the island was granted
as a bone to the Dutch as their last colonial outpost in the Pacific.
Rather than give it autonomy, the Dutch continued exploiting its
prodigious natural resources until the Papuans ousted them in 1961;
for two years, West Papua was self-governing.

In May of 1963, a gathering of Dutch, Indonesian, and United
States governments, plus a UN delegation, met in New York without
including any native Papuans. The assembled dignitaries reached the
so-called "New York Agreement," restoring Indonesia's hegemony
over Irian Jaya. The colonial name Irian comes from from "Ikut
Republik Indonesia Antibi Netherlands" combined with Jaya,
which means "victorious" in Dutch. Since that time, an estimated
600,000 indigenous Papuans have been killed here, either in military
battle, in skirmishes with the Indonesian police, or at the hands of
Indonesian individuals and mobs. Generally, there are no reprisals
for these genocidal killings. They are occurrences of egregious racial
and colonialist slaughter, practically unnoticed in the West.

Marius's harassment by the polisi on our trek was in this tradition,
and this historical context helps us understand his compliant
response. Henki's hushed political history gives grievous weight to

the Papuans' dedication to political autonomy, and to the mood of celebration following the Papuan National Congress's decision to move toward autonomy by changing the country's name back to West Papua. The fact that he periodically looks over his shoulder to check to reassure himself we are not being overheard adds gravitas to the discussion.

I inquire about the formation and constitution of the National Congress. Each local village, he tells me, is governed by a council of adult males who select a chief for his prowess in war, his wealth in material success, and his cunning in resolving conflicts and managing problems. The tribal decision-making process is consensual and emerges out of considerable talking. Along the trail we witnessed this type of negotiation daily, in discussions of each night's lodging and vegetable purchases, as well as permission to pass, photograph, and tape record.

When the time came to convene a National Congress, a similar model was followed on a national level. There was a call for interested parties to convene, and approximately 3,000 Papuans converged on the capital, Jayapura, for a weeklong meeting. There was one major difference, however. Women were not only allowed but also encouraged to participate. Tribal Papuans, male and female, came from the Baliem Valley, the Asmat south coast, and north coastal areas as well as the islands, including Biak, Yapeh, Manokowari, and the Doberai and Bomberai peninsulas. Papuan leaders also returned from work and study in Europe, Canada, the United States, and other parts of Indonesia to lend their voices. The first National Congress concluded this past week under the leadership of Theys H. Eluay, a vigorous leader whom I later met in Jayapura.

The Indonesian legislature, largely comprised of members from the corrupt Suharto era, favors continuing to extract West Papuan gold, copper, diamonds and petroleum. However, the new Indonesian president, Gus Dur Wahid, has recently made public statements about giving the Papuans their freedom. Wahid has even offered financial support to underwrite their Congress meetings. It remains to be seen whether the Papuans, Wahid, and world opinion—led by pro-democracy countries including England, France, Germany, Canada, and the United States—will prevail when the Papuans declare their independence on December 1, 2000. We profoundly hope so, and we pray it comes without further loss of Papuan lives.

We have arrived here literally at a border, boundary, and threshold in this country's history. We would prefer to see this ancient tribal culture undisturbed, and we recognize the massive injustice perpetuated on these people by their colonialist brethren. At the same time, as a psychologist and a woman, I struggle with my observations of the lack of modern education and health care facilities, vast gender inequality, exploitation and maiming of women, and extensive use of child labor for wood gathering and childcare.

Regarding education, tribal learning prevailed for eons until the missionaries built Christian schools and taught Bible studies and hygiene. The Indonesian government added village schools for the teaching of Bahassa Indonesian as a common language, some mathematics and science, and a pro-Indonesian version of history, but school hours are short, holidays are many, and there is no school beyond elementary in the villages. A child must be taken to Wamena for secondary school, and there is virtually no university, so very few children receive education beyond the primary level.

Marius and Henki guess that no more than 100 tribesmen and possibly only two tribal women have received any university education. The two women are Yosina, a bright Dani woman who was adopted and educated by missionaries, and Joseffa Alomang, a Timiki woman, who was similarly educated. Both women have become the first spokespersons for women's rights at the first Congress. Imagine a vast indigenous population entering the second millennium with only two educated women and 100 educated men! In stark juxtaposition, we have seen hundreds and hundreds of stone axes in the Baliem Valley, many made to sell in the optimistic hope that tourists like us will come to observe one of the world's last living Stone Age cultures.

## The Caged Creatures of Jayapura

After surviving the cargo flight back to Jayapura, we meet Henki, again before embarking on our flight back to Jakarta. Henki seems edgy and distant. A disturbing problem emerges regarding my hopes for talking more politics with him over lunch. He manages to whisper to me that an Indonesian police informant owns this lakeside restaurant. Henki says it isn't safe to talk about the Free Papua movement within earshot of anyone employed by the restaurant. I feel a chill, confirming my dark premonitions of the night before. Instead of political enlightenment, we must content ourselves with conversation about the innumerable tropical birds and animals caged in the restaurateur's aviary. Apparently, police informants come into considerable kickbacks, sufficient to purchase such exotic trophies.

Looking at the sad little cuscus, dwarf miniature kangaroos, magnificent parrots, cockatoos, and the plumed bird of paradise imprisoned in the aviary, I have a distinctly uneasy feeling. These unique and extraordinary creatures are held captive for the amusement of dining tourists and the enhancement of the restaurateur's capital investment. Isn't this a metaphor for the West Papuans themselves? Certain Dutch colonialists and Indonesian factotums have positioned themselves as zookeepers who share common values; namely, they deem other people and resources fair game for their personal pleasure or self-aggrandizement. Henki assures me it will be more prudent to continue our political discussion by email. After our whispered luncheon conversation, we bid our final farewell to West Papua, New Guinea, sobered by the almost sure knowledge that our new friends' dreams of freedom will have to be deferred yet again, or there will be a bloodbath. [11]

---

11  After we return to the U.S., anxious to hear follow-up news of the West Papuan struggle for independence, I read with shock and horror that on 11/10//01 the Free Papua leader Theys H. Eluay was assassinated by the Indonesian military and the independence movement had been powerfully suppressed, apparently at the behest of General Suharto. Through 2011, the iron fist of the Indonesian government has continued to brutally smother all attempts toward autonomy of West Papua. There has been a blackout on coverage of this struggle in the foreign press due to Indonesia's denial of travel visas to foreign correspondants wishing to visit West Papua. I wonder if our travel would have been restricted, had the government known of my intention to write about our experience.

## Rudhy and A Last Night in Leks and Linda's Ethnographic Museum

Boarding our Jakarta-bound flight, to our astonishment, we are struck to see other white-skinned people also boarding. We realize that it has been over a month since we were in Kalimantan with Dr. Simone from Provence, Leanora from London, the Irish kids and Ronnie, the American from Guam. Michael Smith was nearly always in diver's skins and mask on Suluwesi. So except for Linda's that night in Jakarta, we haven't seen a white face for weeks.

Arriving five hours later in Jakarta, we are delighted to find Leks and Linda's assistant Rudhy waiting for us with their car and driver, giving us a special opportunity to get better acquainted with Rudhy and learn more about his life as a more-or-less average Indonesian citizen. While he has a white-collar job that puts him in a position of privilege, Rudhy's lot has not been easy.

He is the only son of poor parents who now live on the outskirts of Jakarta with their three adult children. There wasn't enough money to educate all of the children, so his father made an atypical decision. He felt Rudhy was bright enough to make his own way without a college education, but he knew that education would be his daughters' only chance to better themselves in a society where women are subjugated to their husbands. The family scrimped and saved to educate one daughter as a dental assistant and the other as a teacher's aide.

The father's theory appeared to be correct, as Rudhy, a personable, bright and ingratiating young man, was promoted from the ranks within Garruda Airlines. After eight years as public relations officer in charge of taking care of first class passengers, his star appeared to be ascending. However, when Suharto was being ousted, one of his last acts was to take care of his relatives and loyal supporters, assuring them good jobs with the government-owned airline. Rudhy was summarily terminated to make room.

As a member of a small Christian minority in Indonesia, try as he might, Rudhy was unable to find another job for "two years and ten days" until his sister, assigned as an assistant teacher to "Mrs.

Linda," helped gain him access to the Santosos' travel business. After only two and a half months of employment, it appears that this will be a long, mutually satisfying connection between the Santosos and Rudhy. Rudhy is grateful and loyal to his new employers and we can attest he is a natural at handling travelers and their needs.

He proudly tells us that his current Santoso project is planning a trip for a group of Australian professors into Torajaland to observe a spectacular funeral celebration in July. We tell Rudhy that when we were there, we saw these very funeral preparations and heard that 200 water buffalo, including many of the prized pied ones, were being assembled for the funeral. We explain our relief at not having to witness the actual carnage, to which he replies that the Australians have stipulated one condition for their visit. They do not want to see the slaughter in the killing field. Even those from the land of millions of sheep are not inured.

We relish our lovely respite, Chez Museum Santoso, with a cool, long workout swim and a morning yoga practice in their garden among Asmat carvings. I buy a beautiful antique Javanese batik from their collection and two "substitute" skulls from the southern coastal Asmat region of Irian Jaya. Hand-carved wooden skulls have been substituted for human skulls since headhunted skulls are no longer available for initiation rites. Rudhy, who is learning to become the Santosos' museum curator, tells us that when headhunting was banned and skulls were no longer available for Asmat rites, enterprisingly adaptive carvers began carving wooden substitutes.

Ancestors' skulls have always been a reverenced part of daily life throughout the Asmat area. These skulls are decorated for certain feasts but not painted. To keep in constant contact with their ancestors, men often wear them on their backs or breasts, or use them as headrests when sleeping. Although usually inherited by men, the skulls of important headhunters can also be handed down to women who keep them and their powerful medicine wrapped in leaves, hidden in the eaves of the house. They also keep jawbones, breastbones and neck vertebrae of ancestors and tie them in place with interwoven rattan.

On the other hand, trophy skulls collected in battle by Asmat warriors are usually hung in clusters in the doorways of family houses or from crosspieces above the fireplace in a man's house. One side of every trophy skull, pierced by a stone axe to remove the brains, was given to old men and women and war leaders to eat for strength. The jawbones, breastbones and neck vertebrae of all headhunted victims were discarded or thrown to women, who used them as the centerpieces of necklaces.

In some villages, trophy skulls were painted with white, red and black, with a symbol of the mighty cassowary bird on the forehead. The eyes and nose holes of these skulls were filled with beeswax and inset with pale silver coix seeds, red abrus seeds and bits of shell. The top of each skull was decorated with a band of coix seeds and white cockatoo feathers.

Rudhy carefully wraps these priceless trophies for me, helping me inch them into my bulging duffel bag before shepherding us to the airport for the last leg of our Indonesian odyssey. I depart, imagining myself a modern day Freud, carrying incredible artifacts from ancient cultures for the consulting room to which I will one day return. In the meantime, I envision them on the walls of "Cedar Cottage," the cabin at Twin Brooks in the Sierras, where I will have time to write and reflect on having experienced my deferred Irian dream. I know for certain that the finger axe from the Baliem Valley will always haunt me.

# CHAPTER 25
## RE-ENTRY:
### RECRUDESCENCE AND THE RANGDA

RE-ENTRY BEGINS with an overnight stay in a luxurious, thoroughly American airport hotel in Jakarta. We languish with high-pressure hot showers, international cuisine that can be sampled without worry, dancing, and a king-sized bed where we lounge, watching TV re-runs. The next morning we wander the beautifully landscaped grounds dotted with lovely swimming and reflecting pools, fountains and lily ponds. Inside the gracious buildings, gamelan musicians seated on silk cushions greet us with traditional music and lovely Indonesian art adorns the walls. The hotel contains a state-of-the-art fitness center, sauna and yoga room, all of which we avail ourselves of, like true sybarites who have been far, far beyond.

For travelers, fitness is typically catch as catch can. You may climb a mountain one day and sit in a vehicle for the next three days. You may find space to do sit-ups and push-ups, but certainly not on a klotok or in the insect-ridden jungle. Before our trans-Pacific flight from Indonesia, we relish a ninety-minute workout in the weight room and on the track; I follow this with a deliciously long yoga session topped off by a sauna. Feeling fit, rested and deeply satisfied with ourselves and our decision to pull up stakes, we are ready for the return trip home.

My grandmother Jessie Kennedy Prescott, "Sassie" as we called her, bequeathed to me her love of life and hence her love of June

21, summer solstice, the year's longest day of sunshine. Imagine my delight when I realized that our flight home across the international dateline would be on June 21. I would enjoy two days with this special date, one dedicated to flying, the other our first day back in California. Two summer solstices of the millennium year!

Stalwart, minimalist and parsimonious with his frequent flyer miles, Jim is again traveling coach class. Though he will never admit it, he may regret his choice, as coach is full of screaming kids today. Dogged hunter-gatherer of comfort and profligate spender of frequent flyer miles, I return as I had come, in business class. Parting company a tad awkwardly at the departure gate in Jakarta, Jim and I disembark hours later in Singapore for a brief layove.

### Recrudescence: The Rangda Strikes

In Singapore's modern airport, we find an Internet café and successfully retrieve a series of email messages from our office assistant, Martha. News from the home front is pretty bad. While all our loved ones are hale and hearty, Martha's increasingly shrill and distraught emails recount the horrors of the "Tenant from Hell," as she puts it. I find myself recalling the depiction of the cosmic struggle between good and evil in the Balinese Barong Dance. The morphing Rangda, representing all the forces of destruction in the universe, first appeared rather charmingly as a monkey, but with mounting destructive intent. He morphs into an evil, grotesque creature with a lolling flaming tongue, a necklace of human entrails, bulging eyes, red and black snakes thrashing from his bizarre body, and long, red, splintery fingernails. The Rangda serves nicely as my visualization of the unleashed "Tenant from Hell."

Martha's emails, written over the past several weeks, reveal that she has been driven to near hysteria. She feels abandoned in a cyberspace black hole, left alone to single-handedly handle "Hummer Jake" and all the business that we have thankfully left behind. A distressing business it turns out to be. She began sending emailed pleas for guidance in a calm and collected tone. Now, as we haven't been able to retrieve any emails and she couldn't call us in the jungle, her anxiety has mounted.

Not only has our tenant moved all six of his children under thirteen into our once-tranquil abode, but as they're going through their parents' divorce, the children are agitated and acting out. Jake, though adept at directing TV and movie dramas, hasn't a clue how to deal with his own domestic drama.

Martha's last email promises, "More to follow, don't want to spoil your trip." She does say that one or two of the smallest children have wormed their way between the bars of the wrought-iron security gate that locks my office consulting room and managed to pick the lock to my office. Specifically designated as off-limits in the lease, my locked consulting room sanctuary has enticed them to break in and wreak havoc.

Worse, the Rangda's soon-to-be ex-wife feels it incumbent upon herself to micro-manage her soon-to-be ex-husband's living arrangements, particularly the sanitary conditions of the house where he has taken "her children." She has been showing up unannounced when the tenant is away at work and ordering the removal of all dishes, glassware, utensils, spices, flour, sugar, etc., which our tenant had told us he would gratefully appreciate using in his new life as a divorced dad. Ms. Rangda will not have her precious darlings' bodies touched by other people's linens or dishes, so the sheets and towels for five bedrooms and baths have been unceremoniously dumped in trash bags in the garage. And, Martha goes on, "a lot of other belongings are in the trash as 'rubbish.'"

But the very worst is what Martha tells us about our housekeeper. Devoted, sweet Miriam, our San Salvadoran housekeeper of seventeen years, has found herself in the eye of the new tenant's marital hurricane. She had accepted the tenant's offer of a job as housekeeper during his tenancy. She finds herself, however, daily berated by almost ex-Ms. Rangda as a "terrible housekeeper" and "far too old and fat," to boot.

I imagine poor innocent Miriam plunged back into the darkest years of her early childhood in El Salvador, with a mother too burdened by a huge family to raise them all. She farmed Miriam out at age two to a begrudging aunt, to live like Cinderella without benefit of a fairy godmother. She was worked tirelessly yet berated by all. Fiercely loyal to us, her adopted family of seventeen years,

When we contemplate trying to evict a tenant in this era of very protective renter's rights, we aren't optimistic. And what judge would side against a divorcing father who discovers he can spend more time with his kids? Are our peace of mind, our patio cushions and antiques more important than the next generation? We doubt we would win. Even though our neighbors have rushed forth groaning to us about his wild parties with naked women hanging out of upstairs windows, followed by Monday mornings when their clothes and suitcases are heaved out onto the driveway from the same upstairs windows, we pause. We could spend a lot of money and a mortal chunk of our preciously carved-out sabbatical in legal battle. We decide that the purpose of this sabbatical has been to truly let go of everything we have been rooted to. That certainly includes deep attachments to thirty years at Porto Marina and control of our turf.

And so, gazing at each other, breathing deeply, Jim and I vow to "let it be!" If and when we decide to return, we'll devote a lot of good energy to burning sage and purging the wicked vibes that are accumulating in our beloved house. We'll have to fork over more money than we'd planned for re-upholstering, refinishing and repainting. But eventually we'll enjoy the benefits of that expenditure a lot more than time and money down a legal rat hole.

Still, we cannot miss seeing with our own eyes the fruits of the Rangda children's destruction derby: patio cushions lacerated with an X-Acto knife; an oil spill on the patio caused by dribbling bottles of cooking oil up and down the paths; the video tape documenting the house's pristine condition before our departure, complete with welcoming bouquets of flowers, stolen from my private office. We find the remains of a ransacked gift box locked in my consulting room for Gabriel's intended on her 30th birthday, a gold necklace that was my own 21st birthday present. The shredded wrappings we discover scattered in telltale bits in the garden, leading us to the gold necklace draped over the upper branch of a tree. Violations. Violations. Violations.

This is the *crud* in recrudescence. When we draped our own belongings all over Highway 99 because the trailer had a flat tire, that was our own doing. And there was nothing to do but laugh. Since we were transporting most of our toys and worldly goods, I described it as a "transcrudescent" experience. This attack on my sanctuary, our home, and the birthday necklace is not amusing or transcendent. It feels just plain *crude*scent. Though you won't find it in any dictionary crudescent is the antonym of luminescent, . And I hope you don't have much occasion for the word.

Do we regret leasing the house? To the Rangda, of course we do, but in principal, not at all. For without this experience, I'd never have learned one of my life's greatest lessons, a very hard one for me: letting go. *Give it up, move on, let it be,* I keep telling myself with mantra-like rhythmicity. *Remember, when god closes a door, she opens a window!* And so we set off for Twin Brooks with our windows wide open.

# PART VI
# PARTINGS AND IMPARTINGS

# CHAPTER 26
# REST AND A LUMINOUS SUMMER RETREAT

### A *"Poodleluscious" Greeting*

ON OUR ARRIVAL at Twin Brooks, Jullay's glorious poodle greeting amplifies the joy of our return home to the mountains. Her entire body is aquiver in ecstasy—revealed in barks, licks, wiggles, wags and a big puddle in the road by our car. Can we ever grasp the wisdom and devotion of pets? I am taking two and a half years off from a clock oriented profession to discover the experience of unstructured time and how to live fully in the present moment, and our dog already fully understands those concepts! She doesn't think about tomorrow. She doesn't know where we've been or why. All she really knows is that she loves us, and when we show up, she is 100% present for the reunion. And she teaches us the joy of unambivalent adoration. Namaste, Jullay!

Our ranch caretakers, Cathy and Ricky, have outdone themselves preparing for our return and caring for the ranch. With some outside help, they've completed construction of a new garage and storage barn where we can stow the boxes of Rangda "rubbish" Miriam rescued from Porto Marina.

The Sierra woods in late June are beautiful. Dogwood in white blossoming splendor greets our arrival. In the old orchard, apple blossoms are just falling, while wild lupine, golden brodia, Chinese houses, and farewell-to-spring are resplendent in the meadows. The foxglove Sassie started in the garden before I was even born is volunteering all along the road and throughout the forest. Along the creek banks, amongst the Queen Anne's lace, the wild azalea and tiger lilies are budding out in more profusion than I've seen in years. Of course, mice have lavished in our absence, ballooning their population in the house. Jim moves into hunter-gatherer mode, gathering mousetraps and raisins to hunt small game. During our first weeks home he makes the rounds in triumph and announces the body count at breakfast. It is impressive.

We spend our first days of re-entry arranging our life, organizing files, desks, sorting clothes, oiling bicycles and rearranging Twin Brooks for full-time occupation. We have to learn to be fairly self-sufficient, as repair and service calls in the backwoods cost a fortune. Jim has repaired the washer and dryer and I have learned how to deconstruct my computer right down to the motherboard. I love making personal contact with her; it's very satisfying. Slowly, a touch of "feeling on top of things" appears.

### Reflections on the Rangda

As we have more contact with the Rangda, he seems less evil and more flummoxed, even rather pathetic. His family appears certifiably dysfunctional. Though he is a successful moviemaker, he is hopelessly inept at most everything else in life. He literally doesn't know how to change a light bulb and calls electricians to do the job, forwarding the bill, of course. Knowing that I am a psychologist liberates him to confide in me about how overwhelmed he feels about his life and his divorce. *Too much information.*

He divulges the name of a therapist he eagerly reassures me he is seeing "every day." Unfortunately, I recognize the reputation of this "media shrink" whose judgment is documented as questionable and who appeared on the State Board of Professional Psychology's probation list. Though Jake whines about money and his rent is often late, he brags about the therapist's exorbitant fee. I have a slightly juicy dilemma. Do I follow a professional "duty to report" her tenuous credentials and her probation to our tenant? Or do I leave him to the fate he deserves? Eventually, I call the licensing board confirming that the media shrink's license is indeed suspended on probation, but she is allowed to practice under monitored conditions. It's a gray area. I don't *have* to do anything. I can let go.

Slowly regaining email and phone contact with family, friends and patients, it feels good to be home. Ariel is on the ropes, awaiting summer break from an arduous year of bilingual first grade teaching in the inner city. Brooke and Philip have gutted their clapboard house near Seattle and are industriously remodeling it by night as Brooke builds her chiropractic practice by day. Gabe and his fiancée are newly engaged. He has orchestrated an incredibly romantic sunset hike and treasure hunt at Twin Brooks, ending atop Echo Rock where a candlelit table and champagne awaited, set up in advance by Rick and Cathy. By candlelight Gabriel revealed the mystery of the treasure hunt, offering his fiancee an heirloom engagement ring.

As I hear from each of my former patients, I'm relieved to learn that all the work we did in therapy and all the time we spent preparing for a conclusion sounds solid. Though it's been hard sometimes, everyone seems to be doing well. Most are adjusting to "life after therapy." A couple have taken referrals to continue therapy, and a few have requested periodic sessions by telephone or in person.

*Luminescence: A Sixtieth Birthday Retreat*

My birthday is July 3 and we have always celebrated it with family at Twin Brooks. In fact, because it falls on a holiday weekend, I never had a typical birthday party with school age friends. This year, I decided well in advance to make a big deal of it. I wanted to mark not just my 60th birthday, but also that of my closest female friends and our shared passage over the threshold of the new millennium. We have a rare opportunity to gather in a beautiful setting and reflect on a turning point in our lives and a millennial shift. My three daughters, Ariel, Brooke, and Kisha, Gabriel's fiancée, will participate as well. At the same time, there is the poignant absence of friends who cannot be with us, those who have crossed their thresholds early due to cancer When I started planning this, I had no idea that, in one of life's grand serendipities, I would find myself in the midst of an epiphanous moment in the Baliem Valley of Irian Jaya, embraced by a tribe of former headhunters in the dark of night, invited into their grass hut for a sing-sing that was better than any birthday celebration I could ever plan.

For a full year in advance, I've been dreaming of ways to make this observation special. As the date approaches, the fourteen women are coming—some old friends who've known each other for decades, and some from different avenues of my life who haven't met—are emailing each other about details. They're figuring out airport pick-ups, carpooling and borrowing sleeping bags and preparing their unique contributions to the retreat.

Psychologist Erik Erikson outlined how old age is typically marked by an either/or conflict of "integrity vs. despair." Anthropologist Margaret Mead writes of the opportunity for "post-menopausal zest." I often noted, while working as a staff psychologist with hospitalized terminal cancer patients, that people who feel their lives have been well lived enjoy a certain calm about aging and dying. Others, who feel they've forfeited their potential and squandered opportunities and relationships, approach death with despair and often bitterness. These are heavy thoughts to accompany birthday party planning! But reflecting on my good fortune in having friends who add important intellectual, spiritual, emotional and personal depth and dimension to my life, I feel blessed.

The four day retreat washes over me with exquisite poignancy. The days glide by and I am so full of awe I can't even write about it. We have each set off alone each day in the woods for a few hours of silent contemplation and journal writing. Later we hike up Prescott Peak, each friend carrying three helium-filled balloons aloft—a black one representing (pardon) her shit, a white for her hopes and dreams, and a brightly colored one to celebrate what is. On the mountain, we each speak of what we want to release with the black balloon, celebrate with the colored balloon and hope and pledge with the white balloon.

We enjoy an afternoon craft project decorating t-shirts, and a friend's fabulous reading of the opening chapter in her newest book. And after a llama hike and cookout on Echo Rock, I am ambushed by my friends' secretly planned "Angel's Roast," when each one recounts my meaning in her life; they each lovingly give me back parts of myself from times we've spent together over decades. The experience is a total meltdown for me. We fall into hilarity on Saturday night at the arrival of five peroxided and spangled members of the mother-daughter all-girl Western band. We laugh again nervously at the unexpected crashing of that night's party by my son Gabriel and my ex, Donald.

Every morning we do expansive yoga and every evening restorative yoga, and there are hot tubs and afternoons at the swimming hole, cooking and hiking and late night gab fests. What lingers afterward is an amazing blur of intimacy, love, reflection, introspection and celebration. There is no question in my mind but that my greatest birthday gift has been the gift of each of my friends' time out from busy lives—to gather, to reflect, to celebrate our connections, histories, anxieties and affections.

From that extraordinary nocturnal sing-sing in the grass hut among penis-gourded strangers around their campfire, to the sing-sing on Echo Rock among family and friends who know me best, I feel deeply moved, honored, and charged with responsibility to live every moment fully in the present moment, and with regard for Mother Earth. One friend reads a letter Chief Seattle of the Suquamish Indians wrote to the American government in the 1800s, offering the most profound understanding of God in all things. He wrote: "Every part of the earth is sacred to my people. Every shining pine needle, every sandy shore, every mist in the dark woods, every meadow, every humming insect. All are holy in the memory and experience of my people."

Another friend writes a letter conveying the sentiments of many others. "Harriet, I still feel such a strong afterglow one week after we separated from our magical retreat. I am printing your email and saving it to read in the future and perhaps to show to some of whom I've been unable to convey the impact that the weekend had on me and on so many others. I am becoming much more aware of how ephemeral life is, more conscious of how much I treasure my friends and family members and how fortunate I am in so many ways. Thank you. It was unbelievable." My sentiments exactly.

Many of us agree that sixty feels liberating. For me, no more "have to" deadlines of graduate school and writing and parenting. No more of "if onlys" of meeting the love of my life, living in the home of my dreams, finding the right career. Thankfully, those are all givens now. This is the time to sculpt desires with a light touch, hopefully if we're lucky with some years of good health ahead, more resources than in youth, fewer obligations and more freedom.[12] Recognizing the evanescence and fragility of all we have, we can more fully live and celebrate each moment. This is a time to nourish the spirit and protect the earth. Margaret Mead was right about post-menopausal zest!

After our exquisite retreat, I find myself in a mood that mixes zest, poignant awareness of the fragile thread we live by, and gratitude for my time out of the maelstrom and mainstream of ordinary life. I have an unprecedented opportunity to resculpt my desires, to encounter the depth and richness of this global village, to face life's inexorable limitations. I am sobered by the image of women I've met with axed-off fingers and clitoridectomies. Free from the "getting and spending" mode, immersed in spiritual and ephemeral realms as well as social activism, I am able to pause and reconfigure my priorities. I deeply celebrate this chance to open my seventh decade in health and in love, with my pores open. I'm looking forward to savoring every adventure, challenge and meaningful possibility the remaining year and a half of our sabbatical may bring.

---

12  Sadly, between the time of this writing and publication a decade later, already one friend has succumbed to advanced Alzheimers, two to cancer, and another was widowed. Carpe Diem.

Nihal, Jim, Mike, Ruth, John, Susan and H (kneeling) on Summit at Uhuru Peak, the highest point in Africa.

Jim gets his camel lesson, Egypt.

Learning to hookah, Egypt.

Penis gourd Irian man, Indonesia.

My poster boy, Indonesia.

Salt gatherers, Indonesia.

Aiming for my eye, Indonesia.

Wan Tu, Indonesia.

H on KlokTok Writing Book, Indonesia.

Sibling rivalry—Michael and Adung, Indonesia.

Prayer flags and mountain, China.

Litang tribal princess, China.

Jim carried across Dongwang Gorge on litter, China.

Tibetan portrait, Litang, China.

Superb gaited horse, China.

With Gabriel at Twin Brooks.

Cheesemaking Val Buscagna.

Jim and packstring up granite.

Breathe, you are alive.

# CHAPTER 27

## AMAZONIA, ANDES,
## AND ALMOST ANTARCTICA

REPLENISHED and rejuvenated, Jim and I spend the winter on another grand adventure: six months on the road in South America. Vast, rich, and varied, South America remains the "dark continent" to many of its neighbors in North America, including us—until we criss-cross the land in both directions and diagonally, spending one to four weeks each in Ecuador, Peru, Brazil, Venezuela, Chile and Argentina.

Latin America offers wildly divergent and fascinating topography: dry deserts, altiplano, high Andean peaks, Amazon jungles, fjords, glaciers, Patagonian pampas, and tepuis. Local people range from the indigenous poor to the very few rich and powerful. Our activities range from scuba diving with hammerheads and whale sharks, walking the Sendera Sagrada, and making a sacred pilgrimage across Lake Titicaca's Isla Del Sol at 13,000 feet of elevation.

During our winter sojourn in Latin America, we miss the whole debacle of the "hanging chad" election of 2000, flying more than thirty thousand air miles in myriad flying machines, including a 777, a DC3, a Cessna, and an iffy flying Yugo. We trek about two hundred miles, hiking fifteen or twenty thousand feet in altitude and the same back down. We scale Mt. Cotopaxi volcano in Ecuador, Ayuntepui in the Orinoco Basin of Venezuela, Wayna Picchu in Peru, as well as many peaks and a glacier in Chilean and Argentine Patagonia. We paddle on tule reed boats around the isles of Lago Titicaca. We cover uncountable miles while horseback riding, kayaking, canoeing, catariggering (on a four-man canoe-rigged catamaran), paddling a dugout piloted by Pemon Indians, and crossing the wild white water of the Futaleufu River in Chile, suspended upside down by a Tyrolean traverse rope harness.

Besides traveling via planes, boats, ropes, and on horseback, we also journey by train, car, van, and bus. We even tramp several miles behind an oxcart, carrying our duffels into the hinterlands of a wild river in Chile! We hike, paddle and ride horseback with huasos and gauchos through remote Patagonia mountains, where the sheep ranchers' life seems like what my Great-grandpa and Grandma Kennedy must have experienced when they settled in California a century ago.

### Aboard the Ship of Fools

We travel solo and with groups, the most notable being the crazy party with which we summit Angel Falls and Ayuntepui in Venezuela. For starters, I must take full responsibility for chosing this particularly bizarre adventure. I had been invited to give a paper in London at a conference next year on film and psychoanalysis. I love the 1986 British film *The Mission*, about the experiences of a Jesuit missionary in 18th-century South America, and decided to write my paper about *The Mission*. The film, written by Robert Bolt and directed by Roland Joffe, won thePalme d'Or and the Academy Award for Best Cinematography. In it, there is a riveting long scene in which Jesuit priest Father Gabriel (Jeremy Irons), a missionary to the Amazonian tribe of Guarani Indians, challenges slave trader Rodrigo Mendoza (Robert De Niro) to undertake heavy penance for killing his brother Felipe (Aiden Quinn) by lugging a huge burden of arms and a cross up the falls to the mission at the top of the falls.

Somehow I mistakenly think the falls depicted were Angel Falls in Venezuela, the world's highest waterfall. I think it will be uber dramatic and a thrill for my London audience to illustrate my paper about crime and punishment by bringing photographs of our ascent of the same falls. So, I more or less commandeer Jim and daughter Ariel (who is on winter break from her inner city teaching job in

Los Angeles) to join me on a class-five expedition organized by Mountain Travel Sobek, to climb Ayuntepui and Angel Falls, a feat infinitely more arduous than visiting Iguazu Falls where the film was actually shot.

Our unforgettable assemblage—which, had we been at sea, would easily have merited the title "Ship of Fools" —includes a trapeze artist (useful, since we have to climb slippery jungle slopes hanging onto vines and ropes); a brilliant, totally tattooed man (colorful addition to the extraordinarily diverse flora of Ayuntepui); a leggy blonde lawyer (highly entertaining but distracting to the trapeze artist and to the group leader, who practically ignores the rest of us in hours of need); an inventor-physicist with spina bifida (he dyes his few remaining hairs with black shoe polish, which runs down his brow in the daily afternoon rain); and a narcoleptic nymphomaniac (really truly, who snores loudly, prowls nocturnally among our jungle hammocks, and courts every man, gay or straight); and finally, the craziest of all: Jim, Ariel and me, who has misguidedly roped my husband and daughter into this misadventured segment of our Latin sojourn.

Besides the bizarre and colorful cast of characters, the Ayuntepui climb is scared into my cerebral cortex because it is it much harder than summiting Kilimanjaro due to the tangles of vines (including the infamous Medusa's Tangle) and the tropical mud wallows we had to traverse to make it to the top, and also by the after-the-fact discovery that this was the wrong waterfall! What a life lesson in humility and letting go of grandiosity.

Slogging up the slippery slopes of Ayuntepui by Angel Falls, Jim, Ariel and I all become sick with diahrrea and croup and infested with chiggers under our toenails. Meanwhile, the physicist with spina bifida, unable to handle the climb himself, but whose many patents have made him very rich, bribes one of our two guides to carry him to the top. The other guide becomes besotted with the leggy blonde and ignores the rest of us. We accomplish the most difficult climb of our lives, scaling Ayuntepui, from which cascades the world's highest free-falling waterfall, Angel Falls, finally reaching the top of the tepui on Christmas day in a downpour.

Sick, encrusted with mud and totally out of sorts, with a pair of my hiking pants and Tevas actually rotting with mildew, we agree it is the worst Christmas ever. But at least, I sigh rather smugly, still mistakenly believing I have mastered the torturous course of the Robert De Niro character. Metaphorically licking our wounds before guiltily waving goodbye to Ariel, who has devoted her Christmas vacation from teaching in the inner city in Los Angeles, the three of us plus the engaging, leggy blonde spend a week in recovery, snorkeling and sailing around the small Caribbean islands near Las Rochas off the Venezuelan coast.

Months later we discover that the engaging blonde has stiffed us 500 never-to-be recovered dollars; and at the film conference in London, a film scholar righteously corrects my misperception, informing me that everybody knows *The Mission* was in fact filmed in Brazil at Iguazu Falls! Perfect Ship of Fools.

Fleeing the sadomasochistic debacle of Ayuntepui, Jim and I manage two luxuriously recuperative spas in exquisite settings—a Relais et Chateau near Otovallo, Ecuador, and Termes de Puyhuapi on a fjord in Southern Chile. While we spend minimal time in cities—only a few days each in Quito, La Paz, Santiago, Caracas, Buenos Aires, and Ushuaia—for the most part, we are far from populous areas, often in rural areas of agricultural, ranching, fishing and tribal cultures. Whenever possible, we stay with indigenous Quechua and Aymara Indian families.

An especially meaningful contact is our meeting of Prudencio Duran Saraza, a young Aymara Indian who lives in the village of Chicuito on the bank of Lake Titicaca. We meet him working in the nearly empty hotel where we are staying in Puno. He is dying for an opportunity to practice his English, and shows us with great pride the collection of finger puppets his mother knits from colorful yarn, creating a whole Noah's Ark of fanciful animals. Prudencio quickly reveals himself to be an amazing old soul for his nineteen years, and captivates my heart with his depth of spiritual awareness of old teachings, ethnic pride, humility, and fresh enthusiasm. He emanates Aymara pride and love of Pachamama, or Mother Earth. Over several days we form a remarkable bond so strong that it will later lead Jim and me to sponsor him to live with us in the United States.

Throughout our travels we taste delicious fruits we'd never seen before, including passion fruit and dragon fruit, and we pick and eat wild berries, fruits, and fungi on which the indigenous Mapuche peoples of Patagonia lived before they were decimated by the Europeans. We eat conger eel, the most plenteous catch in the waters of central Chile, so many times we get tired of it; the same goes for lamb in Patagonia. White bread is everywhere, as the Latins seem to believe it represents prosperity.

We cut each other's hair, learn conversational Spanish until I begin dreaming *en espanol*, get sick and recover several times. I gain more practice in letting go: giving up control of what once seemed essential, such as daily yoga, health food, and email contact with friends and loved ones. Given my good obsessive-compulsive personality, this letting go is a huge gift. The longer we travel, the lighter my duffel becomes as I give away clothes, learn to simplify, and totally forget that inane, insane swivet of travel wardrobe acquisitiveness that held me in thrall before we set out for the Middle East. With cyber holes, funky haircuts and chiggers laying eggs under Jim's toenails, this odyssey represents what we really set out to do: "pull up stakes," take our chances and encounter a world heretofore unknown to us, over a long period of time that allows us immersion in the new experience.

We worry that will be too much time away from home. We do push the envelope, running out of needed supplies, nearly losing the sale of a property because we can't be reached, and having trouble taking care of business at home. Nevertheless, we find ourselves sad to leave when it's time to head home.

While traveling south of the border, I am writing a first draft of something I am calling *Rivers Run Through It: A South American Odyssey*. I've found writing to be an engaging process, and enjoy watching the slow evolution of this new identity, inspired by my meadow muse in Bench Valley a few years ago. Every time I have crossed a national boundary and filled in passport information, I find myself wondering: *Am I still a psychoanalyst? Have I become a writer? Or shall I go for the hyphenate psychoanalyst-writer?* My dreams have been rich with affirmations of my millennial birthday friends' predictions that writing is to be my pathway for this phase of my life.

*Snowbound Return*

After we return to California, Jim and I are truly homeless. Our Pacific Palisades home is still leased to the Rangda, and we can't really live at Twin Brooks due to massive midwinter snowstorms. The road is impassable except on snowshoes, which we gamely undertake, only to discover that the caretaker's cabins near the front gate look like igloos buried in snowdrifts. Inside, our Twin Brooks house is a cold, dark snow cave, with no light shining through the windows on the first floor. Power and phone lines are iffy as well. The llamas and horses are free to stroll wherever they please, as the pasture fences are completely buried in snow. Fortunately, they know where the hay barn is, so they don't go far. Poor Cathy and Ricky, our caretakers, have been wallowing waist-deep across the pasture to feed the animals, but their spirits are up, if their fresh groceries are down. And next summer we should have a glorious season of full brooks, green growth and the final demise of the dreaded pine beetles we hope are frozen in the snow.

Waiting for the spring thaw, we retrieve Jullay and end up back on the fly, staying with friends and family for most of the rest of spring until the snows melt. We are on the road for eight months before we can get back home to Twin Brooks and finally unload our scuba gear, camping gear and dirty duffels to prepare for our next sojourn, our separate solo summers.

## CHAPTER 28
## FEAR OF WHEELS
## (WHEELER ON WHEELS, THAT IS)

READERS may recall the story of Jim's horrific bike accident, told around the campfire while climbing Kilimanjaro. Here's the backstory: Columbus Day, 1987 was a bank holiday for Jim, but I did not take the day off from my analytic practice. Although he had promised to clean the garage, on a whim he played hooky and took a long bike ride up the coast. I was seeing patients when someone from St. John's Hospital Emergency Room in Santa Monica called and told me, "We have your husband here. He's had a little accident, mostly it's his hands." Right about the hands, wrong about little.

In the blinding setting sun, an uninsured motorist had taken Jim out. Many of the bones in his hands, which took the brunt of the blow, were pulverized, and an artery in his arm was cut. His life was saved by the luck of the draw. An off-duty paramedic happened to be jogging along the remote stretch of highway north of Malibu and was able to stop the bleed. Jim's "little accident" resulted in an emergency ambulance transfer to Cedars Sinai Hospital, where he subsequently underwent twenty-seven hours of state-of-the-art reconstructive hand surgery.

By then I knew Jim Wheeler very well, and had begun to see his denial of his vulnerability, his defensive bullheadedness, and his readiness to choose play over work—unlike me. His parents, whom I dearly loved and had known since my adolescence, were very controlling. Like my kids with me, Jim rebelled mightily against them. As an adult, he often had considerable difficulty differentiating adult responsibility from the feeling that someone was forcing something on him. When I asked for his help, he viewed me as the demanding mother of his childhood; this gave him fodder to take off on his bicycle to play. After the bike crash, it was easy to Monday-morning-quarterback his bike-riding as an accident waiting to happen. I enjoyed claiming entitlement to the moral high ground, but it put the first serious wedge between us.

In our newly emerging family crucible, Jim colluded in a developing unconscious dynamic between us. I was the designated "needy" one with a corner on the family feelings, or the over-conscientious, overcontrolling one; he would be the "good guy," the Spartan, denying he depended on anyone for anything. I, the ever-attuned, diligent and overly responsible psychologist deeply engrained with a Protestant ethic, had a hard time taking even legal holidays off from my practice. At the time of the accident, I was working yet again, while he was out playing.

### Our Psychodynamic Molotov Cocktail

On the surface, our roles were split, but beneath it we each felt unacknowledged guilt and envy of the other. (Once at a street fair, I found a rock carved with the phrase "Carpe Mañana!" and bought it for Jim. He still keeps it on his desk, which is piled high with reminders of his penchant for procrastination.) Just as I envied his ability to lightheartedly take off and play, he envied mine for focus and responsibility. Our split, however, created tension and made a potentially explosive marital cocktail.

After twenty-seven hours of reconstructive hand surgery, Jim— for the first time—could not deny his neediness. It was inarguably difficult for him. He couldn't dress himself, bathe, or even wipe his own bottom for weeks and weeks. On weekdays, I took on the role of his caretaker, rushing upstairs between sessions with patients to help him dress or undress, eat or go to the bathroom. His father and I took turns nursing him on alternate weekends. But once the bandages were off and his physical therapist gave him a handgrip to redevelop his strength, he was back on the road to Sparta, clenching his fists on and off, regaining his strength and the illusion of total independence.

Five years later, our psychodynamic cocktail boiled over again. Jim had another near-fatal head-on collision with a mountain while cycling in the Senior Olympics. An ER tech accompanying him in a helicopter radioed to inform me. I was working again, this time on a Sunday morning. As president of my psychoanalytic institute at the time, I was chairing an annual meeting when I got the message that my husband was being airlifted to the Head Trauma Center of Sharpe Memorial Hospital in San Diego. I dropped my gavel in a nanosecond, called daughter Brooke and we drove off together to San Diego. There was Jim, lying outside the ER on a gurney with his neck in an immobilizing brace and his face looking like a huge, overripe summer squash.

Brooke, seeing her father like that, burst into tears and ran to the bathroom to vomit. She had never seen her dad in such extremis. I had more mixed feelings. I knew that weeks, months or years later, he would deny the gravity of what he had done to himself and potentially to us all. I had the peculiarly sinister presence of mind to take his photo on the spot.

After two days' immobilization, observation, MRIs and CT scans to determine whether he had sustained serious spinal cord and brain injury, and whether he would be quadriplegic or paraplegic, Jim was released from the Head Trauma Center with the rejoinder that he was "one lucky dude." We drove him home to Los Angeles so he could undergo many hours of reconstructive craniofacial plastic surgery repair over the following weeks.

Somewhat jokingly, Jim asked the plastic surgeon if he could straighten his nose a bit (broken several times in accidents before my time), and smooth out a few wrinkles. This time, his eminent surgeon, a friend of ours, told him he'd be lucky if he could even make him recognizable to his friends. He installed new metal eye sockets and plates in his cheekbones, reset his nose and sent Jim to a periodontal surgeon who put braces on his teeth and wired his fractured jaw shut for six weeks.

Though relieved that he was not going to be in a wheelchair for life, I was in a burning swivet, churning between gratitude he'd been spared and wasn't a quadriplegic, and a slow boil that he was thick-headed enough to keep doing such things and denying that they had any impact on me or our relationship. How I wished I could control him! But I knew that such fantasy would be pure folly. I told him that if he wanted to keep our marriage alive, he would have to look at some of these issues in therapy. To his credit, through his wired-shut jaw, Jim agreed to look at some of these issues in therapy.

### The Talking Cure

Jim did not want to go to therapy alone, but agreed to go to couple counseling. We must have been quite a handful for our therapist: me, the psychoanalyst with words and feelings to spare as well as a list of publications on intimacy and relationship, accompanied by a testosterone-triggered, Spartan husband whose jaw had only recently been unwired! "Dr. Larry," to his credit, did a yeoman's job. He addressed each of us on our own terms, got us to talk and listen to each other, reframed conflicts, delved deeper into their roots, and offered us considerable humor and no little sense of irony. We both gained a lot from the experience. A year later, with new metaphors and a couple of working agreements in place, we returned to a blessed kind of normalcy.

Larry introduced Jim to his alter ego, a mountain man named Jeremiah Johnson. Jim had always thought of Johnson as a kind of a hero—a self-sufficient trapper, Indian trader and loner; so initially he was flattered by the comparison. But Larry saw Jeremiah Johnson in an entirely different light. He described him as "a hard-ass, narcissistic son of a gun" who scalped Indians, used anybody and anything without regard except for his own use, and couldn't get along with anyone. Larry suggested a shift in role models.

He also unearthed a childhood memory from a hike Jim took with "Doc," his father, in the high Sierra wilderness. To get him moving, Doc told eight-year-old Jim to toughen up or he'd leave him behind "for the Indians." Larry was able to make contact with a vulnerable little boy who was afraid of being abandoned in the woods. This helped bring about a healthy shift, so that we were no longer polarized as the woman with all the vulnerable feelings and the no-nonsense man of action, the one who "just does it." Therapy saved our marriage and we both knew it.

We reached an agreement that Jim, who finally acknowledged how traumatic his bike accidents were to me, would refrain from cycling for a full year. I wished it would be for good, but Larry figured he couldn't hold Jim's feet to the fire on that. I think he also felt I needed to work on relinquishing anxious control. A year would give us time to reflect and heal, in more ways than one. We agreed to seek out common ground for our shared interests and adventures.

We had met and fallen in love backpacking, and the mountains have always brought us joy. However, with my two torn rotator cuffs, I could no longer shoulder a heavy backpack. I had already had a brainstorm about using llamas for backpacking, but hadn't been able to do anything about it. So the deal was that Jim, who always wants to go the simplest, leanest way, would agree to help me in the purchase, training and packing of a couple of llamas. In exchange, I would put up no fuss about his taking off a couple of weekends a year on his own, on a macho "seeds and nuts, balls-out hike." It was easy for him to agree that I could also take off to give a paper here and a workshop there, or to go to a spa.

I return to the backstory and this pivotal period in our relationship because here we are, almost twenty years of shared history behind us, facing some of the same issues again. After spending months on the road in South America, we've returned to Twin Brooks and spring has sprung. Soon we will embark on another odyssey. This one will be rather huge, churning up dregs of our old emotional issues.

### Solo Voyagers: Jim on Wheels

We reached the decision that as part of this sabbatical, there are things we each want to do very much that the other does not want to do. We have also realized that there is still more psychological homework for us each to do from our work with Larry, now years ago. Therefore, we will each embark on long, solo journeys of our own divination. Each in our own way, we've been preparing for these journeys for months, if not years.

Jim's one year off his bicycle did not, as I might have hoped, cure him of his bicycle mania. He honored the year-long hiatus but let me know that he would resume riding. He pledged several changes in his cycling: no more racing; no more riding on Pacific Coast Highway; and whenever possible, any riding would be with a group, which tends to provide safety in numbers. I have had to work on letting go of my fear, to accept that I have difficulty tolerating something dangerous my true love loves, and I'd best lighten up about it. Up to now, to be truthful, I have cultivated more of a grin-and-bear-it attitude than genuine acceptance. It is time for me to move toward genuine acceptance, because Jim has been planning, with great enthusiasm, to bicycle across America—to ride from the Pacific Ocean to the Atlantic Ocean. I am thankful he'll be with a group.

The ride will take nine weeks, from mid-June until late August. We will drive together to Seattle, near both the starting point of the ride and Brooke and Philip's home. This will give us an opportunity to visit them, in their new house overlooking Puget Sound, and see Brooke's new chiropractic office. Then we will drive to the starting point in Everett, Washington, where we'll camp with the other cyclists assembling for the Transamerica ride, and where Jim will reassemble his recumbent bike.

On Father's Day morning, after he symbolically dips his rear tire in the Pacific Ocean, we will say our final farewells and I will see him off. 4,194 miles of self-propelled cycling later, if all goes well in his northern crossing, he will reach the coast of Maine on August 18, 2001. He plans to cycle with the "EFI" group, the ones who will eschew the sag wagon and cycle "Every Fucking Inch" of the way. He will traverse Washington and Idaho, following the Lewis and Clarke trail into the Rockies in Wyoming. He will cycle across the Bitterroot Valley and over the 8,429-foot Teton Pass to Jackson Hole. He'll ride through the Big Horn Mountains, past Devil's Monument, and through the Black Hills of South Dakota. There, for the first time in his life, he will see Mt. Rushmore and the Crazy Horse monuments.

About halfway across the continent, having traversed innumerable rivers, he will pedal over the great Missouri River, through Minnesota's wooded "Land of 10,000 Lakes," across the mighty Mississippi River, and into Wisconsin. He'll be ferried over

Lake Michigan and Lake Ontario, remounting to ride through Ontario, Canada before dropping down for his first sight of Niagara Falls. Nearing the end of this awesome journey, he will cycle through the Adirondacks and around the Finger Lakes to Lake Placid, New York.

The last week of his odyssey will take him by ferry across Lake Champlain to Burlington, Vermont, then through the Green Mountains and into the White Mountains of New Hampshire. After a nine-week journey of over four thousand miles, he'll reach the Maine coast, where he plans to ceremonially dip his front tire into the Atlantic, commemorating the completion of a grand bicycle pilgrimage. As Jim's cycling goal sinks into my consciousness, I am no longer simply grinning and bearing it. I'm really proud of him, impressed that my love, this man of sixty-four summers, will take on and I have great confidence—surmount this great personal challenge.

# Chapter 29
## Good Medicine: A Parting Ceremony

It is very important to me to be mindful of the impact of a lengthy separation on our relationship. It will be a true and noble challenge for me, for my fears of loss are by no means extinguished. We'll be honoring each other's separate interests. Jim will be cycling for nine weeks, which I would pay handsomely *not* to do. I will be giving a paper at the International Psychoanalytic Congress in France, and more importantly, traveling solo and writing, then spending time in Plum Village monastery in the south of France, which Jim has no interest in doing. I will then odyssey in the Italian Alps, Greece, and Turkey.

I will be taking myself to my own edge by traveling for two months alone, something I've never done. And I will be realizing a sacred trust, to spend time in residence with Zen master Thich Nhat Hanh at Plum Village. This spiritual pilgrimage has become profoundly meaningful to me; it is not only a quest for a deeper sense of the sacred, but also a support for my efforts to lighten up and let go. This may be the heart center of my odyssey.

As Jim and I approach countdown, we talk about how to be separate yet maintain an intimate connection. Today at lunch on the front porch at Twin Brooks, we powwow about time zones and cell phones and email and spirit messages, and discover that for the first month it will be relatively easy to be in close contact. I'll be here at Twin Brooks. Jim will carry his new cell phone and if he's in a place with reception, can call in the evenings before he craters after a long day's riding. We will reach a black hole during the second month, where he'll be cycling and camping and I'll be residing in tiny B&Bs with no telephone number, and at the monastery with a vow of noble silence. We'll be separated by time zones of seven to nine hours' difference. Jim will be pedaling all day, and if he turns his cell phone on in the evening, it will be the middle of the night in France.

I will have my laptop to send and receive emails when I can get on the Internet, but that won't work for Jim. Once a week, when he has a day of rest, he might—even in the smallest burgs of Iowa—find an Internet café to send an email. For the last three weeks, when he comes back to Twin Brooks and I am in the Middle East, if we are lucky, maybe I can call him. Direct communication will be iffy at best.

We will do better to maintain an intimate connection by remaining conscious of each other and practicing mindfulness. To mark this idea, I have an inspiration. If we each carry a "medicine bag" of special talismans and fetishes to remind ourselves of each other, we will protect that fragile connection in our relationship. We talk about this idea and it seems to symbolize something important in the growth steps we are each trying to take. For me, letting go of my anxiety, dependence and need for control, accepting days and maybe weeks of not knowing whether Jim is safe represents a huge step toward letting go of fear and honoring his autonomy. For him, truly acknowledging my importance to him and that we are deeply interconnected, and knowing that this acknowledgment bears daily mindfulness, will be his big growth step.

### A Ceremony and an Omen

We decide to make a ceremony on the evening before our departure to Washington. A long time ago, on a trip to Aspen, Colorado, Jim bought me a beautiful, handmade, beaded and fringed doeskin purse with a little fetish pouch attached to it. That pouch will be my "medicine bag." In Santa Fe I found a soft doeskin bag for Jim. All spring, we have been looking around amongst our things for small totems, fetishes and special objects to put in these pouches for remembrance of each other.

At sunset, we take our medicine bags to the natural swimming hole at Twin Brooks, along with a trowel, a whisk broom and flower clippers. At this time of year the path along the stream to the pool is resplendent with rhododendrons and wild azaleas, and we stop periodically to snip a few spectacularly fragrant blossoms. We arrive at the pool with our medicine bags and flowers, and begin to tend to the ancient circle of Indian grinding holes on the large granite outcropping overlooking the natural pool. More than a dozen holes have been honed into the rock here, probably by Miwok Indians with stone pestles.

This is a powerful site. My family history here is relatively brief, maybe only a hundred and twenty-five years, but in California, such a history is still remarkable. Near the pool and in the surrounding woods are four bronze plaques placed in memorium of my mother, grandmother, father and grandfather. Their newer presence joins this place that has been an ancient Indian hearthstone, where acorn meal was ground and food was prepared, and is still a serene spot in God's country, a sacred site, and a reminder that all lives are brief.

In silence, we clean the grinding holes, using the trowel to clear out weeds and dirt and the broom to sweep the site clean. When we are finished, we each put one or two of the objects we have brought into each of the grinding holes. Jim has brought a Navajo bear fetish with turquoise eyes from my consulting room, a tiny frog fetish with coral eyes, a polished stone inscribed with the word "Love" that he found in Auberry, a scrap of his t-shirt and a good luck dollar bill folded into a tiny square.

I have brought a lock of my blond hair, which my mother cut and saved when I was two years old, and which I discovered last Mother's Day in a drawer of my grandmother's old treadle sewing machine. I also have a small bear fetish from Santa Fe, and a tiny sack of sacred dirt from the old church at Chimayo, brought for the occasion to my birthday retreat by my childhood friend Chris, an artist who lives in nearby Taos. I have also gathered assorted small stones from our travels.

When all our objects are in place, we break silence to tell each other why we have chosen each one. Then we take turns going around the grinding hole circle, selecting a few of each other's offerings that feel most powerful to us and putting them in our medicine pouches. Jim selects the lock of my hair, the Chimayo sacred dirt, and the bear fetish. I select the Love stone, the tiny frog, the dollar bill and the bear fetish he has chosen.

Just as the sun dips behind the tall pines and cedars, Jim says, "Look, Harriet! Look at the pool!" I turn around and see, for the first time in my life of sixty summers here, a mother mallard duck beckoning six tiny ducklings out of hiding from the rushes on the far bank of the pool. With great dignity and apparent pride, she parades them, swimming in widening circles around the pool before our astonished eyes. This time it isn't planned silence; it is utter speechlessness.

If ever we wanted an omen, here it is. I feel ready to cross a new threshold, to trust that as we set out on our separate journeys to grow, to take ourselves to a new level personally and in our relationship, we will return in safety, changed in positive ways. It almost feels guaranteed. For the first time in years, I feel I am stepping into freedom from anxiety.

## Chapter 30
## Spirit, Cheyenne, and Running Bear

AFTER WAVING Jim off in Washington, I return to Twin Brooks to stay for a month until I begin my pilgrimage in mid-July. He calls to tell me the journey started comically. The assembled Ride across America cyclists were camped in tents on the football field the first night at the high school in Everett, Washington. At 3:00 a.m., the sprinklers came on. Pandemonium ensued as sleep-heavy cyclists rousted out of their tents and hopped to the sidelines in sleeping bags, like kids in a three-legged race. Perfect baptism for an auspicious launch.

### Sixty-One Going on Sixteen

Today, July 3, is my birthday again. This is a quiet one, unlike last year's major millennium celebration and retreat. Today I am sixty-one, but feel (and act) like I'm going on sixteen! Since riding horses across the plains of Patagonia and the pampas of Argentina last winter, I've been possessed of memories of myself in sheer bliss as a teenage girl, flying down the road in the Twin Brooks moonlight atop my Palomino Arabian quarter horse, Calypso.

From the time I was an infant in my mother's arms atop her horse, I spent summers here on horseback. In summer camp, I learned to ride English and to jump, and even rode in the prestigious Santa Barbara International Horseshow. Trouble was, my camp horse, "Mon Ami," whose real name was tellingly "Mouse," was a dud who decided to lie down and roll in front of the judges' stand. My showing career ended unharmed but humiliated in a dust heap on the ground, while my parents and grandparents looked on in shock, probably mixed with a tad of stifled amusement.

Over the years at Twin Brooks, my grandfather Punky picked out a series of fine old cow ponies for me. There was Sox, then Daisy, then Gillette (so named for his razor-sharp back). By the time my fourteenth birthday rolled around, I had saved enough money to buy a horse of my own, Calypso, a winsome palamino arab quarter horse mare. With my savings I bought her and a fine-tooled Western saddle at auction. I remember how scared I was, uncertain whether I was choosing the right horse, spending most of my savings on such a major purchase. Once the decision was made, I never regretted it. I spent the summer afternoon of my fourteenth birthday with Calypso, a hose and a bucket of suds, adoringly giving her a bath, scrubbing the tar weed from her flanks and shampooing her flaxen mane and tail until they shone bright in the sun. Riding her in the cool of teenage summer evenings, I loved to flatten out on her warm neck, smell her horsey smell and gallop down the road in the moonlight, telling her my dreams and knowing that I was about as close to heaven as any girl could be. I didn't have a boyfriend yet and saw no need for one. For a couple of years, Calypso was all I needed for perfect happiness.

After high school graduation came college, grad school, teaching, marriage and babies. Except for summers, Calypso spent her later years grazing in the pasture, seldom ridden. One winter in my forties, my children didn't know what was wrong with Mommy. I was lying on my bed sobbing; I had gotten word that Calypso had died.

It had become prohibitively expensive to board horses over the winters, as the former ranch land around Fresno became high-priced suburban real estate. We didn't yet have a year-round caretaker at Twin Brooks, so I had to mourn the definitive end of an era and my youth. Jim is allergic to horses; they make his asthma worse. The only time we did any serious riding together ended traumatically when I was thrown by a rogue gelding on a dude ranch and my shoulder rotator cuff was badly torn. It never occurred to me to consider buying a horse again.

When Calypso died, I figured my riding years were over except for an occasional ride on vacation. That is, until we visited a

Patagonian *estancia* during our travels through South America. On a sheep ranch at the tip of Patagonia, I was treated to a wonderful ride on a very fine horse, accompanied by a sexy gaucho who wore flared black trousers fitted into high black boots and held in place by a wide leather belt in which was tucked a handworked silver-handled knife. Whooee. During our travels throughout Patagonia, I rode at every opportunity. From the huasos in Chile to the gauchos in Argentina, from the pampas to the Andes, I had unforgettable rides and riding partners, and my old horse-loving brain synapses started refiring.

Now, at Twin Brooks by myself, with Jim away on his bicycle, I have become obsessed with buying a horse. I'm acting out "just a bit," with both of us taking highly questionable risks to follow our passions—Jim cycling after two near-death bike accidents, and me contemplating horse riding again after racking my shoulder up in a way that has left me fairly compromised.

I propose to Cathy, our caretaker, who has her two horses pastured here, that we go in together on the cost of training her young mare, Sugar, so we would have two horses to ride around the ranch together. This year we began logging some of the ranch to reduce fire hazard and to increase the health of our forest. To do the job, we hired a seasoned logger and cattleman who happens to be an accomplished horseman with a ranch of his own. We sent Sugar to Mark's ranch for schooling, and he lent us one of his well-trained cow ponies to use in the meantime. Unfortunately, we got word from Mark that Sugar is a "bucker" who won't let anybody saddle her. This is not the horse I need for my comeback. On the other hand, Cathy and I have been having some wonderful trail rides together, she on her old reliable black stallion, Storm, and me on Mark's well-trained cow horse, Blackie. Blackie is well more than sixteen hands high—a big horse. He's willing and handles well, but I need a stepladder or a bale of hay to climb aboard. The ground is just too far down if I fall.

I put out the word that I am in the market for a young, small, easy handling trail mare. On these horse-hunting forays, I've met a couple of horse traders: a big-bellied, gravel-voiced guy who looks and sounds like Burl Ives; an aging rodeo queen whose barn is graced with pictures of cowboys and cowgirls in spangles and fringe; a parson whose private passion is not God but livestock and breeding; and a couple of horse-crazed teenage girls who are growing up, moving away in September, and parting with their beloved horses to pay for college.

I've met all kinds of horses, mostly young trained American Quarter Horses, Morgans, and paints. I have seen a dozen and ridden five candidates in the unrelenting heat of the San Joaquin Valley, including a five-year-old, registered sorrel paint and an unusually beautiful and sweet eight-year-old buckskin/palomino paint who is very pregnant with a foal by a leopard Appaloosa. With my birthday approaching, I decide to make a bid for the pregnant paint. If having baby llamas born here on the ranch has been splendid, having a foal born here would be incredible. Mark agrees, saying it's a bit like an Easter egg hunt. A palomino paint and a leopard Appy could produce an amazing little foal, with splashes of Calypso's color to help me feel the circle was unbroken!

But when I call Rhonda, the paint's owner, she's gotten cold feet about selling her. I take a hike with Jullay to the top of Echo Rock, where I do yoga with a few extra salutes to the sun to bring good energy and fortune. About midday, I decide to bid for the five-year-old sorrel and cast my fate to the winds, telling Mark and Cathy that by sundown today, I'll either have no horses, one horse, or two-and-three-quarters horses. However it goes, I love spending my birthday turning sixty-one and feeling sixteen.

Rhonda, the pregnant buckskin paint's owner, is unable to part with her mare, but my bid for the sorrel is accepted. She is registered by the dopey name of Skipalou, but when she arrived in a light summer rain, another name reveals itself. When I lead her down the road to exercise her and let her familiarize herself with the ranch, I feel her prancing spirits and high temperament, and know that she will be my Rain Spirit of Skipalou. I name her Spirit.

She is elegant of form, a sorrel red beauty with a white blaze on her face and two white socks. I ride her English and Western to get the feel of her, but she feels like a spirited English lady to me; I'm inclined toward riding close to the bone with the Swiss-made English saddle I'd given to Mother years ago. It is in excellent condition, especially after I work it over with saddle soap, and riding it brings me closer to the feel of the horse. Just in case, I ride her wearing a hard hat with my mom's jodhpur boots and riding crop.

Life feels great—especially when, a week later, Rhonda calls to announce that she really can't afford to keep her pregnant mare and would accept the price I offered. I gasp in shock, pissed at the runaround she'd put me through, but I realize her mare was my first choice. I impulsively agree, suddenly finding myself the unexpected owner of two-and-a-half new horses. With a single swipe I have forfeited any credibility arguing against Jim's bike riding.

Rhonda calls her mare Blue for a reason I can't recall. I'm very particular about names; they summon spirits and energy befitting each animal. Witness our llamas: Machu, Pichu, Mica, Hopi, Jambo, Miwok, and Zuni. We named Miwok's cria Llao Llao—a Patagonian Mapuche Indian word, pronounced "zhao zhao," which means "sweet sweet," after a wild woodland delicacy. This is the baby llama that was conceived that hot dusty day on the trail up to Bench Valley. Sweet!

Naming has been a special family tradition; We named our dog Aaballou, a.k.a. Aaballoucious Beastie, and now we have Jullay. All the fish in the aquarium had names, including Leon, Clowny and Angelo Mio. Ariel named her guinea pigs Zeus and Hera, and Gabriel, at age six, named his tye-dyed stuffed fish Ichthyosaurus. This pregnant, eight-year-old buckskin paint mare looks to me like a sturdy Indian pony; I clearly see her name is Cheyenne. I also clearly see her carrying a gorgeous foal, who will be called Running Bear, to offer up the highest tribute to the spirit of the great bear.

The rest of July flies by on Pegasus's wings. I am in horse heaven, riding Spirit on mother's Swiss saddle one day and Cheyenne the next, with the tooled leather Western saddle I'd bought for Calypso when I was fourteen, polished to a gleam. By the time it is time to follow the call of my dream to the south of France, I don't want to go anywhere but down to the barn! But I have a paper to give, and I trust that once I am launched, something else amazing will be in store.

# CHAPTER 31
## PSYCHE ET LA VIE EN ROSE

*Psyche and Salmon*

A FEW HOURS ago I landed in Nice, France for the International Psychoanalytic Congress where I'm to give another paper. I arrive among coveys of psychoanalysts from every continent of the globe. It's easy to pick them out in the airport, converging like salmon genetically programmed to hone in on the mouth of their river—in this case, le Fleuve du IPA Congress. While fewer of the men wear Freudian beards and three-piece dark suits any more and the field is comprised of nearly half women now, my colleagues are clearly identifiable, even in casual wear and without their Congress briefcases and identifying badges.

Even after being away from all this for almost two years since the Freud Congress in Jerusalem, my "psychoanalytic self," intellectual orientation, behaviors, and mode of dress snap back into place—but maybe not exactly the same place. While I have kept my close collegial relationships over the Internet, to converge in the flesh with compatriots like salmon on the river of Nice is a bit jarring. I had to ferret around, looking for "professional" clothes for this segment of my journey, having stowed them deeply away in the store barn at Twin Brooks. My attitude toward packing has transformed totally from the insane traveler's anxiety preparation for the Jerusalem trip. Volume is now less than half and anxiety is practically nil. That's progress.

Within days, I am back in the swing of it and having a good time. I take part, for the first time ever, in a two-day Spanish language work group of training and supervising analysts. Spending last winter in Latin America has given me new confidence speaking Spanish, even when it comes to discussing complex psychoanalytic issues. I delight in discovering that I can follow most of the conversation and participate enough. It is intriguing to meet with colleagues from all over Latin America—there are several Argentines and Brazilians, two Chileans, and one Peruvian and one Bolivian. It feels like a reunion. Truly, over the course of the sabbatical travels, I have exchanged a fixed American identity for citizenship in the world.

There are other reunions, not only with friends and colleagues from the States, but from Canada, Britain, France and Italy as well, and an especially heartening hug from and dinner with Emmanuel, my Israeli colleague who had invited me to the Millennial Freud Conference in Jerusalem in 1999. That invite preceded the Middle East's explosion into violence and strife, and the foiling of Bin Laden's plot to abduct Americans in Petra (which would have been us). I have been very worried about Emanuel and our other Israeli friends since then, as we've had little news. It is truly a pleasure to settle in together to catch up at a Nicoise café for a dinner of aubergine terrine, planked fish, salad and a bottle of wine.

During the IPA Congress, our international film panel gathers to give our papers, screen clips from films and field discussion on our panel topic: the cinematic construction of memory from a psychoanalytic perspective. My paper, about *Limbo* by one of my favorite filmmakers, John Sayles, is called "Constructions of Memory And Desire: Marooned In John Sayles' *Limbo*." After the panel we enjoy a dinner overlooking the Côte d'Azur, and make plans to re-group in London this November for the European Psychoanalytic Film Festival, which is being orchestrated by our Italian friend Andrea.

Andrea is the serious film scholar who burst my bubble after the fact of our last winter's arduous climb of the world's highest free-falling waterfall, Angel Falls in Venezuela. I would prefer to keep my illusions, but as Andrea is so continentally charming, if someone has to burst mine, I suppose he's the one to do it.

## Cellular Connection: A Dogged Quest

When I'm not involved in meetings or panels, I spend far too much time running around Nice in search of a way to keep in contact with Jim, who has cycled his way to the Dakotas by now. He was wonderfully reliable about calling me at Twin Brooks to report on the day's cycling. His adventure is summed up in "95/95/95" and "EFI." 95/95/95 refers to his typical daily ride of ninety-five miles in 95-degree heat and with 95% humidity. Undaunted, Jim has vowed with a few of his newfound mates to uphold the honor of the EFI Club. Unlike most of the other riders who periodically ride for a sensible stretch in the van, the EFI Club pedals every day, all day, in rain, lightning or blistering sun, every inch of road over the Rockies, the Black Hills, and the Midwest, vowing to cycle every inch to the Atlantic Ocean.

Cell phones are a relatively new gadget. This is my first. The cellular phone attached to my Handspring Palm computer, which Jim gave me for my birthday to maintain our nightly communication ritual, managed only one successful call between us. On my pre departure day in Los Angeles I reached his cellular phone in Wyoming before mine went black. I hurriedly made arrangements to replace it, and in a disquieted state of anxiety about entering a relational black hole, took off for Nice. Now, while the company is willing to replace the malfunctioning phone, they will only send it to an address in the U.S., so it must go to my office assistant who will send it to me abroad, if she can get it to me soon enough here in Nice.

This doesn't seem too daunting until I learn that the package will be detained in customs for inspection. I entertain downward spiraling optimism about ever seeing it again, even if it makes it to my hotel in Nice, as the desk clerks have been utterly unable to take or deliver a phone message for me from any colleague. Messages seem to go awry, and if a slip of paper can't make it into my box, I can't fathom how my replacement phone will find me.

Miracle of miracles, on the eve of my departure from the Nice Congress, it shows up, but without the crucial battery or SIM card that mobilizes it. The factory shipped only a replacement for the phone itself, not all of its parts. I send a frenzied email for another battery and SIM card, but not before scouring cellular telephone shops in Nice to see if I can buy a new battery and card. While I discover I can purchase a French Telecom card, which would save me money on transatlantic calls, my phone is a brand new model that the French haven't yet seen. When I show up with my batteryless little device, an excited flurry of French techno-freaks converges on the counter to have a look and exclaim, "Ou, la la!" But they have no battery for it.

My intermittent, transcendental experiences of Zen and the Art of Computer Maintenance must now be applied to my mental state regarding communications with Jim. We've managed to speak only twice since I arrived in France, rising above the arithmetical challenges of a nine-hour time difference, his rigorous bicycling schedule and my conference schedule. He knows I've made it abroad safely, and I know he is distinguishing his career among the diminishing membership in the EFI Club. Jim is not entertaining a Zen approach to cycling the American continent. He is not stopping to "smell the roses," as the bike tour organizers have invited him to do. No, Jim is on a race. He is dedicated to proving the manic proposition that a sixty-four-year-old white American male can be just as well stocked with testosterone as any recent college graduate from any country. He brags he has "taken out" a young Dutchman and several college students, and is doggedly nibbling away at hegemony for the lead position established by the one professional bike racer on the trip. Oh, Jim, *plus ca change, plus c'est la meme chose*. The more we change, the more we discover nothing has changed.

What has changed is my attitude. In past times, I would have been frantic with worry that daily racing would increase the risk of accidents, and furious about his stubbornness. But now, after all the work I've done on letting go, I have a kind of bemused and affectionate interest that is unclouded by anxiety or a wish to change the man. I truly hope I have finally relinquished what my writing partner, Judy Welles described as every woman's intermittent unconscious fantasy: to regard her man as a lump of clay waiting to be shaped to her desire. I do wish I could count on a working cell phone as I set off to navigate solo through the French countryside in a rented Peugeot with nothing but a Michelin #233 regional map and rustic directions. But even toward that prospect, which would ordinarily evoke high anxiety, I notice something has truly shifted. Zen and the Art of Computer Maintenance has permeated my being. I breathe. I smile, and I simply go on going on. If I get lost, if the battery never comes, or if we lose phone contact, we'll both be all right. We'll even be the wiser for it. I am ready for my Peugeot.

### La Vie En Rose: Motoring Toute Seule through the Dordogne

Rivers run all through France. My travels will take me through valleys alongside tributaries of the Dordogne as it wends its way across the southwest of France, past Bordeaux and into the Atlantic. My aim is to experience traveling alone. Though colleagues have invited me to accompany them on enchanting post-Congress trips, I am doggedly chosing to take this time alone, more to explore myself in the world than to sightsee in France. I have been here before, and I know it is lovely and rich with historical sites, but this time, I am looking for solitude, quiet places to alight and read, reflect, and write. I look forward to dusting off the French I studied in college and over one magical sixties summer of French language immersion at "L'Institute des Etudes Etranges" at the old monastery in Carmel, the Carmel Mission.

I am slowly heading for Plum Village, east of Bordeaux in the tiny hamlet of Thenac between Bergerac and Ste. Foy le Grande. My other aim is to reunite with Kevin, our friend from the Patagonia Express trip along the fjords of Chile to the Termes de Puyhuapi and the San Rafael Glacier. Kevin, a British hotelier, was traveling solo. He and Argentina's pre-eminent novelist, Marcos Aguinis, with his companion Nori from Buenos Aires, were among the most magical of our new acquaintances in Latin America. Kevin will be here in the Charante region for two weeks, staying in his flat in the Chateau de Charras. During our ongoing email correspondence, we discovered we would be in the same region of France at the same time and planned to get together.

*Le Vignoble*

With a week to ramble before I am due at Plum Village for a meditation retreat, I am feeling quite spritzy and proud. I manage to pick up my mini silver Peugeot at the airport in Bordeaux, and successfully navigate both the manual gearshift and the map to locate the miniscule hamlet of Celles, where I'll reach Le Vignoble, the home of Nick and Sue, who are to be my hosts for the week. I feel liberated and happy about it all. While Jim merely has to pedal against all odds, EFI, nose to the road, following endless yellow arrows, I pedal on the gas, clutch and brake and proceed sans arrows toward Le Vignoble. Along the way, as I ponder whether I should turn this way or that, I recall an apocryphal story from my days as a grad student in Cambridge, Massachusetts.

According to the story, some New Yorkers driving a big Mercedes found themselves totally lost on the back roads of New England. At a crossroads, they saw an old farmer in the field. The driver called out, "Does it matter which road I take to get to Boston?" "Not to me it don't," came the terse Vermont farmer's reply. This story has always delighted me, not only because it illuminates the cultural divide between New York and New England, but because it sheds light on the journey I am on. No French farmer gives an endive if I get lost. But beyond that, does it really matter which road I take or what my destination, if I travel the road awake and in awareness?

Even lacking yellow arrows, and though many of the roads are unmarked or marked in French, I don't get too lost. Driving up the hill toward Le Vignoble, through fields of corn as high as Babar's eye on one side and luxuriant nodding sunflowers on the other, I arrive quite sure I have found my way to a corner of heaven. The house is a typical French stone farmhouse but Nick and Sue have refurbished it as a permanent home away from their previous home in London. They've added a pool on the slope overlooking the nearby fields, and two new upstairs suites with lovely French windows overlooking the valleys below. My chamber's French doors overlook the Dordogne. All is charming. I meet the other guests, old friends of Nick and Sue on holiday from London: Peter, an Aussie barrister and his partner of nine years, the lovely Leslie.

During the day I am free to write or travel about as I wish. In the evenings, I am embraced and invited into good company with wonderful regional wines and conversation over late gourmet suppers prepared by Sue with fresh vegetables, salad greens, cheeses, wines, patés and fish from the nearby farmer's market in Ribérac. One night, at my urging, they all go out on the town without me, leaving me in charge of their young dachshund, Percy, who's in a deep funk because his sister was fatally bitten last week by an adder in the garden. Sue sets out a dreamy homemade dinner of fingerling pommes, haricots verts, tomates, salmon, flan and chilled Sancerre, and an Internet connection! Not bad. Even better, Jim manages to find me at home with a call from Middle America and we have a lovely overdue catch-up.

The following day, I affirm my fledgling capacity to navigate alone through the country roads of the region to visit Kevin. The only challenge is that Charras is an even tinier hamlet than Thenac. Preoccupied with work, Kevin didn't send me the exact determinants, somewhere between Perigueux and Angoulême. After about an hour and a half nosing along tiny circuitous roads, voila, I make my way to Chateau Charras, where behind great iron gates and down a tree-lined lane, I find Kevin and his chum are in high spirits, preparing an al fresco lunch with champagne in my honor. Lunch occasions a riotously happy reunion—and then we crash out in the sun on chaise lounges near the chateau's old cistern, converted to a swimming pool. Kevin has a perfectly exquisite petit pied-a-terre in Chateau Charras. He was able to come by it at a great price as the former owner, a Madame le Baroness de Charras, was guillotined under Robespierre and her abandoned digs had fallen into considerable disrepair.

Kevin has brought along his friend David, the very cosmopolitan concierge of the Savoy in London, who is terribly English, charming, a campy former actor and retired businessman. David delights his worldly clientele while highly entertaining himself as the Savoy's haute concierge. He insists on taking us under his wing when we come to London for the European Psychoanalytic Film Festival in November, and it seems a wonderful wing to be taken under, so I accept with pleasure.

The days glide by seamlessly. One day is spent with Kevin and David sightseeing in the lovely town of Brantome on the River Dronne. We visit Brantome's prehistoric caves, which came to be inhabited by troglodytes in the early middle ages, and became a medieval abbey with a wonderful carved bas relief the height of a huge wall, showing something like the Day of the Dead presided over by a mystical figure of God. On another day, we visit the farmer's market in Ribérac, where I have an excellent opportunity to photograph local French faces, including my favorite, a close-up of two hale and hearty brothers in the sausage-making business. I manage to email the photo to family and friends as evidence of my good health and spirits.

Taking the leap into solo travel is being amply rewarded thus far. After two weeks enjoying la vie en rose of gastronomic and gustatory pleasures of France, I am fairly nervous about making a dramatic shift into a vegetarian monastic life. I procure a small vial of cognac at the Ribérac farmer's market for the upcoming eight-day Buddhist retreat. It is, however, my solemn intent not to touch it. *Je ne sais pas.*

After a joyful and restful week of writing and exploring at Le Vignoble, I reluctantly say goodbye to Nick and Sue. I move on to Le Sauzade, a B&B in the next valley over, with plans for a quiet transition, writing and practicing walking meditation for a few days until Plum Village. This area is very beautiful and very reasonable; my lovely room at Le Vignoble is 250 francs, or about $30, per day, plus delicious breakfast and dinner for another 100 francs, or $13. *Incroyable.* However, Le Sauzade is charming but not nearly as comfortable, so I return for the rest of the last week to write at Le Vignoble.

Alas, now it is time to pack up, zip up my computer and my lip, cork the wine bottle and enter into solitude and silence for my long-anticipated retreat with the monks and nuns of Plum Village. I am eager and apprehensive, both. I pack a soupçon of cognac, although I know it is more in the spirit of a Benedictine monastery than a Buddhist retreat—and the latter is my intention. To abide by the spirit and the rules of the monks, I will refrain from reading, writing, alcohol and sexual activity (which I have missed for nearly two months since I saw Jim off in Everett, Washington in mid-June), and finally, refrain from talking except on designated occasions. Today I will close my mouth against idle chatter and the fruit of the vine. I hope my restraint will be rewarded with an experience like none I've ever had.

# PART VII
# I HAVE ARRIVED

# Chapter 32
## Cloisters and Pilgrims

Man does not live by bread alone.[13]
There is the hunger for food—and the hunger for meaning.

THICH NHAT HANH established Plum Village, a Zen monastery in the south of France, as a safe haven for hundreds of Vietnamese refugees who fled Vietnam at the end of the war. Thay, as he is affectionately called and which means "teacher" in Vietnamese, is a poet, renowned Zen master and peace activist who was nominated by Martin Luther King for the Nobel Peace Prize in 1967. For nearly forty years, he was exiled from his homeland. During the war, both the communists in North Vietnam and the American-supported government of South Vietnam condemned him for his pacifist activism and refusal to take sides. Plum Village, or Le Village des Pruniers, has grown to include four separate hamlets and is open to pilgrims from all over the world for one month each summer as a meditation retreat center. This month, Thay is hosting a group of young Palestinians and Israelis in an effort to provide a safe refuge, a container for dialogue and healing.

My quest is twofold: to instill a deeper sense of the sacred, and to support my efforts to lighten up and let go of burdensome attachments to things, ideas, outcomes and dependencies. I have been a struggling pilgrim on this path for a long time. My budding interest in Buddhism was watered as a student in the early Sixties at UC Berkeley and nourished at City Lights Bookstore in San

---

13 Deuteronomy 8:2-3 (King James version)..

Francisco, where I found Ferlinghetti's Beat poetry, Jack Kerouac's depiction of Dharma bums, and Alan Watts' books on Zen. My spiritual life was nourished when I lived in Carmel, near Esalen in Big Sur. It took root in the fertile soil left by renouncing the austere teachings of Calvinist-tinged Protestantism—a refusal that reached its apex with my adolescent refusal to throw a pine cone, symbolizing bodily pleasures, into a campfire. How could I abandon physical pleasures? I hadn't even discovered them yet! Zen offered a welcome contrast from Presbyterianism and the constraints of conservative Pasadena. But my Buddhist period in the Sixties was a more "hip" than devotional path. The latter has come more quietly, slowly and unexpectedly over time.

This pilgrimage started anew fifteen years ago, when Jim and I went trekking in Kashmir and Ladakh. In the isolated Himalayas of northern India, we came into contact with many refugee Tibetan Buddhist monks, living in exile from the invasion of Tibet by the Chinese Army. We met them throughout the mountains, for many of their monasteries are located on lonely isolated peaks. We were deeply touched by their incredible gentleness, peaceful natures and tranquility, in spite of the egregious tragedies they'd had to endure.

The monks always greeted us warmly on the high mountain paths, with the musical phrase "Jullay!" which we now say in greeting to our sweet doggie. They invited us to visit their monasteries, to show us the few Buddhist scrolls they managed to secrete in their robes as they fled Tibet. They offered us ancient *thangkas*, rolled devotional paintings on sheepskin or parchment depicting mandalas, prayer wheels, or scenes from the life of the Buddha. Two of these thangkas, a Buddha and a mandala from Ladakh, are now the only art pieces on the wall of my consulting room, giving it the aura of a cloister and reminding me of that spiritual place.

Later, when the Dalai Lama left his exiled refuge in Ladakh and Dharamsala to travel around the world and to raise consciousness about the Chinese Cultural Revolution's genocide and cultural "purging" of Tibetan peoples, especially monks and nuns, I went to hear him whenever I could, and bought and studied his books. A friend introduced me to books by American Buddhist Pema Chodron and by Vietnamese Buddhist Thich Nhat Hanh, including

*Peace is Every Step* and *The Miracle of Mindfulness*. I was so taken with their messages of peace and their teachings about Western society's preoccupation with past and future, which cause us to miss the precious present moment. I found this wisdom very compatible with the yoga practice I have followed for the past thirty years.

Buddhist teachings about embracing what *is*—including acknowledgement and acceptance of the complex soup of conflicting desires, prohibitions and longings that make up our human psyches—are such a wonderful contrast to the Protestant polarization of sin and sanctity. I found the teachings on tolerance incredibly helpful during the painful struggles I faced with my son Gabriel's rebellions and renunciations. I also loved Thich Nhat Hanh's teachings on the meditative potential in ordinary moments during life's most mundane tasks: washing dishes, preparing vegetables, sweeping the floor, walking, even driving a car in traffic. He teaches that if we are conscious, or "mindful," and remain focused on the simple miracle of breathing in and breathing out, we are able to meditate as we engage in these simple daily tasks.

He recounts an ancient Asian fable about a pilgrim who was overtaken by a wild and hungry tiger. The traveler ran for his life and dove into an empty well, where he clung to stones on the walls, but his noises awakened a dragon below. He hung on for dear life while the tiger roared down at him from the mouth of the well and the dragon snapped up at him from below. He knew it was only a matter of time before exhaustion would overpower him, and he would let go and fall into the dragon's mouth. Just as he was about to let go, a shaft of sunlight fell on the wall of the well and he saw a beautiful branch with a few drops of honey on the leaves. In his last gesture, he smiled, opened his mouth and tasted the sweet honey. Here is a parable about living fully and consciously in the present moment, as if it is the last moment.

When Thay came to speak in Santa Monica in the 1980s, I was dumbstruck by the mind-boggling shift in driving behavior on the freeway leading to the Santa Monica Civic Auditorium. Ordinarily contentious LA drivers paused to let other cars change lanes, waiting patiently as they snailed down the off-ramp to the large parking lot. No honking, no squealing tires seizing a hair's advantage over the competition. In all my years of driving in LA, I'd never seen anything like it. It was as if fairy dust had been sprinkled over the freeway. Once we were settled inside the auditorium, a small, humble monk with big Dumbo ears and a sweet childlike smile stepped quietly onto the stage, wearing a simple brown cotton robe, indistinguishable from the robes of the monastics who accompanied him. Hardly the arrival of the Pope. Immediately the audience hushed, touched by his calm, deep, light-hearted energy. It so reminded me of the Dalai Lama and the simple Tibetan monks we met in Ladakh.

I realized that reading the teachings and sitting in my own meditative practice was not enough. I had to go to Plum Village to have my own retreat experience. Fifteen busy years later, when I planned to attend the IPA Congress in the South of France, the long-deferred but perfect moment arose, and I have seized it.

# CHAPTER 33
## PLUM VILLAGE

*Ste. Foy Le Grande, Thenac, France*

EN ROUTE to Plum Village, I motor across Bordeaux. The fields are resplendent with plum orchards dripping with fruit and sunflowers dancing and nodding like droll wee folk brownies in sunbonnets. This is the culinary capital of French hedonism: wineries, tasting rooms, cheese makers, and foie gras farms beckon salaciously to my intemperate, oenophile, former foodie self. Following the instructions in my pre-registration packet, however, I navigate my Peugeot sans stops through the countryside, south from Charante to la Dordogne.

I arrive in less than two hours at the train station at Ste. Foy Le Grande, where I've been told I will recognize one of the brown-robed monks waiting to meet new arrivals on incoming trains. And so I do. I see two men, one holy-looking East Indian man and one very young monk whose head is so shaven it fairly gleams. Dusting off my rusty French from "L'Institute des Etudes Etranger" summer school, having practiced during the car ride, I muster an awkward schoolgirl's courage. "Bonjour! Je m'excuse. Je cherche les Freres des Village des Pruniers parce que j'ai besoin du direcion la."

The East Indian man bows courteously but looks slightly bemused. The young monk smiles. "American? You speak English?"

"Quelle bonne chance! Oh, yes!"

So it is that I meet Shantum Seth, the East Indian who has been an assistant to Thay since 1987, and the young monk of the shining dome, who introduces himself to me: "Phap Diep. It means Brother

Leaf, but I was named William at birth. Does your car have room?"

I lead them outside the station foyer to my mini Peugeot. On a bench in front of the station is a gaggle of Vietnamese children, ranging in age from four to fourteen. Phap Diep, whose name is pronounced "Fop Yip," looks from them to my tiny car and then at Shantum. Phap Diep motions wordlessly, suggesting that Shantum go ahead in the overloaded monastery van, leaving himself and some of the children to work it out with me. Before departing the station, I make an unsuccessful attempt to purchase my train ticket to Domodossola, Italy, for two weeks hence, then we approach the tiny Peugeot. Somehow the five Vietnamese children, whose families in Texas have sent them here for the summer, fold themselves into the back seat like circus clowns into a VW.

Phap Diep offers to drive. In this shy young man I see a person who may not have frequent opportunities to drive a car and would clearly enjoy the chance. I see in his young face depth and kindness, as well as pain, and I am drawn to him. Wilted from negotiating my way across Bordeaux to La Gare du Ste. Foy Le Grande, I happily relinquish the keys.

Driving to Plum Village, he peppers me with questions about who I am and why I have come. Once I've briefly explained that I am a psychoanalyst traveling the world on a pilgrimage, he tells me more about himself. Within minutes, jammed into my tiny silver-blue Peugeot, I begin to learn more about him. He talks about his quest for peace and wisdom. "When I left my Quebec home for Vassar, I—"[14]

I interrupt him. "Vassar! Poughkeepsie? Really! That's where I went to college, and my son Gabriel as well!"

A great grin glides across Phap Diep's face. Monk and Mama give each other a high five.

Life is full of such improbable serendipity. Here I am, six thousand miles from home, trying to get away from it all, en route to a Vietnamese Buddhist retreat, being shepherded by a bald, brown-robed monk from Vassar College. There is something about not only his age but his wry self-conscious way that reminds me of a softer

14  To protect confidentiality, monastic and given names and some details have been changed..

version of Gabriel, who is still heartbreakingly angry and alienated from me. With this newly minted bond, our conversation quickly deepens and we agree to continue to meet during the retreat.

Phap Diep tells me about his childhood difficulties, augmented by his parents' divorce. That sounds familiar. During college, he found a good therapist who helped him connect with the repressed bodily pain and deprivation he felt as a twin whose birth had precipitated their mother's postpartum depression and inability to respond to her babies. I hear his sense of disjuncture as he describes running out of money for therapy just when he was untangling all of this. His therapist, though well intentioned and trying to protect him from debt, advised the young man to discontinue treatment until he could pay for it. He never had a real opportunity to explore this decision with her. I tell him that whether or not her decision was reasonable, it seems he felt cut off yet again from a nurturant mother he deeply needed, and he nods in sad affirmation. Almost without knowing it, we enter into an unlikely and certainly unanticipated relationship that represents a healing pathway for each of us.

The welcoming calligraphy sign at the monastery gate proclaims both a geographical fact and a state of being: "You Have Arrived. You Are Here." I take a deep breath. "I have arrived. I am here!" Plum Village, located among rolling hills of vineyards, is a haven not only for the Vietnamese refugees who settled it but also for legions of enlightened healers, spirit-hungry wanderers, broken souls, and lay pilgrims like myself, from every continent. Once we arrive in Plum Village, Phap Diep leads me to Upper Hamlet, which is to be my home, and introduces me to my Sangha, or the "family" with whom I am to take meals, practice working meditation and engage in daily Dharma discussions. I settle in with my family for the evening supper, served in silence, buffet style on long tables in the dining hall. We each have utensils or chopsticks, a bowl and plate to silently serve ourselves rice or noodles, vegetables, tofu and fruit. I feel happy and full of anticipation and joy that I kept to my decision, made so long ago, to come here. It feels like I have found a heart home.

Unfortunately, when it is time to go to my room, I discover that the Vietnamese monks in the registration office had taken "Dr. Harriet" to be a man, and I have been assigned to share a room in a monastery with two men! This abruptly ends my stay in Upper Hamlet, as it is only for single men and families. Single women stay in Lower Hamlet, so off I am sent, three or four kilometers away, to find space and another family.

I am given a seldom-used loft, "Rising Moon," a tranquil eyrie upstairs in a cottage called "Golden Years," overlooking the fruit-laden treetops of the plum orchard. Although it lacks the cots that the other rooms have, my room has two thin mattresses on the floor; they feel appropriately monastic and comfortable. I am to have the eyrie all to myself, or nearly. The loft is the preferred refuge of two of the monastery's free-roaming cats. At first they regard me as an unwanted interloper, but when they discover I have spread out a fluffy sleeping bag and give good head scratches, they decide I can stay.

I am reassigned to "Fresh Eyes Sangha," my Lower Hamlet family. After having to acknowledge my own sexism in being disappointed that I will live only with nuns and women, I am soon very grateful for the experience. I haven't lived exclusively with a community of women since Vassar.

### The Sangha and the Flow of Days in a Monastery

I didn't come here seeking new friends, but rather to pursue a personal spiritual quest. In all the busy years of raising a family, building a practice, writing a book and many journal articles, losing my parents, getting divorced and remarried, and taking on the psychoanalytic establishment by joining an anti-trust lawsuit as a plaintiff, my spiritual life has taken a back seat. I've nourished it in bits and pieces, cuddling with my children, savoring sunsets, and climbing mountains with Jim, but I haven't given my soul her full due since I refused to throw that pinecone in the fire as a young adolescent.

This time, I vow to try to nourish my soul with a practice of open-heartedness and compassion. My intentions are to quiet, settle and listen, and to learn to honor my soul's needs for depth, simplicity and purity. I am also here to learn more about the teachings of this modest but powerful Vietnamese Zen monk whose socially responsible Buddhist philosophy sounds refreshingly far from the Calvinism of Scottish Presbyterianism.

My new international Sangha of twenty-one women, ranging in age from thirteen to seventy, becomes a wonderful part of that quest. A Sangha is a community of souls—from one's biological or spiritual family to one's community—that gathers to support one another individually and collectively. Here in Lower Hamlet, we meet in our small family groups for working meditation, at least one communal meal each day, and evening Dharma discussions. We gather with the greater Sangha for Thay's daily Dharma talks and Buddhist teachings.

Outside Plum Village, in communities all over the world, such self-selected Buddhist groups meet with regularity in offices, homes and temples. One of several Sanghas here in the Lower Hamlet, our Fresh Eyes Sangha is comprised of three ordained Vietnamese nuns, two very young shy novitiates in training, two longer-term scholarship residents and sixteen lay members—twenty-one women from ten countries in all, plus one very brave young man, Tómas from Germany, who is here with his German girlfriend "to learn to cry".

We make deep connections in ways that are markedly different from "outside." For the duration of the retreat, most of our time together is spent in Noble Silence and meditation, taking silent meals and working quietly at our group's daily tasks, which are to wash and put away the enormous cooking pots and utensils after each meal, and to arrange the washing basins and towels for the community's dishwashing. Other Sanghas are assigned to tending the vegetable garden, cooking, serving, washing dishes, cleaning toilets, and cleaning the living areas or the gathering hall.

With very little conversation, and despite generational, linguistic and cultural differences, our connections are forged simply through practice together, quiet observation during daily routines, occasional eye contact, and nonverbal communication that provides refreshingly "plot-free" acquaintance. I don't know who is married, who has children, what each person's job is, how long or how often each one is here. But I become attuned to *presence*: the presence of suffering or tranquility, distraction or focus, warmth or isolation—in each person and each moment. I sense day-by-day changes among the members of my Sangha and in myself, from our agitated arrivals to a deeper focus, from disquietude to peacefulness.

Days in Plum Village flow into one another like the surrounding Gardonette, Besage, Lescaroux, Dourde and Seignal Rivers flow into the great river that gives this area its name, the Dordogne. There is a rhythm, a pattern and a sound to the daily monastic routine. From the evening sitting meditation following a program or Dharma discussion until after breakfast, the hamlets observe Noble Silence. There is no talking at all from 9:30 or 10:00 p.m. until 7:30 a.m.

Each morning, only the sound of the great bell is heard, ringing at half past five to awaken the hamlet. At ten before six, the deep sonorous gong of the great temple is sounded repeatedly, increasing in pace and volume, awakening the community for sitting meditation. I rouse myself from deep slumber in my eyrie while it is still dark. We all file slowly from our tents and rooms, observing Noble Silence as we walk toward the meditation hall. There we sit on our cushions in meditation for half an hour.

At half past six, the bell sounds for a silent breakfast of fresh fruit, oatmeal with raisins, French bread and jams as well as teas, milk and coffee. Nearly every person pauses, palms together, for a moment of gratitude before taking a plate, and offers a slight bow toward the table of food. We bow our heads again before eating. We sit at long picnic tables around the dining hall, or on the lawn by the lotus pond, or wherever we choose to break our fast. Serenity and mindfulness seem to permeate every move, every measured step, every meal.

I move through the monastic routine almost in a trance. It is so calm and peaceful; the energy is so different from the hurry-hurry-hurry typical in my world. Following breakfast, lunch and dinner, we wash our dishes in quiet mindfulness, a meditation practice itself, standing at long tables. As part of our working meditation, three times each day it is Fresh Eyes Sangha's job to set up five wash basins and towel racks. We fill the first with soapy water, the second with clear water, the third with a purple antibacterial liquid. Each retreatant learns to wait at the purple basin while the dishes are submerged, taking three slow breaths, before moving on to the fourth and fifth rinse basins, then the drying towels, and then to the dining room, where we stack our dishes for the next meal.

The nuns explain that by the end of retreat, we will be offered an opportunity to take a vow to avoid killing. However, this is never totally possible; the purple antibacterial liquid kills microorganisms to prevent sickness from sweeping through the monastic community. In walking meditation, we inevitably step on tiny ants and bugs. The precept to honor all life is a North Star to guide us toward awareness of interbeing and the right of all beings to life.

Every morning after breakfast, hundreds of retreatants gather in one of the hamlets, walking either the short distance to the meditation hall in our own Lower Hamlet or three-and-a-half kilometers uphill through plum orchards, past fields of corn and sunflowers, to Upper Hamlet, or going by bus to New Hamlet, fifteen kilometers away. Dharma talks begin at 8:30 a.m. with a choir of resident nuns and monks chanting in the different languages of the community—Vietnamese, French, German, and English. Thay addresses the whole community, adults and children, but especially the children who are invited up front to sit at his feet. Each day he gives the dharma talk in a different language: Vietnamese, English or French. Translations into many languages, such as Dutch, Italian and Spanish, are offered via headsets. Thay's ease with languages, including Chinese and Sanskrit, as well as the profundity of his energy and his ability to speak so directly to so many widely disparate hearts, reveal his extraordinary intelligence and depth of soul.

Between Dharma talks, a nun leads us in silent stretching. This is often fairly challenging as we have been sitting crowded close together in the meditation hall, with cords and plugs and earphones crossing this way and that. We have barely enough room to stretch, but the nuns have worked out a series of stretches and breathing exercises that one can do in the tiniest space. After a break for tea and using the bathrooms, the children go off with young monks and nuns for their own activities, and Thay resumes the Dharma talk on a more philosophical level, until it is time for walking meditation.

After returning to our individual hamlets for lunch, we have an hour of free time before afternoon working meditation, during which gardening, cleaning, and community laundry are done by the members of each Sangha. Noble Silence is lifted during free time, so clusters of folks sit on the grass and under the trees, visiting. I want to call Jim, cycling somewhere across the Midwest, nine hours apart. Will my phone work here? No, not unless I hike down the road and walk into a neighboring vineyard. Will he be awake? No, he is not answering his phone.

But I retrieve an exuberant voicemail message from him recounting his daily cycling stats. They're all about how far, how fast, how high, how many hours and who won. Oh, we are in different energy vortices! But I am thrilled to learn that he is safe. I wonder how re-entry will be for us—me returning from this slow realm of interbeing and cooperation, him from uber-testosterone surges of rivalry. I leave a message crafted to assure him I am well, without touching on the gulf that's opening up on our separate journeys. I sigh and find the little medicine bag we lovingly prepared snug in my pocket. Feeling peaceful, I return through the vineyard to my eyrie until time for working meditation.

This is an opportunity to practice mindful and appreciative silence doing the most mundane tasks: cleaning toilets, sweeping, cutting vegetables, in palpable contrast to my typical tendency to rush through "chores" to get on to something else. Here, attention to the most ordinary work itself becomes a moving meditation. This, I realize, can be translated to all of life's routine activities, from brushing teeth and washing my face in the morning, to dressing, driving, sorting the mail and going to the grocery store.

The dinner gong sounds at 6:15, inviting individual Sanghas to gather. We bring our bowls to sit in silent circles on the lawn, eating slowly and mindfully together. As all meals are, dinner is initiated with a blessing that I like very much:

> This food is a gift of the whole universe, the earth,
> the sky, and much hard work.
> May we eat in such a way so as to be worthy of it.
> May we transform our unskillful states of mind and
> learn to eat in moderation.
> May we take only foods that nourish us and prevent
> illness.
> May we accept this food to realize the path of
> understanding and love.

After washing the dishes, each evening we gather for Dharma discussion, or a festival celebrating the gathering of cultures, such as the Israelis and Palestineans, or a remembrance, such as the sobering 50th anniversary of the bombing of Hiroshima. Dharma discussions in each Sangha offer good practice in "active listening." A person who wants to speak so indicates, and the nun or monk who is moderating invites that person to speak with a bell. The speaker bows to the encircled group with palms together, and the group responds in kind. The speaker then talks until he or she is finished, again placing palms together and bowing to the group. Like the native American practice with the talking stick, there is no interruption of a speaker. A moment of silence allows thought about what has been said, and then another speaker is acknowledged. It is the same method the Palestineans and Israelis here have been learning to listen and speak with one another. Practicing mindful listening offers real contrast to the type of arm-chewing free-for-all discussions marked by competitiveness, interruption, and lack of deep reflection that I've endured in so many board and committee meetings.

This night, however, two professional mimes from Paris, who discovered each other here, create a delicious surprise. With the lotus pond as their backdrop, they put on a wicked pantomime of life in Plum Village. One mimes the serious, devout practitioner, walking about in mindful silence, eyes averted, bowing respectfully to the passing nuns and monks, arriving early to settle in for the Dharma talks. The other plays the pratfall artist, tripping himself and crashing into the other, bobbing up and down in parody of bowing, causing a great commotion by arriving late for the Dharma talks and stumbling over meditation cushions. He entangles his neighbors in the long cord to his earphones for the translation, and plugs into every language translation box but the French, necessitating more commotion. Then he does a sublime satire of assuming the lotus position, masterfully entangling himself and his neighbor with his long, ungainly legs and arms, while the devout one tries desperately to maintain his composure.

The routine has the whole community in an uproar of laughter on the lawn. Humor, a welcome guest here, delightfully reminds us of the balance between devotion and levity. If we are to practice non-self, we'd best not take ourselves too seriously!

# CHAPTER 34
## THE BUDDHA AND THE DHARMA

### *The Buddha*

WHAT AM I LEARNING of Buddhist philosophy and psychology? Though certainly not steeped from birth in the culture and traditions of Buddhism, as are the Vietnamese monks and nuns here, my pores are open to learning. I often come upon a statue or a drawing of the Buddha here; simply contemplating the face, the posture, the energy that is present, I feel myself absorbing awareness subliminally as if through osmosis.

Through this nonverbal knowing, I am becoming more acquainted with Buddha's evocation of peaceful contemplation of whatever is, pleasant or unpleasant. This is a stark contrast with the crucifix, which emphasizes transgression and suffering, depicting Jesus in the sacrificial agony of death; and with Mohammed, who is never shown in human form but rather in abstract designs representing the transcendent unknowable. Alternately, the Buddha appears as very human—no longer the emaciated ascetic striving for enlightenment. The enlightened Buddha is depicted as ample of girth, seated in the lotus position, grounded, smiling, equanimously receptive to pain, suffering and ease, and always contemplative. Maybe after way too much ascetic denial under the Bodhi tree, he reclaimed his pine cone.

One important teaching is that the Buddha was not a god but just a man who lived, suffered normal human conflicts, and gained enlightenment in India over two and a half millennia ago. The Buddha is also a spirit of consciousness and awareness that is in all of us and in every cell and atom of the cosmos. I learn more about him from Shantum Seth, the East Indian lay member of the Plum Village community I met at the train station. Shantum, whom I'm getting to know better daily, lives here and has been a lay follower and assistant to Thay for over twenty years, both at Plum Village and during his teaching tours in India. Shantum and his spirited Indian wife Gitu have a baby daughter, Nandini.

Shantum often reveals a wry sense of humor. Hanging out during "lazy time" with Phap Diep, some of his monk friends, Shantum and Gitu, I begin to grasp the social complexity of the lay and monastic community in Plum Village.

Every year, Shantum leads pilgrimages to the sites of Buddha's life in India and Nepal.[15] During a slide show of pilgrimages to the holy sites, Shantum, who comes from the region where the Buddha lived, tells stories of Siddhartha's birth to a queen, who dreamed that a white elephant placed a pink lotus in her womb. She died eight days after delivering her son, Siddhartha He shows pictures of modern boys from the same tribal group in Nepal in which Siddhartha was born, to give us a sense of what the young prince probably looked like. Years later, Prince Siddhartha was released from his unhappy arranged marriage to seek enlightenment, after fulfilling his royal husbandly duty to produce a son. Shantum shows artists' images of the starved and emaciated man seeking enlightenment with five ascetics in the forest.

He next shows slides of the Bodhi tree under which Siddhartha, having left the ascetics on the verge of starvation and disillusionment, sat for days. Here, he received enlightenment about the nature of nonbeing, the indestructibility and sanctity of all that is in the cosmos, the paradoxes of self and non-self, and the substance of the Dharma that comprises Buddhist teachings. Shantum explains how Buddha's teachings were preserved through oral tradition for three hundred years after his death, first by his disciples and then by his followers. Finally, texts were written by followers in India and China, and varying traditions of Buddhism emerged; these variations carry on to this day, colored by and embedded in their unique cultures.

---

[15] www.buddhapath.com for guided spiritual pilgrimages to India

Thay teaches a core Buddhist idea: all is one and one is all. In other words, unity and indestructibility pervade every atom, particle and subparticle of the cosmos. Nothing is born and nothing dies; everything is part of everything else and of the fluidity of states of being. Calligraphy in the dining hall proclaims: "Ce morceau de pain est le corps du cosmos," or "The bread in your hand is the body of the cosmos." An anonymous poem I find here teaches:

> The thought manifests as the word
> The word manifests as the deed
> The deed develops into habit
> And the habit hardens into character.
> So watch the thought
> And its ways with care
> And let it spring from love
> Born out of respect for all beings.

Thay's talks with the children here on retreat with their families offer amazingly deep teachings to the whole community. In his own unique, disarmingly simple and poetic way, he tells stories that even the smallest child can understand. His presence is very beautiful; he speaks thoughtfully in a gentle voice and looks to me like a Buddha himself, with his shaved head, huge ears, and beatific smile. One day, for example, he tells the children and us about his own life. As a boy of nine, he first saw a picture of the Buddha on the cover of a magazine. Seeing the calm, peaceful happiness on the face of the Buddha, he vowed that he wanted to become like that. With a bunch of boys from his school, he went on a field trip to climb a mountain and visit a hermit.

"I was so, so happy to have a chance to climb that mountain, to have that chance to actually see a living holy man. I was so, so happy. But I climbed and I climbed and I climbed that mountain, and I got so tired and so thirsty, and it seemed forever, that I wanted to lie down. Now, because I have learned mindful walking, I could walk for hours. But I didn't know how to do that then. If you listen and you practice mindful walking, you will learn you can walk all the day long and you will never be tired.

"And when we finally reached the top and went to the cave, the hermit was not there. I was so disappointed. But now I think that probably the hermit, who lived there and who was there because he wanted to be alone, heard all those boys coming and probably hid himself because he didn't want to be in the middle of a swarm of little boys. (Thay chuckles impishly.) But then I was very disappointed, but also so, so tired and thirsty that I fell asleep. I fell into a deep, deep sleep, I think the deepest sleep I had ever known. And when I awoke, I didn't know where I was, and I didn't see any of the other boys. But I looked and I found a spring, and being so very thirsty, I took a drink.

"Never in my whole life have I tasted anything so sweet as that spring water. It was so beautiful, so fresh, so replenishing. And at that moment, I think I understood that the hermit was there, in that water, in that spring. That the hermit is everywhere if you just can be patient and be present and taste, really taste the sweetness of the water. So today, you have to look to see if you can find the hermit, here in the flowers, in the water, in the eyes of your friend. If you look with your Dharma eyes, not just your flesh eyes, you will see the hermit. So the hermit is the Buddha, and the Buddha IS the water, and the water is in all of us. Did you know that we are 90% water? That means we are all 90% the Buddha!"

He laughs so engagingly that the children and all of us sitting on our meditation cushions around him are chuckling. We laugh with pleasure and with the recognition that in this sweet, simple story is a very deep teaching. One morning during Q&A, when the children are encouraged to ask questions, one small German boy whose feet don't even reach the edge of his chair shyly asks his question: "Dear Thay, why did you become a monk?" Thay pauses thoughtfully for some time, and then replies with a twinkle, "To have fun." The little boy looks puzzled before a wellspring of understanding laughter ripples through the audience, as the depth of this reply sinks in.

Thay explains to the little boy that there is deep joy and pleasure in this life. It is much easier to find the peace and pleasure that comes from mindful meditation within the support of the monastic community than it is outside, where one is surrounded by everything that pulls us away from genuine, true joy and pleasure, and offers false "pleasure" in TV and video games, fast foods, advertising, shopping malls, drugs, alcohol and quick fixes. When we can find, with the support of the monastic community and the teachings, that the Buddha that is everywhere, we are truly joyful and it is a lot of fun.

Thay encourages the little boy to look with his "Dharma eyes" (the third eye that sees beyond ordinary reality) after he leaves Plum Village. "You will see that your mommy is really a boddhisatva with the many arms you have seen in the statues. She has arms to hold you, and arms to cook for you, and arms to dry your tears, and arms to love your daddy, and arms to teach you how to behave. Can you see how many arms your mommy, the boddhisatva has? No? Then let me help you."

He invites a group of children to stand up and come up closer to him to make a boddhisatva for all to see. Nuns materialize to help the children arrange themselves into a line facing the Sangha. The tallest child stands in back with the smaller and smaller ones in front, reaching their arms out wide. Placing implements of the boddhisatva in each of their hands—candles, books, pens, bells—Thay says, "See? You are the boddhisatva yourselves, just like your mommies and daddies, and you have many arms and you can do many things." The children are delighted and we adults can appreciate both the teaching that we all share Buddha nature and that Thay truly does have fun in his life.

After the Dharma talk for the children, Thay invites them to stand up at the sound of the bell, bow to the Buddha, then at the sound of the next bell, turn around and bow to the sangha, and with the third bell, to walk quietly out of the meditation hall. They are met by some of the young nuns and monks, who take them to have fun making art and craft projects inspired by the Dharma talk, leaving the rest of us with Thay to continue in the meditation hall.

A young woman, barely able to speak through her tears and suffering, tells the Sangha how her mother committed suicide when she was one year old. Her father and brothers kept no pictures of her and never allowed her mother's name to be mentioned. She feels cut off from her mother, distraught and confused. If she is to follow the Dharma, which includes teachings about respect and gratitude to her ancestors, and the notion that she *is* her mother and father and brothers, how can she reconcile this? She hasn't even got a picture of her mother and has no memories. She only knows that because of her birth, her mother killed herself by jumping off a bridge. She doesn't want to be like her father, who is cold and cut off, as are her brothers. How can she possibly find peace?

Thay gently soothes her, saying she should understand that her mother's suffering was very, very great. She must have felt completely alone with this husband who was not able to reach out, and no Sangha to support her, and no teachings to support her through her depression. She needs to forgive her mother and to realize that her mother is, in fact, manifest in her. She *is* her mother and her mother is here with her now in Plum Village. She has brought her mother here, now, to this place and to this moment, where her suffering can be contained and held by this Sangha, and where both she and her mother can find peace and understanding. She is lucky, because unlike her mother who was so isolated in her pain, she has found her way to a loving community that can share her pain and help her.

She cannot force her father and her brothers to talk with her. It is not possible if they are not willing. She can only live mindfully in their presence and hope that they will see that their way is not helpful for themselves or for her. In the meantime, she can find new fathers and brothers here who will talk to her about her mother, and who will help her to understand that neither she nor her mother is alone any more.

This latter teaching touches me deeply. I realize I have to face the fact that although I may reach out to my own son, if he is not ready or willing, there is nothing I can do. I can, however, find him in others of his generation, like Phap Diep, and in that way, heal the wounds I carry from our estrangement. Thay says to the young woman that it is also time to invite laughter and joy into her very sad spirit.

As a psychoanalyst, I am impressed by how much psychological wisdom is compressed in Thay's response. Though he works directly through instruction and suggestion, he communicates that we can never have a "parentectomy" as this woman would wish for her father, or a maternal implant as she would wish for her lost mother. He implies that we must reconcile and accept certain identifications, inheritances and internalizations, and learn that it is even possible for one person's therapeutic transformation to encompass and liberate the suffering of those before us, which we carry internalized within us. That process can relieve, heal and enliven us.

The last question comes from a spectrally tall, thin, white-haired English gentleman who approaches Thay very respectfully. Before seating himself, he places a bell on the ground beside him. After a moment of silence, he begins. "Dear Thay, before I ask a question, first I have a confession to make. I am here simply because I wanted to sit near you." There is a murmur of laughter from the audience, and from Thay as well. "Second, before I ask my question, I also wanted to make an offering." He reaches down and picks up the bell. "I wanted to bring you my beautiful bell, which was given to me many, many years ago by my 'Angelina' (referring to a story Thay has told about a loving and patient woman). But since I have been here, I have seen that you already have many bells."

Thay reaches out to take the bell and then slowly sounds it three times as the man, increasingly flummoxed, continues. "So I decided to give you the sound of my bell." Now the man looks pleased, because Thay seems to have understood and has enjoyed making the bell ring. But the man's expression changes as Thay places the bell beside him, among his belongings. There is a pause and then a few chuckles as the assembly grasps that Thay might be teasing the man, who now looks completely bewildered. We wait expectantly for the joke to be over, and the bell returned.

But no, Thay smiles quietly…and keeps the bell. The poor man, who has now given away the meditation bell that his Angelina gave him so many years before, is stumped into silence. A mirthful laugh rolls through the assembly hall. A twinkling-eyed Thay, it now becomes clear, fully plans to keep the bell. It is a rich comic moment marked by the puckish spontanaiety and sense of play that are trademarks of this remarkable man. It's also a fine teaching in letting go of attachments, control, intentionality and plan.

After the morning session ends, as we are walking from the hall, I catch up to the white-haired man to tell him I loved his offering and wonder if his Angelina is here with him to witness the departure of his bell.

He turns to me, still dumbstruck, and says, "No, she is not here. She's still in England. She couldn't come. I don't know what I will tell her!"

I say, "Well, hopefully when you recover from the shock, you and she can celebrate, knowing that your bell is now in the hands of this wonderful Zen master." He still looks flummoxed, so I add, "It wasn't what you planned, but you gave us all a wonderful moment. Why don't you buy the video of this morning's session and take it home to show your Angelina? She'll be delighted and will understand why you haven't brought your bell back home with you."

He appears greatly relieved by this suggestion. Whenever I see him during the rest of the retreat, I enjoy a quiet, delicious chuckle.

# CHAPTER 35

## TOUCHING THE EARTH

### *A Powerful Mindfulness Meditation*

ANOTHER PRACTICE here is called Touching the Earth meditation. It is led by Sister Chan Khong ("True Emptiness"), who ministered to the homeless, broken in spirit, and impoverished in and around Saigon during and after the Vietnam War.[16] She looks like an old Buddha herself with her simple brown robes, shaved head, and round face with a lovely dimple in one wrinkled cheek, and a smile so sweetly disarming, it almost makes me want to cry. She seems like Sister Theresa in her generosity and goodness of spirit, and I feel privileged to be staying near her in Lower Hamlet.

Chan Khong offers a late afternoon Touching the Earth meditation in the meditation hall as is customary, with a bell inviting us to breathe in and breathe out several times. With another bell, we bow to indicate we are gathered and mindfully present, ready to begin the meditation. She instructs us to lie down on the floor, flat on our backs, palms facing upward, as in the *savasana* position in yoga, and to breathe deeply as she guides us into a very deep state of relaxation. This state continues for half an hour or forty-five minutes; I lose track of time and almost of consciousness.

Then she asks us to stand and begin the Touching the Earth practice, which lasts another hour. With her guidance we alternate standing with palms together in a gesture of prayer with complete prostrations, "touching the earth" in humility. Prostrate, belly down, <u>foreheads on th</u>e floor, we invite our parents and grandparents, one

16  Sister Chan Khong, *Learning True Love: Practicing Buddhism In A Time of War,* revised edition. Berkeley: Parallax Press, 2007.

by one, to come into our consciousness as they were when they were young, in their teens or twenties. We greet each one in his or her most fresh, innocent and hopeful state of being. She encourages us to express gratitude to each of them for having given us the life we have to live and to enjoy. This invocation follows for all of the ancestors we do not know, but without whom we wouldn't be alive.

This part of Buddhist practice is natural and familiar to the Vietnamese and Asian practitioners amongst us, but unfamiliar to those of us from the West. I have never addressed my young parents or grandparents, or welcomed them into my present consciousness. It is a moving practice, giving not only a sense of contact with the youth of our parents and grandparents, but also a sense of the finite nature of our time on earth. Those young parents and grandparents have long since moved on, but here they are, parading through my mind, and I am grateful for the opportunity to think about them and genuinely thank them for giving me this life.

My mind travels from this moment in time, here in the south of France, back to my meditation several years ago in the meadow of Bench Valley. It was there that the phrase "pulling up stakes" and the notion of writing about this journey were hatched; and it was there that my parents and grandparents came into my mind freshly and vividly, reminding me of my roots and of why I feel so grounded, so close to them and so at home in the High Sierras of California. In those meditative musings, I was able to see their strengths and weaknesses, and to recognize them in myself.

I am struck by the notion of endless circles of evolving consciousness. While I'd never heard of Touching the Earth meditation in that High Sierra meadow, I was practicing it. At this moment I am present in that meadow two years ago, as well as long ago when my parents, grandparents and great-grandparents walked in that place, and I am also here now, with them, in France. It is as if we are slowly turning on an endless wheel of life, yet always coming back to the same place. If we practice mindfulness, each return is with deeper consciousness and enlightenment, and may offer a transcendent sense of timelessness.

Sister Chan Khong continues, guiding us as we shift back and forth between standing with palms together in prayer to acknowledge our ancestors, and prostrate with belly on the earth, to acknowledge the pain and suffering each of our forbearers may have caused us by his or her ignorance, mindlessness or cruelty. I think of anxieties and fears instilled in me by my grandparents' Presbyterian Calvinism. With each prostration connecting with the earth, I think of the guilt that my mother's indoctrination in those beliefs brought her and then me, when I felt withered by her judgmental Presbyterianism just as my own sexuality was beginning to blossom. I think about my father's narcissism and his capacity to demean my sister, me and others around him, and the extraordinary pain his arrogance and blindness caused many people.

Addressing each person in the generations preceding me, I acknowledge their goodness with a prostration to the earth; I acknowledge their capacity to inflict suffering as well as my own. Over the years, through psychoanalysis and time, I have forgiven my parents and grandparents for whatever resentments or disappointments I've carried. Now reconciled at a deeper level, I feel fresh appreciation, even more at peace with and close to them.

Sister Chan Khong invites us to address others in our current family, our lovers and our children. With daughters Ariel and Brooke, I have had many powerful, private opportunities to be truthful about our impact on each other, to acknowledge the deep suffering, periodic anger and frustration we have caused one another in our "mother-daughter bond or bondage." We've also celebrated the great joy that each of us is to the other. Five years ago at Twin Brooks, during the Summer Solstice Retreat's "Meditations on Our Mothers" at Echo Rock, both Brooke and Ariel publicly shared their feelings, bearing moving witness to the power of our relationships among that collective of women. Last summer at my sixtieth birthday millennial retreat, again on Echo Rock, I had an opportunity to hear them give testimony to me and I offered the same to them. With my daughters, I feel deeply reconciled.

My sabbatical journey has been about letting go, finding and nourishing my spiritual center, deepening my marital relationship, and coming to terms with Jim's and my differences. Occasionally in any intimate relationship, we inevitably hurt each other, usually unconsciously, sometimes painfully. Jim and I have been deepening our tolerance for and appreciation of our differences. I have had to let go of my wish that Jim would want to be here with me at a place like this, and he has had to let go of the wish for a transcontinental cycling partner.

The person with whom I am not yet at peace is my son. When Sister Chang Khong invites us to address that loved one who continues to cause us the most suffering, I feel ambushed by grief and pain. This is the most raw and unresolved of my family relationships. She invites us to tell that person how they have hurt us. Tears streaming down my face, I find myself recounting more than a decade of his intermittent verbal accusations, acts of passive coldness and withdrawals.

His verbal attacks on me peaked toward the end of his high school adolescent years, and then mostly stopped. But they've been replaced by painful distance peppered with anxiety on both of our parts. There have been powerfully hopeful adult moments. Three years ago, Gabriel acknowledged that he has been carrying around his rage at me as if it were a precious baby that he loved and fed, thereby—as Sister Chan Khong would say—watering his seeds of disappointment and rage. He acknowledged that he'd been using this anger to avoid facing his own issues. He told me that this baby had become a heavy burden he wanted to put down. I felt so grateful for this courageous acknowledgement, but despite that deeply meaningful first step, at this moment, it still doesn't feel like he has been able to put that baby down and move on.

Over the years, on many occasions, I have acknowledged to myself and to Gabriel the truth of some of his allegations and asked for forgiveness. My failures as his mother are grounded in the difficult divorce between his father and me, and in the period of his early adolescence when I felt alone, overwhelmed and afraid. I know I felt the need to try to control my children to protect them from drugs or ending up in a fatal accident. During Gabriel's senior year in high school, he attended five funerals for classmates who died in such ways. Because of my mother's fatal car crash, my fear of traumatic loss was almost unmanageable. I exercised an overanxious control that was not helpful to Gabriel or Ariel and made them rebellious and angry teenagers.

Ariel has been aided by a gifted therapist she has bravely and devotedly seen for several years, but Gabriel has, not surprisingly, resisted therapy. So this Touching the Earth meditation stirs up my tears for still-raw wounds. With fresh pain, I recall family holidays and birthdays, including my recent sixtieth and this past Mother's Day, when I hoped for a call seeking reconciliation that did not come. I have been trying to relinquish my attachment to a certain outcome, to put my firstborn baby down, honor his own experience and let him be. But here the old feelings stir again.

Sister Chan Khong brings us back to the present moment, enjoining us with our last prostrations to the earth and our last mindful breaths not only to express love and gratitude to those who bring us comfort and joy, but also to communicate with loved ones with whom we are unreconciled. Together we pray that where there has not been reconciliation, it will come one day, and where there is acceptance and celebration, it will continue daily. At the sounding of the bells, she sends us out from the hall.

Slowly walking back to my eyrie, I realize that I had not come to Plum Village with this wound on my mind. I thought that I'd learned, for the sake of my own peace of mind, to release the pain and the remnants of a hope that is guaranteed to make a part of every birthday and holiday a disappointment. I have tried to soften my heart and not dwell on Gabriel's and my relationship for quite some time, and have felt good about that. But today Sister Chan Khong revealed the fool's errand in the notion that any mother can truly let go of such anguish. It's been sitting on the back burner, waiting to be reignited. Tonight in the Rising Moon cottage, at her suggestion, I write a letter to my son—one of many I have written, and almost as many never sent, for fear they would incite riot in him. But maybe I will send this one. I decide the wiser course will be to send a brief letter simply indicating that I am here, thinking deeply about our relationship, and that I've written him about it and, if he is interested, would like to send him the letter.

*Working Through, Through the Work with Angels of Gabriel*

Many different "Angels of Gabriel" have crossed the threshold to my consulting room or found me in other ways; other women's sons, troubled young men who have given me an opportunity to process and work through some of the ragged pain that passes between mothers and sons, as well as to celebrate some of the delight that mothers and sons can bring to each other. It is always a great privilege to be invited into these deeply private and troubled realms, and to feel deep empathy for both the mothers and the sons. The healing penetrates and nourishes us all.

Today, Phap Diep—just such an angel—has invited me for lunch in Upper Hamlet with Shantum, Gitu, Nandini, Henric, a young Dutch monk, and a lay brother, Franz. He's also invited me to meet with him in private later. What a blessing to have the opportunity to spend informal time with these deep practitioners. It almost seems overdetermined. I have arrived. Everything in the cosmos is alive in the here and in the now.

When I arrive in Upper Hamlet, though I am filled with questions about life in a monastery and about each of their pathways here, Phap Diep, Shantum, and Franz are equally fascinated to learn more about me, about psychoanalysis, and about how I came upon my path as an analyst.

I tell them that when I began my journey toward becoming a psychoanalyst in the early 1970s, it was a "closed shop," locked tighter than a drum by the hegemony of medical doctor-members of the American Psychoanalytic Association, which refused to train anyone except psychiatrists. I hadn't wanted to become a medical doctor and a psychiatrist because my lifelong leanings had been toward the arts and humanities, and my inclination was to come from a developmental rather than a medical or pathological model.

I found myself in the right place at the right time to dive into the eye of the hurricane, giving testimony as a plaintiff in a lawsuit against the American Psychoanalytic Association for restraint of trade. The suit was mounted by an active, smart group known as

GAPP, the Group for the Advancement of Psychoanalysis in Psychology. Though long and arduous, the lawsuit was successful and the outcome has immeasurably changed the path of American psychoanalysis. It opened up psychoanalytic training to lay analysts and thus invited the feminization of the profession, since many social workers and psychologists seeking analytic training are women. There was an infusion of fresh air into a field that was being stifled to death by old-line, chauvinist male psychiatrists.

I speak with Phap Diep, Shantum, Brother Henric and Franz about Freud's enduring contributions: the value of exploring the unconscious and dreams through free association, and of delving into transference and countertransference through analysis. I talk about new breakthroughs in our knowledge from infant observation, as well as my own interest in the earliest unfolding of erotic life in the mother-infant dyad. While we're conversing, a delicious little four-month-old baby girl, Nandini, is held alternately by her mother Gitu and father Shantum, Phap Diep, Brother Henric, and Franz.[17] We're sitting in a living lab of early mother/father/baby erotic life, complete with milk, drools, coos, cuddles, wiggles and diaper changes.

Having done most of the talking, I feel it is my turn to learn more about them. I ask what they know of their earliest relations with their mothers after birth. What emerges is a remarkable sharing about early disturbances in the mother-infant dyad. Franz tells of his very young Turkish mother's inability to recover from being overwhelmed by the birth of her first children, twin boys. His mother and father had left their tiny Turkish village as teenagers, looking for opportunities in Germany. She was around fifteen when the twins were born and eighteen when Franz was born. She was a young adolescent, accustomed to the tight bonds and constraints of family life in a small Turkish village, suddenly free but alone and without support in a foreign land.

Both she and Franz's young father were completely unprepared for parenthood. Franz's father was emotionally constricted, and both were unable to communicate or meet each other's needs. Overwhelmed by twin boys, when she found she was pregnant again,

---

17  Names and certain details are changed to honor the privacy of these compassionate Buddhist practitioners.

she prayed the baby would be a little girl to keep her company in her loneliness. Into this unstable crucible, another disappointment appeared, a baby boy, Franz. She acted as if he were a baby girl, setting him on a painful path of gender identity confusion.

Shantum, who seems a little self-conscious with Nandini, tells how his young mother was similarly displaced. She had come from a traditional urban family in India to the completely different culture of London. She, too, was relatively lost and depressed. In order to take care of her own needs and find self-support, she enrolled in law school before Shantum was born—and, it seems, related to him like an unexpected parcel that had been delivered inopportunely to her doorstep. Shantum and Gitu are both able to recognize how the experience of being an unsolicited parcel is re-created in his self-conscious handling of Nandini.

Shantum's mother is now a grandmother in her seventies. Though still traditionally conservative East Indian, she is in the process of writing a book about her struggles and her life. Hearing this, I feel empathy and identification for both sides—the young, overwhelmed mothers and their young sons, who reflect now on their early pain at the hands of mothers who were unsupported in the daunting task of mothering. I think of my inexperience with my firstborn and how the Touching the Earth meditation has rekindled pain in my heart. We talk about Shantum's opportunity, provided by Nandini's birth and his mother's self-reflections and writing, to rework his own birth narrative.

Phap Diep enjoys serving as Nandini's "uncle" as a way of contacting the baby in himself, yet he holds and plays with her in a noticeably split way. At times he seems relaxed and present; at other times, he and the infant stiffen just perceptibly, averting their gazes. When I ask about his birth, he reveals a story that explains this split and his choice to seek refuge and healing in a spiritual community. Faced with caring for a four-year-old daughter and daunted by the birth of twin boys, Phap Diep's mother fell into a postpartum depression. Though he shared moments of animation with his mother, he was frequently unable to navigate the chasm that her depression cast between them. Used to a noisy rumpus room with his twin brother in the womb, he must have felt cut off both from body-based closeness with his twin, and from a comforting connection with his mother. It shows up in his awkward contact with baby Nandini and with anyone getting close to him.

The afternoon is waning and we are still sitting with our lunch plates and heavy hearts, discussing these deep issues. Franz's and Phap Diep's mothers were each unprepared for motherhood, in shaky marriages with husbands who were unable to meet their isolated young wives' need for mothering. At the same time, these women were called upon to abandon their own girlish needs and minister to very needy babies. Just as I am brimming with the ache of my own mother/son relationship, I marvel that we've been brought together to touch these core conflicts together.

While I do not have time to talk with Brother Henric, we seem to feel a real connection. The next morning, after Thay's Dharma talk on birth and death, I come upon Brother Henric sitting alone under a great tree, quietly sobbing. I simply sit down on the bench next to him, in silence. After a time, I brush the tears streaming down his cheeks with my shawl, but they continue. I sit with him until the sobs finally subside and he slowly opens his eyes, smiling sadly at me. No words are spoken. We squeeze each other's hands and I move on. I do not know what the tears are about, but I do know we have shared a deep moment.

Still raw from Touching the Earth and the freshly revived pain of my failure to breach the chasm with my beloved young adult son, I feel an intense mixture of emotions. I am touched by each of these young men, drawn here from around the world by their spiritual yearnings. On the one hand, feeling empathy for the hurt these sons carry from their mothers' inadequacies, failures and mistakes, I feel deeply for my own son's suffering. At the same time, I identify with their mothers. Each one no doubt struggled deeply with the overwhelming challenges of young motherhood. Imagine Phap Diep's mother, underwater within a postpartum depression while trying to care for her four-year-old and newborn twins. I didn't face anything close to those challenges, but I identify with the sisterhood of mothers struggling to do our best when our best apparently isn't good enough.

### Medea's Child

It is time to attend a talk on the Five Mindfulness Trainings in Lower Hamlet. When I arrive, I realize I've forgotten my headset; as today's talk will be in German and Vietnamese, I'll need it for translations. Walking out of the meditation hall to retrieve my headset, I run into Franz. I can feel his desire to talk and decide to sit with him instead of attending the talk. We find a place on the grass overlooking the lotus pond, and Franz reveals more about his life.

When his older siblings, the twins, were six years old, his mother turned to a lover for comfort. Franz's father flew into a rage, calling her a whore and initiating the terrifyingly explosive rages that became his trademark. He abducted the twins and took them to the Turkish village that he and Franz's mother had left. Before long, he again grew restive and returned to Norway, leaving the twins to be raised by his aged mother and aunt in their provincial village. At that time, laws proclaimed that a child's country of physical residence had jurisdiction over that child, so the twins came under the jurisdiction of Turkish law. Franz, who had remained with his mother in Germany, was under German law.

Franz was alone in Germany with his young mother, who was far more distraught, fearing that if she returned to Turkey for her twins, she would never be allowed to leave and would forfeit the freedom she'd sought by leaving the small village. As I listen, my mind replays the scene from Nikos Kazantzakis' *Zorba the Greek,* in which a lonely young widow—played hauntingly in the film version by Irene Pappas—is stoned by her village for having erotic longings for Zorba. Franz confides that when he reads *Medea*, he cannot refrain from seeing his mother as the title character, the soul murderer of her own children.

When his father took the twin boys to Turkey, four-year-old Franz felt confirmed that he really was not a boy, but the girl as which his mother dressed him. He plunged into a bewildered loneliness. He'd lost not only his father, but also his only comforting close tie: the twin he'd been particularly close to, and whom he so resembled that they were often mistaken as triplets. He is still not sure which fate is worse, being raised by a loutish, unavailable stepfather or by a mother who abandoned her twins and wished he was a girl. Or did the twins suffer a worse fate, abandoned by father and mother, raised by two old ladies, one of whom was nearly deaf and blind, and most likely oblivious to the children's needs? The twins' only encounters with a biological parent were during yearly summer visits from their volatile father, who heaped verbal abuse on the memory of the twins' mother and treated them as outcast children of the "whore who left."

As a small boy in homoerotic flight from an incestuous and confusing tie to his mother, Franz struggled with gender identity problems, taking refuge in solitary masturbation and fantasies of reunion with "men," sealing his homosexual orientation. He had considerable therapy before coming to Plum Village, and here in the monastic community he is gaining palpable solace through meditation and the loving stability of his monastic Sangha. However, what troubles Franz is that he's been told that because of his homosexuality, he cannot seek investiture as a monk. He can remain here but only as a celibate member of the lay community. Because homosexuality is regarded as threatening to a monastic community, Franz has not felt there was anyone with whom he could explore his pain, confusion, frustration, and erotic longings.[18]

We spend a couple of hours sitting together, lotus-like by the lotus pond, "in session." Listening as he details his traumatic early history and current issues, I assure Franz that it is understandable he's come seeking refuge and order in this gentle community, but also that he feels hurt by rejection from monastic training due to his homosexuality. His childhood was so chaotic and his own parents were such children that there was no refuge, no order. The generations were topsy-turvy, the sexes were reversed, and he couldn't find a safe place to grow into manhood. Not surprisingly, his sexuality was inordinately precocious, with early orgasmic masturbation from the age of three. I suggest it is probably a good thing for him to remain here for a time, celibate and spared from dealing with issues of sexuality. He has even more primary and pressing issues to address first, namely his core sense of safety, hope and trust among loved

---

18  Soon after this experience, Plum Village began to accept people who were openly gay as monastics in both the sisters and brothers sanghas.

ones. Perhaps later, I tell him, when he feels more grounded, it will be time to leave this place and take up the thread of his shattered capacity for intimacy and sexual fulfillment in another safe place.

Franz tells me that my interpretation makes sense, and says he feels great relief that he has finally been able to talk about troubling sexual matters that he can't comfortably discuss here. We part, sharing a long embrace. I often wish I felt freer to offer such an embrace to my own patients in pain.

With this privileged conversation, I gain insight into one of the unique stresses of monastic life: there is very little privacy, and the very brothers who are your richest and most generous source of support may be too close for comfort at times. There is a need to inhibit revealing absolutely all about oneself, to hold something of the self in reserve for safekeeping. I realize that I am trying to integrate my own training and beliefs about psychoanalysis with my developing understanding and appreciation about Buddhism. Much is readily compatible: mindful contemplation of one's consciousness, tolerance of differences, working through pain and suffering while inviting joy, taking time out for reflection. I do not know, however, how to integrate psychoanalysis' focus on an individual's unique narrative with Buddhism's emphasis on the universality of the narrative and on non-self.

Later I sit in private conversation with Phap Diep, and he speaks more about his own tormented struggles toward intimacy and his earliest sexual relationships with women, including the one he broke off to pursue monastic training. I am touched and sobered by how much we all, when we are honest, carry raw wounds. I listen as a friend, a maternal presence and a clinician to some of his private anxieties. He tells me of his soul-searching as a result of a wrongful but excruciatingly painful accusation when he was a preschool teacher's aide. A troubled preschooler in his care, who was a victim of childhood sexual abuse, accused him rather than his uncle, the perpetrator.

Phap Diep's longing for safety and connection and his anxieties about intimacy are so close to the surface, I feel a very strong pull to comfort him. At the same time, I sense that as a monk trained to listen, he has the capacity to offer comfort to me, and to hear some of my own sorrow regarding my son who shares our unlikely connection with Vassar. We both appreciate how that ironic connection brought us together in this improbable way. The shadows deepen on the lawn, and soon it is time to gather for silent dinner with my Sangha. As I walk back, I can't help thinking that therapy is a two-way street. Although I have been sitting informally more or less in the role of therapist, saying very little about what was troubling me, through the course of these two afternoon conversations, I feel another level of transformation in myself.

# CHAPTER 36
## THE FIVE MINDFULNESS TRAININGS

TONIGHT'S DHARMA discussion is on the ancient Buddhist precepts, guidelines for daily living reframed in modern language for clearer understanding. We're invited to consider making our pledge to these Five Mindfulness Trainings at a pre-dawn ceremony in the meditation hall on the last morning of this retreat. While most of these ethical teachings have guided my life for a long time, there are a few I am not clear about, or in conflict with, or would struggle to uphold. Going into tonight's discussion, it feels premature for me to make such a commitment. But what are these five precepts, the equivalent of the Ten Commandments in Judeo-Christian tradition?

*The First Training:* Aware of the suffering caused by the destruction of life, I vow to cultivate compassion and learn ways to protect the lives of people, animals, plants and minerals. I am determined not to kill, not to let others kill, and not to condone any act of killing in the world, in my thinking and in my way of life.

*The Second Training:* Aware of the suffering caused by exploitation, social injustice, stealing and oppression, I vow to cultivate loving kindness and learn ways to work for the well-being of people, animals, plants and minerals. I vow to practice generosity by sharing my time, energy and material resources with those in real need. I am determined not to steal and not to possess anything that should belong to others. I will respect the property of others, but I will prevent others from profiting from human suffering or the suffering of other species on earth.

*The Third Training:* Aware of the suffering caused by sexual misconduct, I vow to cultivate responsibility and learn ways to protect the safety and integrity of individuals, couples, families and society. I am determined to respect my commitments and the commitments of others. I will do everything in my power to protect children from sexual abuse and to prevent couples and families from being broken by sexual misconduct.

*The Fourth Training:* Aware of the suffering caused by unmindful speech and the inability to listen to others, I vow to cultivate loving speech and deep listening in order to bring joy and happiness to others and relieve others of suffering. Knowing that words can create happiness or suffering, I vow to learn to speak truthfully with words that inspire self-confidence, joy and hope. I am determined not to spread news that I do not know to be certain and not to criticize or condemn things of which I am not sure. I will refrain from uttering words that can cause division or discord, or words that can cause the family or community to break. I will make all efforts to reconcile and resolve all conflicts, however small.

*The Fifth Training:* Aware of the suffering caused by unmindful consumption, I vow to cultivate good health, both physical and mental, for myself, my family, and my society by practicing mindful eating, drinking and consuming. I will ingest only items that preserve peace, well-being and joy in my body, in my consciousness and in the collective body and consciousness of my family and society. I am determined not to use alcohol or any other intoxicants, or to ingest foods and other items that contain toxins, such as certain TV programs, magazines, books, films and conversations. I am aware that to damage my body or my consciousness with these poisons is to betray my ancestors, my parents, my society and future generations. I will work to transform violence, fear, anger and confusion in myself and in society by practicing a diet for myself and for society. I understand that a proper diet is crucial for self-transformation and for the transformation of society.

These five ethical precepts provoke deep thought. I recognize that I will probably have to struggle with aspects of the first and last. But the second training on injustice, generosity and integrity reflects my core social values; the third on sexual conduct and the fourth on deep listening have been in place in my life for a long time. In my professional life as a therapist, I devote my energy to promoting mindful listening and helping my patients do the same. I observe sexual responsibility and devotion, and believe strongly in social responsibility, voluntary action, sharing of resources and "random acts of kindness."

The other night, Thay invited us all to Upper Hamlet to meditate on his front deck during the rising of the new moon. I looked forward to walking the few kilometers up and back in the dark. It occurred to me, however, that some of the older nuns might be able to use a ride, and without hesitation offered the keys to my car for anyone who wanted to borrow it. In thanks for that small gesture, one of the nuns christened my little silver car "Moon Shuttle," as it was pressed into yeoman's service shuttling nuns and lay guests back and forth for the moonrise. That sort of act is a no-brainer and makes me feel good.

One issue that weighs heavily on me is the question of abortion. As a feminist, I have long argued for every woman's right to make decisions regarding her own body. I believe that rigidly opposing abortion is irresponsible. I have worked in mental health clinics and among orphans at Reiss Davis Child Study Center, and seen much psychological and physical abuse of children born into unstable homes. I firmly believe in responsible sex and birth control, but mistakes happen. They have happened to me and to my daughter. They have happened to my patients, and we have labored for long hours, very mindfully, over their decisions about whether to have an abortion. It is a profoundly painful decision that no woman in her right mind ever forgets, but I support each woman's right to choose. I bring this up in my Sangha. While there are differing views within the group, what is emphasized is the importance of consciousness and mindfulness as opposed to action and reaction without deep contemplation. This I can live with.

I consider whether to practice a completely vegetarian diet. I've been thinking about this for a long time, since my children decided to become vegan, eschewing fish, fowl, meat and dairy products. We have supported their decisions wholeheartedly, and Jim and I now practice a far more vegetarian lifestyle than we were raised with. When serving fish or chicken, I try to buy only humanely farmed poultry or wild-caught fish that are not endangered. But as a guest on a big cattle estancia in the remote pampas of Argentine Patagonia, I temporarily gave up my own injunction against eating beef rather than go hungry. In the same spirit, I will continue to make conscious choices. I vow to be ever more aware of the rights of all living beings and the health of the planet, and to mindfully strive toward a more vegetarian lifestyle.

The fifth training, on the topic of excessive consumption, is a good one for me to think about. Even if I have the means and see something that appeals to me, I want to rethink whether I should "consume" it. This is a change in point of view. As the first professional woman in my family, I used to take pleasure in the autonomy of earning and spending my own "disposable" income. I took the position that being well dressed makes a woman look professional and feel attractive, and that spending provides jobs. And I wasn't alone. During every professional meeting, when a boring panel was anticipated, I've watched (and participated in) a mass exodus for shopping after lunch.

Now I begin to think about the grievous sweatshop conditions of third world women laborers who produce the clothes that Western women find in the "nicest" shops and boutiques. I think about the acreage required to graze sheep for wool, and cattle for not only beef but leather. I think about our shrinking rainforests, and then contemplate those barges in Borneo, hauling vanquished trees downriver to become paper pulp to make price tags for the dresses in "nice" boutiques. The more I think about these realities, the more unsupportable my consumption becomes. It seems like an unconscionable waste of natural resources and habitat.

When Jim and I packed up our worldly goods of twenty-seven years to lease our Pacific Palisades house, I was shocked at the volume of our possessions. Certain closets looked like the havens of a pack rat, gathering for the sake of gathering. Even socially conscious manufacturers like Patagonia, whose catalogs are printed on recycled paper and whose clothing is made from melted-down, recycled plastics, can easily pander to the consumer mentality. I know. In eco-conscious Santa Cruz, I have waited in feeding frenzy lines for Patagonia's Labor Day sale. I have been too affected by consumerism and advertising. I resolve to welcome the Fifth Mindfulness Training into my life. This will be an ongoing mindfulness struggle; just this summer, with two new horses as my excuse, I regressed to the level of a fifth grader gathering outfits for a Barbie doll, assembling saddle blankets, bridles, halter gear, winter blankets, and lead ropes for Cheyenne and Spirit.

While never tempted by gluttony or drugs, I enjoy wine. I don't think I'm ready to give it up. The teaching is very clear: "I am determined not to use alcohol." It is bizarre that every time I begin to type this teaching onto my laptop, my computer literally crashes. Last night, typing this, I had eight crashes, and I haven't had one for months! Is the Buddha sitting on my shoulder like Calvin used to? I hope not! I don't know what to make of it, but the peculiarity of these crashes gives me pause.

Alcoholism and drug addiction are rampant in our society. Clearly, as Thay teaches and I know firsthand from years of clinical practice, they cause untold suffering in families and damage in the workplace. But he speaks of alcohol only as a toxin, not of the sociable pleasure of wine in moderation, nor of its benefits to health. He also makes a very good point that with world hunger as it is, we must use our agricultural land judiciously. At the same time, we have close friends who grow and harvest their grapes biodynamically and who provide jobs, good housing and education to their workers' families.

As a psychologist, I am dedicated to avoiding moral absolutes and injunctions, honoring honing one's own personal discretion and the capacity to tolerate ambiguity. I support each individual's thoughtful process at arriving at values of moderation and balance. I run periodic reality checks with those near and dear to me to make sure they are not bothered if I drink wine. This training, like my laptop's crashes, will continue to give me pause. Talking about it in Sangha tonight, I think I can accept the training and make a pledge of ongoing open mindfulness regarding consumption rather than skirting the issue.

As my Sangha discusses issues around the Five Mindfulness Trainings, I learn that perhaps no one, not even the most devout nuns, feels they can observe them perfectly. What they attest to is making a commitment to be guided by them, to strive toward ever-more complete mindfulness in their daily practice, and most importantly, to approach decisions which entail these precepts thoughtfully and consciously. They liken the trainings to the North Star, a point to guide one's path.

I revisit my conflict about taking life. I have personally taken a life and suffered over it, killing the marauding bear at Twin Brooks, but over the years I've been coming to terms with it. Since Jim and I parted in June, how often have I fingered my fetish bear? How deeply do I honor the spirit of the bear? I plan on naming Cheyenne's new foal Running Bear. But how many mosquitoes have I slapped as they feasted on my flesh in the mountains? Yet even here, the most devout monastic Buddhists use an antibacterial in the dishwater, choosing to kill germs rather than transmit disease through the community. Now I will not automatically swat a fly or kill a mosquito. I'll take precautions to wear long sleeves and long pants in mosquito-ridden places, or use bug spray to repel unwanted insects. Just yesterday, as an ant crawled up my neck, I gently moved it onto the grass. I truly value the notion of conscious intention toward the North Star.

As the Sangha's discussion unfolds, I am able to relax and become clearer that making a pledge during this retreat, which is having such profound impact on my spiritual life, is a privilege and an important step. Long after night has fallen and by the end of our Sangha's Dharma discussion, I reach the decision that I will arise in the darkness tomorrow to take the Five Mindfulness Trainings.

### Tam Hoi Hy

Although it is pitch black and I am really tempted to sleep another hour, I get up at the first sound of the pre-dawn bell. Soon I am grateful that I didn't give in to that impulse to sleep. The ceremony in the darkened meditation hall, lit only by candles and attended to by nuns wearing saffron robes, is truly emotional for me. I am called forth by name to kneel and prostrate before the community and to take my place toward the front of the assembly, near the altar. We are invited to hear each of the five vows; we listen in solemnity, and are invited to pledge. At the end, we are reminded that we must read the Five Mindfulness Trainings aloud, preferably with our Sangha at home, at least one time per month. If we fail to repeat the trainings for three months, they are nullified. At the end of the ceremony, we receive our certificates and our new Dharma names, chosen for us by Thay and the nuns in our sangha. My Dharma name is Tam Hoi Hy. I like it. It means "Joyful Celebration of the Heart."

After breakfast, Thay gives his last Dharma Talk of this summer's retreat; it is titled "Being and Nonbeing, Birth and Death." He talks about how life is fleeting, cyclical, transitory, like water molecules that gather to form a cloud, then coalesce into droplets of rain, fall into rivers and oceans and evaporate, over and over in an eternal cycle. No individual has permanent identity, any more than an individual water molecule has; but like water molecules, forming and reforming as water, ice, rain, snow, rivers and oceans, we remain always part of the vast cycle of nature.

I remember Aldous Huxley's lectures in my physics class at UC Berkeley. Huxley explained that everything in the cosmos never dies; it just goes through changes and transformations, like the clouds in the sky. He used the analogy of water, describing how a pool of water forms into ice, or evaporates and becomes steam, rain or sleet. When we see a cloud, we can be sure it has been rain, ice, snow, river, ocean, or water in our bodies. We go round and round in a perpetual cycle, no birth, no death, just changing forms. When a person dies, the atoms are dispersed into the soil to become a tree, a pebble, an ant, a leaf, a cloud, and so on. We can appreciate what John Muir taught, the unity and sacredness of everything in the cosmos. I love discovering I am a cloud!

I listen to the Dharma talk, stretched out on a blanket in the sun with Franz, Brother Henric, Phap Diep and Shantum Seth, who is cradling little Nandini to his chest, occasionally getting up to walk with her. During the talk, I compose this poem in my journal:

Dharma: "Dear Cloud"

Can anyone know the day of your birth?
Or is Not Knowing the cause of your mirth?

Cloud, rain, ice and snow
Water, rivers, oceans, go
Back to cloud, to rain and snow.

Birth and rebirth, death and dying
Endless circles, blissful sighing.

Every atom, every drop
Never truly starts, or stops.
So with the endless turning wheel,
Mindfulness shows us what is real.

Cloud, rain, ice and snow
Water, rivers, oceans, go
Back to cloud, to rain and snow.

I am life without limit
Inter being—Ultimate.
This body, mind, senses—not me.
Meditating deeply, I am free.

Every atom, every drop
Never truly starts, or stops.
So with the endless turning wheel,
Mindfulness shows us what is real.

Cloud, rain, ice and snow
Water, rivers, oceans go
Back to cloud, to rain and snow.

When I realize this summer retreat is nearly over, I can't imagine where the time has flown. I never opened my knapsack with the cognac I brought, "just in case." I never even thought about it. But I do think about the Five Mindfulness Trainings and my commitments.

For our last night together in Fresh Eyes Sangha, we celebrate Beginning Anew, a practice that provides an opportunity to constructively air feelings toward each other. Because our Sangha has been remarkably harmonious—much more so than the crucible of my biological family and the intense relationships with close friends at home—our sharing turns out to be a love fest. We have all been together in quietly positive ways. The power of cross-cultural sharing in total silence, except for Dharma discussions, has been as remark-able for us as we have witnessed it in the Palestinian-Israeli Sangha. During their month together here, that group has moved slowly from red-hot rage through paranoia and distrust, to grief, compassion and empathy, and finally to trust. Toward the end of the retreat, they composed and sang the following *"Thanksgiving Song"* to all of us, bringing tears to nearly everyone gathered:

> Branches of the same tree
> Jew and Arab, you and me
> Being quiet, gentle, slow
> This space helps me learn to know.
>
> Breathing in, Breathing out,
> Abraham's Children
> Breathing together.
>
> Each branch suffers and has joy
> In each a little girl and boy
> Compassion, understanding
> Deep wounds need tending.
> Breathing in, Breathing out,
> Abraham's Children,
> Walking together.
>
> Bury garbage of the past
> Plant a seed of peace to last
> Solid, clear and free,
> To change the world begins with me.
> Each moment mindfully
> Knowing peace begins with me.
>
> Breathing in, Breathing out,
> Abraham's Children,
> Planting together.

Our closing celebration goes on until nearly midnight, as did the meditations on the new moon a few nights ago. By the time I finally crawl into my bed, I am thoroughly exhausted.

I remember Joseph Campbell, the great teacher, mythologist and psychologist, with whom I had the great pleasure to dine one special evening before we were on a panel together at UCLA. Campbell has talked about the importance of "following your bliss," by which he meant your passion, the deepest thirst for meaning in your soul. He's written of the three stages in the archetypal hero's journey: separation, initiation, and return. I think of those stages at this phase of my sabbatical journey.

Although I'm certainly not a hero or heroine but just a devoted wayfarer, I realize that this journey, made sacred by the rites at Plum Village, is taking on an archetypal form. Jim and I marked our separation with a rite, and he has undergone an initiation in his solo journey. Now I have been initiated as well, and I emerge with a changed identity, symbolized by my new name. We are both altered. Jim tells me his whole body has changed its shape, and I feel my spirit and psyche have transformed deeply. What remains ahead are the steps toward return and reintegration.

# Chapter 37
## L'Enclos

In French, "l'enclos" means enclosure or cloister. Moon Shuttle has ferried me away from Plum Village, and I am ensconced in the tiny, stone-walled hamlet of Pragelier near Hauteforte, this time for a planned weeklong solo retreat at L'Enclos. I'm staying alone in a 250-year-old stone building, a former *boulangerie*. I am meditating, walking, reflecting on my experience at Plum Village, and writing and making photographs to relish from the Dordogne, the Charante, Perigord and surrounds.

Although I am in Bordeaux and Perigord, I have recovered surprisingly little taste for wine and none for foie gras. Plum Village taught me to exchange one joy for another. After seeing a woman here force-feed a struggling goose, I can't imagine eating foie gras. I have new ways of calming myself when I see something like that that distresses me. Through my meditation practice, I'm finding myself able to breathe through most stressful situations.

I also have some incredible photographs, thanks to faithfully practicing "Zen and the Art of Computer Maintenance" this past spring, when Jim and I returned from our nearly six-month peregrinations through South America. During our "snowed out or snowbound" spring, after working my way through the sort of serial computer disasters that can make one rant and rave in impotence, I learned how to take the nonsense as an opportunity for breathing meditation. Discovering the definitive superiority of deep breathing over ranting, I have been rewarded with learning new art forms that only a springtime of devoted computer use could yield.

During our travels there has been a technical revolution; cell phones, smaller laptops, and digital photography have all become widely available. I transformed my love of photography—making slides with my 35 mm Nikon and telephoto and macro lenses—to making digital images with my new compact camera, the one that miraculously survived my tumble down the Ayuntepui River waterfall into total immersion in a pool below. Without knowing how the end products would compare, I was impressed by the digital camera's capacity for instant editing and by my liberation from carrying x-ray-proof lead bags of film canisters on every trip. I have replaced that hassle with postage stamp-sized mega memory cards. Before I left Twin Brooks, I mastered Photoshop sufficiently to download my Latin American digital images onto my laptop and edit, crop, enhance and save them. This has been like studying yet another new language; daunted but intrigued, I've already enrolled in a Photoshop master class in Santa Fe for next winter. For now, at least I am up and running.

I'm placing photographs as screensavers on my laptop, and it serves as an ersatz meditation altar. When the spirit moves me, I can meditate anywhere on the grounds of this medieval village. I sit cross-legged on my Crazy Creek backpacking chair with my inflated "Relax the Back pillow" tucked in behind me, facing the screen, contemplating Thich Nhat Hanh's smile or the face of Sister Chan Khong, or a lotus blossom growing in the pond near my eyrie, or a photograph of my Sangha in front of the huge Plum Village temple bell.

At L'Enclos I celebrate uninterrupted days composing my own "Book of Hours"—inscribing reflections in my travel journal. I take time to work on my photography. Not only do I have writing meditation as a way of reliving and metabolizing my experiences, sifting through them, highlighting what matters most to me, letting go of what doesn't, but I also have photography meditation, the careful process of sorting through new images, organizing and saving them for various uses.

An important part of my sabbatical practice is to bring pilgrimage home—to make an altar, arrange photographs, collect talismans and touchstones, to share my experiences via email, and to devise small formal rituals to keep the sacred alive. Now, as I'm travelling solo, when I dine alone, I open my doeskin fetish bag and arrange the fetishes Jim chose for me, communing with him over the weeks when we cannot be in direct telephone contact. I also take out the tiny stone Buddha Shantum Seth pressed into my palm when we said our goodbyes at Plum Village. Just as I've learned the importance of allowing time to sit on your luggage for half an hour to collect yourself before departing, I've also learned the necessity of time for re-entry and reintegration—to always stop for a time at "L'Enclos," the figurative enclosure, before crossing the threshold into routine.

I am growing bolder and more seasoned as a solo traveler, and have decided I will cancel my flight to Milan and instead drive my Moon Shuttle into Switzerland, across the Alps into Domodossola. There I'll meet Lucas, my young climbing buddy and mountaineering guide from the Andes; Lucas lives near his sister Cecelia's *refugio* in Alpe Devero, learning to make cheese high up on the mountain. Then I'll go to Greece to visit the monasteries of Meteora and the Isle of Samothraki off the coast of Macedonia, and on to Turkey, travelling alone in trains, planes, rental cars, ferries and on foot from convent to cheese to cloister to Kasbah, before I carry my doeskin bag back to our own mountain and into the arms of my beloved.

Phil Cousineau, writing of the "thump and the lift of the heart" that he feels on pilgrimage, says: "It's for moments like this that you left home—to no longer feel like a stranger in the world, to test your mettle against the strength of the fates, to find the unmet friends and hear that no matter how far you wander as a pilgrim, 'You'll Never Walk Alone.'" [19]

---

19   Cousineau, Phil, *The Art of the Pilgrimage*. Berkeley: Conari Press, 1998, 228-229.

# CHAPTER 38

## OLD CHEESE

*Putting Pedal to the Metal: Testing My Mettle*

In a propulsive blur, Moon Shuttle ferries me across Bordeaux. When I optimistically arrive at the car rental bureau to extend my rental and arrange drop-off in Milan, the laconic station agent, amplifying my stereotype of French beaurocrats, wearily leans on his elbow and emits a nasal "Mais NON, Madame." Moon Shuttle is not allowed to cross any borders. I must leave her, but hopefully not my newfound equanimity, here. "Absolument, Madame."

I buy a ticket and board a train to Paris, then a sleeper riding the rails overnight to Milan. In the morning, rather mop-haired myself, I have another day's travel to Domodossola, where I'll go by taxi and on foot into the Italian Alps to visit Lucas, the mop-haired Italian wilderness guide who led us on horseback through the Argentine Andes. I continue from Domodossola by taxi up a winding, rocky alpine canyon alongside a riotous and rocky tumbling stream, up a paved road that becomes a dirt track. A narrow hiking trail signals the definitive end of my taxi ride. I bid *arrivederci* to the cabbie, gather my rolling suitcase, which is flagrantly inappropriate for this terrain, and continue trudging up the trail with my bag bumping, clicking, thumping, and dragging along behind.

I hope I am indeed headed for Alpe Devero and Lucas's sister's refugio. I am also proud of having accomplished a reversal of plan, managing schedules in French, and purchasing train tickets from French vending machines. Noisily bumping along or not, I've made it here. I've never navigated such a traveler's challenge alone before.

After half an hour the trail gives way to a gorgeous alpine meadow. Before me stands a tall stone refugio, its windowsills bedecked with geraniums, clotheslines beside it with freshly laundered sheets flapping aloft. In front are picnic tables, all occupied by hikers and mountain bikers who have trekked or cycled up here from Domodossala. There is the bright aura of a summer festival, and when I enter the refugio I discover a chaotic tumble of guests: Lucas's sister Silvina from Tenarife, his other sister Cecelia, her husband, Luca, who owns Refugio Alpe Devero, and his parents, all in full tilt with aprons on, sleeves rolled up, providing guests with food and drink. Lucas's girlfriend Eleonora is helping out in the kitchen, along with Cecilia and Lucas's three young children, Frederico, Carolina and Valentina.

### Enveloped by a Warm Italian Family

Cecelia greets me with a warm embrace, apologizing profusely for her broken English and the commotion. She explain that Lucas is way up the mountain, helping the eighty-year-old cheesemaker herd and milk the cows and make cheese, and that I have arrived in the midst of the busiest week of their summer, for indeed it is festival time, and all the beds in the refugio are full. If I don't mind, they've made up a cot for me in the loft of the cow barn with Silvina and Eleonora. Do I mind? Not at all! It sounds like the beginning of another adventure.

I arrange my belongings in the loft, get settled, and return to don an apron, roll up my sleeves, and jump into the fracas of running an Italian alpine refugio! I soon join in peeling vegetables, stirring sauces, working the cappuccino machine, waiting tables, loading and unloading the dishwasher, taking down and folding dry sheets and hanging up wet ones in a nonstop whirl that begins at sunrise and goes until midnight. We take time out for our meals, shared convivially as a family after the lunch crowd has left and after the dinner crowd has been fed. Cecilia's cuisine is fabulous, the international merriment of the hikers and bikers is infectious, the family embraces me as its own and I love my cow barn!

## *Heidi Revisited—the End of an Era*

We are in such a whirlwind of busyness that it is several days before I can find time to climb to the top of the mountain and visit Lucas, who has thirty cows to milk morning and evening and can't come down to the refugio. One sunny morning, feeling a solo traveler's confidence, I set off with my knapsack to climb the mountain and find the valley where Lucas is milking his cows and learning to make cheese in the old-style way. Never mind that there are goat, horse and cow paths this way and that, and the directions I am following were given in Italian, which I don't speak; the mountain is spectacular. I find a path following the rivulets that feed the stream I followed up from Domodossola. Along the banks are wild blue delphiniums and a riot of other alpine flowers. Nearing the top of the ridge, I hear a bell and look up to behold a horned ruminant, a bearded billy goat with his bell ringing from a leather collar. He is standing sentinel-like, guarding the narrow way into the verdant valley where some of his lady friends are munching in rhythmic summer satisfaction.

My nonverbal conversation with old Bill seems to give him the idea to yield to me, so I continue past him, down into a hidden hanging valley evocative of Shangri La. I pass two more sentinels, solitary horses posing with their front hooves planted up on hillocks, manes in the wind, tossing their heads in greeting. I am stunned by the sylvan beauty of this glimpse into a hidden pastoral era long since past. I wouldn't be stunned to see Heidi skip across the path or Julie Andrews stride out into the middle of the meadow and burst into song.

Standing beside the stream are a few small stone huts and two barns. I approach, stick my head in the doorway of one of the huts and find Lucas preparing lunch. His matted blond Argentine dreadlocks have considerably lengthened since I saw him in the Andes. He knew I would visit sometime in August but had no idea when, as he's cut off from contact with the outside world in his alpine hideaway. He gives me a great bear hug and beckons me inside his rustic abode to finish preparing the noon meal, a more than ample reward for my newly minted courage.

It feels very good to be here with this unique young man. Lucas is Argentinian by birth but Italian by culture, and he marches to his own drummer. Ever since my years as a high school English teacher, I have been drawn to interesting young people who have questing hearts. Jim and I have several very special ongoing relationships with my former students, male and female. Considering the painful wound in my relationship with my own son, I'm aware how much I am drawn into mother-son relationships with young men like Lucas, Phap Diep, Franz, or Brother Henric. Such men often find an unconventional "out there" mother like me a fresh contrast to their stay-at-home moms.

### Cheese the Old Way

I learn that Lucas's routine is to arise at 4:00 a.m. with Alejandro and Gregorio, the other cowherds, to milk the great bovine beasts. After the cows are milked and the milk pails emptied into a huge cauldron in the cheese shed, the men break their fast with slabs of cheese and wedges of hard crusty bread. Then they drive the cows further up the mountain to pasture for the day. They return for lunch and the chores associated with cheesemaking: stoking a slow, wood-burning fire, stirring the ancient carbon-encrusted cauldron with a paddle the size of a broom; skimming the curds off the simmering milk; gathering up the cheese and pouring it into round wooden forms, which are set to age on drying shelves in the cheese shed; turning the older, aging cheeses by hand. In mid-afternoon, they head up the mountain again to herd the cows back for their evening milking before supper. After supper, the four men fall exhausted into their beds to sleep until 4:00 a.m. comes again. The four are Lucas, the other two cowherds, and Dominico, the old man who supervises them and has been making cheese in this valley, as did his father and grandfathers, for most of the summers of his eighty-three years.

While we are slicing bread and salami and setting up the noon repast, Lucas tells me that as of this summer, the Italian commission that oversees dairies and cheesemaking will close down this centuries-old operation unless Dominico switches to aluminum vats and milking machines. It seems they believe human hands on teats and an old iron cauldron that cooks cheese over an open fire do not belong in the 21st century. I am witnessing the very terminus of this wonderful, ancient process of handmaking cheese.

Lunch is soon readied. I meet Dominico—a sunburned, deeply wrinkled, white-haired man with forearms like hams from a lifetime of milking cows—and his son Gregorio and nephew, the goatherd Alejandro. We gather round the oilcloth-covered kitchen table, eat bread, cheese, sundried tomatoes, salami and olives, and drink red wine from old jelly glasses. The wine was carried up the mountain in an old ceramic crock by one of the horses I saw, whose weekly work is to pack several hundred pounds of cheese down the mountain for sale or further aging in the barn where I sleep. When the wine is offered, I smile and not "No thank you," remembering the Fifth Mindfulness Training and my return hike down that precipitous trail.

Conversation is not a developed art form at this table. These are men of hard work and few words. I suspect there is a layer of sadness as the August days roll inexorably by, spelling the end of this historic era. Dominico manages to communicate to me in Italian that he will comply very half-heartedly with the government edict. After lunch, he takes me into the barn to show me elements for milking machines and assemblies for the new vats, carried by the horses when they returned from cheese deliveries. He says the worst thing will be losing the physical contact with his great beauties, and the intrusion of machinery noise, which will shatter the peace and calm he loves about this hidden place.

### Beastly Beauty

Soon it is time to climb up to the upper meadows and gather the cows; Lucas, Alejandro, Gregorio and I set off. When we reach the first cows, I am amazed by their huge size. They look more like oxen than dairy cows. Their heads are enormous, and each wears a thick, wide, leather collar with a handsome handmade brass bell whose deep timber ensures they can always be found. They are robustly healthy and wonderfully colored, some tawny, some black and white, some brindled. Though their brown eyes and long lashes speak of pastoral calm, I am nervous about herding these huge beasts, but soon discover that they are totally tame. From their twice-daily milking and routine of moving from pasture to barn, they seem patiently prepared to teach me how it's done. I hardly have to do anything but walk, following the west side of the stream alongside my docile teachers, relishing this opportunity for walking meditation as I hear and feel their rhythmic inhalations and exhalations.

Back in the stone barn, Gregorio introduces me to the one-legged milking stool and shows me the strokes he deftly employs to send robust streams of milk frothing into his milking pail. He fills bucket after bucket while the cows stand compliant and untied, waiting for the relief his milking brings them. Milking is a completely different skill, a world away from being a cowherd. Lucas tells me Gregorio is definitely the best of the three of them, and that Alejandro, who milks not only the cows but also his goats, is considerably better than he is. Even after a full summer here, Lucas assures me he still is a novice milker, but he insists on teaching me. At least for one day, someone else can be the lowest of the low.

He picks out one particularly bountiful bovine for me, and then cracks up as I teeter around, perilously imbalanced on the one-legged stool. I try and try the moves, but get zero yield; this delights all three of the milkers, whose varying prowess at coaxing milk from their cows seems to amp up their testosterone. After half an hour, I manage a couple of cups of milk from my Bessie before Lucas takes over and brings her the relief she desires.

I step back from hands-on mammary kneading to watch each of these young men balance on his stool and lean into the warm furry flanks of his enormous female companion, quietly coaxing her to give up her milk. There is something tender, intimate, and gender-bending about these privileged relationships between man and cow which both parties seem to enjoy, and which I am privileged to enjoy vicariously.

I've relished this unique relationship with our young Argentinean mountaineer, and invite him to come stay with us in Pacific Palisades. Knowing his adventuring spirit, I'm pretty sure he will turn up on our doorstep sometime. I hate that the shadows are lengthening and the day will be soon drawing to a close, but as the path is perilous, I must be on my way down to my cow shed for the night. I will sleep amidst the musty aroma of aging cheese with much deeper appreciation and gratitude that my wanderlust fostered this serendipitous meeting with Lucas and allowed me to experience this poignant end of a pastoral era.

Already missing this place and these people, I'm also looking forward to re-embarking solo for my writing respite on the island of Samothraki in Northern Greece before heading to Turkey, then home to greet Jim who will already be at Twin Brooks, ripe from his own adventure.

### The Best Laid Plans . . . Are Aftly Gang Awry, Again

After touching down on the tarmac in Athens with the sun low in the sky, I rent another car and brave the angry, fist-waving drivers of Athenian rush hour, queuing through a dizzying plethora of roads whose signs are all in Greek, to find my way north to Meteora. I arrive at my hotel around midnight, sighing deeply with amazement and relief as I sink into bed and a night of deep slumber.

In the morning, I begin my visit to a series of intriguing medieval monasteries and nunneries perilously perched throughout a long winding valley, each atop an isolated spire. Nourished by spending a few days in the peace within them, and by the deep sonorant chanting of the monks, I set out driving across Greek Macedonia along the north coast of the Aegean to the port city of Alexandroupouli to book a ferry to Samothraki.

With three hours to wait for the next ferry, I stroll the waterfront of the port of Alexandria and settle on one of the few cafés that promises Internet, hoping to send an email home with my journal entries and photos from Plum Village, L'Enclos and Alpe Devero. Joyfully I hear the *whoosh* of emails being sent, and feel relief in knowing that I am no longer the holder of the only copy of my journal. I order a cappuccino and settle down in the warm Aegean sun to continue writing, readying myself for my stint, contentedly imagining myself as a female version of Gerald or Lawrence Durrell, inspired by the Greek Islands.

Out of the corner of my eye, I catch sight of the young barista approaching my table carrying a tray loaded with coffees and cappuccinos. Wearing skin-tight, elasticized pencil jeans, lots of make-up and a banal smile, she is clippity-clacking across the patio in three-inch, red stiletto heels. I turn in my chair to survey her approach. She doesn't seem to be focusing on her task. Suddenly, her heel catches in one of the grooves in the patio and she pitches into me, drenching me and my laptop with hot coffee, whipped cream and despair. Spluttering, I reach to rescue my laptop from the deluge, but it is already too late. The screen has gone black and I can see milky liquid seeping through the keyboard into the motherboard. I am sunk. Drowned. Killed.

The barista picks herself up and smooths out her elasti-tight jeans. I look at her as coolly and calmly as I can, expecting profuse apologies, but she comes at me with a towel and starts roughly mopping my laptop, saying rather casually in heavily accented English, "Don't worry, it's nothing." After I take the computer apart and dry the insides as best I can, I discover it's not "nothing," and there's no one in Alexandroupouli who knows anything about Mac computers.

I realize that I haven't been traveling solo all this time. I've always had a wonderful companion, sitting in cafes, propped up against pillows in various beds and cots. I've always had my "twin," my laptop, my journal, to whom I talked about the day, about what I was feeling and experiencing. She has been my pilgrimage partner. And now she is *dead,* along with something in my heart.

Was it not enough to let go of my house and my psychoanalytic practice? Bid farewell to our friends and family and then to my beloved Jim, and to learn to let go of anxieties and fears? Was that not enough? Apparently not. For the next several weeks, I must travel without even the companionship of my laptop, and without knowing whether her contents can be resuscitated when I return home.

So, dear reader, I share with you the black hole that accompanied me to Samothraki and through the amazing byways, coastline, deserts, villages and towns of my travels through Turkey. And which I brought home with me as the corpse of my laptop, carried aboard the plane from Istanbul, Turkey to New York on September 9, 2001. Only two days later, back at Twin Brooks after returning home, the mere loss of my laptop is hugely overshadowed by the searing images of the Twin Towers falling. What an enormous opportunity to practice everything I have learned.

PART VIII

RE-ENTRY:

LOSS AND LUMINOSITY

# CHAPTER 39
## TRIPPING INTO THE BODYMIND

THRILLED TO BE safely reunited after our three-month separation, but also both shaken by the vivid televised images of the Twin Towers falling and so many tragic deaths, Jim and I "hole up" together in the cabin to await the birth of Cheyenne's foal. When her foal is born, I plan to name it Running Bear and dedicate it to the spirit of the Great Bear.

Why? It's a long answer, found deeply embedded in the bodymind. I found myself thinking about a winter snowstorm about three years ago when our car slid off the road into a ditch, and we had to shovel snow to get it out. As I was hoisting a heavy shovel full of snow, I heard a *snap*. I had re-torn my shoulder rotator cuff yet again. The next morning I couldn't lift even a hairbrush to waist height. Initially I'd injured that shoulder in a skiing fall, and again shoveling llama dung, and finally suffered a complete rotator cuff tear when thrown by a rogue horse. It had completely debilitated my shoulder motion and necessitated a total shoulder arthrotomy.

After the snow-shoveling episode I went to see my high school friend Mike, the orthopedic surgeon who had performed the original surgery. Viewing my new MRI, Mike told me that the reason I couldn't lift my arm above my waist was because my shoulder cuff was totally "destroyed." There was so much residual scar tissue from the previous surgery that even if he'd tried, there would be nothing firm to sew anything to, and the procedure and post-op would be draconian. He could block the pain, but that was about all. I would have to accommodate to life without much use of my right arm.

I couldn't tolerate the notion of being unable to even brush my own hair or lift a spoon to my mouth. Our sabbatical dreams had been hatching at the time and would have been severely compromised by my disability, so I decided to undertake every reasonable alternative to surgery. This path led me to homeopathy, physical therapy, yoga, acupressure, chiropractic and massage, Jungian Authentic Movement therapy, and magnetic pulse therapy in Mexico. I have no doubt that each of these alternatives were helpful in some measure; over several months, I began to notice some improvement, but the most unusual and profound treatment brought me in touch with the depths of my somatic psyche and my inner mother bear.

One day in yoga class, one of my classmates noticed my avoidance of shoulder stands and other shoulder-stressing postures. After class, she asked if I'd injured my shoulder in a traumatic accident. As a psychoanalyst well-versed in "true" trauma such as rape, incest, satanic practices and war combat, I didn't think shoveling snow qualified as a trauma, and said I hadn't. Painful and disappointing? Yes. Frustrating? Certainly. But not emotionally traumatic. She explained that she worked as a trauma therapist for an orthopedic surgeon. I was open to every alternative available, and I became curious. The psychologist in me, who had written her Ph.D. dissertation on "The Belief Systems of Women with Breast Cancer," was intrigued by the mind-body connection.

I agreed to a session with Beverly, whom I came to call "the lizard lady" because of her interest in the primitive limbic brain, the central nervous system, involuntary musculature, cardiovascular and respiratory systems. I surely wasn't expecting what transpired. My experience of my somato-psychic body detonated two deeply buried traumas into mind- and body-altering explosions. Under Beverly's gentle guidance, I was metaphorically visiting my body and discovering intensely painful and conflictual stored secrets about my shoulder.

Beverly's approach to working with body-based trauma is to completely relax you and bring your mind into focus on physical sensations in the afflicted area and any imagery that comes up in relation to that area. She told me not to talk or even "think" about it, but to stay closely attuned to any muscular twitches, sensations in the skin, changes in temperature or circulation, to notice respiration, and to observe any other bodily expressions or visual imagery that occurred.

### Unearthing Somato-Psychic Trauma

In the first session, I followed my mind into my shoulder and noticed a series of physiologic expressions I would normally have never noticed. It was like turning over an old, rotting log with a magnifying glass in hand—there's a crazy, hidden civilization down there! I observed nervous twitches, quivers, and pulsations. Eventually, I began to experience mysterious visual imagery. Bringing my mind into my shoulder, I experienced a kind of splat, like a jar of red ink had been thrown and broken. Or was it blood? It spread through my consciousness like the red ink of a Rorschach in an abstract explosion, a splash of blood, bone, skin. Suddenly I was awash in a flood of tears, overwhelmed with shock and pain. I started to speak, but Beverly hushed me and told me not to "think," just to stay with the sensations in my body.

After the session, within moments, I associated to my mother's fatal and bloody car accident twenty years earlier. She had been driving Dad from Twin Brooks to Los Angeles for a doctor's appointment. Traversing small farm roads through familiar miles of orchards, vineyards and farms between the foothills of the Sierra Nevada and the central San Joaquin Valley, she had come to an intersection. It was not the four-way stop she habitually took. At this two-way stop, she did not realize the oncoming truck had no stop sign. Pulling out, she was instantly crushed by the Mack truck that demolished her car, hitting the driver's door and no doubt smashing her shoulder first. My father, on the passenger's side, miraculously survived the wreck with only broken ribs and lacerations.

As I later processed my overwhelmed response in the session, I realized that perhaps I had unconsciously taken her unmetabolized trauma into my own body and stored it as a somatic wound, identifying with her horrific death, maybe feeling guilty for being alive. Maybe I unconsciously set out to metabolize it or atone through my own accidents. I was struck by the fact that my wound was in the part of my body that would reach out to embrace my mother. My injury left me like a helpless infant, unable to reach out for a hug, blow my own nose or brush my hair.

Mother's accident had occurred while I was still in my own analysis. We spent months and months on my grief, the loss and the impact of her death on me and my family, but we had never discovered its psychosomatic implications. Most of the injuries to my shoulder happened a few years later.

I felt compelled to return for another session with Beverly. In the second session, I expected to revisit my empathic bodily identification with that mortal trauma. But instead, Beverly insisted, we were without an agenda and I must simply pay close attention to any somatic phenomena. After becoming conscious of neurological twitches in my shoulder, I experienced a rank fetid smell, then the vague image of a snout. I felt shivers and twitches and then something like lightning or a jolt of electricity in my shoulder, and the image of blood again, and immersion in an associative sense memory. I associated to an animal's foul breath and stinking wet fur.

### The Primordial Mother Bear

What was a bear's snout doing in my shoulder? I flashed on the connection to shooting the bear at Twin Brooks, two or three years before mother's death, when I spent the whole summer finishing my dissertation in the Tiger Lily Creek cabin at Twin Brooks with Gabriel, then eight years old, and Ariel, five. That was the summer the renegade bear I spoke of earlier broke into our cabin and ransacked the kitchen. It was terrifying for the children and I'd felt a primordial urge arise within me, like a mother bear on an instinctual mission to protect her cubs. When the bear returned, my inner Annie Oakley and I were ready. With a hunting rifle, I shot the bear inthe heart. (Please do remember, this occurred before I had taken the Five Mindfulness Trainings.)

In the middle of the night following the shooting, replaying the scene over and over, it occurred to me that in a different time and place, my action might be narrated entirely differently. Perhaps I had shown courage as well as unexpected skill as a sharpshooter I had gotten up at dawn and made my way to the caretaker, asking if he would dig up the carcass and save me some evidence, teeth or claws. That evening, he had brought me ten bear claws and had confided that before burying the remains, he had butchered the carcass and had a winter's full of bear meat in his freezer if I wanted some. Making the claws into a beautiful necklace for my unborn grandchildren, I supporessed the entire thing. That is, until the trauma therapist invited my body to speak.

I realized that the gut-wrenching psychosomatic explosion in my shoulder during the session was a body memory of the recoil of the hunting rifle against my shoulder. It was also, I realized, my own murderous guilt, embedded in my shoulder behind the grief over my mother's fatal accident. The rank smell was the bear's breath, and the fetid smell was the bear's fur. Making the claws into a beautiful necklace for my unborn grandchildren, following my father's "don't tell" injunction, I had repressed the entire thing. That is, until the trauma therapist invited my body to speak.

Though we had explored these traumas in my analysis, we had never contacted them in this body-based way. While I did learn that at a different time and place, my action might be narrated entirely differently, that maybe instead of something my father insisted must be hidden, I had shown courage as well as unexpected skill as a sharpshooter. But with the help of the lizard lady I was dumbstruck to discover my body speaking in a way that my analysis had been unable to access. It was a profound experience, finding these intensely painful and conflictual psychic secrets about my shoulders buried in them, perhaps creating the proclivity for subsequent repeated shoulder injuries.

It was meaningful to me that the somatization included both sides of the conflict—love and hate—a daughter's grief over loss, feelings of helpless abandonment and rage, and a mother's primal capacity for murder to protect her children. I'd never thought of myself as somatizing emotional pain, but here was irrefutable evidence of my own mind-body connection. After these two sessions, my other therapeutic work on the shoulder became effective, and over the course of many months of intense preoccupation with my body, I slowly regained nearly complete movement and strength in my shoulder.

### *Another Trip into the Body/Mind*

Remembering trauma therapy brought another powerful journey back into my bodymind, one that I had taken almost forty years earlier, but hadn't thought about in years. These incidents were psychically connected, marrying the identifications of myself as a victim and a perpetrator in two episodes involving death. But this earlier one involving LSD brought me a feeling of peacefulness about my own intrauterine experience before the trauma of my breech birth, along with my first inkling of peace of mind about my own death. It happened in San Francisco at the beginning of the psychedelic Sixties, when I was a student at UC Berkeley. I volunteered for a research project on LSD and had one incredibly good trip.

Two indelible body-based memories remain with me from that LSD-induced experience. In the first, I experienced myself curled up in utero. I could feel everything about it as if it were present time; my little knees were folded up against my chest; warm, viscous amniotic fluid was all around me; my umbilical cord was draped over my shoulder. I could feel the gentle shifting movements of my mother's body, the drumbeat of her heart and occasionally a muffled but echoing sound that must have been her voice. Even while I was totally, speechlessly immersed in that intrauterine memory, I also had a sense of how amazing it was.

Later, during that LSD day, still floating on acid, I went to the bathroom and looked into the mirror to behold an old woman looking at me. I was startled and pulled back a bit, as did she. I kept gazing at her in the mirror and she steadfastly returned my gaze. I studied her very wrinkled skin, which was soft and even a bit furry, like my grandmother's when she was in her eighties. Her hair was nearly white. Her hazel blue eyes seemed incredibly calm, even smiling. In astonishment, I realized that I was looking into my own very aged face.

Something in the psychotropics altered my brain and perception in such a way that it was as if I were able to access genetic information stored at a cellular level in my body and see my own aging process right before my eyes. It seemed that at a cellular or DNA level, potentiated by the drug, the plan map of my body from pre-birth to near death, past and future opened to my sensorium. The encounter had a powerful, centering impact on me. I felt no desire to repeat the experience with LSD because it had been so profoundly moving and illuminating. I didn't feel I needed to know any more. It changed my entire perspective about aging, relieving me of anxiety, for these aspects of my unborn and aged self seemed at peace. What struck me most was how the somatic body stores so much psychic information. If only we could easily access it.

Not only did the LSD vision offer me a sense of peace about and acceptance of my own personal biological destiny or map, but it also gave me greater reverence and humility for my place in the natural world. Ever since shooting the bear, I have wanted to atone for that violation of nature by honoring the spirit of the Great Bear. Bears have joined horses to take on great meaning in my personal pantheon, and a bear has become my guardian spirit and my fetish. I not only have the the letter written by Uncle Amaziah Clark about being clawed by the grizzley bear and the bear claw necklace I made from the bear I shot, but also a beautiful Navajo grizzly bear claw and silver squash blossom necklace and bracelet. I have collected several small Zuni bear fetishes and offered them on occasion to patients in need of strength. When Cheyenne births her foal, which could be any day now, Running Bear will be dedicated to that Great Spirit.

# Chapter 40

## Running Bear: A Brief Candle

Cheyenne has taken her own sweet time giving her foal to the world. Has she been waiting for the most auspicious moment? Since we didn't know when she was bred, we were left guessing. By the size of her belly, everyone thought she would deliver while I was away over the summer, but she has held on…and on…and on. Did she realize that just a few days ago that our world changed forever with the fall of the Twin Towers? Probably not, but for me, carrying the magnitude and horror of that loss, it has been incredibly comforting to imagine that she waited until now to bless our devastated world with a birth.

At dawn this morning, Ricky calls me to rush down to the barn; she has just delivered. I jump into my jeans and work boots and throw on a warm coat and practically fly down the mile-long road to the barn and the manger. There, still wet and curled up misty-eyed in the straw, is the most beautiful little foal I have ever seen. He is the perfect image of his beautiful buckskin paint mama, with a little white tail, long eyelashes, big beautiful eyes, and long gangly legs. He struggles to stand as I approach, but crumples in newborn exhaustion.

We are all prepared to begin the bonding process we've been studying. Foals that are welcomed into the world by their mothers and other horses, and are also held, massaged and caressed routinely by their human caretakers, learn to accept people as naturally as other horses. I drop down into the straw and envelop him in my arms, greeting him by his new name: "Running Bear!" I stroke his head and explore his ears, nostrils and belly while he gazes up at me with his huge brown eyes. As I was with Dr. Adung's adoring gaze, I am utterly smitten.

Soon, he is ready to stand up and begin his first wobbly lurching traverse across the straw to his mother's side. She waits patiently as he flounders around, looking for her teat, so I stroke her and, remembering milking the cow in Domodossola, collect some of her milk to put to his lips, guiding him to the teat. Before long, they are connected and he feeds beautifully, then sets out on his first unsteady romp around the manger. I spend most of the day in awed rapture, watching this miracle of nature and experiencing the power of a new life to heal the still-raw wounds of September 11.

I take gazillions of still photographs and even record his sucking sounds with my video camera. I am infatuated. Although all the equine birth manuals speak of bonding as helpful for the foal, none of them speak about the intensity of bond that the human caretaker experiences. I could pick him out from any other foal by his sweet smell alone; I am awash with memories of childbirth and the milky tumble of bodily feelings Ariel and Gabriel's births brought forth.

Every day, Running Bear grows stronger and more robust. He meets the llamas and horses in the pasture, and they nose him gently and curiously. He is soon steady enough on his long legs to playfully prance around his mother and me. Four days go by in a blur of bliss. Even though Apple informs me it has regretfully "misplaced" the hard drive and data from my destroyed computer, and even though the daily news is still flooded with September 11th, Running Bear helps me forget about all that. Jim is tolerant of my "equine berzerkitude" and smiles indulgently. He doesn't get how I could feel this way about a pooping, hay-eating little horsey creature that can grow up and dump me at any time, when a bicycle is so inert, obedient and tidy. Jim and I are just different and we've come to appreciate those differences more and more.

I'll tell the rest in emails, as I can barely bear to write it again:

Dear Friends and Family—
   Just hours ago, I got a call from Cathy and Ricky, our

ranch caretakers telling me to come quick—Little Running Bear our newborn colt was down—I rushed all the way down to the barn and there he was—our beautiful four-day-old foal suddenly really sick—Unable to get up, he was groaning and struggling to breathe—Naturally it is Sunday and we couldn't reach any vet—both of our regulars are away at the huge annual animal veterinary conference, so we gave him penicillin, electrolytes and hooked up the trailer. We led a very confused Cheyenne into the trailer and I got a blanket and wrapped Running Bear in it and carried him into the back of the Explorer. Jim started driving out toward a vet clinic, but before we were five miles from our ranch, my precious little love died in my arms.

It is wrenchingly sad. Yesterday he was a perfect little buckskin paint colt, frolicking and beautiful, and in a few hours today he is dead. We are all in mourning. He brought such sunshine and joy to the ranch—we all are in love with him—to have him mysteriously just die—maybe an anomaly, bacterial infection, or something—we don't know yet—is such a terrible blow. What have I been saying about learning to let go—How much more do we have to learn to let go of?

I can't write more right now—just feel so mournful. We are scheduled to leave the ranch on Friday for another several months of travel in Latin America—some professional speaking engagements—some adventure—but of course I don't feel like going anywhere at the moment. We'll have a burial tomorrow—today Jim and I are going for a llama hike with Miwok and her new baby, Llao Llao. As he looks just like his grandmother Hopi, who we lost to plant poisoning two summers ago, we'll see if that helps.

In the meantime, poor Cheyenne is just standing with her head hung low beside Running Bear's little body. The vet says we should give her 24 hours with him—she's grieving and all the other animals know something is lost.

Namaste, and a Lotus to you from a Pilgrim Wayfarer,

Harriet

❖✧❖

Ooohhh, Harriet Dearest!

I am sending love and warm thoughts and can only say you wrote the most beautiful poem when you were on retreat in France. Reading that was very comforting to me three weeks ago when I had my loss. What a terrible mystery. One minute alive and then gone. Your dear mother and my Mama are looking after Running Bear and so many wonderful spirits are welcoming this little baby colt. I am aching for you and Jim.
Love, SVG

Dear Harriet,

I was so sorry to hear about the death of Running Bear. What a sad event to occur just as you are leaving and with the world in such turmoil. Things in New York continue to be tense but at a lower level. The anthrax scare keeps people on edge, but we are keeping life as regular as possible, and enjoying small gatherings of family and friends as well as big events like Bar Mitzvahs. But everywhere there are still funerals with sad-eyed lovely young people spilling out onto the streets, their eyes prematurely saddened, their faces brave but drawn. And then there are the memorial services for the firemen going on still and at every fire station, shrines of flowers, food, messages etc. Today I brought over a gift certificate for free therapy for firemen and families for two hours a week. It is still inspiring to be here.
Love, DD

Dear M & S—

Thank you so much for your compassionate reply. You're right. It is so painful. And with Running Bear, we had inaugurated a new technique which I am very impressed with—it is a bonding and attachment program whereby within the first hour of birth the human caretakers cuddle, touch, talk and hold the newborn—exploring every tender part and orifice—to enable the babe to develop trust—so

Running Bear had experienced that and clearly moved easily between us, his human caretakers, and his wonderful mom, Cheyenne—I wish I had done it with LLao Llao—as he is far more skittish about being handled than Running Bear was—but I wasn't here for his birth. The theory is that as they are herd animals, as long as the critical early window of timing is open, they can bond to more than one creature without going berserk. Makes sense, yes? Anyway, of course with his death, I realized I was so totally bonded to HIM; I've been grieving as if he were my own! It's been hard. Love, H.

Dear Rhonda (Cheyenne's former and devoted owner) —
   Jim and I are far, far away—and we hope you are well, and the upcoming holidays will be warm. I am still grieving for our beautiful little colt and imagine you are too. Thank you for the beautiful tulips and the sentiment. Did I send you pictures of him and Cheyenne? Let me know if I didn't. In the meantime, I thought you might enjoy reading some of the kind and comforting words other friends have written—and a poem I wrote in a Buddhist retreat in France before his birth—but which I have turned to, to remind me of the cycle of birth and death. So though his time on this earth was brief, he has already touched many.     –H.

Harriet,
   I felt with you about the death of Running Bear. He did not have much of a chance to run, I fear, with so little time on this earth! Have grieved the death of many pets over the years—mostly of dogs, though one was a macaw brought back to me by my uncle who spent some years in Venezuela...But it also evokes memories of the death of my own little four-year-old sister when I was six, and her burial on a Christmas day.
   Cheyenne's grieving reminds me of my parents' grieving, and how the 25th of Decembers were never the same after

that. Do we think Cheyenne's sorrow may be time-limit-ed, or will she always remember, as we human beings do? Missing you, but happy that you will return to us some day.

Dear Harriet,
What you said about letting go is the truth. And some people and foals are for longer than others. Our memories are never measured or perceived in time, but the wholeness is stored within us, always accessible and in full color, timeless.

When I looked at my lovely little, conscious, granddaughter Keely, I had new fear, to keep her safe, to bundle her properly, lay her properly on the bed so she would breathe, keep her from theTaliban... attachment is a curiosity, so mysterious that we can't know it, and all we can do is to cry, even for happiness, but especially when we are sad. And don't forget, when we die, we are only missing from one place...

I'm so sad you are suffering like this, Harriet, so unexpectedly and so seemingly unnecessarily. We keep learning the lessons until the last day, don't you think? And perhaps we can only hope that we can appreciate souls while they are with us— and as they are, when we can no longer see them.

Now, you know more. Take care, my friend.

Dear Harriet,
I just now read your email and couldn't help but shed a tear. How very, very sad; so sudden and unexpected. And now to watch the mare also grieve. Such grief, Harriet. The bonding process is so unique and powerful. I am always humbled by the trust it builds and that our animal friends bless us with their trust and friendship. A good friend shared the following with me when I lost two of our horses in 1996:

We who choose to surround ourselves
With lives even more temporary than
Our own, live within a fragile circle,
Easily and often breached.
Unable to accept its awful gaps,
We still would live no other way.
We cherish memory as the only certain
Immortality, never fully understanding
The necessary plan...

"The Once Again Prince" –Irving Townsend

Dearest Harriet,

Oh, how awful and sad...Such a beautiful little spirit. He looks wise and sad in the photo. I will print it up and put it on my altar. You and I know this little teacher will be back.

I had had you on my mind for some time, as I knew the birth was to be soon after you returned home. My mind now finds itself up on Echo Rock... one of the special places in my life. In 1990, at the Twin Brooks reunion, Dad had only been gone a couple of months, and I had had no time to myself, no time to let the spirits heal. I spent one afternoon, by myself, up on Echo Rock, lying on my back, watching sky and clouds intermingle. To experience what you just have... Echo Rock is a wonderful place to communicate with the heavens and the spirits of our animal friends. Take care my friend, and know that I send you much shared sorrow, and a sad heart.

# CHAPTER 41
## FALLING FROM A ROOF
## ON THE ROOF OF THE WORLD

APPROACHING three peripatetic years traveling the globe, including the winter of wandering, paddling, dancing, sailing, riding and hiking through beautiful Latin America, we are forever uncured. The travel bug bites us once again when a travel journalist friend describes an annual tribal gathering and horse festival in the remotest corner of Tibetan Szechuan China. It offers everything needed to make our hearts sing: an exotic, unvisited part of the world; one of the few remaining unspoiled enclaves of Buddhist monasteries; horses; and time with the kind hearts of the persecuted people of Tibet. Jim is enticed by the idea of hiking and camping for a week along a remote gorge of the Yangtze River. So in July, we set off again. Little do we know that this journey will be another pregnant combination of awesome and its close cousin, awful.


We fly to Kunming province in Southwestern China to spend a few days exploring the region's fantastic geology and cultural richness. More ethnic tribes live in this area than in the rest of China combined, and they are beautifully represented in the Cultural Arts Museum in Kunming. There we see life-sized dioramas of tribal villages, and watch artisans create baskets, pottery and weavings. We spend an entire day as students at the University of Tea and learn the history of the tea trade, as well as the growing, collecting, curing, transporting and economics of tea. We are introduced to tea tastings offered with exquisite style by one of the slim-boned, graceful young female students at the university. I'll never forget how beautifully and delicately she poured the aromatic golden tea into tiny tea bowls for us to taste. She exemplified a lovely practice of mindfulness.

Kunming is a city of "rivers of bicycles" such as we have never witnessed. In the early morning, the streets below our hotel window are teeming with bicycle riders on their way to work. We see cyclists carrying baskets of chickens, sheaves of plumbing pipe, plates of glass, balloons, flowers, myriad children and families. They flow like salmon heading upstream, widening around obstacles, narrowing, then widening again. As cyclists fearful of catching a wheel from riding too close to another bicycle, we are incredulous. It is meditative to watch this extraordinary flow of humanity on wheels.

### Tashi Delek, Tashi Phuntsok!

After a few days, we fly north to Tibetan Szechuan. With our small airplane's wings dipping dizzyingly close to the Himalayan peaks, we drop into the enchanted hidden valley of Dzong Zhien, the mythical Shangri La of World War II fame. We are met by our guide, Tashi Phuntsok, a tall, nut-brown young man who offers us rare insights into his people. Tashi is the youngest child in a large farming family that couldn't afford to send all the children to school. He was very apt and desperate to learn, so he would secretly accompany his more fortunate older brother to school and sit unobtrusively in class, drinking in whatever teaching was offered the older boys. His parents were so overburdened they hardly noticed his absence.

Tashi is a deep-hearted soul who, as he grew, craved the opportunity to learn more about Tibetan Buddhism and to sit at the feet of the exiled Dalai Lama. At age eighteen, with only a pair of old sneakers and a shabby sweatshirt, he ran away from his village and into hiding. It took him six months of near-starvation and freezing to cross the Himalayan range from his village to Dharmasala. All along the way, traveling under cover of darkness, he practiced prostrations of devotion, facing Dharamsala on his pilgrimage to bow at the feet of the Dalai Lama. Once there, he found refuge in an exiled Tibetan community and learned to cook and speak English. He remained for seven years before returning home to Dzong Zhien, where he was hired as an English-speaking guide. It is our immense good fortune to partake in one of his earliest adventure guiding experiences.

With a jeep driver as unmindful as Tashi is mindful, we spend several bumpy, winding days of four-wheeling through the rugged valleys and slopes of the Himal. Tashi guides us through a land of wonderful monasteries that offer opportunities for quiet sitting meditation with chanting monastics. I inflate the beach ball inside my portable meditation cushion and find several opportunities to play catch with the shy but impish young monks.

Finally road rattled and road weary, we arrive on the Himalayan plateau to witness an awesome annual Tibetan tribal gathering, the Litang Horse Festival. As we enter the valley, we see lines of vehicles approaching. They are small, slow-moving, three-wheeled tractors that sound like lawnmowers, pulling trailers full of extended families. Galloping alongside are horsemen on sturdy ponies. The people are handsome, high-cheekboned, dark-skinned, with warm brown eyes, often wearing colorful tribal dress. Large dump trucks transport portable yurts into the open field, and the people pitch these beautiful tent-like yurts, complete with Tibetan rugs, trunks and beds. Cooking tents are set up, offering the delicious, hot chili seasoned foods of Szechuan. As we walk through the camp, all the locals smilingly greet Tashi and us with the familiar Tibetan greeting, "Tashi Delek!" which means something like Shalom, Aloha, Hello, Blessings. May all auspicious signs come to this environment!

In this remote Tibetan area annexed by Red China, ancient feudal costumes hidden during the Chinese takeover are donned for days of dancing. Men and women wear fur boots, tiger skin wraps, pendulous coral beads and gorgeous tweny-four karat hammered gold medallions. Hundreds of gaily decorated sturdy Tibetan ponies and their fearless riders thunder across the plain, competing in races, stunts, and archery feats, all at recklessly high speeds without helmets. We see only two other Westerners the whole time.

Most of the events are races across the wide plane. A cadre of riders on ponies bursts forth at the sound of the starting gun, racing into a field to pick up scattered treasures—packs of cigarettes and white silk scarves bound around coins. At a dead run, the riders lean way down over their ponies' shoulders, touching the ground and scooping up their booty to the hoots and huzzahs of the crowd. We see more than one heart-stopping accident, and one man is agonizingly trampled and dragged to death by his frightened pony. Pushed along in a groundswell of excited Tibetan spectators then driven back quite ruthlessly by the Chinese police, I am nearly clubbed to the ground by Chinese militia as the ages-old antipathy of the Han Chinese for the Tibetans surfaces.

Spectators who are not on the playing field are clambering to get aboard the dump trucks, clinging to their slanted sides, gaining a viewing advantage over those on the ground. When the horses are not racing, there are large teams of tribal dancers—each group wearing the silken color of its tribe—moving across the field in serpentine fashion.

### Dongwang Gorge

More than rewarded by the bone-crunching ride to the Litang Festival, Jim and I set out again with Tashi Dalek on a weeklong trek into the remote Dongwang River Gorge, a tributary of the Yangtze. In this isolated but breathtaking part of Tibetan Szechuan, adventure trekking is still virtually unheard of, so we are to become outback guinea pigs. We figure this out when we arrive at a trailhead where, theoretically, there would be horses or mules waiting to carry the tents, food and other equipment for the week. However, there are none. No one has informed Tashi that in the summer months, all the able-bodied villagers and their livestock leave the villages for the high Himal to gather maitake mushrooms, a cash crop that provides income through the long, cruel winters.

After scouring the village, Tashi sends word to the high camp that a group below will pay handsomely for the use of a pair of mules. They materialize by nightfall. We settle in for the night with the news that tomorrow will probably be easy, maybe five to eight miles. Not so. Once we set out, we follow a precipitous trail along a thin gorge dynamited out in the narrowest places, one to two thousand feet above a river. There is no possibility of camping along the narrow ledge. On the first day of this ill-planned trek, we slog over twenty precipitous miles along the narrow gorge, climbing more than 5,000 feet in altitude.

After eleven hours on the rugged trail, as rain begins to fall, an opening appears at the side of the gorge. We follow a tributary to reach a tiny village where Tashi arranges for us to stay. Children, dogs, and village elders rush out to greet the strangers and look at us in awe. They have never had white-skinned visitors, only the occasional wandering *bikkhu* or monk. We are invited to pitch our tent on the flat roof of the village headman's house. In a Tibetan home, the ground floor shelters yaks, horses, and pigs. The second floor is the space for family cooking, eating and sleeping, all arranged around a central firepit with a vent through the roof. The roofs of Tibetan family houses are open to the sky and festooned with prayer flags, but have walls on three sides. They are considered the place of honor for visiting monks, and for meditation and prayer. We are grateful and fascinated by this tradition, but so utterly exhausted, we decline the headman's offer of a celebratory dinner in our honor, and beg his permission to pitch our tent and fall into our sleeping bags for the night.

Just before crawling into bed, it occurs to me to ask where the toilet is. (In China, that means, "Where's the slit in the floor?") Our host motions to the anteroom off the earthen roof. We go to check it out. Tashi and I walk gingerly onto an extension off the rain-dampened roof toward the slit, but the roof sways with each step. We step back to call Jim, who walks along the edge, where he supposes there is structural support. And then I watch in speechless horror as the whole mud roof collapses under him. He falls three stories into, yes, the Tibetan toilet. Terrified he might have been killed, I find my voice and scream out to him—and in vintage humor, Jim moans back from the bottom of the pit, "Well, now you can really call me shithead."

The eighteen-foot fall results in three broken ribs and a badly torqued foot. There is no ordinary means for evacuation. Tashi descends into the hole on a ladder and carries Jim back up to the roof on his back, carefully finding his footing on the primitive ladder. The codeine in our kit allows Jim moments of fitful sleep, and in the morning, we get to see how a true village works. We tell Tashi that Jim will need to be evacuated by helicopter, assuming that our trip and evacuation insurance will cover the expense. Ashamed to tell us that because there is no phone, there is no way to contact the outside world, and probably no helicopter anyway, Tashi and his assistant retreat to another part of the village. After an hour, our host nervously signals that all the strong young men of this village are up in the high mountains gathering mushrooms, the village's sole source of income. We offer to pay handsomely for their return if they can carry Jim out.

After a couple of hours, the summoned young men arrive for a powwow that results in the construction of a comically rustic litter. Fortunately we have more codeine, as broken ribs are very painful, especially as Jim has started a cold with a cough. After three tries to make the litter wide enough for the hips of a Westerner, he is roped onto the litter of rough-hewn saplings, and twelve young men form three teams of four to take turns carrying him twenty rugged miles. I beg for a mule to ride, as our pack mules have been returned to the village at the trailhead. Following the previous day's twenty-some-mile hike, plus the night of anguish over Jim's fall, I am completely done in. After hemming and hawing, a mule is reluctantly proffered. (I later discover that no one in the village's memory had ever dared ride an animal along the sheer gorge.)

Coming to the Litang Horse Festival, I never imagined a ride like this one. On the mule, who hugs the outer edge of the heart-stopping dropoff, I manage my stomach-turning vertigo by remembering the advice of a savvy horsewoman: "Be like the lead mare; always keep your eyes on the horizon, never look down or back. This steadfastness will be communicated to the animal." Eleven hours of alternating rain and sun later, in the dark, my mule and I drag to the trailhead behind Jim's litter and twelve helpers. Tashi's assistant has jogged ahead to call for a jeep. After gratefully purchasing a crate of beers for our bearers and paying them, we get Jim into the jeep. We jostle for seven grinding hours to the nearest "hospital" in Shangri

La. The antique X-ray machine confirms broken ribs, but indicates no broken bones in Jim's swollen black, blue and green foot.

### Tibetan Outback Medicine

The hospital's Han Chinese doctor advises us that the local shaman is far more experienced than he with orthopedic injuries, as the shaman is the fourth in his line of healers and knows the most. Jim reluctantly leaves the hospital to enter the care of the best available local treatment: a shaman. This wizened Tibetan man arrives, bowing, with his bag of herbs, poultices and needles. His first clinical move is to grab Jim's toes and yank on the foot, ostensibly to realign the displaced ligaments and torn tendons. Jim shrieks in pain, but before he can protest or I can intervene, the shaman pulls a needle from a rumpled paper bag and quickly plunges it repeatedly into the top of the swollen foot. He applies suction cups—bowing to the modern world in preference to leeches for bleeding. Wasted from the fall, from morphine, and from the helpless struggle against being yanked and stabbed and bled, Jim falls into slumber.

It is another week before Jim can tolerate the twenty-three-hour plane trip home, where three orthopedists and an MRI diagnose the foot trauma as a serious Lisfranc dislocation. This injury is uncommon in the West since cavalry days, when horsemen fell and were dragged by a foot caught in the stirrup, but is common among the horsemen of Litang. It tears all the tendons from the cuboid and metatarsal bones and dislocates the joints along the top of the arch, and requires a complex and seldom-performed surgery to freeze the joints on the top of the foot. Literally screwed, Jim spends twelve weeks on crutches. The prognosis for hiking again is bleak, but Jim is granted yet another of his dramatically expended nine lives, which we eventually celebrate with a five-mile hike. Not so fortunate are the Litang horsemen who suffer this injury; it is highly unlikely that poultices, leeches and prayer alone could repair such a ravaged foot to full function.

God or life or the Buddha doesn't close a door without opening a window. This journey to the back of beyond and the ensuing catastrophe open our pores so wide, we can feel the whole universe coming in. The opportunity to live, laugh, love, chant, meditate, hike, and sing with the lovely, persecuted Tibetan people in a remote outpost will sober and nourish me for the rest of my life. We emerge grateful for the safety and comfort of our lives and the medical care here, yet still uncured from the powerful bite of the travel bug that poignantly brings the awful and the awesome into our lives.

# PART IX
# CHALLENGES TO FAITH

# Chapter 42
## Cancer and the Bears

I'd just returned, ebullient, from the fortieth reunion of my class at Vassar College when Jim gets a call confirming that he has prostate cancer. The good news: it is encapsulated, slow growth. We need to wait until the biopsy scars heal, then make a choice between surgery and implanted radiation seeds. Jim chooses surgery. It's daunting to think of going through surgery in LA without living in our own home there, so maybe it can wait three months until our tenant's lease expires. In the meantime, we receive an auspicious omen.

### Bear Medicine

An hour after Jim gets the news of his cancer, we take a mental health hike to the very top of Echo Rock. Suddenly, Jullay charges off, barking wildly. For the first time in years without bear sightings, we see one. It's an adorable, tiny bear cub, leaping onto a huge fir tree and scrambling nimbly up. Thirty seconds later, there is his or her twin, right behind the first cub. The two healthy spring cubs roar up to the top of this awesome, hundred-foot tree. They are a sight for sore eyes. Worried and wondering where Mama Bear is, we urgently whistle Jullay back. We don't need to wait long; we hear Mama, moaning and roaring out to her cubs. Hearts pounding with a naturopathic cocktail of adrenaline and endorphins, we listen in awe to their anxious dialogue for twenty minutes.

I know in my heart that this is a grand omen. I sigh deeply and think, "The universe is finished extracting payment from me for the bear I killed." The little bears with their remarkably youthful energy, roaring up the most phallic of phalluses, a healthy tall tree, are etched in our minds' eyes. We can envision them whenever we need an infusion of the life force. And in the background is the power of the great Mother Bear, calling out protectively, as I was called forth to act protectively of my own cubs so many years ago. We walk home via a long, respectful detour around the tree, holding hands and feeling remarkably at peace and blessed. And the omen proves to be a good and true one. Jim's cancer is encapsulated and completely removed.

### Owl Medicine

Nine months later, back in our house after an extensive sage smudging and refurbishment to purify Porto Marina and to clear her of any psychic residue of the Rangda, we put her on the market with the intention of moving away from Los Angeles. Many things have changed for us over what became a three-year sabbatical. We've let go of so much, literally and emotionally, that we no longer feel attached to the past. We want to live in a more healthful environment.

We drive up to Twin Brooks to enjoy a beautiful fall weekend. Driving amidst the tall trees of the grand forest, with dogwood and maple leaves turning along the way in on our long winding road, I get a call on my cell phone from my gynecologist. "It sounds like you're driving. We can talk later."

"No," I say. "My husband Jim is driving and we're about to lose cell contact. You can talk to me. Please."

"Well, Harriet. I'm really sorry to tell you this way, but you have breast cancer."

Just then, we lose cell contact.

Breathing in short, shallow, tight gasps, I ask Jim to stop the truck. I tell him what she has just told me. He looks as stricken as I feel. I never expected this—I, who wrote my doctoral dissertation on "The Belief Systems of Women with Breast Cancer," looking for variables that might impinge on the immune system. As we sit in stunned silence, we suddenly hear a great whooshing of wings. A shadow passes overhead just as a great horned owl swoops down from above and lands on an overhanging branch not ten feet from the windshield. She just sits there, staring at us for several minutes while we stare back in numb disbelief.

My first thought is *not* that this is a good omen, like Jim's vibrant baby bears and the massive tree. I think of the phrase, "I heard the owl call my name," and of the Native American lore of the owl as a harbinger of death. Finally, she lifts her great wings and takes flight. With one cell phone call and the whoosh of the great bird's wings, I am thrust into what is to become a nearly year-long saga of cancer treatment—multiple surgeries, chemotherapy and radiation—and a house sale precipitously postponed.

The next morning I awake to a Twin Brooks resplendent with fall colors, hearing the sound of the brooks splashing and chortling over the stones in the streambeds that divide around the house, creating our natural island sanctuary. I arise from my bed and go straight to my meditation cushion. Within minutes I begin to feel a tectonic shift from the shock of the day before, from fear and rejection to acceptance and embrace. "What an opportunity to practice!" I think. I remember how the Dalai Lama, when asked about the Tibetan people's egregious persecution by the Chinese Communists, replied, "They provide a deep opportunity for practice." Whatever brought that owl to alight so close and stare at me so assiduously, I know it was some kind of powerful, good medicine that combined very well with the teachings that washed over me from Plum Village. I think of the books I have read: *No Death, No Fear* and *The Places that Scare You*. I remember my teachers' encouragement to enter the fear and embrace it.

After a deeply restorative sit, I get up, fix breakfast, then go for a hike in the beautiful woods with Jim. That afternoon, I take Cheyenne out for a ride. The autumn woods are staggeringly beautiful. I feel ready for whatever lies ahead.

We return home to LA, take the house off the market, and meet Nora, a highly respected surgeon at the John Wayne Cancer Center in Santa Monica. She is very reassuring and competent, but she discovers more bad news. Palpating my right breast, she finds another lump and immediately orders an ultrasound, a mammogram and a needle biopsy. Within two hours we learn that I have bilateral cancer, though the pathology of the two lumps is different, so it isn't metastatic. Nora says she can operate the following day. What a relief. So many women have to wait for weeks of disquietude and anxiety between initial diagnosis and treatment.

At almost warp speed, I have a bilateral lumpectomy and removal of the sentinel lymph nodes. I learn that while the cancer was Stage One, slow to moderate growing, one lump was 1.4 and the other was .8 centimeters, and there were some malignant cells in the nodes, so I need additional surgeries to clear the margins. Carol, my new oncologist, studying the path reports and consulting with my surgeon, recommends a course of chemotherapy and radiation. I consult with two other oncologists and explore several alternative treatments, but decide for now that I will follow Carol's advice.

My faith is buoyed after consulting Madeleine, a UCLA gastroenterologist who has moved beyond Western medicine and has been embraced as a shaman by the Lakota Sioux. Madeleine assures me that the owl that came to me represents not a call to my death, but a visitation by a totem of wisdom and knowing. This cancer journey, she counsels, will take me on a path of deep wisdom.

The remarkable thing is that all three—Carol, Nora and Madeleine—concur that chemotherapy must wait a month until all the surgery scars are completely healed. I am free to embark on my intended trip to Bhutan next week. When they learn that I have long planned this pilgrimage to Bhutan, the land of "Gross National Happiness," with my dear friend, yoga and meditation teacher Phyllis Pilgrim who underwent treatment for breast cancer just six months ago, they all feel such a journey will do more for my healing than chemo. Blessings to be cared for by doctors who are on the path.

We schedule the surgical implantation of a chemo shunt on the same afternoon my flight will return from Bhutan. Nora sends me off with syringes and antibiotics in case of infection. Suddenly, I am out of my hospital gown and in my travel khakis. I pack my traveling altar: my inflatable meditation cushion, my small rosewood Buddha, Jim's fetish bag and the tiny stone Buddha given me by Shantum Seth. The next thing I know, Jim is waving a tearful goodbye to me at the LA airport.

# Chapter 43

## Bhutan: Midnight Musings

*The Guest House*

This being human is a guest house.
Every morning a new arrival.

A joy, a depression, a meanness,
some momentary awareness comes
as an unexpected visitor.

Welcome and entertain them all!
Even if they're a crowd of sorrows,
who violently sweep your house
empty of its furniture,
still, treat each guest honorably.
He may be clearing you out
for some new delight.

The dark thought, the shame, the malice,
meet them at the door laughing,
and invite them in.

Be grateful for whoever comes,
because each has been sent
as a guide from beyond.
　　　　　　　　—Rumi[20]

---

20  Rumi, Jelaluddin, trans. by Coleman Barks. *The Illuminated Rumi*. New York: Random House, 1997.

IT'S 4:00 A.M. and I lie awake on a hard, monastic-style bed in a cold room in a small Bhutanese cabin in Bumthang Valley. My monkey mind is making sure I won't go back to sleep. With the diagnosis of breast cancer exactly one month ago, a double lumpectomy and nodal dissection, and two oncologists' recommendation that I undertake a "short" twelve-week course of chemotherapy to be followed by fourteen weeks of radiation, I'm lying here churning. *What has just happened to me? What might happen? What are my alternatives? Dare I turn my back or at least one shoulder on the conventional Western medical advice? Is the potential damage to my healthy body worth this draconian chemo treatment, which is favored only because of statistical possibilities of recurrence or death?*

Phyllis Pilgrim, my roommate and travel guide on this auspiciously timed pilgrimage to the tiny Himalayan Buddhist kingdom of Bhutan, snores softly on her bed. Our fire has gone out and the room is freezing. If I get up to build a fire, I might wake her. But I secretly wish she'd wake up to talk, as she went through her own journey with breast cancer over the past year. She knows a great deal about alternative healing, and I'm dying to ask her a million questions. But I keep still. My busy brain whirs over the past year and the stresses that might have taken their toll on my immune system.

What cunning irony! My doctoral dissertation, entitled "The Belief Systems of Women with Breast Cancer," demonstrated a possible link between diseases of the immune system and our beliefs about what constitutes psychic trauma. In 1978, when medical science was paramount, that thesis was definitely not mainstream. But a quarter of a century later, the mind-body connection has been well established. Every doctor I've seen since my diagnosis has not blinked when I've mentioned the possible connection between the cancer and severe psychic distress. Since my diagnosis, I've been mulling this over in the middle of the night, trying to imagine if there is any way to address or redress the two hard hits I have felt and to promote healing.

We carry malignant and "deranged" cells in our bodies all the time, and it is the job of our healthy immune systems to survey and knock them out. The problem arises when the immune system itself is distressed and doesn't function fully. Most of us are familiar with getting colds when we're not taking care of ourselves or are overloaded or distressed. Serious diseases of the immune system, like cancer, sometimes occur when there's an increase in the kind of distress that goes to the jugular of the somato-psyche. Add other causes, such as genetic predisposition, strong birth control pills like the ones I took in the 1960s, hormone replacement therapy, and carcinogens in our diet and environment, and you can have a malignant cocktail.

Over the past year, my immune system has had three blows: two painful losses, plus Jim's bizarre and terrifying free-fall accident in Tibet. If I can undertake healing and repair on these fronts, will my immune defenses return to full functioning and surmount this cancer?

The two losses were so traumatic that within minutes of my cancer diagnosis, my mind instinctively lurched back to those palpable body blows. Both experiences assaulted my core identity, my sense of myself as a competent mother, assaulting the maternally protective power in me when the bear broke into our cabin. Instead, I was left feeling impotent, failed, and deeply depressed. Utter powerlessness and defenselessness could have dealt a decisive blow to my immune system's defenses.

My mind rolls back to the first loss, last January. I stood in the international arrivals terminal at LAX, eagerly awaiting the return of Prudencio, the young Aymara Indian from Lago Titicaca whom we had sponsored to live with us as a guest and helper, and who had become a beloved member of our family during that year. Prudencio, abiding by the terms of his ten-year visitor's visa, had returned to his village in Peru to be with his family for the winter. I waited and waited, scanning the droves of incoming international passengers coming up the ramp after immigration clearance. I kept looking for his huge smile and his red backpack, watching the tide of returning Americans and foreign visitors from all around the globe. No sign of Prudencio.

There is no way to get information from INS as to the where-abouts of an arriving passenger. In the space of that endless vigil, I experienced the first direct hit from my own government. Immigration officials refused to speak to me, even to tell me if he had been on the flight. I finally had a taste of the impotence many disenfranchised persons routinely experience—of being treated like a zero, a cipher, or worse.

After eight hours of building agony, an official relented and gave me a guarded phone number—under injunctions that I never disclose how I got it. I reached our dear Prudencio in detention and learned that INS had detained him, questioned him, and harrassed him with escalating threats of imprisonment for himself and his family in Chiquito, if he did not confess to traveling to the U.S. to work illegally. Out of panic that his family would be imprisoned, Prudencio, a true innocent who hates to oppose anyone, finally said he did help us some around the house. The INS informed him they were rescinding his ten-year tourist visa and sending him out of the country as a persona non grata. He could make one phone call and then he would be on the next plane back to Peru. Our shared sense of impotent loss triggered depression in both of us, as he had become part of our family.

Though only twenty-one, Prudencio is a wise old soul but an innocent in the ways of the modern world. Until he came to live with us as his sponsoring family, he had never left his little pueblo, much less seen an airplane. While he was a great help around the house and at Twin Brooks, my trauma came from the loss of his purity of spirit, his fresh-eyed look into our culture, and the long hikes and horseback rides we'd shared as I learned of his fascination with dreams, the unconscious and spirituality. In my midnight mulling, I try to figure out if there is any way we will ever reunite with our dear Prudencio.

My mulling also gravitates to the deeply troubling relationship with my only son. He never responded to the letter I wrote him from Plum Village. Last May, I wrote to him again, this time urging him to consider starting some kind of therapy. To him, unfortunately my effort to offer therapy as a relief for his suffering apparently felt like I was criticizing him. Stung by the suggestion, he replied with a searing seven-page email to everyone in our family, detailing his rage at me and his decision to cut off all communications. I vividly remember receiving the letter, feeling faint, clammy, grief-stricken and filled with shame and humiliation. I distinctly felt stabbed in the breast.

I despaired for Gabriel and for our relationship, feeling it spoiled by a gulf of misunderstanding, and knew there was nothing I could do but let go of my desire to connect and "help." I would have to honor his decision and truly let go permanently, relinquishing hope, even more than I already had over the past fifteen years. I had to release—finally and for all time—any of my own agendas or desires for him. His pain was so unmitigated, I knew that further communication would be futile and destabilizing for both of us. After a wave of depression, I really let it go. It was over.

Years ago, in my own analysis, I had explored many dysfunctional aspects of the relationship between my ex-husband and me and how they had permeated our children. Now, release could only come through yoga and meditation practice, and in both I practiced *tonglen*, taking in his suffering and sending back compassion. He never needed to know. This was between me and the universe.

With a heavy heart, I gratefully acknowlege that I'm a pilgrim seeking solace in this peaceful country whose monarchy places "Gross National Happiness" as its highest priority. What a dramatic contrast to the demoralizing conflict we left in America, in the throes of Bush's pro-war obsession with Iraq. *Here in tranquil Bhutan, will I be able to gain perspective on this past year in a way that will foster my healing? Can traumas be repaired, or can I release my attachment to such outcomes?*

After an hour of midnight ruminations, I hear Phyllis' sleepy voice say, "Are you awake?" Joyfully, I roll out of bed and cross the cold plank floor to light a morning fire in the wood stove. Pine logs are crackling and a refreshing scent fills the room as I crawl back into bed. For the next hour and a half, while awaiting the dawn, Phyllis and I talk about traumas that preceded each of our diagnoses. I hear about treatment alternatives she has explored on her pathway to wellness. We note the bitter irony in the fact that as caretakers of others in our careers, we share this same diagnosis with three of our own caretakers/female doctors—my radiologist, my "soul doctor," and her nutritionist. When I was writing my dissertation, many of the women I interviewed with breast cancer were caretakers, including a prostitute.

### A Great Day of Big Medicine

We finally rise at 6:30 and push off down the grassy slope to do yoga in the open space of the dining hall. Phyllis is a gifted yogi, and her teachings are gentle, expansive and freeing. As we move through the poses with Ujjayi Pranayama breathing, I feel my travel-weary body open up, relinquishing the crimps and knots from riding several days in a minivan on winding mountain roads. I think of yoga at home with my dear friend and teacher Cat, who likes to say, "The most powerful part of yin yoga is what you cannot see: intention, awareness, and breathing." Phyllis closes our practice with the following invocation from Kalidasa, a 5th century Sanskrit poet:

Salutation to the Dawn

Look to this day, for it is life, the very life of life.
In its course, like all the verities and realities of your existence,
the bliss of growth, the glory of action, the splendor of beauty.

For yesterday is but a dream, and tomorrow is only a vision.

But today, well lived, makes every yesterday a dream of happiness,
and every tomorrow a vision of hope.

Look well, therefore, to this day.
Such is the salutation of the dawn.[21]

Returning to our room, we take quick showers and dress for the day. We have a specially prepared "American" breakfast of scrambled

---

21 A Sanskrit proverb for serenity and peace written by Kalidasa.

eggs and white toast (more than overcome by the thick, dark floral honey that is unique to this valley) and set off with three other pilgrims, Aviva, Bonnie and Christine, plus Renzin our guide and Tenzin our driver, to visit the most important and beautiful monastery in all of Bhutan, Kurjey Gompa.

*Leki, the Master Weaver*

First we have a special stop to meet Leki Wangmo, master weaver and owner of Leki's Guesthouse. I have been carrying a box of business cards for Leki, designed by my friend Mary, who visited here last spring. Mary, who loves textiles, found Leki's studio here in Bumthang and was so taken with her, she offered to design her business cards; I am the bearer. Leki is a graceful, youthful-looking middle-aged woman who sweeps me up with her warm welcome and broad gap-toothed smile. As Mary's emissary, I receive a royal welcome. This turns out to be fortuitous. Renzin, our guide, has petitioned His Majesty Jigme Singye Wangchuck for permits to visit the most sacred monasteries of Bumthang, but they have not come through. Leki, as the Chair of the Bumthang Women's Association and a member of an important council on natural resources, as well as a devout supporter of Kurjey Monastery here in Bumthang, insists on personally guiding us to the three principal Bumthang monasteries today, with a midday luncheon at her guesthouse.

Leki is dressed in the women's traditional Bhutanese *kira*, made of the conservative checked fabric worn by men and women alike, though the woman's robe wraps around like a complicated sarong, fastened at each shoulder over an underblouse with a gold clasp. Over her left shoulder, Leki is wearing one of her own handwoven fringed silk shawls in a stunning shade of rose. She and her daughter have packed a generous bag of guavas from their orchard to offer to the monks.

Everything here moves at a slow and simple pace, like good meditation practice, fostering just slowing down and taking notice. Founded in the 8th century, Kurjey Lhakhang sits on the side of the mountain and at the mouth of the cave where Guru Rinpoche, its founder, reportedly sat in deep meditation just before he brought Buddhism to Bhutan. As the Crown Prince is due to arrive here tomorrow, having just been invested as Governor ("Ghotse Penlop") of Trongsa, feverish preparations are underway. Two elderly ladies are here, filling hundreds of brass lamps with yak butter and candlewicks to be lit in the monastery by the expected hundreds of devout pilgrims. Young monks are decorating a wood-framed entry gate erected for the occasion with brilliantly colored silken banners, and others are out in the sunshine polishing enormous brass and copper ceremonial vessels. We cross the courtyard lined with tall pine poles painted silver, flying the Bhutanese-style vertical white prayer flags indicative of mourning, marking the site of the cremation and burial of the Royal Grandmother here last year.

By nature, Leki smiles broadly at everyone she passes, although I think her smiles are self-conscious with us, as her teeth are stained red from betel nut. She puts her arm around my waist in a warm, sisterly way and guides me up the steep stairs toward the first chapel, built in the 8th century. Today is another brilliantly clear, blue-skied Himalayan morning, and flocks of crows swoop in and out from under the monastery's eaves. We remove our shoes at the door and are greeted by the caretaker monk. Leki offers him the large bag of guavas from her tree, in the traditional way of locals making offerings to their monasteries.

Inside the chapel, behind glass, is an eyrie at the mouth of the cave where Guru Rinpoche (Precious Master) meditated on his arrival here. We see the mouth of the ancient cave with a clear outline of a seated figure, reportedly burned into the grotto's entrance by the guru's devoted presence. In Bhutan, animistic legends and legendary signs abound from a mythical past that remains unrecorded with conventional historical accuracy. Every school child knows the stories about the heroes, demons, mythic monsters and deities, the stuff of their cultural education. Modern intellectual skepticism aside, there is something very powerful at this site of the origin of Buddhism in Bhutan. We are respectfully silent.

Next, we walk to the chapel next door, built in the 1800s. Re-moving shoes and hats, we enter the small, heavy, wood-framed doorway and emerge into a beautiful, open room. Behold, a delicious surprise! Several monks are "skating" around on the burnished pine planks, polishing the floor to a golden orange with fragrant acanthus juice, scooting around on foot cloths woven of yak hair, grinning as they glide. I love the impish, playful side of Buddhist monks and nuns throughout the Mahayana world. Renzin tells us that when he was a little boy visiting his uncle, a high lama in his own local monastery, they used to set all the little boys out on yak cloth cushions to play a sort of human skittles game on the floor, giving the boys freedom to play while they polished the floor with their skidding cushions at the same time.

The walls are covered with beautiful traditional murals painted in brilliant hand-ground pigments in the stylized Bhutanese fashion, often depicting cautionary or mythological tales. Most show the myriad forms of Buddha and the pantheon of Tantric deities, including carryovers from the Bon period of animistic worship here in this valley. The murals are painted on fine linen cloth and then applied to the walls so they can be taken down every few hundred years when a building needs refurbishing. What a contrast to our disposable culture. All the murals are protectively covered by large, light yellow, silk hangings with red and navy designs. The same pattern appears in many aspects of this culture. The skirts of festival dancers are made of layer upon layer of multi-hued silk scarves, draped from the waist and topped with scarves of the yellow pattern.

## A Totem Shattered

Following Leki's and Renzin's examples, moved by the atmosphere here in the monastery, instead of offering three bows, I do three full prostrations, stretching my body out completely on the polished floor, rising to face the gigantic gold statue of Guru Rinpoche with his attendants and consorts. Rising from the third prostration, I approach the altar where a monk is ready to bless us with saffron-scented sacred water, poured into the cupped palm to be tasted and then applied to the head, and in my case, to my stitched breasts. In so doing, I instinctively look down at the small, delicately carved, ivory Buddha pendant I wear on a chain around my neck, inherited from my mother. Shocked, I see the halo from which it hangs break into three pieces, which fall, saved from tumbling to the floor by the fanny pack I wear on the front of my waist.

I can't describe the complex reaction I feel, but the main feeling is horror. This small Buddha from my mother has come to mean so much to me. What does its shattering portend? I feel tears welling up. I'd been moving into faith and optimism, into a state of reverent transport. In this land of magical animistic beliefs, demons and miracles, I am increasingly aware that I'm here on a pilgrimage to find a spiritual support for the next six months of chemotherapy and radiation and to heal fully from this cancer. *What if my interpretation of the owl's penetrating gaze on the day of my diagnosis is not a harbinger of protective eyes overseeing my treatment, but instead an omen of my death from cancer? What if I have got it all wrong? What if in my optimism, I've imagined that those penetrating eyes represent all the loving and vigilant caretaking eyes of my radiologist, oncologist, surgeon and other doctors, and I'm dead wrong? I've got my totem all wrong!?*

Tears well up for the first time since my diagnosis a month ago. Leki turns to me and I show her my broken Buddha. "This was my mother's, maybe even my grandmother's. It means so much to me. Leki, I just discovered I have breast cancer. Is this an omen? I'm scared!"

Leki rocks back on her bare heels, then forward into me, then she laughs in a whisper, embraces me and says, "Don't worry, Harriet! We'll get Super Glue!" I'm incredulous! I'd expected something entirely different. Everyone here talks all the time about karma, bad fate, transmogrifications, signs and omens...and Leki cracks me up. Flushed with a marginally hysterical energy, I'm drying my tears. "Of course! Super Glue!"

We move into the courtyard, where the long white prayer flags of mourning are fluttering in the morning sun. Leki asks me about my cancer and I explain how two lumps were found, one in each breast, only four weeks ago. I have had surgery, and immediately on my return to the U.S., I am to begin chemotherapy.

"Then I'm taking you to the sacred spring. Right now. It is not too far to walk. There are so many stories from the time of Guru Rinpoche until now, of pilgrims coming from so far away to this spring, to drink and bathe in this holy healing water. It has stopped many cancers."

I tell her that both Phyllis and I have breast cancer. Together, our little procession climbs up the winding trail to the top, where we behold a man and his wife, no doubt here for the biggest festival of the year, the Jambay Lhakhang Festival, bathing under the pipe that carries the water up from the spring. Leki says, "They are typical of the many pilgrims who come here to recover from or protect themselves from disease. There are many stories of healing here." Phyllis and I take turns washing our hair, arms, and all that we can manage to wash while remaining decorous. We drink from the sweet, cooling spring and thus join the thousands of supplicants who have sought health here. We fill our water bottles and return back down the trail, where we say goodbye to Leki for now. We will visit Tamshing and Kunchosum Monasteries while she returns to her guesthouse to prepare lunch for us. Renzin assures me now will be a good opportunity for sitting meditation.

As we arrive at Tamshing Lhakhang, monks of all ages are in a flurry of preparations for tomorrow's arrival of the Crown Prince in honor of his investiture as the Ghotse Penlop, Governor of Trongsa, the position habitually occupied by a crown prince in preparation for his coronation as king. Two monks struggle on top of an elaborate frame constructed for the occasion, battling the afternoon winds of Bumthang Valley as they try to wrap the gate with ceremonial silk banners. Further down the road, pairs of young monks with iron rods are attempting to dig holes in the rocky soil to place poles for banners lining the entry to the monastery. At the door to the monastery's courtyard, two young adult monks are meticulously folding, braiding and thumbtacking three long interweaving banners—red, yellow and white—as adornments along the portal. Two others are hanging a drape over the archway. Once inside, we cross the courtyard, where other monks are preparing for winter, slicing a pumpkin in slivers for sun-drying on saffron-colored cloth on the grass. Across the courtyard is the entrance to the holy of holies.

I've inflated my travel meditation cushion, looking forward to this chance to meditate within a Bhutanese sanctuary. Like the monks skating in the temple, I carry along my own bit of sacred comedy, as my inflatable cushion is actually a brightly colored beach ball stuffed inside green fabric covering. I recall many merry moments, playing ball with young monks in Tibetan Szechuan, marking the fine line between the sublime and the ridiculous, the sacred and the playfully profane.

This temple was founded in 1501 by Pema Lingpa, Bhutan's most esteemed reincarnation of Guru Rinpoche, the lotus-born spiritual ancestor of Bhutanese Buddhism whose form we encountered earlier at Kurjey Gompa. Tamshing Lhakhang houses not only the oldest extant paintings in Bhutan, but also a remarkable twenty-five kilogram cape of chain mail said to have been handcrafted by Pema Lingpa. Legend has it that if a penitent dons this heavy metal cape and walks three times clockwise around the sanctuary, part of his or her sins will be wiped away. Inside, noisy preparations are underway for the Crown Prince's arrival. After circumnambulating the altar in the requisite clockwise fashion, I search for a relatively quiet corner to meditate. In the dark passageway behind the altar, I find Pema Lingpa's metal linked cape piled on a large flat stone. This will be my spot.

Settling cross-legged on my cushion, I prepare to meditate, but I still hear hammering, chattering and distracting merriment from the sanctuary. I realize that tucked into my fanny pack is my iPod, loaded with with a number of meditation tracks. Serendipity! Just before I left California, my friend Daishin, a psychoanalyst Zen monk and one of my Sangha mates, recorded himself and our Sangha chanting the *Enmei Jukku Kanzeon Gyo* or Prolonging Life Sutra for his wife, my dear friend Concetta, who underwent brain surgery the same week as my breast surgery. My Sangha sent me off with the recording, which I transferred to my iPod.

Losing myself in time and space, I have the privilege of sitting here for at least an hour in deep meditation, with soft eyes. I quietly chant the Kanzeon sutra with my Sangha. The droning chant is mesmerizing. I sit, following my breath and chanting in this musty, dark, ancient hallway redolent with stories of demons, magic and miracles, gazing at Pema Lingpa's chain mail cape, suspended between heaven and Earth in this high Himalayan country, the last autonomous Buddhist kingdom on Earth. I lose all sense of time. Finally, I feel someone gently squeezing my shoulder and look up to see Renzin telling me it is time to return to wakefulness. We must move on. I squint as we walk out into the bright sunlight, knowing that I have already found the calm and well being I came for.

But many treasures await in this land where Tertons, reincarnated sons of Guru Rinpoche, found many of the spiritual treasures he hid for the benefit of all beings. Approaching late afternoon, we wend our way back down the road to Leki's guesthouse for lunch and a tour of her weaving establishment.

### *The Sole Domain of Women*

Leki's home, like so many Bhutanese houses, clings to the side of a hill overlooking the Bumthang Valley. In steppes down the hill she grows vegetables for her family and the guesthouse table—chilis, onions, radishes, cabbages, broccoli rabe, and fresh guavas. Her guesthouse is finished in white plaster with traditional windows in Bhutanese style, with exquisitely carved and painted lintels and sills. Roof shingles are weighed down against the wind by large stones; the particularly Bhutanese surprise, suspended from the corner of the roof overlooking the valley, is a flying phallus, hung there to ward off mountain demons. In this land, ancient animistic Bon beliefs were carried forward and interwoven with the 6th-century teachings of Buddha, brought here 1,000 years later.

In Leki's studio, two young weavers from Assam in Eastern Bhutan are seated cross-legged on the floor, working with backstrap looms before them, shuttles and fingers flying deftly as they pull silver and gold threads to articulate a fine, intricate pattern in the silk-threaded warp and woof. Textiles are the summa qua non of

Buddhist art, the sole domain of women who have traditionally lived very restricted lives in this land of flying phalluses. Women weave their own *kiras*—three woven panels sewn together and wrapped over a blouse, toga style, pinned at the shoulder and belted by a contrasting handwoven sash. They also weave the ample, A-line, long-sleeved *ghos* worn by the men, which are lifted to knee length and belted to create a generous chest pocket for storage of anything from cash to cough drops. Women have this one vehicle to express their creative artistry.

Leki is one of a growing handful of entrepreneurial women we meet in Bhutan that includes our local travel agent, Sonam, who owns her own business in the newly privatized travel industry here. Another is Pema, a wild animal veterinarian whom I met on the plane, and who has studied in London with, of all people, Rosa Garriga, the orangutan vet Jim and I traveled with four years ago in Kalimantan, Borneo.

There are women in the royal pantheon as well. The late Royal Grandmother, a commoner discovered to be a reincarnated spiritual being, is worshiped as a goddess here, held in the same great esteem as many manifestations of Tara, the goddess of safe journeys to whom Tashi prayed in a less-than-successful entreaty in Tibetan Szechuan.

Bhutan's fourth king, King Jigme Singye Wangchuk, has married four gorgeous, highborn sisters who have borne him ten children. The third sister bore his first son, the Crown Prince Jigme Gesar Namgyal Wangchuck, whom we hope to meet tomorrow on his royal tour of his new domain. Although we hear of the domestic harmony of this unique royal arrangement, I learn that the king mainly lives alone in a log cabin in the royal woods where he can meditate daily in silence, and each of the queens has her own private palace compound. The psychoanalyst in me can only marvel at what stories I might hear, were I appointed the nonexistent role of Court Psychoanalyst to attend to the dreams of queens.

Leki invites us into the dining room, which also serves as a showroom for her textiles, and we are treated to a typical multi-course repast of Bhutanese red rice and beans, noodles, plates of freshly prepared vegetables, chicken, *amugatsi*, the ubiquitous Bhutanese hot chili and cheese side dish, and pancakes of locally grown buckwheat served with rich amber Bumthang honey, followed by fresh guavas for desert.

After lunch, a transformation occurs: we five pilgrims manifest ourselves as five American shoppers. Textiles are stroked, colors compared, prices queried, kiras modeled, shawls and scarves draped and financial transactions executed. We invent an instant banking system, as those cash-heavy among us trade with those who are cash-poor. Leki promises that before tomorrow's Jambah Lhakhang festival and the "secret fireside ecstatic monastic naked dancing" (Whoa, we can't miss that!), she will accompany me to her friend's stall in the main square, where the only Mastercard in the valley can be pressed into service.

## A String of Pearls

These are days of grace beyond all measure. They glide by like pearls on a necklace as we move through spectacular traditional Bhutanese dancing festivals in Prakhar and Chodar, hike through the Ura Valley, have lunch with a poor farm family before the altar in their modest farm house, practice daily yoga and sitting meditation, and receive blessings from lamas and the handsome young Crown Prince, who goes out of his way to welcome us to his country. To top it off, we traverse 12,000 foot passes through the jagged mountains that have kept this kingdom a hidden jewel, the last of the vanishing Buddhist kingdoms of the Himalaya, closed to the outside world until thirty years ago.

As our days turn into weeks and we move closer to the end of our journey, I feel more and more blessed, my heart and spirit stilled to a calm that feels deeper than I could have fathomed. I feel as ready as I can imagine being, to begin the infusions of toxins that will destroy any remaining cancer cells throughout my body.

## Coup de Grace

On our last day, back in Paro, we arise early for our final and most spectacular hike up the craggy mountain overlooking the Paro Valley, on whose rock face hangs the fabled Tiger's Nest Monastery. As this will be a three-hour hike, Aviva opts for a horse to carry her. The others and I choose to walk. Donning hiking boots and hiking poles, we set off in the cloudy dawn up a long switchback trail from the forest below. At Renzin's suggestion, I opt to hike ahead to a special outlook over the famous monastery for my last sitting meditation. For three solitary hours I climb, listening on my iPod to the sounds of Tibetan singing bowls and to a Dharma talk by Thich Nhat Hanh, taped at Plum Village Monastery. By the time I reach my destination, the morning fog has burned off the valley below and the sky is crystal clear. Tiger's Nest's golden roofs glitter in the sunlight.

Tiger's Nest, or Taktsang Monastery, is perched on a rocky ledge across a deep canyon from me, halfway down a sheer cliff with a drop of nearly 800 meters. More magic. To this day, Bhutanese believe that in the second half of the 8th century, Guru Padma Sambawa alighted here upon the back of a tigress and decided to build a monastery. On a rocky overlook, I settle in on my green cushion for an hour I'll never forget. I feel the sun on my shoulders, my cushion under me, the canyon quiet except for the call of ravens from time to time. The power of this place is phenomenal. I will surely call forth this experience whenever I feel the need as I go through treatment, or any of life's other challenges.

With Renzin's official government invi-tation in hand, we are given permission to climb across the last canyon, past another sacred spring where I refill my water bottle, and climb up into the monastery itself. Ten years ago, Tiger's Nest caught fire and burned. The reconstruction was only completed this year and the monastery re-opened in January; we are fortunate to be able to visit. Though many of its precious scrolls and paintings were destroyed, their art forms are widely taught here, and many artists and craftsmen have been enlisted to reproduce the most famous paintings and carvings. Tiger's Nest transcends the list of the many high points of this trip.

On the way down, reflecting on all the blessings I have received and the omen of the broken Buddha, I can't avoid wondering if I will be one of the 80% who will long survive this diagnosis, or whether it is my lot to be one of the 20% who will not. I screw up my courage to ask Renzin a question. "Renzin, the day I was diagnosed with breast cancer, a giant owl swooped down in front of our truck and alighted on a low branch not ten feet from the windshield, and just sat there, staring at me. What does such an omen mean here in Bhutan?"

Rinzin hesitates and his face clouds visibly. "Oh, dear. It is a very dark portent. We believe the owl brings very bad news." Immediately, I wish I had never asked. *Well, I'd better accept and embrace that other possibility, which, to tell the truth, I don't dread. Loving life and my loved ones, I definitely don't want to leave, and until my last breath I am sure I will always be wildly curious about what the next chapter on this planet holds, but one day it is time for each of us and we don't get to choose.*

I don't believe in heaven or hell, except the ones we create and discover here on Earth, but I do believe that at death, we are transformed into another aspect of the physical and spiritual universe, not as ourselves, bound to our egos, but like molecules of water in a piece of ice, melting and returning to the rivers, the clouds, the rain. I find myself somehow ready for whatever, and pledge to live each day to its absolute fullness, realizing that in this moment I have probably never felt more alive—except perhaps in those inestimable moments of childbirth. I am very grateful.

# CHAPTER 44
## RETURN AND RE-ENTRY: HAIRLESS IN LA LA LAND

I'M IN DOWNWARD-facing dog pose at my morning yoga class with Cat in Pacific Palisades. The early winter sun is streaming in the window. Cat opens our class with a poem by an eleven-year-old boy:

> Do the best that you can
> With what you have
> In the time that you have
> And the place where you are

I look forward between my hands to see little glimmers of light catching something falling. Oh, no! Today is day number eighteen since I started chemo, and what is glimmering like snowflakes are my silver hairs, drifting onto my yoga mat. There is something mesmerizing about this unlikely, sparkling snowfall. In an epiphanic moment, it occurs to me that I am about to witness an age regression. All the silver will fall first and I'll be back to pure brunette. After that, I'll manifest as a bald baby. This is not all bad. I smile, quite moved.

Next I do a headstand. When I am finished, I glance back at my yoga mat to discover a perfect crown of brown hair surrounding the spot where I stood on my head. That regression was fast! I feel my scalp. There's a bald spot on the crown of my head, surrounded by a Benedictine-like fringe. My Yogi Cat witnesses the circle of hair on my mat and nods knowingly. I feel like I'm in the seventh grade and just got my first period. *Do I want anyone to notice? Do I not want everyone to notice? I don't know!* After class, Cat says, "We've got to do some kind of ceremony with that hair." I entrust the thatch to her, knowing she will come up with something creative.

Things have been moving fast. My second chemo treatment will be this Friday. God, I hope it won't be like the first one, which I now describe.

### A Hellacious Re-Entry

After Phyllis and I said our farewells to our fellow Bhutan pilgrims and to Renzin and Tenzin, we began our twenty-something-hour return home via Bangkok. It was Tuesday, November 9. With the extra day gained crossing the International Dateline, I would arrive in time for the port to be placed in my chest and to meet with my oncologist to prepare for chemotherapy.

On the flight, however, I noticed a rash on both arms. What could it possibly be? As the hours passed, it looked familiarly like the dreaded poison oak to which I am highly susceptible. Oh, no. Where could I have possibly gotten it? In the woods, climbing up to Tiger's Leap Monastery? Maybe in the dormant season it looked like no-harm twigs. By the next afternoon arriving in Bangkok, I was very sick. Barely registered in our hotel, I rushed to vomit into the five-star sink. Phyllis was right there with me, holding my forehead. When I finished heaving, she put on her best Scottish brogue and said, "Well, me wee Scottish grandmother used to say at times like this: 'Better an empty hoose, than a baad tenant!'"

It was a hellacious re-entry. Buddhism teaches nonattachment and impermanence. I could have become very attached to the sublime bliss I felt meditating over Tiger's Nest, but I realized that the shitty side of life was also part of it all. I took it as a preview of what was to come.

Jim collected all of me at the airport: the grateful traveler, happy to have squeezed this Bhutanese pilgrimage into a three-week window between surgery and chemo; the sublimely inspired writer and dreamer; and the clammy, sick patient covered in rashes. We headed to the oncologist's office, where I learned that both Thursday's and Friday's procedures had been bumped from afternoon to morning.

I had to call all of my patients, who I'd been seeing since we ended our sabbatical, to regretfully cancel sessions and try to reschedule. I felt sad; I had carried my patients and supervisees and their concerns with me, and was looking forward to resuming my "normal" life with few disruptions. But reschedule, I did.

Early Thursday morning, I entered St. Johns Hospital for an echocardiogram, followed by a surgical procedure in which they placed a euphemistically named "passport" in my chest. This was a subcutaneous valve with tubes entering an artery near the heart. It would be the port of entry for a needle carrying the chemotherapy drip into my system; it was placed near the heart pump for rapid and effective distribution through the body.

By the afternoon, home from the hospital, I'd recovered enough from local anesthesia and the procedure to see a few rescheduled patients. That felt good, though the rash on my arms was starting to rage; blisters were forming. Did I brush with a poison oak bush? Or did the prostrations on the monastery floor put my forearms in contact with oils someone tracked in? However I got it, cooking it in that farewell hot stones bath surely set it up for its fullest potential.

### Of Red Bombs and 'Frigerators'

On Friday morning, daughter Ariel met Jim and me at Santa Monica Hospital for my first round of chemo. It was to be here because my oncologist's office was closed for the Veterans' Day holiday. Jim, who had seen me through all my visits with the surgeon, my surgeries and meetings with doctors, but who is faint of heart where needles are involved, planned to take the day off and leave me in Ariel's good hands. He kissed me goodbye and we were left waiting, to walk into unknown territory.

And wait we did. First, it turned out we were in the wrong waiting room. In the next waiting room, wondering who among those waiting were there for chemo, like me, I hoped not that young mother with the baby! Or that young man with the cane. I have been fortunate to receive amazing medical care at warp-speed efficiency, but that morning, I got a taste of clinic medicine. Finally the nurse came in, escorted me into the curtained-off cubicle that would be mine for the day, and strapped me into a large recliner.

No matter how ready I thought I was, my heart was *not* ready. My typically low 110 over 60 blood pressure rocketed off the charts. I was convinced the cuff and monitor were broken and asked the nurse to measure Ariel as she registered completely normal. It wasn't broken. Due to my recent lumpectomy, the nurse avoided using my arms and placed the cuff around my leg and tried again. 208 over 95. The procedure couldn't start until the patient calms down. I put on my iPod and began listening to the soothing sounds of Tibetan singing bowls, imagining myself overlooking Tiger's Nest. Within the hour, my pressure had dropped to 140 over 75 and the pharmacy had a green light to mix the two IV cocktails I was to receive—Cytosine and Adriamycin. We waited another hour. Finally, the nurse rolled in two IVs, the clear liquid Cytosine and the red liquid Adriamycin. In a thick Chinese accent punctuated by a very blunt style, she proffered several kitchen wisdom sayings that were bizarre and relatively indecipherable.

"You have to fill the 'frigerator a lot cause the bomb is coming. Maybe big fire. Maybe terrorist. Maybe big quake. Never know. Get that 'frigerator so full. Big trouble coming. I tell you. I tell you. Need full 'frigerator."

I looked wanly at Ariel, who was trying to maintain her most neutral, appreciative face. But I knew she was thinking, "What!?" Finally, Ariel translated, "I think she's saying you need to eat a lot because hard times are ahead." Oh. We're all trying our best.

I nodded at the Chinese nurse and we began. She inserted the needle through my skin into the port in my chest. The Adriamycin drip went slowly but steadily through the port and into my veins. *Dathump, dathump, dathump,* my overactive heart pumped the chemo through my body. The nurse watched me closely to make sure there was no adverse reaction. She titrated the drip to flow very slowly, just in case. Nothing untoward happened. She took off to tend to other patients. The red liquid looked like what we put in our hummingbird feeder, but I didn't think this was sugar water. At the same time, I didn't feel any more affected than the birds at feeding time. *Drip. Drip. Drip. Drip.* The drip continued.

The nurse returned and switched me over to the Cytosine. *Drip. Drip. Drip. Drip. Drip.* Ariel held my hand and we talked. I found myself telling her things that had been in my heart for a long time, but that I'd never told her. Fears and hopes and dreams and all manner of stories about my life came tumbling out. She was completely present, offering back an infusion of daughter energy, the sort of thing that truly heals. When the procedure was finally finished, we had been there for seven hours. Ariel had gone out to feed her parking meter many times. We had turned a deep corner of closeness, our roles were switched, and tables had turned from my caring for her to her caring for me. We were both grateful.

Before we went home, my daughter insisted she would teach me how to smoke marijuana: another major role change. We picked up some grass for medicinal use and stopped by a head shop for the apparatus. By the time we got back on the freeway in Friday evening rush hour traffic, I was sinking fast. I felt like the flu was coming on like a Mack truck. I felt clammy, achy and nauseous in increasing waves that built and ebbed and built and ebbed through the night, the next day and night, and all day Sunday. I could barely imagine looking at anything to put in my "frigerator" and it was difficult to sleep. The thought of the Monty Python and Buster Keaton comedies I'd stocked to watch turned my stomach. For three days, I hung onto the spars and tried not to be pitched off the roiling deck of the ship. Ariel taught me to use the water pipe with the marijuana and came and went with ginger and mint tea and sympathy. Jim held my hand and brought me cold compresses. I rolled and pitched. By Monday, I was better.

### Wigging Out

On Monday a couple of friends called and said, "So, what are you gonna do about a wig?" I hadn't even thought about that! I'd just come back from Bhutan, where I traveled amidst droves of beatific bald-headed monks. Why not just go bald? But I'd probably scare my patients. The same day, a fat envelope arrived from my friend Pam, the knitting queen who, after going on a llama pack trip with us in the Sierras, took our llamas' spun fibers and knitted me the most beautiful llama shawl. In this envelope was a jaunty, white knitted cap with a note about every stitch being taken with love. With Pam at the needle, I didn't think I'd need a wig.

But I got the name of a wig maker and decided to make an appointment. This wig maker said he hand-tied human hair into wigs, but it would take him five or six weeks to make a wig, as many of Hollywood's most famous heads were in line ahead of me. And it would be very pricy at $1500. I'd be halfway through chemo by then. My friend Jeanie told me to go to the store at UCLA Medical Plaza. When I called "Reflections" at UCLA, a very warm voice invited me to come right on over. "We have ready-mades in stock for around $100." That was more like it. I asked Jim, "How do you feel about an outing to the wig store?" After a weekend on the roiling seas of chemo, Jim was happy to hear me completing sentences, and he good-naturedly drove me there.

I'd never tried on a wig before, not even for Halloween. We started looking for wigs to approximate my own look. But I looked like Joan Collins in a fright wig. I looked at Jim pleadingly, "Hey—this isn't working. Let's color way outside the box. What's your fantasy? Redhead? Blonde bombshell? Who is she?"

Jim warmed up to the task and started collecting wigs from all around the room. We began to get the giggles. I went through more changes than the twenty-three manifestations of the Goddess Tara and more transmogrifications than Guru Rinpoche riding his tiger. We were laughing such great belly laughs that I forgot my chemo belly. Finally, utterly unable to choose, we settled on two wildly different looks. One was a retro, long, honey blond, the color and length of my hair in my twenties, but with a richness and volume I never had—why not indulge in a fantasy and turn back the clock to the swinging Sixties? We called her "Veronica," evoking that Forties bombshell of our childhood, Veronica Lake. The other, the "Silver Fox," was a short bobbed number in a foxy silver-gray I could only dream of becoming in another decade or two.

The total tab came to 15% of the human hair wig and these were washable with permanent styling. Too much fun! I asked Jim whom he'd like to ride home with, and without skipping a beat, he intoned, "Veronica." This became our gig through the chemo process. Jim could decide who he felt like taking out. The only problem with Veronica and the movies was that if I leaned back in the seat, then looked down at my lap, Veronica's long locks would get caught between my back and the chair and oops, off would slide the wig. So Veronica could only go dancing and on stand-up dates.

Well, not exactly dancing. Jim was celebrating phenomenal progress in the healing of his foot, but not dancing yet. He got off his crutches the same week we bought the wigs; his foot was healing much better and faster than his surgeon ever dreamed, and it looked like we might both be right as rain before a year was up.

### Dame Nausea Comes and Goes

Tuesday was a good day and I saw patients all day, from 9:00 until 6:00 p.m. I thought I was free and clear. Not so fast. Wednesday dawned with Dame Nausea at the helm, and she took command of my boat off and on for the next week. On day ten, Tuesday of Thanksgiving week, I finally sent her off to sea in a flimsy, sinkable leaf boat with clear instructions to drown before she reached Catalina and inflicted my nausea on any hapless souls there. She complied and I have been feeling fine ever since.

She left me free and clear to enjoy a wonderful Thanksgiving weekend with a family potluck dinner at Porto Marina, with much to celebrate. In late September after Jim's foot surgery, we had been relaxing at the family beach house in Santa Cruz and found a beautiful home for sale. We were ready to make a move so we'd hastily put Porto Marina Way on the trial market for three days. It generated a lot of interest but we learned of my cancer the same week, thank God, before any offers were formally written up, so we took her off the market. We have our beloved home in which to go through this process and to celebrate Thanksgiving.

## *Formative and Deformative Narratives*

After Thanksgiving, still feeling better, but quietly disquieted by the dissolution of my Buddha in the monastery and the dark Bhutanese version of owl omens, I called Madeleine, my shaman soul doctor who'd calmed me with both the Lakota and Greek Athena version of owls as a signal of wisdom. I told her that my mother's ivory Buddha pendant had fragmented just after I'd done three full body prostrations before the altar and was receiving the blessing of sacred saffron-scented water. I explained how unsettled I'd been. Madeleine paused just a beat, then said, "Whoa, Harriet. That is so portentous. The Lakota believe that at certain moments of great power, when you actually become what it is your totem represents, it will break into pieces. You don't need it anymore. You have become the spirit of the thing. In fact, it is nothing to be mourned. It calls for a celebration. It is even time to consider passing your mother's Buddha on to someone else on the path. This is wonderful."

As she spoke, a lightness came over me. Indeed, in that moment in the sanctuary, I had felt deeply embraced by the spirit of the Buddha. In fact, I felt I had found what I'd come for and took in the blessing in a very profound way. What an amazingly transformative power narrative has! Formative and deformative narrative scripts have been at the core of my psychoanalytic practice, writing and teaching. But I was surely about to get caught in a dark one myself. With a sigh, I accepted her offering of such a powerfully tectonic narrative shift.

I told Madeleine of my fear that maybe I had been wrong about the large owl that landed on a branch in front of our truck the day of my cancer diagnosis. The great bird's behavior was so unusual; in my whole life at Twin Brooks, I'd never seen one sit so close, and in daylight, too! I'd felt a surge of peace descend as if wrapped in a protective force of nature; later, I interpreted the owl's intense gaze as representing the watchful eyes of doctors who had taken steps to save my life, from finding the lump, to reading the mammograms and ultrasounds, to interpreting the biopsy. But in Bhutan, both Leki and our guide Renzin's faces had clouded over when I queried them about the meaning of owls to the Bhutanese. Back at home, when I pressed a Mexican friend about how Zapateca Indians interpret the owl, he had reluctantly replied, "When the owl lands on your roof, we believe it means someone in the house will die soon."

Nervously, I asked Madeleine again about what the Lakota Sioux believed. She reassured me, "True, some Indians believe the owl is the harbinger of ill tidings. But that is not our belief. To us, the owl is a powerful signal of enormous transformation about to take place. You are on the cusp of something tremendous. The owl symbolizes deep change and that can be very positive. And you are right, think of the ancient Greeks. Athena bore the owl as a symbol of great wisdom."

I felt a spine-tingling chill course down my back as I realized that this was exactly what cancer had already potentiated in me, from the morning after the diagnosis, sitting on my meditation cushion, when I felt that huge shift from panic and resistance to open acceptance, even welcoming cancer as an opportunity for very big practice.

"Madeleine, for the most part, my life has been almost as if I have lived in a ray of sunlight under a bell jar. As a woman, I have had so many rare opportunities, wonderful love and support, the finest education, professional fulfillment, athletic adventures and extraordinary cultural explorations. My life, by comparison to the lives of 98% of the downtrodden women I have met all over the world, has been charmed. Now I face a real test of my mettle. Education, love and success cannot inoculate me against cancer. I am ready. During the course of this, whichever way it takes me, I feel an opportunity for growth, depth and wisdom, maybe like I have never witnessed before. I think you are right about that owl. She came to me to signal deep transformation. Thank you.

"And," I continue, "maybe Renzin and my Zapateca friend's narrative versions of owl sightings also came to remind me to get serious. This is cancer. You could die. It has helped me to face that possibility, and has reminded me of my own earlier reflections on death and dying, expressed in the poem I wrote on retreat at Plum Village in France. 'Dear Cloud' once again takes on more intense personal meaning." I repeated some of the lines for her.

> Birth and rebirth, death and dying
> Endless circles, blissful sighing.

Every atom, every drop
Never truly starts, or stops.
So with the endless turning wheel,
Mindfulness shows us what is real.

The following morning, my lightness of heart continued. Several sessions with patients felt particularly connected and meaningful. In the last one before lunch, in which I served as a consultant to a respected analyst, I found myself uncharacteristically more revealing about the impact of my spiritual journey since my sabbatical, because I sensed her parallel quest in her own personal life and with her patients. It opened up a rich vein for us to explore, and a very moving session unfolded for both of us.

Right after our session, in the day's mail came an uncanny card from the edge, whose message and timing I couldn't believe. It was a letter addressed to me, in my own handwriting, dated exactly one year earlier. Puzzled, I slowly opened it to read:

My intention is to deepen my mindfulness practice with consciousness in daily living, mundane acts, random acts of kindness, deeper and more regular meditation practice and to practice tonglen—the active prayer for the cessation of pain and suffering in all sentient beings. I intend to let this permeate my very being, my body, my yoga practice, and my interaction with strangers, family, and friends. I also intend as appropriately as possible to communicate my intention to my patients, supervisees and colleagues. Finally, I plan to let my practice encompass travel, walking and meditation.

Namaste, Harriet

I was fully puzzled—did I write this? When? Then it came back to me. The year before, when Jim and I were guest lecturers at Rancho La Puerta, the retreat/spa in Tecate, Mexico where we have been going for years, I had taken Phyllis Pilgrim's meditation workshops. On the last day of the retreat, Phyllis had asked us to formulate our intentions for the coming year and to write a letter to ourselves indicating what we intended to do with our lives. She asked us to address an envelope to ourselves that she would mail the following fall. We could see whether we had been true to our intentions.

The letter expressed exactly what I had been trying to do over the past year. Another good chill coursed down my spine. What a relief not to encounter broken New Years' resolutions, but rather intentions that had guided me.

### Opening My Pores

Cancer has been opening my pores to much more than poison oak. Things I've heard before have taken on new meaning. I've connected with people I had lost track of, in ways we never connected before. Having trekked in the jungles of Borneo, Irian Jaya and the Amazon among Stone Age tribal people, Jim and I were burned out by the prospect of returning to our old life in Los Angeles, seeing only giant SUVs and Hummers in Pacific Palisades and feeling the compulsive pressure vibrating off too many people. By now, we were more than ready to sell the house and move to Santa Cruz. That dream has had to be deferred for now. But I have found new circles and new friends here, plus my soul doctor, my oncology team, my acupuncturist and Chinese herbologist. I feel stimulated by the presence of mind in all of these people. My sense of alienation is dissolving daily.

Today after yoga, when I give her that thatch of my fallen hair, Cat and I sit down to talk. Though I've been taking her yoga class for a few years, just now we discover an unexpected six degrees of separation. I taught Honors/AP English at Beverly Hills High School when she was a gifted but floundering student. She tells me how her friends urged her to try to get into my English classes, sensing we would connect. Instead she dropped out, struggled with her family's craziness, before finally finding a pathway to wisdom and the capacity to inspire as a yoga teacher. We have been given a second chance and we both vow to seize it.

This is simply one of the ways chemo has opened my pores and led me to connect with someone on a deeper level than we had before. I ask Cat to recite again the poem she quoted in class, by the eleven-year-old boy, and ask how she came to learn it. After reciting it again, and letting its simple yet profound wisdom wash over us, she says, "That wise young boy is dying of AIDS. That's how I met him."

### Chemo II

With blessings washing over and upon me, I go for my second chemo on Friday. This time, free of poison oak, I sit in my oncologist's office instead of the hospital. My friend Judy, having heard of the very difficult time I went through the first time, accompanies me this time in my doctor's own office and marvels. The staff is inviting and the setting restful. My oncologist sits down with me to ask how I've been and to answer any questions I might have. We are led into the chemo room, which we have completely to ourselves. I settle into a commodious version of a Barcalounger and after we chat merrily for a while, I nearly fall asleep.

In no time, the nurse says, "Okay, you can go now."

Judy looks as startled as me. I blurt out, "But have you started?"

The nurse hastens to assure me, "Yes, and it's all over."

Other than an intense "retch" on Saturday that prompts Jim to drive me to my acupuncturist's house for emergency anti-nausea treatment, and to the Chinese herb store for a collection of twigs and pods for a concoction, I emerge much more quickly from the nausea. Day by day I feel more myself. I surmise that the first course hit me so hard because of the poison oak.

### My Giggle Therapist

Jim and I decide that one of the best medicines—right up there with love, pilgrimages, transformational narratives, bosom buddies, and great care—is laughter. What is the surest way to laughter? We agree unanimously that it's time for a puppy. Jullay is nine years old; a young companion could be great for her. Like a teenager who's been grounded, I am uncharacteristically stuck at home anyway, so it would be a perfect time to housebreak a puppy.

After a careful search we locate a promising litter and a beautiful black miniature poodle puppy and name him Tashi Delek, which, of course, means "Shalom!" or "Aloha!" in Tibetan. It reminds us of our wonderful guide, Tashi, from Tibetan Sezchuan. Since Jullay was the littlest of her litter of Standard Poodles, we choose the Miniature Poodle puppy with the hugest paws and hope he rises to his small stature. Already, Tashi's name has morphed from Tashi Dalek to Tashi Da Lick, since he is one big irrepressible kisser. He's also already earned his second name, The Giggle Therapist, and proven himself to be exceptionally good, curly, black, wiggly medicine.

There's other fun to be had as well, such as yesterday, when I was out doing errands wearing "The Silver Fox." Waiting for a light to change in the crosswalk on Olympic Boulevard, I saw a sassy young black woman pull up to the intersection in a sports car. She began honking and waving. I swiveled around to see whom she was waving at. There was no one on the curb but me. I looked at her and she shouted, "Hey, your hair is really foxy!" As the light changed, she sped off, leaving me to laugh incredulously. No one's *ever* said that to me before! *And the times, they are a-changing...*

Still chuckling about that curbside honk, I am also smiling broadly because tomorrow, I will toss off my wig, put on my brown temple robes and drive to Escondido, bald as a billiard ball, for a retreat at Deer Park Monastery with Ariel. I laugh to myself at the pun as I imagine joyfully blending in as a reNUNciate with the bald nuns and monks of the Plum Village West Sangha.

# CHAPTER 45

## RADIATION TO RADIANCE

Suffering—whether physical, emotional, spiritual,
or as is often the case, all three—can be a doorway
to transformation. Telling stories can be healing. We
all have within us access to a greater wisdom and we
may not even know that until we speak out loud.
                    —Rachel Naomi Remen, M.D[22].

### *The Setup*

I'M ON MY back on a cold metal table, trying to decide whether to make eye contact with the man who is leaning over me, scrutinizing my bare breasts as if gold might be hidden there. Don't we both wish! He's probably scrutinizing my five surgical scars to see where the cancer was, so he can decide where to aim the radiation beam. The physical proximity is too close for comfort between strangers. I want to create psychological distance between us, and it is tempting to fall back on old tropes like "inscrutable Oriental," as the man is Asian. But that would be defensive and culturally indefensible, especially for a world-traveling feminist mindfulness practitioner.

Suddenly I recognize the dilemma that will trouble me for some time. Is this the time to deploy my psychological defenses, to distance myself, to be "not here" mentally? Should I remove my gaze and my consciousness from this room? Or is this an opportunity to practice mindful presence, to "be here now" fully in this moment? I face forms of this dilemma repeatedly during fourteen weeks of my five-times-a-week radiation treatment for bilateral breast cancer.

22  Remen, Rachel Naomi, *Kitchen Table Wisdom: Stories that Heal.* New York: Riverhead Books, 1997.

Once I calm myself and gain perspective, I acknowledge that it's not the cold or this stranger that frightens me; it is the radiation. Haven't we all been warned about too much sun exposure? Don't those of us born before World War II remember the horror of pictures of radiated victims in Nagasaki and Hiroshima?

I soon realize that this radiation technician, who is "setting me up" today, is probably struggling with his own dilemmas. He may be asking himself: "How do I, a young man, carry out my job, which requires me to ask a woman I do not know, perhaps old enough to be my mother, to bare her breast and lie still while I peer all over her, my nose not three inches from her nipple? How do I carry out a job in which I must tattoo this woman so that for fourteen weeks, my radiation team will know exactly where to point the equipment to accurately deliver the right dose of radiation to kill errant cancer cells that might have survived her surgery and chemotherapy?"

Realizing that we are together in a rather ticklish—no, awkward—situation helps me gather my cool. Speaking of cool, this room is freezing. The man is dressed warmly, but I'm bare-breasted. I ask him if there is some reason the room is so cold. He replies matter-of-factly, "Because the machines like it that way." Now that I understand the machine's comfort trumps mine, I can try to begin to settle in to this situation. But it appears he and the cancer have the upper hand.

Henry, as he tells me he is called, explains that he is sorry for my discomfort. In so doing, he makes contact as a human being with a name and a feeling of concern. This surreal situation takes a step toward something more tolerable. Henry explains that he will draw diagrams all over my left breast with a black magic marker. Then he and Dr. Lisa, my radiologist, will confer on the strategy for improving the odds that I will recover and resume my normal life—a life that stopped in its tracks last September, when I got the call that my tumor was malignant and the harbinger owl stared in my windshield. With my doctor's approval, Henry will tattoo certain points on the pattern as markers. He will use a gun to create the tattoo. "It will make a sound like a staple gun. Is that okay?" He asks.

Just last week I had my fifth surgery, to remove the subcutaneous "passport" from my chest, where the chemo had been administered. While I love my real passport with its stamps from countries all over the globe, this one was hard to take. I tried welcoming that alien appliance, but last week's removal surgery was a celebration, as I am greatly relieved to have it out of my chest. I can handle this minor discomfort; by now, I've surrendered to everything. I meekly nod, "Okay. Yes."

Ever professional, Henry tells me, "Good. After we've got you tattooed, I'll paste small metal markers on your tattoos, then we will go downstairs together to the imaging center where I'll put you on another table for a CAT scan to make sure the marks are precisely where they should be in relation to your tumor sites."

Fortunately I don't get claustrophobic, so I make it through the CAT scan easily. Satisfied, Henry tells me I can go upstairs and get dressed; we're finished. I'm formally "set up" on the left side. "We" will do the right side in several weeks' time, as it has been shown that radiating both breasts simultaneously delivers too much radiation to the body. "This afternoon, we'll put all the data into the computer so the machines will be programmed with precision. No chance of radiation error. You need to come back tomorrow morning at 5:00 a.m. for a run-through to test everything out, okay?"

After years of freedom and autonomy, I have to accept the extent to which my life and schedule are no longer my own. Next week, radiation will begin every weekday at noon, and it will happen five times a week for fourteen weeks, with one week out so I can go to New York to give a psychoanalytic paper and receive an award.

### Experiencing Radiation

Monday rolls around and I go in for my treatment. I've been worried about noon appointments, wondering if there'll be a backlog from the morning, and whether I'll have to wait my turn in a waiting room full of cancer patients, and whether I'll make it back to my office in time for my afternoon patients. But the office runs like clockwork. I go right in, change into a pink demi-gown and ask, "Can I listen to my iPod?" The three male techs all nod.

Relieved, I'm up on the table listening to the sounds that calm me more than anything I know, Tibetan singing bowls and chanting.

The table is moved up and down, left and right by electronic sensors responding to commands on a handheld programming device. Each of the three radiation machines moves in on an orchestrated computer-run cue, red laser lights finding the marks on my breast. Images of meat packing plants and assembly lines come to mind. I feel like chicken breasts being processed and packaged by a team of white-coated workers.

Days and weeks roll by inexorably. I stretch out daily on the slab-like table in the freezing cold room, my breast bared to huge, silent, white, slow-moving machines, their red lasers finding and marking my tattoos. The techs leave me alone behind the lead-shielded wall while radiation pulses into my breast. On the first day of treatment, I feel stressed by the unlikely intimacy with strangers and awkward in the presence of three young male techs peering over my poor boobie. But over time, I slowly find myself relaxing my resistance.

The young men are all foreigners. As the days turn into weeks, I learn more about each one and they learn more of me. Jason is Cambodian. He's thirty-something, very handsome and friendly. Earle, the senior member of the team, is Chinese and reveals a courtly manner as he extends his hand elegantly to me each time I ascend and descend the table. As the machines slide into place and the red laser lights find their marks, he always utters reassuringly, "Good, good, good." Alexi, a Ukrainian bear of a man with a sardonic sense of humor and short, cropped, graying hair, is gruff and direct. He wants me to bring souvenirs from New York.

They all seem to get a rise out of my varying noontime garb, guessing where I've been or where I'm going. As I do most consultations by telephone, except on days when I see my patients in person and don professional garb, I may show up in jeans, yoga duds, horseback riding tights and boots, or bike tights and bike shoes.

They make it clear to me that I mustn't be late, as I am the last female patient of the day. Right after me, they switch the machines for men getting radiation treatment for prostate cancer. The male patients arrive with full bladders and they get cranky if there's any untoward delay. Fair enough. I will make sure not to keep them waiting. I learn that some patients have a three- to four-hour daily round trip for ten to fifteen minutes of radiation. Others live so far away, they have to pack up their lives and take up residence in a nearby motel for the duration of treatment. I have no reason to be late or to complain about my fifteen-minute drive.

## *Radiating through My Mind*

I reflect on my anxious resistance and alienation from this process, my defensive desire to make Henry an "inscrutable Oriental." As we see each other day in and day out, week in and week out, I learn his story. He is Vietnamese, the youngest son of a family of refugee boat people. He cannot understand why Americans complain so much about insignificant things. People come in complaining about the lines at Starbucks, or "because they got nonfat instead of low-fat in their cappuccinos. People here don't keep their clothes until they're worn out. They just go buy new clothes every year whether they need them or not. They have no idea. When I was a little boy in Vietnam we had nothing. I had old flip-flops, one shirt and one pair of pants. I walked to school almost two hours and home for two hours. I wouldn't have missed school for anything! I can't get over how people take so much for granted here!"

I am very moved as I come to know Henry and the other three men, discovering their deep humanity and the hardships they have struggled through to get here. They value the opportunity to save lives while they earn good wages in a high-tech field. As my treatment unfolds, I am increasingly grateful for their kindness, warmth and care. They are generous with their healing energy. From them, and from my weekly consultations with two wonderful radiologists who are responsible for my state-of-the-art treatment, I understand that I am truly lucky to have all this available to me. As the weeks go by, instead of anxiety and alienation, I feel connection and appreciation.

## *New York Perspectives*

My trip to New York is an exhilarating and welcome weeklong reprieve. It's a relief to give my French-fried breasts time to recuperate.

I forget to bring my Silver Fox wig, and almost wig out until the baggage guy sees my now very, very short hair, grins, and tells me not to worry: "Hey, you look real Euro!" Jim and Ariel attend the conference on "Women's Fear of Success: Psychoanalytic Explorations of the Unconscious Saboteur." The paper I've been struggling to pull together goes very well; Ariel blurts out afterward, as if totally surprised, "Mom, you're so smart!" It's wonderful to feel wrapped up in their loving support and to realize how much it has meant along the pathway of my own professional ambition.

Ariel does a quick New York turnaround, returning to her bilingual second grade class in Echo Park on Monday. Jim and I stay on to enjoy the wonderful hospitality of my colleagues in Greenwich Village. We take the subway all over the city and walk miles in glorious spring sunshine every day. The city still has a spruced-up look from the makeover it enjoyed for last summer's presidential nominating convention. Daffodils, tulips and flowering fruit trees are buoying everyone's mood. Dogs are sniffing and tailwagging, and people are smiling and helpful to *auslanders*. We have lunches and dinners with friends and colleagues, pig out on great theater and appreciatively prowl the new MOMA (Museum of Modern Art) and the disposable Nomad Museum on the banks of the Hudson River.

Jim leaves Thursday, and I move uptown to the Waldorf Astoria. I feel warmly feted by my colleagues at a reception where I'm given an award for contributions to the field. Meetings are stimulating and the aura is pure New York Intense. I'm beginning to miss my team in Santa Monica—my shaman, Dr. Madeleine, my radiologists Dr. Lisa and Dr. Michael, my oncologist Dr. Carole, and my surgeon Dr. Nora. I really miss the guys at the radiation center, and I've picked out a gift for each one. Following Alexi's request, I prowl the streets for interesting NYC refrigerator magnets, and come up with a New York taxi, a Broadway ticket, a big apple, and a NY Fire Department badge. I also miss riding Cheyenne and Spirit, playing with Tashi and Jullay, my early morning meditation beach walks, my organic healthy diet, restorative acupuncture with Clinton realigning my qi, and yin yoga with Cat.

*Radiance: A Life Lesson*

On Sunday, as I am Jetting Blue back to the small, user-friendly, 1940s Long Beach Airport, I lean back in my seat and an inspiration comes to me. *Let's plan a Radiance Party!* We'll host it on the deck at Porto Marina at the end of May, after my treatment ends and before we go to Twin Brooks for the summer. There is so much to celebrate. Jim easily walked miles along the Hudson River on that screwed foot, not even looking back over his shoulder at memories from two years ago, when he was the one undergoing cancer treatment. Ariel and her partner are choosing rings and talking about wedding plans for next year. Brooke's pregnancy is going beautifully, and guess what… it's a girl! I will soon enough have hair enough, and radiation will give way to radiance.

Monday morning, I am back on the table. Henry, Jacob, Earle and Alexi are there to greet me. I pass out the magnets. The table moves into position and we're back in the groove. With only two weeks of radiation left, I acknowledge that it has been a rather amazing psychological journey. The clear, hands-down choice is to be fully present in this radiant moment. I celebrate this new life lesson, reflected in a quote by Shizen Young: "The amount of suffering we experience is in direct proportion to our resistance to pain."

# CHAPTER 46

## DAMNATION AND FAUST,
## OR HOW I LEARNED ABOUT AFGO

WE CELEBRATE the end of May with a Radiance Party on a sunny Sunday afternoon on our deck in Pacific Palisades, joyfully marking the completion of my radiation treatments, daughter Ariel and her partner Sarah's betrothal, Brooke and Philip's pregnancy with our first grandchild and Jim's first successful eight-mile hike on his "screwed foot." It is a gorgeous spring afternoon with the sun shining on the azure sea, making it a great and convivial gathering.

A week later, continuing the celebration and return to health, Ariel, Jim and I take off for the Big Sur coast for a weeklong yoga retreat at Esalen. It is beautiful. Five hours of yoga each day, scrumptious organic meals from Esalen's vegetable gardens, and soaks in natural hot springs open every pore to the universe. I am feeling myself again: light, strong, frisky and full of beans. The winter of our discontent is fading mercifully into the sunset, leaving me with a profoundly deepened sense of connection to each moment and each loving relationship in my life.

Thursday evening, June 10, Jim and I arrive at Twin Brooks, hauling the horse trailer with Spirit and Cheyenne. Everything in the Sierras is lush after the second heaviest winter on record. The mountains are heavenly with wildflowers and brimming streams, the water in the swimming pool is spilling over its dam like an infinity pool, shades of green are everywhere. Joyful anticipation abounds for a wonderful post-cancer summer of horses, llama packing, and a yoga/meditation retreat.

Ariel and Sarah are standing at the front gate under the Twin Brooks sign with big smiles, waving to greet us. "Hey, dinner's ready! We'll help you unload your stuff. Great to see you!" We unload the horses. They show their happiness by whinnying and kicking up their heels, visiting every nook, cranny and apple tree of their seven-acre pasture. Dinner is another delicious celebration. The next morning the horses are eager to hit the trail. Over the weekend we take two celebration rides. One day, I ride Spirit and Sarah rides Cheyenne; the next, Ariel rides Spirit and I ride Cheyenne.

We all hike up Echo Rock and around a soul-replenishing loop, following the creek trail back down to the house. On Saturday we drive to Huntington Lake for a bluegrass dinner concert with a fine banjo, mandolin, fiddle and bass group called Lost Highways. Jim and I dance the night away on his well-healed foot while Sarah and Ariel, scoping out potential rednecks in the mountain crowd, unfortunately have to decide it prudent not to publicly dance together. After brunch on Sunday, we wave goodbye to Ariel and Sarah as they head back to Los Angeles for teaching and summer school, and we begin settling in for the summer.

### Thwack

On Monday, a gorgeous morning just four blessed weeks past radiation, Jim and I set out together on a mountain bike ride. Our biking routes are in bad shape from winter's torrential rains. About five miles out, happily whistling along, I round a bend and plough into a wicked car-tire-sized pothole hidden in the shade. *What's happening? Can I stay upright?* In split seconds, as these thoughts race through my brain, my front tire hits the far side of the hole as my back tire drops deep into it. Bike and all, I take a slow, nasty, sideways-skidding dive landing, with a dull, bone-crunching whomp on my hip.

Jim often goes on ahead to complete a longer loop, but fortunately, this time he is behind me. As he rounds the bend and sees me crumpled in the road, I hear him let out an agonized, "Oh, Harriet, no!" He slides to a stop and runs over. In shock, I'm still thinking, *This will all pass and in a minute I'll pop up and climb up on my bike.* But after trying unsuccessfully to get me out of the road and off to the shoulder, we both know it's bad. He quickly ascertains that I may have broken my hip, as I can't be moved without mega-bone-shattering pain. Jim has no choice but to leave me and my bike, lying where I fell in the middle of the road, while he rides home for help.

With my bike semi-blocking me in the middle of the road, I lie there for a long hour under the watchful and comforting eyes of Tashi and Jullay, waiting for dear Jim to come back for me with the car. I am awed by animal wisdom. Tashi, a puppy who loves nothing better than to jump all over me and lick my face, knows I'm badly hurt and lies stock-still next to Jullay. Their four brown poodle eyes watch over me like sentinels.

As the minutes crawl by, sliding in and out of pain, I am flooded by images of past accidents. I remember the stricken look on Gabriel's face as his knee ripped in a family game of Capture the Flag on Fourth of July ten years ago. I remember my mother, lying broken on the Meadow Trail beside her horse, Stormy, her shoulder fractured from a freak fall in 1947. I don't remember how I, her seven-year-old daughter, got help, but I do remember the plaster upper body cast she wore for a couple of months, her arm braced up by a plastered stanchion. I remember the agonizing months of exercises after the cast came off, as she stood in the doorway of their tiny rented bedroom in Altadena, inching her arm up the doorframe. Another Twin Brooks accident drifts into my mind. Since the early days, we've heard the apocryphal story of my mother's childhood friend, Lois Allen, who was thrown by her horse onto her head, landing on an iron nail on the bridge, which has ever since been called the Lois Allen Bridge.

And then I shiver, remembering the call five years earlier when Ariel was in a car crash on the way up to Twin Brooks. I still feel the anguished groan that swelled up from the depths of my belly when I heard how the SUV rolled and she was catapulted feet first through the passenger window and across two highway lanes, and laid down gently, as if by guardian angels, on the grassy shoulder by the oleander hedges of Highway 99.

Despite these horror stories, there are the facts: Lois Allen didn't die, Mother's shoulder recovered completely, and after extensive knee surgery, Gabriel has run more than one marathon, and running is his exercise of choice. And here is Ariel, vibrant and passionate about her life, her partner, her teaching, convinced she was spared to live a life of conscious purpose.

Still wearing the bicycle helmet I heard bounce protectively a couple of times as I hit the pavement, and with a mosquito net still tied on to keep from inhaling clouds of gnats, I slowly examine myself for wounds. I have a road-rashed bloody forearm dotted with gravel and scratches on my leg, but the main injury is invisible and internal. I listen apprehensively for the sound or road tremor of a vehicle. I teeter between hope that it will be my own personal chariot and terror that the rumble will be a redneck screaming around the back roads in his pickup, about to squash me like a bug.

I hear sounds before I felt the deep reverberations of a vehicle coming, and sigh in relief as I realize it is Jim, back with the Subaru and Edgar, our Filipino house helper. Edgar is strong and good-natured. Together, they carefully lift me into the car and we set off back down the painfully bumpy road to offload Edgar, the dogs, and my bike, and to pick up my wallet and Blue Cross card. I curse audibly, realizing I'm still only two and a half weeks shy of Medicare!

Jim carefully chauffeurs me the hour and a half drive to the ER in Fresno. After a few hours of waiting on a gurney with no painkillers, X-rays confirm I have broken my hip. It's not just a neat fracture but "the worst kind in the worst place." The good fortune is that during my sabbatical, when we were living up here on the ranch, we found a fine local internist. Dr. Julie is one of our llama hiking buddies. I reach her on my cell phone en route to the hospital, and she arranges everything including Dr. Steve, the orthopedist who shakes his head in wonder that he is about to operate on a sixty-five-year old woman who flew off her mountain bike. "This will be a new one," he quips.

He can't get operating room space for that night, so schedules surgery for the next morning and finally, thankfully, shoots my hip full of morphine. The X-rays reveal that the bone was too badly shattered to pin back together. The fracture runs vertically from the ball through the neck of the femur attached to the ball and they are in lots of pieces. Dr. Steve will do a partial hip replacement, as the socket and pelvis are still good.

A very exhausted Jim bids me adieu and heads back up the mountain for the night while I am wheeled into my room on the orthopedic floor and hooked up to an exquisite on-demand morphine drip. Next morning, Jim is back to accompany me as far as he is allowed toward the OR, where I wake up in recovery several hours and a new hip later.

Dr. Steve comes in post-op to report that everything went well, but he can't believe how flexible my hips are. This worries him a bit; he's concerned that I might dislocate the new joint. I am both proud and chagrined. My hard-won flexibility comes from over thirty years of yoga practice and the recent week of intensive Esalen yoga. My next thought is, "What if I can't go back to my beloved yoga practice?" Dr. Steve is not sure. However, he delivers the excellent news that the bone fragments showed no sign of osteoporosis or damage from chemo and radiation or metastatic bone disease. It's just good, healthy, smashed bone.

Dr. Steve tells me, "I'd estimate your short term recovery to take six to twelve weeks. During that time you will have to be very careful." *Read:* I won't be able to do most of the physical activities I was looking forward to to celebrate my "radiance" and return to post-cancer health—no horseback riding, no yoga, no hiking, no llama pack trip. The orthopedist says it may take a full year for complete recovery, but the prospects are very good given my physical condition and the indomitable Wrye/Wheeler survival tactics. He is cautionary, however, about my yoga; my hips are as open as any he's worked on, and he's afraid of the new ball popping out of the socket. That would be excruciating and require surgery to return it into place, so we *don't* want that!

I have absolutely no excuses not to get back to this manuscript. No excuses whatsoever. Over a year ago, I finished a first draft of *Pulling Up Stakes* and sent it to my editor, who underwent several major life transitions and a serious illness and couldn't read it for a long time. But she did get to it last summer, and sent me suggestions for tightening and focusing. My book and her editorial suggestions have been resting quietly on the back burner over the past year of cancer treatments. Since I "finished" it, of course, everything has changed again. My original ending, right after Plum Village, has to yield and all my new growth experiences must be woven in. The past year has provided a huge opportunity to practice everything my sabbatical has taught me, letting go on an even deeper level. However, I feel stupid to have hit that pothole. Clinging to a happy ending is yet another attachment to let go of. Besides, one of my patients who is a much-published writer tells me that happy endings are boring. "What you want is the real stuff."

### A Definite AFGO

It's hard to believe what can occur in a hospital in the name of caregiving. As I lay in agony on a gurney in the emergency room, the young ER doc greeted me with, "So, what about your medical history?" I told him about my five cancer surgeries this past winter, twelve weeks of Cytoxin and Adriamycine, followed by fourteen weeks of bilateral breast radiation. Then I proudly told him my oncologist and radiologist's wonderful parting words: "You're cured!" He snorted contemptuously, "No way. You're not cured! No one can say that for five years!"

That formerly attractive ER doc instantly became my psychological nemesis. Any day under the rainbow I'll take a doc who understands the healing power of affirmative narratives! Who did he think he was, an ER doc with no knowledge of my cancer, my treatments or anything specific, and no reason to attack my highly qualified oncologist and radiologist's diagnosis? Not good medical practice, and a definite downer.

To frost the cake, the day after surgery, a volunteer chaplain comes in to visit. I had indicated "Buddhist" on my intake preference, also writing that I did not wish religious counseling. This chaplain is a zealot who asks pointed questions about my beliefs, including, "Do you believe in heaven and hell?"

Lying weakly under the covers, I gather myself the best I can and say, "Well, not exactly. No, I don't believe in some geographical place of hell fire and damnation, or a realm with angels, halos and wings in the sky somewhere, but I do believe there are heavens and hells here on Earth, many of which are man-made, and I believe there is sacred spirit in all of us and in all things."

He harumphs and snorts, "Well, I can see that you don't believe in the literal words of the Good Book. You are a pagan!"

Stunned by this assault, my left hip quivers in pain and I ask him, "Sir, did you read in my chart that I have not requested spiritual counseling while in the hospital? Did you read my religious preference as Buddhist?"

"Yes," he snaps, "but I just had to hear for myself what them Asian pagans that don't even believe in God over there think."

I compose myself and say firmly, "I think it best to leave it here, sir."

He does me the favor of semi-slithering, semi-slinking from my room.

Next, my blue-haired roommate offers me, free of charge, a big life lesson in how *not* to handle adversity. Following knee replacement surgery the same day I got my hip, Budge salivates at the chance to repose in a convalescent home, as she had set her heart on a course of doing "absolutely nothing for a month." When her doctor tells her that in order to regain the use of the knee, she needs to walk daily and take on activities, Budge harangues him. "You young things think you know everything. My neighbor has a friend in Texas who has a cousin in Oklahoma who had this done and he took to some gardening and he swears he'll never walk again. No, thank you, doctor. I'm not moving!" I see him standing at the foot of her bed rolling his eyes at me. Budge (as in "I'm not budging") is a textbook case in milking secondary gain from an injury by projecting her negative feelings about pain, suffering, and aging into the doctor, the nurses, the food, the treatment plan and the way the pillows are arranged. They are all worthy of her contempt.

Jim brings my laptop so I can email my bosom buddies about the hospital experience. One good-humored and enlightened friend quips reassuringly: "But pagans are wonderful!" An irrepressible biking buddy replies that her Texan sister would say this whole debacle deserves a genuine "Golly damn holy shitfire!! (Yes. They really do say those things in Texas!)". A yoga buddy labels this as a definite AFGO (Another Fucking Growth Opportunity)—a crackup, and an excellent Zen koan. With that, plus a lot of humility, I've begun practicing with my new walker, crutches, and long-handled tongs for reaching to the ground. I know this must be another opportunity to integrate my huge life lessons: *I'm not in control. I won't get attached to outcomes. I'll celebrate each precious breath and moment of the life I have as I live it, the good, bad and the ugly.*

With the help of physical therapy staff, I am up and about with my new accoutrements: walkers, crutches, wheelchairs, and even a commode on wheels, for which another friend has promised to send me a horn. An occupational therapist offers me the choice between a convalescent home and release. Figuring a convalescent home full of the likes of Budge would do me more harm than the ER doc and the chaplain put together, I opt for direct exit home to the ranch.

It is heaven to be back at Twin Brooks. Edgar and Jim carry me in my wheelchair up the steps and I wheel myself into our bedroom. Jim doesn't send me roses, but he's another kind of amazing lover. Over life's long and yet short intervals, our intimacy shifts gears each time we go through one of these life-threatening episodes. Formerly driven solely by pheromones, hormones and young and passionate bodies, our love shifted to the heart and finally settles somewhere deep in the soul. He empties my commode each morning without a single comment or complaint. In my book that's at least a dozen red roses. It makes me weep.

I am also fortunate because my dear friend Mary materializes at Twin Brooks to look after me during my first weekend home. Mary has had double hip replacements, and in the process became the director of Operation Walk, a traveling medical ship whose orthopedic surgeons operate on Third World people who can't walk. What a perfect angel she is! Mary inspires me by doing deep knee bends and high kicks to assure me that this, too, shall pass.

I quickly settle into a new form of mindfulness meditation. Every basic move is slow, thoughtful and conscious. I must do walking meditation with "peace as every step." My morning ritual unfolds at a relative snail's pace, but it feels amazing to notice an increment in healing every day. I downgrade from morphine to codeine to extra-strength Tylenol, and then to long gaps without pain medication.

I only miss one and a half days' telephone sessions with my patients and supervisees. Meeting with them in our regular time slots gives me back a sense of normalcy, so I can feel like the doctor rather than the patient and broaden my horizons beyond my hip. I find myself "shooting from the hip" much more freely in sessions; I feel I must give an account to each one of what has happened, as it affects them too. I feel freer to speak my mind about the insights I have been assimilating, and am amazed to experience how meaningful it can be to practice a more relational form of psychoanalytic work, in which there is space to weave together their experience and my own, offering food from my journey for their thought.

What is it I feel freer to say? Dependant upon the issues of the person with whom I am speaking, it goes something like this:

*Suffering laces its way into every life, no matter what. This is what Freud called 'ordinary unhappiness.' It's not the neurotic, self-indulgent misery we work to relinquish, but existential angst. It's death, vulnerability, cancer, divorce, broken bones, West Nile virus, the devastation of war, poverty, crime and the effects of pollution.*

*It touches us all: rich, poor, franchised, privileged, outcast alike. It is not our task to try to insulate ourselves from suffering. Of course we try to avoid needless suffering and work assiduously to prevent the preventable. But it is ours rather, to embrace as an inevitable part of human experience. If we can breathe into it when we are in its throes, it offers us much rich fodder for growth and acceptance of what we cannot control. It liberates us from obsessional needs for control, from denial and projection of our own "yucky stuff" onto "them," those others, those foreigners, whomever we don't like—and it frees us from seeking manic escapes, and anxious, paranoid avoidance of living fully. It is, all of it, heaven on Earth.*

# PART X

# REFLECTIONS:

# STEPPING INTO FREEDOM

## CHAPTER 47

## THE HOMELESS MAN AND THE FLIGHTLESS DUCK

WITH MY HIP healed, our cancer treatments behind us and summer drawing to a close, we return to the Palisades. In one serendipitous week, we put our house on the market, get the offer we want, and have our own offer accepted on a beautiful home on twelve acres in a lovely valley with redwoods and meadows in the Santa Cruz mountains. It's just what we've been dreaming of. We will be less than ten minutes from the ocean, yet we'll have a meditation grove, lots of space, lovely neighbors and room for the horses and llamas to be with us year round.

One sunny morning before we leave Los Angeles, I set off nostalgically for the beach in front of Porto Marina Way. The dogs trot along nicely in tandem, Jullay like a grand lady with Tashi, her jaunty little gentleman partner, completing the walk down the road from our house, across the bridge, down the stairs to the patch of grass by the sand, where they know to sit still until I release them to glorious doggie freedom. The surf, seagulls and sandpipers beckon and they're off! I'm left to my solitude, breathing in the sea air, listening to the call of the gulls, moved by the timeless beauty of the wide uninterrupted oceanic horizon, flooded with memories of almost forty years living, loving, working, and raising our children in this place.

The sand crunches under each footstep, inviting deep immersion in the moment—in reverie about the slenderness of the threads by which we are held to this life. Lost in time, I arrive at the rocky end of the cove, where I see a remarkable duo. For nearly a year, a homeless man has been living in a makeshift tarpaulin shelter in this rocky enclave. I wave and he waves back. But this time, I realize that the duck I've seen up in this end of the cove is actually with him. She never flies. Once, Jullay chased her and she rushed away awkwardly on her waddling duck feet. Now, with more presence of mind it occurs to me that the homeless man and the flightless duck are actually partners.

What an image! He sits bundled in his dark blue sleeping bag while she stands sentinel nearby, her bright yellow beak and feet in marked contrast to her soft white and beige feathered body. They sit watching my slow progress, apparently calm and observant. I am overcome. They have nothing much in the material world, but they have each other, and they have this beautiful cove in which to share whatever time they have and whatever they offer to one another. They look utterly peaceful.

Suddenly, as if this is a pool of meditative peacefulness disrupted by monkey mind, Jullay and Tashi spy the duck. Jullay knows better, but puppy Tashi bounds off after the biggest wind-up toy he's ever seen. Oh, no! The duck's tranquility is disrupted and in a panic, she tries to flee, flapping her useless wings, running in spirals. I shout to Tashi the new command we only started to learn yesterday in obedience training: "Leave it!!" I shout it three times to no avail, but the fourth time, in a heart-stopping moment, just as he's on her tail, Tashi stops in his tracks. Sits down. Looks back at me and turns to stone. I can't believe it. I don't have any treats but I praise him lavishly. The stunned duck stops in relief. The crisis is over.

The whole sequence stays with me as a living contemplation, a metaphor for life and for meditation. In stillness, we can find the presence of mind to appreciate such unexpected but big lessons as the homeless man and the flightless duck have to teach us. What a model of interbeing and nonattachment! Here is an unlikely interspecies couple providing each other comfort; where, I wonder, do they take refuge during the torrential storms? They probably snuggle together under the tarp or a bridge, testament to how little we really need in the material world.

And then, I think, our rare lucid moments of apprehending these lessons are steeped in impermanence. Tashi broke the moment off just as during sitting meditation, our monkey minds disrupt moments of calm lucidity with intrusive thoughts. It is possible, however, during the interference that breaks our mindful presence, to tell our internal mental puppies to "leave it!" This is not a clicker command, but a simple and quiet instruction to let it go, to release those compulsive, intrusive thoughts. When we do, we are brought back to a reflecting pool of potential lucidity in the richness of the present moment.

Smiling in gratitude, I savor my last beach walk on these familiar sands before pulling up stakes again to begin a new, quieter life.

# CHAPTER 48
## ORDINATION BY SCORPION

IT'S 2:00 A.M. at Deer Park Monastery, and later today, Thich Nhat Hanh will ordain me as a lay member of the Order of Interbeing. I'm lying wide awake on my bunk, not yet sure if I'll make it. More specifically, not sure if I'll be able to be there.

Jim is fast asleep in the men's bunkhouse. Ariel is sleeping soundly two bunks away. Part of me is so touched and grateful for her presence, but another part of me feels like throttling her. I am afraid, extremely afraid, that she has done something beyond foolish which could cause my imminent death.

### No Death, No Fear

Last night, after evening meditation, we all walked back to our dorms. Maintaining noble silence, my five bunkmates and I removed our shoes before entering. We took turns using the bathroom and I was last, after Ariel. When I closed the door, I saw a note above the sink written in her handwriting. It said:

> Please be aware. I discovered a small scorpion on the floor near the toilet. Of course I wouldn't violate the precepts to kill it, and having no way to capture it, I shooed it under the sink cabinet where I am sure it will enjoy a peaceful night's safe sleep.

A scorpion! Loose in the bathroom where we walk barefoot? In the spirit of the retreat, I practiced calming my rising pique with measured breathing, brushed my teeth, and climbed into bed, where I fell promptly into a deep sleep.

About an hour ago, around 1:00 a.m, I awoke, padded sleepily into the bathroom, and sat down on the toilet. Just as I relaxed, I felt a blazing, piercing sting on the side of my right foot. I barely stopped myself from screaming aloud. It jolted me awake like an electric shock, and I turned on the light. There on the floor next to my bare foot, with its tail arched menacingly over its horny body, was the scorpion. I imploded with a rush of feelings: panic, fear, and rage. What to do?

Deer Park, miles from town, generally doesn't have cell phone coverage. I had no idea where Sister (doctor) Dang Nghiem was sleeping, only that it was too far away in Lower Hamlet. Shaking with fear, I reacted impulsively. Gathering a huge wad of toilet paper, I scooped up the scorpion and flushed her down the toilet. Trembling, hoping maybe she would survive the flush, I turned out the light and climbed back onto my bunk. Hadn't I just broken the sacred precept not to kill?

Probably the one I really wanted to flush down the toilet was my own beloved daughter! What was she thinking?! I thought about waking her, but decided that would be self-indulgent acting out. There wasn't anything she could do for me now. I'd have been waking her up out of pique. A fleeting thought crossed my mind: "Won't she feel horrible when she discovers my lifeless body." I chastised myself for that petty thought.

From John Steinbeck's novel *The Pearl*, I know that scorpion stings could be deadly. I used to teach it to ninth graders at Beverly Hills High School. I love the story. I remember the legendary devotion of Kino, the pearl diver whose baby boy, Coyotito, is stung by a deadly scorpion. Kino cannot afford medical treatment until he dives and discovers the Pearl of the World, bringing epic tragedy to the family. The story pits innocence and poverty against greed and evil. Remembering that baby rattlesnakes deliver more fatal venom than grown ones, I wonder nervously if small scorpions are the same.

There is more than one irony to this predicament. For years, I was sure I didn't want to be ordained. My Buddhist practice had been both beautiful and sustaining, but it was also something private and personal. Now, once I'd made this commitment, maybe I wouldn't survive long enough to attend the ceremony. A further twist: one of the things that had helped me change my mind was Thay's incredible talk, "No Death, No Fear," at the UCLA Mindfulness and Psychotherapy Conference I helped to organize in 2006. So, I decide simply to breathe deeply, meditate, and wait. I would practice Thay's teaching: face death without fear. If this is to be my fate, I would embrace it.

### In the Here and Now

So, I have been lying here in my sleeping bag for an hour, tracking every sensation in my foot, ankle, and leg. I feel them throbbing and swelling up. My leg feels hot, and I 'm aware of a pulsing sensation. But I am not dead, yet.

At the same time, I find myself smiling. What a beautiful ending to my blessed life. Here I am, held safe in this spiritual sanctuary, my loved ones nearby, about to be ordained by Thay, who teaches us how to face death utterly fearlessly. There doesn't seem to be much I can do right now anyway, but simply watch and wait. If the pain really amps up, I'll ask for help. But it continues, steadily throbbing, yet stable.

I continue breathing deeply, smiling into fear, calmly watching my thoughts like a movie in my mind. I realize I am deeply meditating. I am fully present. I am here in the now. I am fearless. I am happy. And then I smile to myself. I have been ordained by a scorpion!

### A True Precious Smile

By 3:00 a.m., I decide that I will survive the bite. I will limp, and it will hurt, but I'll be fine. Amazed and grateful that the teaching, "This too shall pass," is yet again revealed to be wise and true, I fall into a short but deep sleep before the bell sounds for morning meditation and the day of my ordination.

The ceremony is profoundly moving. Fourteen of us are seated in the center of the great meditation hall on our zafus and zabutons. Behind the monks and nuns are all those who have come for the ceremony. I can't turn around to find Jim and Ariel, but I feel their presence and it lifts me.

The ceremony begins with chanting, then a recitation of the Heart Sutra, and an invitation to receive the Fourteen Mindfulness Trainings. All the ordinees are called to stand and come forward to "touch the earth," to make three full prostrations in gratitude for our parents, our teachers and dharma mentors, our friends, and all beings who have guided and supported us. That is easy, as my heart is brimming with gratitude.

We are vowing to commit to practicing open-mindedness and tolerance; nonattachment to views; respecting freedom of thought; developing compassion for all beings; simple healthy living; dealing with anger by softening and transforming it; dwelling happily in the present moment; resolving all conflicts through deep listening and mindful speech; promising to always be truthful; to addressing oppression and injustice; right livelihood through a vocation that benefits humans and the planet; practicing non-violence; practicing generosity; and maintaining sexual responsibility. As each of the Fourteen Trainings is read, we make our pledge to practice it, prostrating our bodies.

Reciting each one, I realize I am finally fully owning my values and holding myself responsible to these philosophical and spiritual precepts. Performing seventeen deep prostrations is a real challenge to my old knees and shoulders, but I feel tears of gratitude that I can do it, and that, for this moment, I have completely forgotten my other ordination. I hope the scorpion swam to safety and is out in the field where she belongs. If she has died, I ask forgiveness and send her gratitude for her deep teaching, knowing that truly, like the bear I shot, we inter-are.

Finally Thay calls us forward, one by one, to give us our certificates of ordination and to bestow Dharma names, chosen by our mentors and Dharma teachers with Thay. When I step forward and kneel before him, Thay hands me my certificate and grins broadly, his eyes twinkling at me as he says my Dharma name: "True Precious Smile."

May I never forget today's deep teaching—no death, no fear—and the preciousness of a smile. May I practice breathing with deep gratitude for each being who supports me intentionally or accidentally, and for each present moment throughout the rest of my wakeful life.

# CHAPTER 49

## TEMAZCAL IN TULUM

FOR YEARS I've wanted to participate in a sweat lodge ceremony, but nothing auspicious has presented itself. Attending a tribal gathering in the Sixties in New Mexico, I wished someone would invite me to a sweat lodge, but no one did. Then there was the Miwok Indian who stopped me on the way into the tiny feed store in Auberry and invited me to a sweat lodge at his rancheria. I was sorely tempted, but thought with a slight shiver, *I've never seen this man before in my life. I have no idea if this is legitimate or a peyote fest or a great spiritual awakening or an opportunity to be fleeced and rolled. We're too close to Table Mountain Casino. Maybe he's a gambler. No, this is not the time.* Now, back in Tulum on the Yucatan Peninsula in Mexico after forty years' absence, the opportunity to enter a windowless kiva seems perfect. I'd much rather experience a spiritual cleanse in this tiny beachfront village than witness the high-rises and hawkers that have sprung up around Cancun in my absence.

There are thirteen supplicants, most relative strangers to each other, waiting in the tropical night air for Fabian, a Mayan shaman, to lead us across the white sand and through the forest of palm trees to the sweat lodge for a Temazcal ritual purification and dedication. I've heard amazing things about him from my yogi friends and teachers, Jenni and Paul, and feel I will be in good hands. I've cleared my mind and opened my body with an intensive week of yoga and meditation, and today consumed only fruits, vegetables, juices and the requisite two or three liters of water to prepare for this ceremony.

There is hushed sweetness to the jungle night, softened by the sound of the gentle wind and waves. With waist-length, midnight-black hair bound in a ponytail, a lithe and slender brown body and a deep, unfamiliar accent, Fabian arrives, playing a haunting melody on his wooden flute. He invites us into this ancient Mezzo American ceremony of his ancestors, bidding us follow him single file further into the palm forest. We reach an altar of ceremonial items laid out on grass mats around a small, clay, goblet-sized brazier brimming with hot coals. In a mesmerizing voice that is part incantation and part transmission from the elders, moving back and forth between his Mayan dialect, Spanish and English, Fabian invokes the four elements in our sacred bodies. "Bring your heart and mind into awareness of these elements in your home, your body: earth for muscle and bone; water for the blood that courses through our veins; air for the breath that signifies life; and fire for the powerful creative and destructive energy that moves us and moves through us." By his presence alone, any residual anxiety I felt has been released. I know I've chosen wisely to wait until now, the middle of my seventieth year, for this transmission of the sweat lodge.

Fabian invokes the sacred authority of the four directions and their corresponding power and energy. From the East, the white light of purity, insight and intelligence. From the West, the red glow of the sunset, the fire of passion and fertility that animates us. From the North, the blackness that signifies privacy and introspection. And from the South, the blue light that comes from all the ancestors, the collective wisdom, the traditions that sustain and unite all peoples, men, women, old and young, of all time. Fabian explains that we will dedicate this practice to Mother Earth, Pachamama, who provides without complaint or judgment everything we need to sustain life. It is our duty to honor our mother, to acknowledge how we have misused her and to pledge to take care of her myriad resources and wounds.

We are brought into a circle to announce our names and our intentions in being present. Following my journaling and reflections, I declare my intentions for this Temazcal: to embrace what is and to relinquish fear. I mean to continue my never-perfectible practice of letting go, of breathing into what is. I intend to continue to try to let go of fear about whether Jim will kill himself with a misplaced burst of testosterone in a fourth road biking accident; whether Ariel will recover from the heartbreak of her divorce from Sarah and finally find her soulmate and become the mommy she has always dreamed of being; whether Brooke and Philip will get out from under their ponderous mortgage; whether Gabriel will continue his own auspicious journey letting go of resentments, softening his heart and moving back to the dear closeness we shared and savored when he was a boy; whether Prudencio will ever be able to leave Peru and make it back to us in North America; and whether I will be able to grow old—or just grow—with grace.

When we have each spoken, Fabian invites us to come forward to be prepared for the sweat lodge. He circles us one by one with smoke from the embers in a ceramic vessel of smoking coals. He then makes an offering and invites us to crawl through the small door into the kiva, a circular domelike lodge. We sit on a carpet of palm fronds laid out around the fire pit, tucked in very close to one another with our backs against the brick wall and our feet literally to the rim of the fire pit. It felt oddly trusting and strangely intimate to scrunch in, bare arms and legs to bare arms and legs of total strangers. Fabian explains the purpose of the sweat lodge: to cleanse our minds and bodies of toxins, to purify us to receive the insight from the East, the passion and creativity from the West, the privacy and introspection from the North and the South's collective wisdom of all the ancestors and our own familial line, and to express our gratitude and dedication to Pachamama, Mother Earth, the great provider.

I listen with my eyes nearly closed, until I begin to wonder if this collection of strangers is "with" this, or if they are holding back in fear of something unfamiliar. But when I glance around, it seems as if all present are mesmerized by Fabian's devotion to this ancestral practice and his generous offering to share it with us.

After we are all settled, he makes offerings in Mayan, blows a long, deep blast on a conch shell and instructs us to shout "*Piedras calientes!*" He calls his helpers to cover the hole in the top of the lodge and bring in the first wave of red-hot volcanic rocks, representing the East. As the helpers shovel in each load of glowing rocks, we gamely shout, "*Ajo!*" They bring in a cauldron of water with bundles of fresh, aromatic, medicinal herbs, and closing the entry port, depart, leaving us in utter darkness except for the stones.

Following each of the four subsequent rounds of fresh hot rocks, they reseal the kiva door. Fabian chants in Mayan, throwing water and medicinal herbs on sizzling coals while the heat and energy slowly build up to a crescendo in the sweat lodge. Midway through, three young women ask to be excused, saying they feel like fainting or vomiting. Without judgment, our shaman gently explains that each of us will get as much from this ceremony as we want or can bear.

As we move through the four directions and the heat rises, I feel sweat pouring from my body. My bathing suit is drenched and my hair is stuck to my scalp. In the timeless darkness of the cramped kiva, I try to adjust my body; the palm fronds cut into my sitting bones and legs. I have no idea how much time had elapsed, but tell myself: *This is why you are here…to sweat not only bodily but also to relinquish mental toxins, to continue releasing habits and beliefs that hold you back from being free and fully present. This ancient ritual, celebrated by the first peoples throughout the western hemisphere, represents everything you have devoted yourself to realizing through this entire odyssey. What is a cleanse but a letting go of burdens and stepping into freedom?*

Fabian urges us to invite the loved ones we have lost to come to us from the ancestral South to guide us, to forgive those we have been hurt by, and to find wisdom and clarity in the purity we are bringing to our bodies and hearts. I am flooded by a parade of loved ones who have died—my grandparents, my mother and father, many dear friends and two who are presently on a threshold toward death. As I did in the Touching the Earth Ceremony at Plum Village, I feel their palpable presence, especially my mother, my dad and my beloved grandparents, but this time I am awash with an unambivalent calm and sense of well being. Fabian, whose long black hair is now loose and sweat-drenched in tendrils over his face, bare shoulders, chest and back, says in a voice that sounds almost spent, "Now it is time to let them go. They are here for you and very happy to be summoned here to this sweat lodge, but they also are well where they are…Let them go in peace."

Finally he says, "It is time to leave the kiva—rise slowly and circle back around the fire pit as you came in. Move outside to the cool shower then take your place lying down on the grass mats behind the kiva." Ten of us who have remained throughout file out, bowing before exiting into the bracing night air. The water of the outdoor shower, like a morning wake-up call, is invigorating. I feel each cool drop on my skin as a call to awareness. As I step back, one of Fabian's helpers encircles me with a big towel. I lie on the grass mat with the others, feeling a white cotton sheet offered as a covering. It is ghostly and protective at the same time; I'm not sure whether I feel like a newborn swaddled in the sheet or a body in a shroud.

Limp and exhausted in my swaddling shroud, I have a vision of my "two sons." My almost forty-year-old, beloved blood son, Gabriel, a gifted filmmaker, is on his way to Haiti to volunteer as an earthquake disaster worker. After twenty years' touch-and-go alienation, finally, after a brief but powerful bout of therapy together that softened both of our hearts and gave us hope, he has recently reconnected with me with love and gratitude. I am so relieved, melting into a healing mother-son repair, proud of his brave and generous heart beyond measure. My spiritual Aymara son, Prudencio from Lago Titicaca, Peru, joins him in the vision, though they barely know each other. Prudencio, an old soul himself, has chosen me and I him. Our separation was traumatically induced six years ago by the immigration *federales* at the LA airport, where they refused his re-entry visa. I imagine Gabriel and Prudencio, though grown men now, as little brothers in my vision, and me as a Pachamama, nursing them in harmony at my breast—healing all our wounds and trauma. That is the image that comes and stays with me, a beautiful reunion across psychological, generational, ethnic and national borders.

Fabian offers us sweet tea and fresh fruit, reminds us to drink coconut water to replenish the minerals we've lost, and tells us we will probably "sleep like babies"—unless we are rocketed by huge dreams, and in either case, it was all part of the process of the sweat lodge. The next day I continue this journey with a long massage by one of his healer brothers, Leo, whose grandmother has instructed him in the art of *root keene*, a penetrating healing therapy developed by the ancient Mayans. It is a form of bodywork that acknowledges the importance of the navel region as the body's power center, deeply manipulating the internal abdominal organs to release tension and blockages. Like the sweat lodge, it is an exercise in trust, as Leo reaches deep into my soft inner belly cavity and manipulates the intestines and organs. But as a veteran of the Turkish baths of Wadi Musa, I give myself over to it and emerge feeling energized, focused and in touch with my heart's intentions.

### Into the Depths of the Cenote

To seal it all, two days later, after many hours of challenging and restorative yoga, I follow another impulse. I literally swim into the belly of the earth, into the magical underground caverns of the recently discovered Cenote Dos Osos, no longer stuck as when I relived my breech birth scuba diving in the Red Sea, or in the tight passage in the colored canyons of the Sinai. Guided by Guzman, a local Mayan diver, I swim freely and strongly into my seventieth birthday year with my titanium hip, torn rotator cuffs and cancer survivor breasts. I swim in sweet, crystal clear, aquamarine water, through caves of stalactites and stalagmites, through narrow passages into vaulted rooms, through bat caves and with schools of fish, marveling in silence at the beauty, mystery and transformative power of this primordial and sacred place.

Ajo!!

# CHAPTER 50
## ROLLER COASTER RIDE ON THE RAPIDS

I HEAR THE HORSES' heavy breathing and feel the powerful thrust of Shambhala's strong hindquarters beneath me, moving us upward along the narrow, rarely used trail. We are climbing a switchback through the redwoods, up the spine of a steep mountain in Big Basin in the Santa Cruz Mountains. Every so often, we have to slide off our horses onto the ledge to navigate our way on foot around a fallen tree or limb. I doubt that Jim, who was thrilled to find this trail on a hike last week, realized how challenging it would be on horseback, primarily because it is so narrow and the dropoff is so sheer. But it is Mother's Day weekend, and as a gift he has agreed to show me the way to Chalk Mountain and its extraordinary overlook of the entire sweep of the Monterey Bay.

I am thrilled with this gift, as it really comes from the heart. Jim does not share my passion for horses, but with this present of a nearly unknown trail, he is honoring me and my two beautiful horses, Cheyenne and my new Rocky Mountain Horse, Shambhala, who has taken Spirit's place. It is a clear spring morning. We have packed a picnic lunch and fortified the horses' hooves with Renegade boots against the promise of rugged terrain. Tashi Delek, my "giggle therapist" poodle pup from my successful battle with breast cancer five years ago, bounds exuberantly and carelessly up the zigzag trail, threading between the horses and their hooves as if no harm could come to him. Miraculously, thus far, no harm ever has.

As we climb above the valley floor and the small creek below, the primeval darkness of the redwood sorrel-carpeted forest begins to lighten. Through the treetops, as we gain ground on the switchbacks, we begin to see blue sky. Soon we reach the ridgeline and the flora changes dramatically. Instead of lush sorrel and redwoods, we are in a scrub plain of manzanita, deer brush, Indian paintbrush, lupine, sticky monkey flowers, California sunflowers, popcorn flowers and pearly everlasting. The scent of the ocean greets us. The dark mulch gives way to lighter soil and finally we find the chalky shale that has given this peak its name.

Following the ridgeline, Jim leads me to an outlook and we see Chalk Mountain ahead. We continue climbing, giving the horses a breather from time to time while pausing to marvel at the beauty of this pristine place. Tashi yelps gleefully, bounding after a small marmot, but the local native aces him and slides tauntingly into its hole. Through the scrub we continue into full sun and a whipping coastal wind and finally arrive at the peak of the mountain. The vista is breathtaking. I gaze along the horizon line with the eyes of a doe, shuddering with the climb, nostrils quivering, ever alert for a lurking cougar; and then with the wise eyes of an ancient Ohlone woman, gathering berries, pausing to take in the huge expanse of bay that has sustained my people for millennia; then I survey the coastline with the eyes of my Scottish forbearers, sheep ranchers and lumbermen, settlers who came in the 1800s to establish their wives and children for summers in Santa Cruz on the Monterey Bay to escape the relentless summer heat of the San Joaquin Valley.

I imagine that of late, there haven't been many eyes in this place taking in the sweep of the central coastline and Monterey peninsula. It is one of those Technicolor days. The air is sweet with spring and my heart is nearly melting with love for my husband and for these beautiful animals who have carried us here, and quietly, in gratitude and celebration on this Mother's Day, for all my children who have given me the precious gift of motherhood.

*Love Letters in Cyberspace*

Wednesday, May 13, 2010

Dear Ones—

Take a deep, sweet breath and do sit down. Monday morning after a beautiful Mother's Day weekend, we suddenly found ourselves on a psychic roller coaster—

Out of the blue on my way home from my Monday Pilates class, I felt acute abdominal pain, like very powerful menstrual cramps. Within an hour I couldn't even walk and before long began vomiting, heaving in pain though my stomach was empty. What could it be? Appendicitis? Kidney stones? What? Jim rushed me to our internist, Grace, who did a pelvic exam and felt a mass around my right ovary. She sent us to Dominican Hospital for an ultrasound, where they found a grapefruit-sized mass apparently around or in the ovary. Receiving the findings, Grace called Dominican radiology to tell us to come straight back to her office. A delicious chocolate-black woman with very spirited dreadlocks, Grace entered the examination room looking grey, and as if the very curl would let go in her hair. She sat down heavily, took a huge deep breath and said, "Guys, it doesn't look good."

Having spent six years as the staff psychologist in the Oncology Unit at Cedars Sinai Hospital in Los Angeles, I knew exactly what she feared. Not only have I lost two dear friends to ovarian cancer, but I knew that by the time the mass was palpable, it was probably too late.

Jim and I looked at each other in abject shock. How could this be? In four days we're supposed to be launching the many-month celebration of my upcoming 70th birthday with a river rafting and hiking trip down the Colorado River through the Grand Canyon! My god, will I even make it to seventy? My beloved mother was snatched from life way too early at seventy-three. Am I to depart even earlier than she?

As we looked at each other in disbelief, the tears welling up in both of our eyes, I took a breath and said, "Damn. This is the last thing I expected. I survived cancer and a scorpion bite. But if it is to be, I'm not afraid. It's just what is. I don't think either of us have any regrets. We have truly sculpted our lives over the past decade and a half exactly as we have wanted. We have traveled far and wide in the world, we have loved and raised our children, we have cherished each other and we have found the perfect valley for our golden years. I feel solid in my Buddhist practice, and know "No Death, No Fear" of death. Learning that has been the subject of the deepest core of my pilgrimage. I only feel major disappointment that my ride will be cut short so abruptly.

"What I do know is that this is different from breast cancer. Then, diagnosed with stage one cancer, even presenting bilaterally and with sentinel node involvement, there was no question but aggressive treatment: the full court press with herbs, acupuncture, meditation and yoga as an East/West complement to conventional surgeries, chemo, radiation. This time, I don't think so. I don't want to spend the last chapter of this beautiful life chasing chemo rainbows and vomiting. I have seen it all over those years among the dying on the oncology ward at Cedars Sinai. I just know that if in fact this is late stage ovarian cancer, I want to know I have a way out when the time is right."

Grace looked at me evenly and said, "Don't worry about a thing." I felt a huge sigh of relief, as one of my biggest worries has not been about death and dying, but about getting stuck in a hospital as I saw so many oncology patients caught, hoping, talked into trying for miracles, desperately chasing one more month. I don't need that. I am fully alive in the present moment. Grace's assurance offered a huge relief.

By midnight I was admitted to Dominican Hospital to manage the pain with morphine while we waited for a CT scan on Tuesday. By this time I had begun vomiting some blood. Jim and I held steady on our course. We called the children, my sister and my cousin. We held each other and he tearfully stroked my belly. Strong, clear-headed, open-hearted and focused.

Tuesday afternoon the tide turned as suddenly as it had come in, The results came back from the CT scan showing an encapsulated mass (whew) and the CA125 (marker for ovarian cancer) came back at 19, not indicating cancer. The odds of cancer suddenly dropped from 80+% probability to 25%. We'll take that! Grace then ordered an endoscopy to see where the blood was coming from and found two small new ulcers, in the esophagus and in the stomach, likely caused not by metastatic abdominal cancer but by twenty-four hours of uber-stress-caused acid-induced vomiting on an empty stomach. We'll take that too! The uber-stress dissolved like the outgoing tide.

Unfortunately, of course, we've had to bail on our Grand Canyon rafting and hiking trip. We were due to leave on Thursday to make our descent. This has come totally out of left field as I have been feeling on top of the world, physically, emotionally and spiritually! Just this very Mother's Day weekend Jim and I and the horses had surmounted that fabulous steep switchback trail through the redwoods up to the top of Chalk Mountain overlooking the whole Monterey Bay. It was thrilling. Who would have ever thought there could be such a cosmic turnaround?

Looks like another "AFGO" (Remember when I shattered my hip mountain biking? "Another Fucking Growth Opportunity.") But it is true; my mindfulness practice is solid and sustaining. Ariel cancelled work and flew up here immediately and has been a wonderful mommy. Gabriel has been checking flight schedules from Louisville, poised to come to my bedside as well, but with this relieving turn, may wait to come in on the weekend. Brooke immediately offered to close her chiropractic office and fly down from Tacoma, but with this auspicious turn, we agreed to wait til our planned family gathering at Twin Brooks in July. Jim throughout has totally been a rock to lean on, but with no camouflage for his tender feelings. Very present.

Ariel checked me out of Dominican hospital yesterday and drove me to see my new oncologist at Stanford for a five-year follow-up from the breast cancer. She says there is nothing at all to worry about regarding breast cancer;

all is perfectly clear and whatever this is, it is unrelated to that. She also agrees it is very probably a non-malignant cystic neoplasm in the ovary. The procedure can be done by laparoscopy, but must be done by an expert, an ob-gyn oncologist surgeon. Finding that doctor is what's slowed us down on the timing. The surgeon will decide during surgery whether to perform simple ovarectomy or total hysterectomy.

After a flurry of efforts to find an ob-gyn oncology surgeon, I am scheduled with Katie O'Hanlan, MD from Stanford for emergency ovarian surgery this Saturday. They'll have a preliminary pathology report at the time and the definitive path report should be back within a week of that. Oh, impermanence! Oh, opportunities to practice mindful breathing! Now it's just pain management until then.

So, with love and gratitude for you in my life and your prayers and healing energy, I'm calm and very optimistic about celebrating my upcoming 70th birthday with flying colors. This does bring me dramatically into the present moment. Please don't worry. We'll keep you in the loop.

–Harriet

Friday, May 14:

Dear Ones—

We are heading up tonight to check into a hotel near the hospital in Redwood City, as I have the big pre-op bowel purge to do and guess driving in the Friday traffic with legs crossed in knots isn't the best plan. I talked to my surgeon and am REALLY impressed with her—she does not think it is cancer but she also recommends a total hysterectomy and appendectomy "while I'm in there."

I'll be in hospital till Monday sometime. I am still growing but I didn't request this AFGO!     –H

Saturday, May 15:

Dear Ones—

Whoo-ee, are we gonna ride! All's well. Everything's gone. Benign. What a joyous end to this roller coaster week. Amazing doc—she clearly saw my pain level and came in on the weekend. She picked up on what no one else had diagnosed, that my ovary had gone into "torsion." The mass may have been there, even for years, but something finally happened in Pilates and it twisted around and pulled off the abdominal wall, causing the acute pain. Am I ever grateful. Of course the morphine could be entering into this glee but I'll take that.

I'm quite a bit loopy but deeply grateful for all your loving support and concern and wanted to let you know the good news. When I said :everything," that means ovaries, tubes, uterus and cervix and an appendectomy, too, while we're at it. So there should be no more worries at all. I'll probably be here in Sequoia Hospital in Redwood City through Sunday, then home to Aptos to reunite with the doggies, horses, llamas, redwoods and meadows for two weeks' recovery, where lots of walking and activity is part of the recovery routine.

Ariel and Jim are here joining me in sending love and gratitude for this and to you for being such beautiful presences in our lives.                                                     –H

Sunday, May 16:
Where is the end of them, the fishermen sailing
Into the wind's tail, where the fog cowers?
We cannot think of a time that is oceanless
Or of an ocean not littered with wastage
Or of a future that is not liable
Like the past, to have no destination'
            –T.S.Eliot, "The Dry Salvages," *Four Quartets*

Dear Christine—

Blessings to you, dear Taos friend! It appears we abide

in the miracle of cyberspace clouds. Medicine is amazing grace, as you among us all surely know. And I am sending my grounded prayers for all that I have seen, felt and learned to bring back from this brief journey to abide with us all. Patience for going with the river, trust, hope, and gratitude for what is, has been and will be.

My crisis appeared dramatically with the bleakest outlook and then suddenly began shifting and every day got better. I think I landed in the hands of the best possible ob-gyn oncology surgeon. Katie O'Hanlan is a marvel—fun, brilliant, expert researcher, clinician, teacher, et al. Though we'd never laid eyes on each other before, she had us laughing on the way into the OR. By 7:30 a.m., while they rolled me toward the operating room on the gurney, Jim and Ariel walked alongside, holding my hands. Ariel had my iPhone in her pocket and it beeped to announce a text from Gabriel. It said, "Can you ask if you get to keep your uterus after they take it out? I have fond memories of my first apartment."

Ariel read this aloud. Katie guffawed aloud and snorted, "No way, kid. You can't have it because every cell I remove is going to the pathology lab. But I will take a photograph for you!" With that, Jim and Ariel released my hands and patted my legs good luck.

"Fond memories of my first apartment," coming from Gabriel, was a huge sendoff. In his own wry style, he's telling me he loves his mommy and the womb that he took form in. After years, really since he was a rebellious, depressed and angry teenager, the air between us has been tense and pained. Desperately needing a father, he sided with his dad in the divorce, blaming me as the cause of all pain. My anxious overprotectiveness felt to him like a lack of trust and cast me as a Gestapo mom. It has taken years of patience, self-reflection, forgiveness and trust to heal this painful wound. Gabriel's short text expressing love for his first apartment speaks volumes to me. Jim, Ariel and Katie rolled the gurney through the double doors, laughing, and soon I was under.

Later that afternoon Katie stopped by with the photograph she promised she'd take for Gabriel and to reconfirm that everything was benign. The photo showed a rosy pink healthy uterus in the ominous shadow of a Darth Vader-looking purplish blue-black torsioned and swollen mass. I felt like Dorothy looking at the body of the wicked witch of the North. Now that witchy serous adenoma is shrunken, scraped off the walls of the nearby tissues it had been draining blood from, and has been sent unceremoniously to the pathology lab with the other six no-longer-needed body parts (tubes, uterus, ovaries, cervix and, for good measure, the appendix) she'd removed. Ding dong, the witch is dead!

Katie said I was doing so well, and since I had had the full day to recover, if I could "walk and pee" I would be much happier at home. With that encouragement, I managed both and by 8:30 p.m. the day of the surgery, I was home in Aptos! My regimen now is to pretty much do everything normally. Walk, walk, walk through the pain. Exercise, etc. Because it was all done by laparoscopy, the recovery is a miracle and there are no stitches.

When I called my wonderful doctor Grace here in Santa Cruz after the surgery yesterday to thank her for her Herculean efforts all last week, she closed by saying she's on her way to Spain for a week. She apologized for speaking too soon of her fear, saying that with a presentation like mine she'd never seen anything but advanced malignancy. She'd told us her fear because she loves us and was overcome. I told her never to regret giving me what she did. I know absolutely now I will never fear death.

In its own wild way, this week has been an amazing gift and she is full of Grace! She reminded me that I would have been hiking and river rafting in the Grand Canyon as of now as well. Can we only imagine the scenarios if this had presented tomorrow instead of last Monday! And this afternoon, though it wasn't the Grand Canyon hiking we'd planned or the rapids we'd expected to run on the Colorado River, we hiked this canyon at home, a mile and a half loop with the dogs leaping and playing, glad to have me home and the familiar returned, up through the redwood meditation grove, pausing for gratitude at the altar of Avalokiteshvara, the boddhisatva of compassion and deep listening.

We will miss you so much in person for my 70th birthday at Twin Brooks next month, but I feel your love, our deep connection and the soft flutter of angel wings that pass between us. Honor your art and be well, my dear friend.

Oh, I forgot to tell you about the sweet poignant farewell Ariel offered to her "nest" and Gabriel's "first apartment."

Before they came to collect me for the surgery, Ariel climbed on my hospital bed and cuddled in. I put on my iPod and we each took one earbud and listened together to the monastics at Deer Park Monastery chanting "Namo Avalokiteshvara Ya." It was soothing and centering. Then we listened as Sister Jewel sang the beautiful "Don't ask the way to peace, peace is the way," and finally, Ariel, stroking our "nest," sang me the words to the round:

"Standing like a tree with my roots down deep,
My branches wide and open.
Come, come the rain,
Come, come the sun,
Return to the earth,
Return to the one who is
Standing like a tree with my roots down deep,
My branches wide and open…"

With abiding love,
Breathing and smiling,
Harriet

◆◇◆

July 3, 2010
Dear Gabriel,

Thank you beyond words for such an amazing time

together at Twin Brooks. I loved seeing you with your beloved Kentucky family—and seeing what a wonderful dad you are to Esme and Levi. They are growing beautifully. I am very proud of you. More than anything, I celebrate our healing heart connection in the place we both love so deeply, Twin Brooks, with lifetimes of memories and family roots.

Among the flood of happy images from my birthday gathering are you, Heather and the kids laughing and playing with Ariel, Brooke, Philip and Chloe and Tatum; riding the horses; you building the raft for all the kids; and us all packing and leading the llamas up to Echo Rock for the cookout. It's as if I have a hopeful dream glimpse of the time long after Jim and I are gone, seeing you all functioning together and enjoying being a family.

But the very best moment was you and me riding Cheyenne and Shambhala, hell bent for leather—galloping free as the wind, shouting "Yee haw!!" We used to love to ride the horses and for so many years, I missed it with you keeping distance, not sharing anything as unbuttoned and freewheeling as a crazy wild gallop together through the forest till now, with you on the threshold of your fortieth birthday, celebrating me and my seventieth.

I can't help but remember quite vividly that July 3$^{rd}$ day here at Twin Brooks in 1976 when I turned thirty-six. Ariel was just three and you were almost six. It was a magical time when all seemed right with the world. Our beloved "Ma" was still alive, baking and frosting the birthday cake. Your Poppy was on location, at the peak of his directorial game filming *The Entertainer* with Jack Lemmon, Ray Bolger, Sada Thompson and Tyne Daly. I was in graduate school in psychology and we still had Stormy and Calypso, the horses you were learning to ride.

You, Ariel and I were staying at Tiger Lily cottage, getting ready to go to the Twin Brooks house for the birthday dinner with Ma and Dad. We three were in the outside shower house, getting cleaned up after swimming in the creek. The summer sun slanted in between the trees through the open gap between the roof and the shower walls. The golden sunlit-washed walls were decorated with the whimsical paintings Susan and I had done of frolicking hippos and frogs taking their baths. You said, "Mima, please promise you'll just stay thirty-six for another thirty years…I'll catch up to you. I love you."

Well, our current forty/seventy arithmetic is a bit more real and grounded, but the shared joy of this summer's gathering feels like the fulfillment of a long-deferred and cherished dream. What a birthday!

My love to you, Es, Levi and Heather,
Mima

Stepping into freedom, with gratitude I humbly close my odyssey with a quotation from one of my very favorite, most inspiring poets, Rainer Maria Rilke:[23]

> God speaks to each of us as he makes us,
> then walks with us silently out of the night.
>
> These are the words we dimly hear:
>
> You, sent out beyond your recall,
> go to the limits of your longing.
> Embody me.
>
> Flare up like flame
> and make big shadows I can move in.
>
> Let everything happen to you: beauty and terror.
> Just keep going. No feeling is final.
> Don't let yourself lose me.
>
> Nearby is the country they call life.
> You will know it by its seriousness.
>
> Give me your hand.

23  Rilke, Rainer Maria. *Book of Hours,* trans. by Joanna Macy and Anita Barrows. New York: Riverhead Books, 1996, 59.

HARRIET KIMBLE WRYE, PH.D. is a Training and Supervising Psychoanalyst Emerita at the Los Angeles Institute and Society for Psychoanalytic Studies. She has been ordained by Zen master Thich Nhat Hanh as a Member of the Order of Interbeing.

Dr. Wrye, co-author of *The Narration of Desire* and author of more than 25 articles, lives with her husband, Jim Wheeler, their five llamas, two horses and two dogs in Santa Cruz, California, where she practices mindfulness and psychotherapy.

Visit her website at www.pullingupstakesbook.com.